Spain at the Polls, 1977, 1979, and 1982

Spain at the Polls 1977, 1979, and 1982

A Study of the National Elections

EDITED BY
HOWARD R. PENNIMAN AND
EUSEBIO M. MUJAL-LEÓN

An American Enterprise Institute Book

Published by Duke University Press

1985

© 1985 AEI (American Enterprise Institute
for Public Policy Research)
All rights reserved
Printed in the United States of America
Library of Congress Cataloging in Publication Data
appear on the last printed page of this book.

Contents

Preface   Howard Penniman   xi

1   Representative Government in Spain: The Historical Background
    STANLEY PAYNE   1

2   Shaping the Constitution   ANTONIO LÓPEZ PINA   30

3   Electoral Rules and Candidate Selection   JORGE DE ESTEBAN and
    LUIS LÓPEZ GUERRA   48

4   The Transition from Below: Public Opinion Among the Spanish
    Population from 1977 to 1979   JOSÉ IGNACIO WERT ORTEGA   73

5   The Democratic Center and Christian Democracy in the Elections of
    1977 and 1979   JAVIER TUSELL GÓMEZ   88

6   The Socialist Alternative: The Policies and Electorate of the PSOE
    JOSÉ MARÍA MARAVALL   129

7   The Spanish Communists and the Search for Electoral Space
    EUSEBIO M. MUJAL-LEÓN   160

8   Francoist Reformers in Democratic Spain: The Popular Alliance and the
    Democratic Coalition   RAFAEL LÓPEZ-PINTOR   188

9   Catalan Nationalism and the Spanish Elections
    JUAN F. MARSAL and JAVIER ROIZ   206

10 Regional Nationalism and the Elections in the Basque Country
    JOHN F. COVERDALE   226

11 The Media and the Elections   JUAN ROLDÁN ROS   253

12 Spanish Politics: Between the Old Regime and the New Majority
    EUSEBIO M. MUJAL-LEÓN   274

13 The October 1982 General Election and the Evolution of the Spanish Party System   RAFAEL LÓPEZ-PINTOR   293

14 Conclusion   EUSEBIO M. MUJAL-LEÓN and RAFAEL LÓPEZ-PINTOR   314

Appendix A   319

Appendix B   324

Appendix C   330

Notes   335

Index   367

Contributors   371

Tables and Figures

TABLES

1.1 Variations in Spanish Suffrage, 1812–1927   3
1.2 Distribution of the Vote, 1936 Elections   12
1.3 Party Composition of the Spanish Parliament, 1936   13
1.4 Composition of Franco's Cortes, 1942, 1946, and 1967   22
3.1 Chamber and Senate Seats and Population per Seat, by Province   52
3.2 Cortes Incumbents in the 1979 Election   65
3.3 Women Candidates and Total Seats Won, Chamber of Deputies Elections, by Party 1979   66
3.4 Candidates and Winners, by Sex, National Elections of 1977 and 1979   67
4.1 Attitudes on "Democratic" versus "Authoritarian" Principles of Government, 1966–1976   74
4.2 Attitudes on the Desirability of Democracy in the Aftermath of Franco's Death, May and December 1975   75
4.3 Attitudes toward the Future March 1975–January 1976   75
4.4 Correlations between Right or Left Vote, by Province, February 1936 and June 1977   77
4.5 Evaluation of the Moncloa Agreements among Technicians, Clerks, and Manual Workers, April–May 1978   79
4.6 Opinions on the Economic Measures of the Moncloa Agreements, January 1978   79
4.7 Attitudes toward Modernizing Policies, July 1978   81
4.8 Knowledge about the Constitution, October–December 1978   81
4.9 Voting Intentions in the Constitutional Referendum, July–December 1978   82
4.10 Popular Support for Democracy, November 1980   83
4.11 Perception of Effectiveness of Democracy, September 1979   83

4.12 Evaluation of the Present and Future Political Situation, June 1978   84
4.13 Perception of Change in Political Situation, October 1978   84
4.14 Voting Intentions for the General Elections, September 1977–February 1979   85
4.15 Voting Intentions for the Local Elections, August 1978–January 1979   86
4.16 Evaluation of Major Political Leaders, 1978   87
4.17 Self-Placement on the Left-Right Dimension, July 1978 and July 1979   87
5.1 Performance of Centrist Parties, Chamber of Deputies Election, 1977   109
5.2 Performance of the Center Parties, Chamber of Deputies Election, 15 June 1977, by Province   110
6.1 Vote Switching, 1977–79: Where the Votes Came From   141
6.2 Vote Switching, 1977–79: Where the Votes Went   141
6.3 Ecological Correlations of the PSOE, UCD, and PCE   144
6.4 Correlations between Pre- and Post-Francoist Left Wing Vote   147
6.5 PSOE or UGT Background of Delegates to the Twenty-Eighth PSOE Congress, 1979   147
6.6 Delegates with Socialist-Affiliated Parents, Twenty-Eighth PSOE Congress, 1979, by Region and Occupation   148
6.7 Socioeconomic Background of Party Supporters   150
6.8 Party Vote of Occupational Groups, May 1979   151
6.9 How "Left" Is the PSOE?   156
6.10 Support for Ideological and Strategic Tendencies within the PSOE   156
6.11 Change Expected under a Socialist Government   157
8.1 Popular Alliance and Democratic Coalition Election Returns by Region and Province, 1977 and 1979   202
9.1 Results of the 1977 Chamber Election in the Catalan Provinces, by Party   215
9.2 Results of the 1979 Chamber Elections in the Catalan Provinces, by Party   219
10.1 Estimated Population and Population Density of the Basque Country, 1975   226
10.2 Per Capita Income in the Basque Country, 1971   227
10.3 Spanish Immigrants in the Basque Provinces, 1970   228
10.4 Results of the Referendum on Political Reform in the Basque Country, December 1976   233
10.5 Basque Seats in the Chamber, by Party and Province, June 1977   235

10.6 Results of the Chamber Elections in the Basque Country, June 1977   236
10.7 Distribution of the Vote for the Chamber in the Basque Provinces, June 1977   237
10.8 Results of the Constitutional Referendum in the Basque Primaries, December 1978   241
10.9 "Positive Abstention" in the Basque Provinces, December 1978, Referendum   242
10.10 Results of the Referendum on the Constitution in the Basque Country, December 1978   243
10.11 Basque Sects in the Chamber, March 1979   246
10.12 Results of the Chamber Elections in the Basque Country, March 1979   247
10.13 Distribution of the Vote for the Chamber in the Basque Provinces, March 1979   248
11.1 News Coverage of Candidates or Parties on TVE during First Half of Campaign   271
11.2 Pages of Party Advertising on 15 February 1979   272
13.1 Results of Elections to Spanish Chamber of Deputies, 1977–1982   294
13.2 Results of Elections to Spanish Senate, 1977–1982   296
13.3 Distribution of Seats in the Chamber of Deputies, Spanish Regions and Provinces, 1982   299
13.4 Voting Intentions, by Occupational Sector, 1980 and 1982   306
13.5 Voting Intentions and Evaluation of the Political Conditions, 1979 and 1982   309
13.6 Ideological Self-Identification on an Abstract Scale and a Semantic Scale, 1979 and 1982   310
13.7 Reasons Given for Change in Vote by Former UCD Voters Who Turned to PSOE or AP before and after the Election of 1982, April and November 1982   312

FIGURES

5.1 The UCD Vote, by Province, June 1977   112
5.2 The ECD Vote, by Province, June 1977   114
6.1 The Socialists' Electoral Strongholds, 1977–79   143
6.2 Left-Right Self-Placement of Party Voter   152
6.3 Left-Right Self-Placement of Party Militants   153
6.4 Voters' Left-Right Placement of Parties   154
6.5 Militants' Left-Right Placement of Parties   155

9.1 Distribution of Chamber Seats in Catalonia and the Four Catalan Provinces, by Party, 1977 216
9.2 Socialist Votes in the City of Barcelona, 1977 Chamber Elections 217
9.3 Communist Votes in the City of Barcelona, 1977 Chamber Elections 218
9.4 Distribution of Chamber Seats in Catalonia and the Four Catalan Provinces, by Party, 1979 220

Preface

———*Spain at the Polls, 1977, 1979, and 1982: A Study of the National Elections* is another in the series of national election studies prepared by the American Enterprise Institute for Public Policy Research (AEI). In the first volume of the series, *Britain at the Polls: The Parliamentary Elections of 1974*, the preface stated that AEI was undertaking the series because it believed the "democratic elections have enough in common that an understanding of the laws and practices of one democracy makes possible a more sophisticated analysis of political institutions in others. By publishing descriptions of elections in a number of sometimes quite dissimilar democratic societies, AEI hopes to provide its readers a better sense of democratic institutions at work and help to inform those who are striving to improve electoral institutions and processes around the world." AEI believes that these studies continue to fulfill their intended functions.

The present volume covers the first three national elections in Spain after the death of General Francisco Franco, who had ruled that nation from 1939 to 1975. These post-Franco elections occurred within a period of less than five and one-half years. They followed one another in such rapid succession that it was never possible to complete one study before another election had been called. After the 1979 election, all chapters on the 1977 election were returned to the authors for revision. After the 1982 election, Eusebio M. Mujal-León and Rafael López-Pintor took over the task of updating the study in a transition chapter, an essay on the 1982 election, and the conclusion.

The unexpected expansion from one to three elections, though frustrating, has had some important advantages. The elections taken together carry the nation's politics through at least two important stages of a developing democracy.

In 1977 the voters chose a Cortes whose members were responsible for writing a democratic constitution. As Antonio López Pina has noted in his chapter on the work of the constituent Cortes, it produced a document that could accommodate a government of any democratic party or coalition whether of the left, right, or center. The proposed constitution was approved by a huge majority in a referendum in December 1978.

A second parliament was elected three months later to be the first to make public policy within the rules of the new constitution. To the surprise of some observers, the governing coalition, at first led by Adolfo Suárez, who had guided the earlier Cortes, began to collapse shortly after taking office in 1979 —at first slowly and then with increasing speed until the coalition disintegrated. The parliament was dissolved, and new elections were called for October 1982.

This time the voters gave the center-left Spanish Socialist Workers' party (PSOE) a clear majority in the lower house under the leadership of the young, dynamic Felipe González. This shift from a government controlled by a center-right coalition that included many officials of the latter years of the Franco regime to one dominated by the center-left party marked the first "alternance" of power, a successful change that most analysts believe marks a major step forward for a new democracy, particularly, as in this instance, if it means a significant change in the policy commitments by the new government. This development has been accomplished without serious crisis.

Democracy in Spanish History

Although Spain has held elections for most of the last century and one-half, it has nevertheless had very limited democratic experience. In the introductory essay to this volume, Stanley Payne points out that "until about the time of World War I, Spanish politics remained highly elitist. The use of universal male suffrage between 1869 and 1885, and once more after 1890, did not alter this situation, since illiterate Spanish peasants were in most cases unprepared to participate actively and beyond that, the electoral mechanisms developed by nineteenth-century Spanish liberalism were controlled, manipulated, and corrupted."

Spain twice proclaimed republics, but both failed. The First Republic elected a Cortes in 1873 that fell even before it could write a constitution. The Second Republic was born in 1931 after the demise of the dictatorship of Lieutenant General Miguel Primo de Rivera in 1930. Local municipal elections were called for 12 April 1931. Parties of the left were voted into power in all the major cities although they won less than a majority of the vote nationwide. Immediately after the elections 103 churches were burned in the nation's six largest cities, and more were destroyed elsewhere in the country. King Alfonso XIII hastened into exile. The Second Republic was proclaimed on 14 April 1931, and elections were called to choose members of the Cortes to write a democratic constitution.

Although no fighting or bloodshed followed the proclamation of the new republic, conditions for building a democracy were far from ideal. The economy, based largely on agriculture, suffered more than the economies of other Western countries also caught up in the Great Depression. The PSOE was the only party with a long history in the country, yet it commanded only about 15 percent of the popular votes. Worse, the PSOE was sharply divided between the moderate, pragmatic socialists and the so-called maximalists or Bolshevisers. José María Maravall in his chapter on the PSOE speaks of the latter as the "revolutionary soul [of the party] that defended revolutionary objectives." The attempt to reconcile the revolutionary and reformist wings of the party "by combining institutional politics with extraparliamentary and mass-mobilization strategies, was fraught with tension, manifested in internecine disputes." The leader of the PSOE left, Francisco Largo Caballero, believed that "socialism could only be revolutionary, following a strategy of mass mobilization and leading to the collapse of the bourgeois order."

This segment of the PSOE and three left republican parties won enough seats in the first Cortes to have a working majority. Payne says that they wished to do more than abolish the monarchy and establish democratic institutions. They also wanted to ensure the separation of church and state, along with the "banning of all religious displays and expelling of teaching orders from Spain." Their goal was "to cripple Catholic schools and destroy Catholic culture in Spain." They also wanted to liberalize the army and provide for major economic changes. In other words, they were at least as concerned about ensuring a broad social revolution in the country as in simply creating formal democratic institutions.

Curiously, the Catholics were almost totally unprepared for the first developments after the proclamation of the new republic. Juan J. Linz notes in one of his many excellent essays on the politics of Spain that "in 1931, Spanish Catholics found themselves without any institution or party that could protect them from the onslaught of the anticlerical Republican politicians (like Azaña), the anticlerical extremism of the Socialists, and even the violence of the masses, particularly the anarchosyndicalists."[1]

It was only after the constitution had been written that the Catholic church entered national elective politics seriously. It became a major supporter of the newly organized Spanish Confederation of Autonomist Rightist Groups (CEDA). In the 1933 national elections CEDA won more seats than any other party. For a period it supported the government of the conservative Radicals. Its later attempts to solve agrarian, employment, and education problems were unsuccessful.[2]

The election law for members of the Cortes could have had a serious effect on party representation. Under the rules, the party winning the most votes in all mainland districts received between 67 and 80 percent of the seats. Generally speaking, the larger the number of seats assigned to a district, the larger the percentage given to the winning party. The second largest party in the district received all the remaining seats. In Madrid in 1931, for example, seventeen seats were to be filled. The PSOE received 175,000 votes and thirteen seats; the conservative coalition won 170,000 votes but only four seats; and the Left Republicans and the Radicals won 100,000 votes and no seats. Even in close contests such as the one in Madrid, a few votes automatically gave the larger party more than twice as many seats as the runner-up received. A handful of miscounted votes could change a national election outcome. In 1936 the election count was challenged in several districts. "Minor irregularities," according to Payne, "interfered with the final outcome of the electoral procedure, as large leftist crowds took over the streets in many cities, beginning on the evening of the election itself. Jails were forcibly opened, and within three days the caretaker government in charge of the elections resigned in fright before all the ballots had been finally registered." The Popular Front leadership took control of the government and managed the recount that ensured its victory.

The level of violence, usually led by units of the left, increased dramatically in the spring and summer of 1936. In early July a Communist lieutenant in the shock troops was killed. Shortly thereafter José Calvo Sotelo, a former official in the Primo de Rivera government and an outspoken leader of the radical right, was arrested and murdered by men in officers' uniforms. Four days later the Civil War began. In Juan Linz's view, "the addition of Socialist maximalism to the anarchosyndicalist opposition was decisive in the breakdown of democracy in 1936."[3]

General Francisco Franco headed the troops that returned to Spain from Morocco in July 1936. In October he was named leader of all Nationalist troops. After the Nationalists' victory that followed the fall of Madrid in the spring of 1939, Franco became head of the new government, a post that he held until his death thirty-six years later. Javier Tusell Gómez says "the government [the nationalists] set up was more like a traditional dictatorship than it was like either of its allies, Hitler's Germany or Mussolini's Italy, and after the Second World War the Franco regime stripped off the fascist attributes thrust upon it by circumstance."

The Parliamentary Monarchy

In spite of the unusually violent and brutal Civil War (no doubt more cruel because it was fought over religious and ideological issues) and nearly four decades of an authoritarian regime under the general who had led the revolt, the transition from dictatorship to democracy was remarkably smooth and peaceful. With the exception of a brief though dangerous threat of a military coup in 1981, the transition to the new regime has remained generally calm.

Rafael López-Pintor and Eusebio M. Mujal-León, in the concluding chapter of this volume, stress that the Franco government decided in the late 1950s "to pursue an aggressive program of modernization and industrialization." Mujal-León speaks elsewhere of the drastic changes "in economic and social policies pursued after [the introduction] of a group of technocrats affiliated with Opus Dei into the cabinet and adjunct administrative organs." This development was accompanied by a reduction in the influence of the Falangists in the decision-making process.

The new policy called for serious efforts to increase tourism, to expand trade with other Western countries, and to encourage the emigration of Spanish workers to Germany. The programs were intended to provide more jobs and more income to the country and its people. And they succeeded. The per capita income of the Spanish people moved up from $290 in 1960 to $2,485 in 1975. (This figure more than doubled by 1982.) The share of the work force employed in agriculture dropped from 51 percent in 1940 to 21 percent in 1976. Some 2.3 million Spaniards emigrated to other European countries between 1960 and 1973. Mujal-León suggests that in these programs the "'popular' component complemented what was in many ways the 'revolution from above' that cleared the way for the elections in June 1977." Between 1960 and 1965 the number of tourists visiting Spain rose from 4.3 million to 11.1 million; in the same period the number of Spaniards visiting other countries rose from 2.1 million to 3.9 million.

In their chapter on "Electoral Rules and Candidate Selection," Jorge de Esteban and Luis López Guerra offer an argument that covers at least two related issues that are similar to those of other authors.

> Only in a country whose cultural history had been identical with Spain's in the last forty years—one that had passed from underdevelopment to a position of considerable economic and industrial power—could the Spanish way to democracy be repeated. Spain's rapid modernization was brought about by a dictatorship that, though it denied all political liberties and fundamental rights, allowed and stimulated economic development. Theoretically the evolution might have taken another course, but in fact what needs to be clearly understood is that political modernization in Spain was possible only *after* economic modernization. [emphasis in original]

A number of the authors refer to the "limited pluralism" allowed by the Franco regime. After the first four or five years of the regime, the government generally allowed increased freedom to organize and press for changes in government policy or to seek improvement in one's personal condition without interference from the government. More often than not the government did not repeal any legislation to achieve this result. Rather, it tolerated change by not enforcing the laws limiting organizational practices or prohibiting the organizations themselves.

A few examples will serve to make the point. Although trade unions and strikes were forbidden, strikes in Spain numbered 2,063 in 1963–66 and rose to 3,156 in 1975 alone. Political parties were illegal, but the leaders of most parties met in the coffee shops of Madrid and elsewhere to plan for the day when elections would once again be held.

Books at odds with authoritarian regimes in general and the Franco regime in particular were entirely forbidden. Linz, however, in an essay published in 1973, said, "Bookstores are full of translations of Marxist works; Hilferding, Lukács, and even Marx, Marcuse, and Che Guevara sell well; and publishing of books in non-Castilian languages flourishes. In the press and particularly in small magazines some political issues are discussed more or less explicitly, while criticism of the social and economic system is frequent. Unfavorable comment on the Axis in the forties could lead to trouble, but criticism of Spain's ally, the United States, is commonplace today."[4]

In a related development of the late 1960s and early 1970s, the press printed some survey research data even when the information could hardly have been pleasing to the regime. A 1973 poll published in the Madrid papers told their readers that 60 percent of Spaniards had agreed that "we should make ourselves heard" on political issues and 82 percent "felt this could best be accomplished if government officials were elected rather than appointed."

By no means were all the actions aiding the transition, however unwittingly, products of the later years of the Franco regime. Ultimately the burden of democratization fell on the shoulders of those who followed the Franco government. Virtually all contributors to this study have given credit to King Juan Carlos for aiding the democratization of Spain.

Mujal-León says, "Juan Carlos demonstrated rare political judgment by judiciously using the vast powers Franco had placed at his disposal (especially those that made him the real as well as the symbolic commander of the armed forces) and by choosing Suárez as prime minister in 1976." It was shortly after the death of Franco that the king replaced Carlos Arias Navarro, whom Franco had recently appointed prime minister, with Suárez, who was generally thought to be more able and more committed to democratization. Even before Franco's death the king and Suárez had apparently agreed upon this arrangement.

Many give highest praise to the king for his role in preventing the very dangerous coup attempt of 1981 from getting out of hand. He took a strong stand for continued parliamentary government, both publicly and directly to top-level military personnel. It is possible that he was the only person then capable of preventing a return to military dictatorship.

The party leaders who led the constituent Cortes elected in 1977 also contributed to peaceful change by their moderation. They held the Cortes to the task of creating rules for a democracy and guaranteeing rights to the Spanish citizens rather than making divisive substantive decisions. Felipe González was critical, according to Mujal-León, in insisting that although the "PSOE was the party of change . . . there would be no social or political convulsions, [and] that the PSOE's objective was simply to make things work better."

González was also important in keeping religious issues from playing the same distinctive role as in 1931. He was prepared to meet privately with the more conservative supporters of the church to help work out compromises that could be supported by a large majority of the Cortes, including the PSOE members, without at the same time creating unforgiving bitterness on the part of those who wanted stronger action against the church.[5]

One final item of note was the replacement of the electoral law that had caused some of the problems of the Second Republic. In the referendum that called for the election of the constituent Cortes and in the constitution, Spain has turned to the venerable d'Hondt system of proportional representation. Its proportionality was somewhat reduced because each of the fifty mainland provinces, however small, was granted a minimum of three seats. This arrangement, in the view of the PSOE, would be greatly to the advantage of the conservatives and make it extremely difficult for the Socialists to win control of the Chamber of Deputies. Socialists may be less concerned about this issue since their victory in 1982.

Samuel P. Huntington's argument has a reasonable ring when he says: "The older an organization is, the more likely it is to continue to exist through any specified future time period. The probability that an organization which is one hundred years old will survive one additional year, it might be hypothesized, is perhaps one hundred times greater than the probability that an organization one year old will survive one additional year."[6]

There is no absolute assurance that democracy will last in Spain, just as there is no assurance that it will continue in any other country. Nevertheless, in spite of the continuing uncertainty and instability of the parties on the center-left, there is increasing hope of its success. After seven years of successful democracy in Spain, the chances of its continuing look very good indeed.

Ten Spanish and four American authors have contributed to this volume. Stanley Payne, professor of history at the University of Wisconsin and longtime student of Spanish politics, provides the historical setting for the election. Antonio López Pina, a professor at the Universidad Autónoma and an elected member of the constituent Cortes in 1977, discusses the work of that constitutional body. Jorge de Esteban, currently Spanish ambassador to Italy and formerly professor of law at the University of Madrid, is coauthor of the chapter on electoral rules and the conduct of the 1977 and 1979 elections. Joining him in writing this chapter is Luis López Guerra, professor and chairman of the department of law at the University of Extremadura and coauthor of a volume on election campaigns in the West. José Ignacio Wert Ortega, who teaches at the Universidad Autónoma, is a member of the city council of Madrid and is a former research specialist at the Center for Sociological Research, discusses the Spanish electorate. Javier Tusell Gómez, professor of history at the Universidad Nacional de Educación a Distancia and director general of fine arts in the ministry of culture from 1978 to 1982, analyzes the government of the Union of the Democratic Center (UCD). José María Maravall, minister of education since 1982, professor of sociology at the University of Madrid, and author of a number of books on recent Spanish government and politics, writes on the Socialist Workers' party (PSOE) in which he has been a high official. Eusebio M. Mujal-León, associate professor of government at Georgetown University and author of books and articles on Spanish and Portuguese politics, writes the chapters on the Communist party (PCE) and on the changes in Spanish politics from the death of General Francisco Franco to the Socialist victory in the 1982 election. Rafael López Pintor, professor at the Universidad Autónoma in Madrid, former director of the Spanish Institute of Public Opinion and also of the Center for Sociological Research, contributes the chapters on the Popular Alliance (AP) and on the 1982 election, and coauthors the concluding chapter of this book with Mujal-León. John F. Coverdale, former associate professor of history at Northwestern University and more recently clerk for a federal judge, discusses the Basque country and its politics. Juan F. Marsal, formerly a professor and chairman of the sociology department at the Universite Autónoma of Barcelona and a prolific writer on Spanish politics, analyzes Catalonian politics in the 1977 elections. Shortly after the 1979 elections he was killed in an automobile accident. His former student and assistant at the University and author of sociological studies on Spanish politics, Javier Roiz, extended the essay begun by Marsal to include the 1979 elections. Juan Roldán Ros, director of Radio El País after 1984 and previously a Washington correspondent for the Spanish News Agency (EFE), discusses the media and its role in Spanish politics. Richard M. Scammon, president of the Elections Research Center and for many years student of comparative election systems, has supplied the appendix electoral data.

I wish to thank Juan J. Linz for the hours he gave me in Madrid discussing authors who might contribute to this volume. His own voluminous writing, especially on the Franco and post-Franco period, is of great value to anyone who wishes to understand modern Spain.

Eusebio M. Mujal-León deserves special credit and my deepest thanks for his work as coeditor of this volume. His knowledge of the country, the politicians, the authors, and his willingness to give generously of his time have greatly enhanced the quality of this volume.

Howard R. Penniman, General Editor
At the Polls Series

Representative Government in Spain:
The Historical Background
STANLEY PAYNE

───────The modern liberal constitutional system in Spain is technically one of the oldest in the world, for it dates back to 1810, well before liberal parliamentary government had been introduced in the majority of Western European countries. Yet the development of parliamentary constitutionalism in Spain has been sporadic, and during the twentieth century it was interrupted by forty years of institutionalized authoritarian rule under General Francisco Franco. Parliamentary government in Spain thus has both a long history and a weak record.

This contradiction stems from a basic sociocultural paradox or conflict in modern Spain itself. Although Spain was the only large Western country to live in close contact with oriental culture during the Middle Ages, its legal institutions and the theoretical norms of its higher philosophy and culture have always been intrinsically Western and—except, perhaps, during the seventeenth-century decline—closely identified and aligned with the predominant norms of Western Europe. Conversely, since the seventeenth century its economy and social structure have failed to keep pace with those of northwestern Europe; as a backward, unindustrialized, agrarian society, Spain more nearly resembled similarly rural and unevolved societies in southern and eastern Europe. This fundamental contradiction between advanced cultural and institutional-juridical norms on the one hand and a weak, backward social economic structure on the other has sometimes produced severe internal conflict and helped to promote breakdown. By the 1970s, however, for the first time in modern Spanish history, the terms of the contradiction had seemingly been reversed: Spain had finally become a largely industrialized society with a reasonably advanced standard of living; yet it continued to live under an anachronistic and restrictive authoritative regime. Rather than being too advanced, the government was too backward for the society it governed.

The Representative Polity of Nineteenth-Century Spanish Liberalism

Modern representative government was introduced in 1810 largely as a result of the breakdown of the old regime under foreign invasion, which permitted a small elite of the liberal intelligentsia and upper-middle class to seize power. Throughout the nineteenth century, however, Spanish society remained largely illiterate and civically uninvolved. Representative politics was normally, though not always, restricted to a minority from the middle and upper classes. During the first half of the nineteenth century, strong opposition was expressed by sectors of the monarchist ultraright, the clergy, and the traditionalist peasantry. This resulted in a series of liberal-traditionalist civil wars, usually known as the Carlist wars (from the name of the first traditionalist pretender), between 1821 and 1876.

For sixty-five years, from 1810 to 1875, parliamentary government was unstable and convulsive in the extreme. This was a result not merely of civil war but at least equally of dissidence within the elite and conflict among the liberals. Five constitutions were written during the century (1812, 1837, 1845, 1869, 1876). That of 1869 was the most advanced, providing for direct universal male suffrage, but the basic document was the 1845 constitution, which was readopted with liberal modifications in 1876. With only one brief hiatus, this served as Spain's charter of government from 1845 until the downfall of the constitutional monarchy in 1931.

Throughout this lengthy period Spanish politics was dominated by conservative liberalism, based on the cosovereignty of Crown and Parliament, a respectful modus vivendi with the Catholic church (Catholicism remaining the official religion until 1931), economic protectionism for the predominant agrarian and northeastern industrial interests, and an electoral structure based for most of the century on "censitary" or restricted suffrage.

Until about the time of World War I, Spanish politics remained highly elitist. The use of universal male suffrage between 1869 and 1875, and once more after 1890, did not alter this situation, since illiterate Spanish peasants were in most cases unprepared to participate actively and, beyond that, the electoral mechanisms developed by nineteenth-century Spanish liberalism were controlled, manipulated, and corrupted.

The common slang term for the oligarchic Spanish electoral practices of the nineteenth and early twentieth centuries was *caciquismo*, derived from *cacique*, originally a Caribbean Indian term for "chief" or "boss." Even within the system of restricted elite suffrage that normally obtained between 1834 and 1890, electoral mechanisms were rarely allowed to work spontaneously but

Table 1.1 Variations in Spanish Suffrage, 1812–1927

Years	Extent of suffrage
1812–14	Indirect universal male householders' suffrage
1820–23	Indirect universal male householders' suffrage
1834–36	18,000 electors, 0.15 percent of total population
1836	30,000–50,000 electors, 0.35–0.4 percent of total population
1837–39	265,000 electors, 2.1 percent of total population
1840–43	424,000 electors, 3.5 percent of total population
1846–54	100,000 electors, 0.6 percent of total population
1854–56	700,000 electors, 5 percent of total population
1856–60	100,000 electors, 0.6 percent of total population
1860–64	160,000 electors, 1.0 percent of total population
1864–68	420,000 electors, 2.4 percent of total population
1869–75	Direct universal male suffrage
1876–89	850,000 electors, 5.1 percent of total population
1890–1923	Direct universal male suffrage
1931–33	Direct universal male suffrage
1933–36	Direct universal suffrage
1942–75	Indirect, organic corporative representation
1977–	Direct universal suffrage

Source: Stanley G. Payne, *A History of Spain and Portugal* (Madison: University of Wisconsin Press, 1973), vol. 2.

were regulated by central control, false ballot counting, restricted candidate lists, and other forms of denial of access to the opposition. Later, after universal male suffrage was permanently established in law, wholesale bribery and buying of votes were added to the list of corrupt practices (see table 1.1).[1]

By the beginning of the twentieth century, the shortcomings of the electoral system and malfeasance of electoral officials were widely denounced; yet the system itself changed little before the complete overthrow of the democratic regime by the Primo de Rivera dictatorship in 1923. First, the restrictions and corruption of *caciquismo* were the not unnatural product of an illiterate, divided, and extremely unevenly developed society. It must be remembered that similar conditions prevailed in all other southern European countries—as well as in certain parts of the United States—in the late nineteenth and early twentieth centuries. Second, the two parliamentary parties—the Liberal and the Conservative—had established a virtual monopoly of association and representation of the major social and economic interests, with only a few exceptions. Opposition to the system was divided among worker revolutionaries, middle-class radicals, regionalists, and the reactionary right, who managed to cancel each other out and leave the established oligarchies largely in control until 1923.[2]

The Primo de Rivera Dictatorship (1923-30)

Criticism of the nineteenth-century Spanish liberal system was already becoming widespread by the 1890s. The disaster of 1898, in which Spanish military forces were crushed by the United States and the country lost the last major remnants of its historic empire, inflicted a national trauma and provoked sweeping demands for "regeneration." Reform became the order of the day in early twentieth-century Spain. Every manner of remedy and nostrum was suggested, ranging from the mildest cosmetic treatments to wholesale social and institutional revolution. Denunciation of the corruption of the parliamentary and electoral systems became commonplace and was sometimes considerably exaggerated. Nonetheless, for the reasons enumerated above, no reformist or revolutionary coalition was able to generate enough strength to alter the status quo. Many specific reforms were passed, and Spanish government became increasingly liberal and in a few respects almost democratic, but the established factions of the old Conservative and Liberal parties still dominated public affairs.

In part because of its geographic situation, Spain escaped involvement in World War I, but after 1918 it was plunged into a major postwar social crisis with the rise of violent, revolutionary anarchosyndicalism. At the same time a revolt in the new protectorate of northern Morocco, which represented Spain's only effort to reemerge in the international arena, sorely pressed the government. Abdul Karim's Riff revolt proved by far the most potent anticolonial rebellion in any part of Africa or Asia during that era. Spain's ill-prepared and inept military forces suffered a major defeat in 1921, provoking a more severe political crisis than had anarchosyndicalist revolutionism. As the political structure slowly became more liberal and more open, the weight of problems cast upon it rapidly increased, overloading the system beyond its capacity to function. Elections became more honest and genuine, but the broadened electorate grew steadily more disenchanted with the seeming ineffectiveness both of the government and of the opposition reform parties. The rate of electoral abstention steadily increased.

This climate of confusion, conflict, and political despair was dramatically ended in September 1923 when Lieutenant General Miguel Primo de Rivera stepped forward to establish a temporary military dictatorship that would rule for ninety days by decree. When the Primo de Rivera regime began, it had no definite ideology and only a very general program. Dictatorship in early twentieth-century Spain was conceived as "Cincinnatian," that is, as a temporary device to confront short-term emergencies. Primo de Rivera promised to resolve the Moroccan conflict, purge the political system of corruption, and restore unity once more before returning government to its normal constitutional channels.

The only clear-cut achievement of the Dictatorship, as it came to be called, was military victory in Morocco. Political reform proved no easier under authoritarian rule than under the parliament, and no alternative system was at hand. Nonetheless, the Dictatorship at first enjoyed general public acquiescence and even the direct support of leading intellectuals, such as José Ortega y Gasset, for it promised to "throw the rascals out" and introduce some of the drastic systemic reforms that had been discussed, however vaguely, for thirty years.

Thus the "ninety days" originally stipulated by the Dictatorship came and went and turned into years. Primo de Rivera's appetite for power steadily increased, and, as the regime rode the wave of international prosperity in the mid-1920s, funds were at hand for large-scale public works and a number of worthwhile economic reforms.

What the Dictatorship never achieved was a political doctrine or philosophy, much less a system. Primo de Rivera himself was a bluff, sometimes shrewd product of the late nineteenth-century reform era. He could conceive of no real alternative to parliamentary liberalism under constitutional monarchy, for the doctrines of corporatism and nationalist authoritarianism that had emerged in central and eastern Europe at first found no counterpart in Spain. After four years, however, the search for a political alternative could no longer be postponed. A new National Assembly was convened in 1927, selected not on the basis of direct elections but by government appointment and corporative suffrage exercised by local administrative, economic, and cultural institutions. The National Assembly was charged with the elaboration of a new constitution to reform or replace the existing document of 1876. The crux of its deliberations had to do with the powers of executive government and the nature of a new representative assembly. The result was a compromise constitutional recommendation in 1929. This proposed to restore parliamentary government on the basis of a new chamber, half of whose members would be elected by direct male suffrage, as under the old constitution, and half by indirect corporative elections. The new proposals would have further enhanced the power of the executive and given the crown greater authority than under the last liberal constitution.

The constitutional reform project was the work of a small group of monarchist neoconservatives and Carlists with very little support in Spanish society at large. When the proposals were opened to public debate in the press in mid-1929, they were almost universally condemned. In fact, they were largely rejected by the dictator himself, who never managed to free himself fully from the norms and concepts of liberalism. Primo agreed with the critics that the proposal was too "monarchist" and perhaps also too restrictive. No effort was made to translate the constitutional reform into law.[3]

Primo de Rivera's failure to find any political alternative to the liberal system sounded the death knell of his regime. Rather than the beginning of a modern authoritarian system, it turned out to have been a Latin American or Greek-style military dictatorship, an arbitrary hiatus without institutional roots. By the beginning of 1930 the regime had lost its reason for being: the Moroccan problem had been solved, and the old politicians had been punished by the temporary abolition of the parliament. But the national budget was heavily in the red, the era of prosperity was over, and Primo no longer had anything to offer. Nearly all political sectors, and not least the army command, agreed that the dictator must go, and he resigned at the end of January 1930.

This returned power to the hands of Alfonso XIII, reigning monarch since 1902. Under the Spanish liberal constitutions, sovereignty lay "with Crown and Parliament," and Don Alfonso's intention was to restore parliamentary government as it had existed before 1923. Dictatorship, however, was a tiger from which the Spanish government could not easily dismount. The old Liberal and Conservative parties no longer existed, for they had been loose confederations of notables and electoral activists. Lacking the catalyst of elections, after several years they fell into dissolution. All the while resentment mounted against the crown for having acquiesced in the Dictatorship in the first place, and the king's new appointees feared the results of direct parliamentary elections before reliable new monarchist groups could be organized. Hence they procrastinated for more than a year, until April 1931, when elections were finally held—on the municipal level only, for the selection of new city governments throughout Spain.

During the intervening year a new wave of middle-class republican sentiment had been rapidly gathering strength. The new republicanism was not socially radical, indeed was economically at first rather conservative, but it was moralistic and doctrinaire, rejecting not merely the fallen dictatorship but the entire system of monarchy and the old liberal constitution of 1876. Although the republican candidates won less than half the votes in the municipal elections of April 1931, they swept the balloting in the larger cities. For the past generation there had been a rule of thumb that the cities were the natural leaders of national opinion, for elections tended to be more competitive and honest there than elsewhere, a truer reflection of political opinion. The outcome of municipal elections was thus a mortal blow to the monarchy, which was deserted by the military commanders and also by most of the monarchist politicians. Don Alfonso left the country in less than forty-eight hours, and the Second Spanish Republic was proclaimed without bloodshed on 14 April 1931.[4]

The Second Republic (1931-36)

The five-year drama of the Second Republic brought to a climax the political history of early twentieth-century Spain. It was unique in two important respects. First, it initially ran directly counter to the trend of politics and government in nearly all other southern European countries, which almost without exception were falling under authoritarian rule when Spain moved to full liberal democracy. Later, however, the Second Republic offered the grim spectacle of total breakdown into civil war between revolutionary and counterrevolutionary forces, perhaps the only modern polity to suffer this fate without the impact of foreign war or direct outside interference.

This democratization of Spanish political life in a depression era when the movement elsewhere was mostly toward authoritarianism was a natural product both of the long history of Spanish liberalism and of the relatively sheltered situation of Spain in the early part of the century. Undisturbed by war and nationalism, Spain had not been affected by major new pressures toward authoritarianism. This was true on the left as well as the right; Marxist parties were slow to develop, and the mass anarchosyndicalist movement of 1917-23 lacked the potential to pose a decisive revolutionary threat by itself. Thus as late as 1931 government in Spain could still be dominated, albeit now only temporarily, by the liberal middle classes, elsewhere largely fallen into political or cultural decline.

The monarchy collapsed so precipitately that power fell to the new middle-class republican parties almost by default, and in the first parliamentary elections of the Second Republic, held in June 1931, they won a strong majority. Yet the republicans were severely divided among themselves, forming various potentially antagonistic groups. Chief among them were the middle-class Republican Left led by Manuel Azaña, the Republican moderates led by Niceto Alcalá Zamora and Miguel Maura, and the Republican Radicals, led by Alejandro Lerroux. These last, contrary to their title, were the main Republican conservatives. They stood to the right of their French namesake and in the years 1931-34 served as a kind of republican umbrella party for diverse middle-class moderates. The republicans' main ally to the left was the Spanish Socialist Workers' party (PSOE), Spain's principal Marxist party, which had a long but weak history and rose to prominence only in the new leftist wave of 1930-31, generating a mass peasant following and becoming the largest single political party in the country, though with no more than 15 percent of the popular vote.

The republicans intended much more than the ouster of the monarchy and the democratization of government institutions, for in addition they proposed four major reforms: separation of church and state, reform and liberalization of the army, limited regional autonomy for Catalonia (and perhaps for several other regions), and economic reforms for the lower classes, especially land reform. Each of these changes produced great tension and bitterness, with the partial exception of the army reform. During 1931-32 the officer corps was reduced by half through a liberal retirement policy, and more liberal-minded commanders were appointed to top positions.

The separation of church and state, provided in the republican constitution of December 1931, was attended by legislation banning all public religious displays and expelling the teaching orders from Spain. The intent of the latter provision was to cripple Catholic schools and destroy Catholic culture in Spain. Though not all the attendant provisions were immediately put into effect, the results of this anticlerical legislation—which went beyond mere separation of church and state—roused intense Catholic opposition to the new political system, and this opposition took major organized form in 1933.

By the 1930s the issue of regional nationalism had become one of the two or three major civic problems of modern Spain. What made it so serious was that the two areas where regional nationalism was strongest—Catalonia and the Basque country—not only had their own languages and to some extent their own cultures and institutions but also were the most industrially advanced in the peninsula. Indeed, regional nationalism in Spain was unique in that it pitted the few advanced regions against the more backward Spanish majority. In the 1930s Catalan and Basque nationalists were demanding full autonomy (and some of them insisted on outright independence) to govern their own interests. Catalan nationalism had become the dominant political force in that region, encountering its stiffest opposition from the revolutionary anarchosyndicalists. By cooperating with the new Republic, the Catalans gained a broad autonomy statute in September 1932, given them extensive self-government. Basque nationalists, though weaker, demanded equal treatment, and similar claims were made by the less-developed regions of Galicia and Valencia, which also possessed regional languages and some degree of cultural differentiation. Spanish nationalists and conservatives, on the other hand, proclaimed that the Republic was breaking up Spain.

The economic reforms of the Republic can be divided into two parts. Dramatic improvement of wage rates and working conditions for industrial labor and farm workers was promoted by the first republican minister of labor, the Socialist Francisco Largo Caballero, through a series of new prolabor arbitration committees. The more serious problem, however, was that of more than half a million completely landless peasant families in southern and central Spain. Their plight was so severe that nearly all republicans agreed with the Socialists on the need for a land reform, but the new ruling coalition could not come to terms on its exact extent. The socialists wished to develop collectivist agriculture, but the republicans stood for a limited reform organized around private family farms. The result was a weak hybrid measure in 1933 that was badly designed and accomplished very little.

After two years, disillusionment with the new republic was widespread. Catholic opinion was being mobilized behind the new Spanish Confederation of Autonomous Rightist Groups (CEDA), which promised to make a strong showing in new elections. The republican alliance itself had completely splintered. The moderate Alcalá Zamora was elected president, the Left Republican Azaña had become prime minister, and the more conservative Lerroux had eventually gone into opposition. The Socialists were beginning to turn against their own coalition with the governing republicans, since it seemed increasingly unlikely that the present system was going to lead to socialism. The other strong leftist force, the anarchosyndicalist National Confederation of Labor (CNT), had declared war on the "bourgeois" republic from the outset, and carried out three major as well as various minor revolutionary insurrections between 1931 and 1933.

The second republican elections were held in November 1933. The outcome was influenced by the complicated electoral system. This was organized on the basis of large-city and provincial list voting, in which the top list received a premium—67 percent of the deputies for the district if it took at least 40 percent of the votes cast, 80 percent of the deputies if it won 50 percent or more. Such an electoral system made coalitions a virtual necessity for victory, and in many provinces the Catholic CEDA and the moderate Radicals established temporary electoral alliances. On the other side, however, Left Republicans and Socialists split apart in bitterness over the limited achievements of the first republican biennium and ran on separate tickets. The outcome was a surprise and a bitter disappointment for all the left. The CEDA replaced the Socialists as the largest political party in Spain; the Radicals took advantage of the situation to gain disproportionate representation for themselves; and the Left Republicans, deprived of allies and worker support, were nearly wiped out. Altogether, rightist forces held 185 seats in the new parliament, the Radicals and other centrists approximately 150, and the various leftist parties barely 100.

This outcome created a profound dilemma for the republican system and its president, Alcalá Zamora. According to democratic parliamentary norms, they party with the largest number of votes, the CEDA, should lead the new government. The CEDA, however, while adhering strictly to legal tactics, refused to endorse the existing republican system and seemed to be headed toward a Catholic corporative regime, denounced by the left as "fascist." To avoid this problem, Alcalá Zamora first appointed a minority Radical government, led by Lerroux, which, amid a series of crises and reorganizations, limped through the first nine months of 1934. Ultimately parliamentary government can function only on the basis of voting majorities, and the CEDA eventually announced it would bring the minority Radical ministry down if it were not given a share of power. Thus at the beginning of October 1934 a CEDA-Radical coalition ministry was formed under Lerroux, only three of ten seats going to the CEDA.

This was met by cries of "Fascism in power!" and the outbreak of revolutionary insurrection in Catalonia and the northwestern mining region of Asturias. The Catalan nationalist revolt in Barcelona, aimed at total autonomy for the region, was more opéra bouffe than insurrection and was easily suppressed. The insurrection in Asturias was an entirely different story, for it constituted the most serious revolutionary outburst in Western Europe since the days of the Paris Commune.

Efforts had begun in 1933 to form a workers' alliance of the various left revolutionary groups in Spain, but what finally lent partial success to the enterprise, at least in Asturias, was the leadership of the Socialists. The history of the PSOE has always been—and is still—an ambiguous one. It was founded and developed as an orthodox Marxist party of the Second International but stoutly resisted the blandishments of Leninism after 1917. Its leaders decided to collaborate with the republic in 1931 not because they had adopted an explicit creed of social democratic parliamentary reformism but simply as a tactical measure to create a situation more conducive to socialism. After the Republic swung to the right in 1933, many Socialists were profoundly disillusioned and advocated what they called *bolchevización* ("bolshevization") of the party to convert it into an instrument of direct revolution.

Only in Asturias was a full-scale workers' alliance created. It embraced the Socialists, the anarchosyndicalist CNT (which normally rejected association with Marxists as much as with "bourgeois" parties), the very small Communist party, and the tiny Leninist but anti-Stalinist Workers' party of Marxist Unification (POUM). After two weeks the Asturian insurrection was suppressed by the Spanish army; but by the time it ended, the revolt had become a symbol and a hope for all the left and the horror of all the right, polarizing Spanish politics as nothing had done since the Carlist civil wars.[5]

During 1935 the weight of government tilted more sharply to the right.[6] The leftist forces were partially repressed (though not so severely as their propaganda claimed), and some of the earlier republican reforms were partially undone or rescinded. Alcalá Zamora, however, through the discretionary powers of the presidency, refused to allow the CEDA to assume the leadership of the Spanish government, while the other major parliamentary force, the Radicals, was being rapidly discredited by a series of minor financial scandals. The CEDA finally demanded to form a government of its own or it would refuse further coalition support, and the president decided to take the gamble calling new elections for February 1936.

The Popular Front Elections of February 1936

The political process of early twentieth-century Spain entered its final phase in the elections of February 1936. President Alcalá Zamora originally convened them with the intention of forming a new center coalition that would win at least a balance of power and prevent victory by either left or right. This expectation failed completely, for the only real center party, the Radicals of Lerroux, had been restrained by the president himself and then generally discredited by the scandals and frustrations of 1934-35. The CEDA attempted to construct a right-wing coalition, the National Front, but achieved no more than a very limited success. The radicals could no longer be counted on for a right-center alliance, and other moderate conservative subgroups were not effectively coordinated. The extreme right was willing to cooperate but had comparatively little voter appeal.

By contrast with the elections of 1933, all the leftist forces were effectively organized behind the new Popular Front. By 1936 the idea of a popular front had been espoused by the Communist Third International (at the urging of French Communists), and Communists later claimed credit for having originated the Popular Front in Spain, but as a matter of fact the Spanish Popular Front was developed by the moderate left, not by the revolutionary parties. In late 1935 Indalecio Prieto, leader of the moderate social democratic sector of the socialists, began to establish a working liaison with the middle-class republican left of Azaña to create a broad, moderate leftist alliance that could win the next elections and regain control of the republican system. After the date of elections was officially announced at the start of 1936, other leftist groups showed interest in joining. The fashionable new title of Popular Front was adopted and, at the instigation of the "bolshevized" sectors of the Socialists, the small Spanish Communist party was admitted. By the time that the electoral campaign got under way, the Popular Front was composed of the middle-class Republican Left and several of the radical regionalist groups, the Socialists, the Communists, and the small Leninist POUM. As usual, the anarchosyndicalist CNT refused to cooperate with the left-wing parties—as distinct from worker syndicates—and once more rejected any formal participation in elections, but many of the CNT leaders had learned a lesson from the division that had so weakened the left in the 1933 elections. This time anarchosyndicalist workers were advised to vote for the Popular Front in their districts simply to prevent a victory by the right.

Nonetheless, the electoral effectiveness of the Popular Front coalition, as well as its likelihood of support from the nearly 1 million anarchosyndicalist workers in Spain, were in doubt right down to election day on 16 February 1936. The strength of the CEDA as the largest party in the country, together with the electoral wiles of smaller centrist and moderate conservative groups, was reinforced by memories of the discordant leftist debacle in the last contest. Most observers forecast a modest victory for the right, and even some of the top Socialists revealed skepticism about a Popular Front victory.

The campaign of the right was based on the slogan "Against the Revolution and Its Accomplices!" Invoking memories of the great revolutionary insurrection of 1934, the right asked for a victory to "save Spain," defeat the onslaught of the revolutionary left, and by implication move toward a more conservative, possibly authoritarian corporatist system. The minimal platform of the Popu-

Table 1.2 Distribution of the Vote, 1936 Elections

	Totals	Percentage of eligible voters
Eligible voters	13,553,710	—
Ballots cast	9,864,783	72.8
Valid vote	9,684,236	71.4
Popular Front	4,555,401	34.3
Popular Front with center[a]	98,715	
Basque Nationalists	125,714	3.9
Center	400,901	
Right	1,866,981	33.2
Right with center	2,636,524	

[a] Only in Lugo province.
Source: Javier Tusell, et al., *Las elecciónes del Frente Popular* [The Popular Front elections], vol. 2. (Madrid: Editorial *Cuadernos para el Diálogo*, 1971), p. 13.

lar Front called for a return to the policies of the original left-liberal republican biennium of 1931–33, a purge of republican government to remove all conservative influence, punishment for those who had resisted the 1934 insurrection, and a Popular Front takeover of all institutions, including the judiciary.

The results of the voting on 16 February came at least as a mild surprise, and one of the main turning points seems to have been the addition of anarchosyndicalist votes for the Popular Front in many of the larger cities and industrial centers. The right, by contrast, never achieved full electoral unity and so did not combine its votes as effectively as the Popular Front. Conversely, the extremely weak vote for the center has usually been explained by the fact that moderate opinion knew that both right and left were individually stronger and did not want to waste votes by voting for the center alone.

Minor irregularities interfered with the final outcome of the electoral procedure as, beginning on the evening of election day itself, large leftist crowds took over the streets in many cities. Jails were forcibly opened, and within three days the caretaker government in charge of the elections resigned in fright before all the ballots had been finally registered. The government in charge of conducting an election normally completed the second round of voting (in districts where no list had obtained 40 percent in the first round), but in this case a new Republican Left government under Azaña quickly took office and completed supervision of its own election to power.

The Popular Front's slender plurality in the popular vote was translated into a strong majority in the new parliament through the working of the plurality/majority list system (see table 1.2). The Popular Front was better able to concentrate its support and so gained an additional premium in parliamentary seats. Moreover, when the new Parliament met in March, it decided to cancel a total of twenty seats won by the right and center, on the grounds of alleged fraud or irregularities. Conversely, no notice was taken of irregularities in the Azaña government or Popular Front electoral procedure after 16 February. When new elections for the annulled seats were held under Popular Front auspices on 5 May 1936, they were swept by the left. The eventual composition of the Popular Front parliament is shown in table 1.3.

The Civil War, 1936–39

The elections of February 1936 were the third reasonably democratic elections in Spain within five years; yet the experience of direct democracy did not stabilize a constitutional republic because large minorities refused to accept the results. Anarchosyndicalists, like communists, had always rejected "bourgeois democracy" and "parliamentary cretinism" and voted for the Popular Front only as a temporary tactic. The Socialists, big winners in 1931, had rejected the legitimacy of the 1933 elections basically because in that contest they had lost. After 1931 the Catholic right, while adhering to technical constitutional legality, was seeking a corporative alternative to direct democracy.

The two-thirds majority of the Popular Front parties in the 1936 Parliament

Table 1.3 Party Composition of the Spanish Parliament, 1936

Party	Seats		
Popular Front		**Center**	
Republican Left Coalition	117	Portela Valladares group	14
Socialists	90	Basque Nationalists	9
Catalan Left	38	Radicals	6
Communists	16	Progressives	6
Syndicalist Party	2	Miguel Maura group	3
POUM	1	Liberal Democrats	1
Left Independents	7	Federalists	1
Total	271	Total	40
Right			
CEDA	86		
Agrarians	13		
League of Catalonia	13		
Renovación Española	11		
Carlists	8		
Independent Monarchists	3		
Independent Conservatives	3		
Total	137		

Source: Payne, *Spanish Revolution*, p. 184.

did not produce a unified majoritarian Popular Front government. Although the Popular Front coalition maintained organizational liaison, it was essentially an electoral alliance and not a thorough political entente. The Socialists were still dominated by revolutionary "bolshevizers" who refused to participate in "bourgeois" regimes. Therefore Azaña's new cabinet was composed exclusively of minority Left Republicans and survived only at the sufferance of the other Popular Front parties.

Immediately after the elections the revolutionary parties initiated a broad campaign of radical strikes, church burnings, and land seizures that have been described by most historians as a "prerevolutionary" wave. Over a million acres of land were seized by land-hungry peasants and leftist organizations in southern Spain during the next few months. Strikes increased markedly in nearly all cities and industrial districts. By June nearly a million workers were on strike, and the Spanish economy, already hard-hit by the world depression, was driven further into severe recession.

Azaña's Left Republican government was no advocate of social revolution, but it hated the right as much as or more than it feared the left and had based its entire program on a "republican" polarization between left and right. Thus Azaña and his party had made themselves prisoners of the left and had no alternative but to go along with the prerevolutionary wave, legitimizing most radical activities or be overthrown by their erstwhile allies.

The CEDA, the main force of the Spanish right, had in turn based its strategy on first winning power through parliamentary means before changing the republican system. After defeat in the February elections, the CEDA fell into complete disarray, and the initiative passed to forces of the radical right, the Alfonsine monarchists (*Renovación Española*) and the Carlists. There was also a small fascist movement, Spanish Falange (*Falange Española*), but it proved extremely weak, lacking support among either workers or the middle classes, and gained only 0.44 percent of the vote in the February elections.

Since all the radical antileftist forces lacked both popular appeal and parliamentary strength, the task of stopping the left—if the left was indeed to be defeated—passed to the more radical and nationalist sectors of the army officer corps. Despite its long history as a praetorian institution, the Spanish army had for the most part tried to stay out of politics under the Republic. In general the officer corps was as politically divided as most of Spanish society. The senior commanding generals were for the most part moderates, and the antileftist, anti-Azaña conspiracy that was eventually organized by General Emilio Mola in May and June 1936 was primarily supported by younger radical officers of junior and middle rank.

Throughout the spring of 1936 the revolutionary parties gathered momentum, proclaiming that the Republic was but the prelude to "socialism" or "libertarian communism." Yet a lull in the frenzied cycle of strikes, disorders, and street violence between the extremes of right and left occurred in late June. Moderates still hoped for a cooling of political passions, but after a Communist captain in the republican shock police (Assault Guards) was murdered on 12 July, revolutionaries who had been appointed to positions in the republican police arrested the parliamentary leader of the radical right, José Calvo Sotelo, and murdered him in turn. This was a political crime without precedent in the annals of European parliamentary government: never before had the leading spokesman of the parliamentary opposition been murdered by the state police of any European parliamentary regime, however "bourgeois" or "cretinous." It convinced some of the more moderate antileftists that the political situation had degenerated beyond hope and served as the final spark to ignite the Civil War. Indalecio Prieto, leader of the moderate minority of the Socialists, gloomily predicted, "We shall merit disaster because of our stupidity."[7]

The Spanish Civil War began on 17 July 1936, with the revolt of the section of the army stationed in the Spanish protectorate of northern Morocco. Within approximately forty-eight hours, more than one-third of the garrisons in peninsular Spain also revolted—although scarcely 50 percent of the regular army supported this action. Instead of a rapid coup that could have been completed in a week or two, the revolt led to complete internal division and civil war, an outcome that the rebels had hoped to avoid. Although the uprising was almost exclusively a military affair, it would not have achieved even partial success had it not soon been supported by right-wing civilians and Carlist and Falangist militias.

The military revolt that began the Civil War provoked precisely what it was designed to avoid: whereas its goal was to overthrow the Azaña Left Republican government before the latter gave way to, or was replaced by, direct revolution, in fact the military revolt completed the destruction of constitutional order in Spain, overthrowing the last governmental restraint and opening the way for the seizure of power by the revolutionaries in the leftist or republican zone.

In July and August 1936, as all of Spain was divided into revolutionary (Republican or Loyalist) and counterrevolutionary (Nationalist) zones, the Left Republican government lost nearly all its remaining authority in the republican zone and was replaced as de facto governing authority in almost every province by local revolutionary juntas or coalitions. In areas where the anarchosyndicalist CNT was strong, it dominated local affairs. Some provinces were more strongly influenced by the Socialists or other leftist parties, and a number of them were ruled by mixed juntas.

The revolutionary parties immediately initiated a widespread process of social and economic revolution, either collectivizing industry and farm land directly or taking it under political or governmental control. The revolution went furthest in Catalonia, where most industry was seized by the revolutionaries, and it was extensive in such regions as Asturias, Valencia, eastern Aragon, and New Castile. In the Madrid region, the revolution was more moderate, as the shell of a Republican government struggled to regain control, and in the Basque industrial province of Vizcaya middle-class Basque nationalists took charge and largely prevented a revolution.

The great weakness of the main phase of the Spanish revolution in 1936–37 was that its chief animators, the anarchosyndicalist CNT and the revolutionary Socialists, tended at first to concentrate on the socioeconomic revolution while ignoring the military conflict. What was left of the Spanish army in the Republican zone was largely disbanded in favor of leftist militia battalions that were full of revolutionary zeal and reasonably well-equipped but lacked discipline, leadership, or military skill. Thus the battles of August and September 1936 were uniform disasters for the leftist forces, who in the south were steadily driven back toward Madrid by the small advancing columns of veterans from the Moroccan garrisons.

Only belatedly did some of the leftist leaders realize that they must achieve greater political unity and concentrate on the military struggle. The first true Popular Front government was organized in September 1936 under the "bolshevized" Socialist Francisco Largo Caballero and was later joined by CNT cabinet members. In the months that followed, the wartime Republican government strove to develop an effective mass army that could do battle with the professionally guided Nationalist forces, now under the supreme command of General Francisco Franco.

The new Republican People's Army of 1936–39 mobilized more than a million men and tried to combine the principles of disciplined military organization with revolutionary consciousness, replacing the traditional military salute with the clenched fist and adopting the Red Army symbol of the red star as well as its system of political commissars. It was this need to develop a major military force that first brought Spanish communism to the fore. Before the Civil War the Spanish Communist party had been small and weak, unable to compete in popular appeal with the anarchosyndicalists or the Socialists. It stood at the extreme left of the political spectrum, calling for a "worker-peasant" united front regime to replace the Republic, but after the beginning of the Civil War it moderated its position to concentrate on Republican unity and the military conflict.

During the 1930s and for long afterward, the Spanish Communist party was completely under Soviet control. (The party of independent "Spanish" communism was the POUM, concentrated mainly in Catalonia.) Its strength mounted steadily after September 1936 because the Republic's main—sometimes only—source of military supplies was the Soviet Union and because, thanks to Soviet training and advice, the Communists proved more effective than any other leftist party in military mobilization and leadership.

By contrast, the Western democracies tried to avoid any kind of involvement in the Civil War. Once it had become clear that Italy and Germany were providing military support to the right-wing nationalists, Britain and France organized a nonintervention committee of representatives of major powers. Meeting regularly in London after September 1936, it had no influence on Italy, Germany, or the Soviet Union but did serve to localize the war and preclude any involvement by the North Atlantic democracies.

The Soviet Union's policy in Spain, by contrast, was first of all to promote a leftist victory through limited support, second to establish Communist politicomilitary hegemony within the Republican zone, and third, and most important of all, to advance the foreign policy of the Soviet Union by checking the interests of Germany and Italy while seeking to gain some understanding about collective security with France and Britain. The only one of these goals that was achieved was the second, the establishment of a limited Communist hegemony in the Republican zone.

Communist leaders soon demanded that the revolution be moderated to concentrate on the desperate military situation, and the extreme left in turn charged the communists with sabotaging the revolution. The truth was more complex. Communist propaganda and policy during the Civil War operated on three levels. On the international level, the Communists insisted that there was no revolution in process in Spain at all, that the Civil War merely constituted a struggle between Western democracy and fascism. Within Republican Spain as a whole, the Communist program was to replace the prewar parliamentary Republic with a new hybrid "People's Republic," the first of its kind, that would be partially socialist and under Communist tutelage. In the most hyperrevolutionary region, Catalonia, the Communists engaged in revolutionary competition with the anarchosyndicalists while striving to channel and discipline the revolution.

The semimonopoly of military supplies at their disposal, combined with their discipline and military strength, enabled the Communists to enforce their will on the Popular Front parties by 1937. By May of that year government control had been reestablished over several of the regions dominated by revolutionaries, and the Communists forced Largo Caballero from power in favor of the more moderate and pragmatic Socialist Juan Negrín, who was willing to cooperate with them fully in order to win the war. From the spring of 1937 until the winter of 1939 their power and influence steadily increased in the Republican zone.

So long as Soviet support might make it possible to win the Civil War, the other leftist parties reluctantly agreed to the united front Negrín government and mostly cooperated in a more disciplined military effort. The Republican People's Army, however, despite its numerical strength, never became as disciplined and skilled as Franco's Nationalist army. Though at first not as well supplied as the Republicans, Franco's units used their resources more effectively, and by 1938 the weight of foreign support had clearly swung in their favor. The Republican zone was cut in two, and total military victory seemed only a matter of time. Uninterrupted military defeat had undermined faith in the revolution in much of the remaining Republican zone; yet the Negrín government pressed for resistance to the bitter end, hoping that if worst came to worst and the Spanish left held on long enough, the outbreak of world war in Europe would bring British and French intervention. By February 1939, however, half the original Republican zone had been overrun, and a series of new appointments further increased Communist influence in the People's Army.

That was the last straw for many anarchosyndicalists and Socialists, and so the Civil War ended in March 1939 much as it had begun, with an anti-Communist rebellion by sectors of the Republican army that aimed to save Spain from communism. Although the Communist units were defeated by the anarchosyndicalist and Socialist sectors of the People's Army, the victors were so weak that they sought only to surrender to Franco, who won a complete and unconditional victory.[8]

The Franco Regime, 1936-75

The revolt against the Left Republican government in July 1936 began primarily as a military undertaking, with only marginal assistance from rightwing monarchists and the fascistic Falange party. The military conspirators, led by General Emilio Mola, themselves lacked political unity and were held together only by the negative goal of overthrowing the leftist regime. They did not originally intend to destroy the Republic per se but to eliminate leftist influence and give the Republic a more conservative, authoritarian, and nationalist cast.

The military pronunciamiento's failure to seize full power and the development of a mass civil war radicalized the political structure of both sides. Revolution in the Republican zone was met by reorganization and a new political identity in the Nationalist zone. The military rebels were joined by nearly all the foes of the left, ranging from ultrareactionary Carlists to moderate liberals and nonpolitical sectors of the middle classes.

By September 1936 the Nationalist commanders had to face the prospect of lengthy civil war and the need for strong leadership if they were to achieve victory. As commander in chief they chose the most respected young general in the Spanish army, Francisco Franco. He took office on 1 October 1936 and immediately proclaimed himself chief of state as well as commander in chief of the incipient Nationalist regime, becoming its dictator both in fact and in law.

Born in 1892, Franco was forty-three years of age when he became *caudillo*, or supreme leader of the Spanish counterrevolution. He came from a traditional upper-middle-class family connected with the naval officer corps and had made a national reputation as a hero in the Moroccan campaigns of the 1920s. He was promoted to brigadier at thirty-three and became the youngest general in Europe in 1926. His ascendancy within the Spanish army was not due to his political activity, however, for Franco made a fetish of iron discipline and strict professionalism. Ostracized and momentarily demoted by the Republic for his record under the monarchy, he had been quickly rehabilitated and then briefly appointed chief of the Spanish general staff under the right-center government of 1935.

Franco, like many other middle-class Spaniards, became intensely politicized by the polarization of the Second Republic. Seeking an alternative to the democratic parliamentary system, he gravitated not toward fascistic Falangism but toward the Catholic authoritarian and corporative right, and by 1936 he espoused a philosophy of traditionalist nationalism and authoritarianism. Even so, he carefully eschewed responsibility in political conspiracies during 1935-36, prudently avoiding involvement until he finally decided in early July 1936 that it would be more dangerous to stay out of the rebellion than to join it.

When the Civil War began, Franco became commander of the elite professional forces in Spanish Morocco, the most important sector of the Nationalist army. His representatives initiated contacts with Hitler and Mussolini to gain military support for the Nationalist cause, and by September 1936 his selection as Nationalist chief had become practically a foregone conclusion.[9]

From the very beginning Franco was keenly aware that a mere military dictatorship might be able to win the war but would have no possibility of long-term survival. He was determined to avoid what he termed "el error Primo de Rivera," that is, the failure to develop a fully organized and institutionalized new system. The new Nationalist state could survive neither as a simple monarchy nor as a praetorian dictatorship but must have an ideology and evolve a new political economic system.

The old moderate and conservative parties had collapsed under the impact of civil war. Franco's main civilian support came from the Falangist party, which had swelled into a mass organization only after the fighting began, and secondarily from the Carlist militia. In April 1937 Franco laid the political basis for his system by merging the two groups into the *Falange Española Tradicionalista* (the latter adjective added for the sake of the Carlists), whose Twenty-Six-Point Doctrine was declared to be the ideology of the new state. In creating a state party, however, Franco did not in any way let the Falangists take over his regime. Many of their original leaders and militants had already been killed by the Republicans, and the new Falangist activists were purged and co-opted to serve the Franco regime; they were taken over by the new state rather than vice versa. More specifically, despite the use of the fascist salute and an extreme leadership principle based on the cult of Franco's personality, Franco denied that the system was fascist, saying that the Falangist ideology was merely a point of departure that would be elaborated and modified in the future.

Although Franco won the Civil War because he had a better army, that in turn was conditioned by the degree and quality of German and Italian support. Once his victory was complete in 1939, the future course and the very survival of the Francoist system depended very much on international events. Hitler's invasion of right-wing Catholic Poland, whose government was very similar to Franco's, shocked the Spanish dictator, and during the first year of World War II, Spain was genuinely neutral. At the same time, Franco fully realized that the hostility of Western liberals to his dictatorship might well lead to its overthrow if the liberal democracies won the war in Europe. After the fall of France in 1940, he switched from neutrality to nonbelligerence, an official status favoring Germany and Italy. For two years, from 1941 to 1943, a Spanish division fought beside the German army in Russia as a gesture of enmity toward the Soviet Union, which had intervened in the Spanish war on the Republican side.

By the end of 1943, however, it was becoming clearer that Germany might well lose the war. Anglo-American forces dominated North Africa and would soon invade Italy and France. Franco found it expedient to trim his sails further and emphasize the conservative, legalistic, and nonfascist nature of his regime. The Falangist state party was downgraded and soon became know vaguely as the "Movement," to give it a neutral, bureaucratic flavor.

In 1942 the Spanish government charted plans to create a new controlled, indirect, and "organic" corporative Cortes to replace the old democratic Parliament overthrown in 1936. The Francoist state was founded on the belief that all political parties were divisive and destructive per se. It espoused the doctrine common among the Catholic and conservative right in Europe that true representation should rest on the natural, organic units of society—the family, local government, and economic, professional, religious, and cultural associations. It was not until 1967—an entire quarter-century later—that the regime went so far as to allow heads of families to vote directly for two Cortes members per province. Before that time and for most Cortes seats even after 1967, members were elected by organizations that were themselves subject to government appointment and control. Moreover, a number of *procuradores* (deputies), varying from twenty-five to fifty, were named directly by Franco. This guaranteed a thoroughly controlled and largely unrepresentative national assembly (see table 1.4).

After 1945 Franco was under severe pressure from most of the victorious wartime Allies as the last surviving "fascist" dictator in Europe. During this period of ostracism he moved to regularize and legitimize the structure of his regime by declaring the Spanish state a monarchy. A popular referendum was arranged in 1947, which approved Franco's continued exercise of the powers of chief of state as regent for life. This, together with subsequent legislation, established a complicated succession mechanism whereby the Spanish state would revert to monarchist rule under a descendant (at first unspecified) of the Spanish Bourbon dynasty upon the death of Franco.

The onset of the cold war rescued Franco from ostracism after 1947, and Spain soon became a valued associate of the United States in its strategic competition with the Soviet Union. A special bilateral pact between the United States and Spain was signed in 1953, providing for the construction of major American air and naval bases, together with sizable military and financial assistance. The relationship has been maintained in somewhat revised form ever since and in 1976 was raised to the level of an official treaty between the two countries.

For ten years after the Civil War the Spanish economy suffered from deep depression, but it began to recover in the late 1940s and moved ahead in the 1950s under the stimulus of foreign investment and new opportunities. For twenty years Franco maintained an elaborate series of autarkic state economic controls, somewhat similar to those of the last years of fascist Italy, but in 1959 most of these were eliminated and the whole economic system liberalized. Foreign investment and international trade and tourism increased at a vertiginous rate during the 1960s, producing a Spanish "economic miracle" that momentarily achieved one of the highest growth rates in the world and continued without interruption until the international recession of 1973.

Until his death in November 1975, Franco's rule was never seriously challenged from within Spain. The strength of his grip on the Spanish state was due to many factors: (1) the unconditional military victory in the Civil War, (2) Franco's complete ascendancy over his own army, which became fully identified with him, (3) the extreme polarization and trauma produced by the Civil War, which discouraged most of his original followers from turning against him and led non-Francoists sometimes to acquiesce in authoritarian rule rather than risk more conflict, (4) the internal division of the opposition, magnified by the Civil War but never overcome afterward, (5) the partial rehabilitation of Franco's international position by the United States, and (6) the unprecedented wave of prosperity in the 1950s and 1960s, which encouraged general depoliticization and substituted economic gratification for civic freedom.

While never altering its fundamental authoritarian structure, the regime became increasingly moderate in later years. Several minor reforms were introduced in the mid-1960s. Illegal labor strikes sometimes enjoyed de facto tolerance if they were not associated with political protest. Censorship was lightened in 1967, and heads of families were allowed to vote directly for a

Table 1.4 Composition of Franco's Cortes, 1942, 1946, and 1967

	1942		1946
1	All government ministers	1	All government ministers
2	National councilors of Falange Española Tradicionalista	2	National councilors
3	Presidents of the Council of State, the Supreme Court, the Supreme Council of Military Justice	3	Presidents of the Council of State, the Supreme Court, the Supreme Council of Military Justice
4	Representatives of the national syndicates (their numbers to be no more than a third of the Cortes)	4	Representatives of the national syndicates
5	Mayors of all provincial capitals and of Ceuta and Melilla	5	Mayors of all provincial capitals and of Ceuta and Melilla
	One representative of the municipalities of each province to be appointed by the provincial council		One representative of the municipalities of each province One representative of each provincial council
6	Rectors of all Spanish universities	6	Rectors of all Spanish universities
7	President of the Institute of Spain	7	President of the Institute of Spain
	Presidents of the royal academies		representatives of the royal academies
	Chancellors of Hispanidad		President and two repesentatives of the Supreme Council for Scientific Research
8	Seven representatives of professional bodies	8	Sixteen representatives of professional bodies
9	Fifty members appointed by the head of state	9	Fifty members appointed by the head of state

Source: José Amodia, *Franco's Political Legacy* (London: Allen Lane, 1977), p. 97.

	1967
1	All government ministers
2	National councilors
3	Presidents of the Council of State, the Supreme Court, the Supreme Council of Military Justice, the Court of Accounts, the National Economic Council
4	150 representatives of the syndical organization
5	One representative for the municipalities of each province
	One representative for each municipality with more than 300,000 inhabitants
	One representative each for Ceuta and Melilla
	One representative for each provincial council
6	Rectors of all Spanish universities
7	President of the Institute of Spain
	Two representatives of the royal academies
	President and two representatives of the Supreme Council for Scientific Research
8	Twenty-one representatives of professional bodies
9	Twenty-five members appointed by the head of state
10	Two representatives elected by heads of families in each province

minority of Cortes deputies. The whole tone of Spanish life became more open and informal under the impact of mass tourism and socioeconomic change.

Franco long delayed naming an official successor, but he intended that the structure of his system should survive him. The son and heir of Alfonso XIII, Don Juan, was unacceptable to Franco because Don Juan believed in constitutional parliamentary monarchy of the British type. In 1948 Franco therefore made arrangements to bring Don Juan's own son and heir, Prince Juan Carlos (b. 1938), to be educated inside Spain and specially trained as Franco's successor. Satisfied with the serious and dutiful attitude displayed by the prince, in 1969 he officially designated Juan Carlos to succeed him as king of Spain upon his death. Franco never fully appreciated how much Juan Carlos sympathize with his father's liberal principles or how supple and pragmatic the young prince's own political talents were.

For thirty-seven years Franco combined the office of president of government, or prime minister, with that of chief of state or regent. At the beginning of 1973, however, he finally relinquished the prime ministership to his closest personal and political associate, Admiral Luis Carrero Blanco, whom he intended to have continue as prime minister even after his own death and thus guarantee the regime's institutional integrity under the reign of Juan Carlos. This plan came to naught when Carrero Blanco was assassinated in a spectacular *attentat* by members of the Basque nationalist terrorist organization, Basque Land and Liberty (ETA).

Rather than turning more sharply to the right, Franco chose as Carrero Blanco's successor a loyal but reasonably moderate bureaucrat, Carlos Arias Navarro. During the two years that followed Arias tried to conciliate the growing restiveness of a transformed Spanish society by announcing a new series of reforms, which would include freedom to form limited new "political associations" for the Cortes while avoiding the hated political "parties." This reform quickly stalled, however, and had not gone into effect by the time that Franco died in November 1975.

The last months of Franco's life were a time of renewed tension and confrontation, when the aged dictator decided to defy Western European democratic opinion by ratifying the execution of five convicted leftist terrorists. This elicited protests throughout Western Europe and a temporary boycott of Spanish commerce but provided Franco with the opportunity to demonstrate once again that his regime and his principles remained basically unchanged to the end.

By the time he finally died most Spaniards no longer had any personal memories of the Civil War. Their society had been almost totally transformed during the past quarter-century; an agrarian land had changed into a predominantly urban and industrial country. A regime that had once been part of the "new order" of corporatist right authoritarian systems that were predominant in most of Europe in 1939 had become the last dinosaur from an archaic pre-World War II era. Spain, whose government had been more advanced than its society for a hundred years, now had a society considerably more advanced than its backward, 1939-style political system.

The Democratization of Spain, 1976-79

The democratization of Spain that has occurred since 1976 constitutes a political transformation without any clear parallel or analogy in twentieth-century systems, for an established, institutionalized authoritarian system—no mere ad hoc Caribbean military dictatorship—has been totally transformed from the inside out by means of the personnel, institutions, and mechanism of the regime itself, led by the head of state. The only analogy that has sometimes been mentioned, Turkey after Kemal Atatürk, does not bear comparison; the Turkish republic was not a European authoritarian state but the first twentieth-century expression of guided democracy in a third-world mold. Nor is the recent Portuguese revolution similar, either. The Portuguese dictatorship suffered the standard fate of institutionalized modern European authoritarian systems: its overthrow was due to pressures stemming from foreign (in this case, colonial) affairs.

The democratization of Spain after Franco has depended on two fundamental variables: (1) the semisophisticated new society of urban and industrial Spain, which felt itself to be in full consonance with an overwhelmingly social democratic Western European political culture; and (2) the leadership of the new king, Juan Carlos, the "motor of the change." Franco had not fully trusted his successor and had thought to tie his hands through a set of complicated constitutional provisions making it difficult to name a new prime minister soon after Franco's own passing. Yet Franco's closest associate and truest political successor, Admiral Carrero Blanco, had been assassinated two years earlier, and the new prime minister, Arias Navarro, proved a weak leader.

Juan Carlos began the change in December 1975, the month after Franco's death, by forcing Arias Navarro to accept a new cabinet of moderate reformist liberals and charging them with the task of introducing a complete liberalization of Spanish institutions while working in conformity with existing laws. Broad civil liberties began to be restored by the first months of 1976, but the new Arias Navarro government made little progress in direct democratization of political institutions. By July 1976 Juan Carlos held sufficient control to impose his own prime minister. Arias was forced to resign, and the king's own designee, Adolfo Suárez, became prime minister, at the head of a completely new cabinet of democratic reformers.

Though Suárez had enjoyed a long administrative career under the Franco regime, he was a comparative political unknown on the national level. Many commentators forecast doom for the liberalization program at the hands of a Francoist bureaucrat. What was not known was that the new prime minister and the royal executive had come to a private understanding before Franco's death, and Suárez in fact had been carefully selected to complete the institutional transformation. The photogenic Suárez was only forty-three, a member of the post-Civil War generation. He was endowed with both a detailed knowledge of the inner working of the old regime and the political sense to inaugurate a new system.

Suárez's first major feat was to induce the Francoist parliament to commit suicide by approving a new law for the democratic reform of the Cortes in October 1976. When the referendum on the recasting of Spain's political institutions was submitted to the nation in December 1976, it was approved by an overwhelming majority. The next major step was convening of democratic parliamentary elections, Spain's first in forty-one years. Before that could be done, however, their scope had to be determined and broader guarantees provided. A partial amnesty for political prisoners was declared and the extension of civil liberties made complete. The final hurdle concerned the legalization of potentially nondemocratic political organizations, especially the Spanish Communist party (PCE). The major mass formation of the democratic left, the Socialists (PSOE), insisted that they could not accept the legitimacy of a system that excluded the Communists. Suárez took the plunge by legalizing the Spanish Communist party in April 1977.

This opened the way for parliamentary elections in June. To face the opposition of a newly burgeoning left, Suárez encouraged and co-opted the formation of a new liberal democratic party, the Union of the Democratic Center (UCD), which emerged from the new elections as Spain's largest political force, with nearly 35 percent of the popular vote. It was followed rather closely by the Socialists, while the Communists and the new right-wing party, the Popular Alliance, trailed badly.

For the next eighteen months, Spain's first elected Parliament since the Civil War was preoccupied with drawing up a new democratic constitution for a parliamentary monarchy amid worsening economic conditions and a mounting campaign of terrorism, waged primarily by Basque separatists (the ETA). The economy had begun to deteriorate before the death of Franco, as declining investment and shrinking markets resulted in mounting unemployment combined with steep inflation. By 1977 the Spanish inflation rate was more than 25 percent, while worker demands and the government's desire to conciliate the left made it very hard to limit production costs. By 1978, however, a devaluation of the peseta combined with more moderate economic agreements stimulated the export trade, and the rate of inflation began to lessen.

More intractable was the problem of terrorism and domestic order. The more complete the extension of the democratic process within the country, the greater the incidence of political violence. An overwhelming majority of Spaniards applauded the democratization and in varying degrees sought to cooperate, but sectors of the extreme left demanded total capitulation. In the three Basque provinces nationalist opinion became steadily more extreme, and the Basque revolutionary left, operating from secure sanctuaries inside France, increased its activities.

The constitution was eventually completed in the autumn of 1978 and approved by popular referendum at the close of that year. Spain's new charter of government established all the regular conditions and guarantees for a standard Western European parliamentary democracy under a monarchy that reigned but did not rule. Church and state were separated, but the bitter anticlericalism of the Republican era had disappeared, and the rights of the Catholic church were fully protected. The new constitution was a negotiated document, not imposed on parliament by a dominant party but mutually arranged by representatives of all the main national groups. Thus it did not fully resolve each point of every major issue by specification, but it provided a framework under which the details of major problems might be resolved by subsequent legislation. Regional autonomy for general areas of Spain was recognized as a right, but the terms of autonomy for any specific region would have to be negotiated subsequently for each case.

What had initially surprised many observers was the weakness of rightwing Francoist opposition to the entire program of democratization. This was due above all to the transformation of Spanish society and culture during the preceding generation, eroding the social basis of Francoism even before the generalissimo had died. Without Franco himself, the remaining minority of Francoists proved impotent in the face of legitimate government accompanied by political stability and massive popular approval.

The stronghold of Francoism was supposed to have been the army, commonly held to be an irreducible obstacle to the dismantling of the old regime. Despite much murmuring, however, the military command accepted the transformation without so much as a single serious effort at conspiracy or revolt. Franco himself had been careful to remove the military from ordinary government and politics. He had also reduced the proportionate size of the armed forces and their budget, encouraging an attitude of professionalism and depoliticization. And the Generalíssimo had been careful to divide the power of senior commanders, thus avoiding the coalescence of military authority under a major figure or small united group.

As it turned out, the military had neither the opportunity nor the genuine inclination to intervene in the political process. Historically, the Spanish army officer corps has never been an independent force, contrary to popular image. It has normally been drawn into politics by the breakdown—or threatened breakdown—of regular government, rather than by any spontaneous promptings of its own. Though the democratization was not popular with most officers, the military was not uninfluenced by the social and cultural changes that affected the rest of society. Since the transformation was carried out under legitimate, hierarchical institutions of the crown, proceeded with general smoothness and stability, scarcely ever threatened to get out of control, and was strongly supported by the great majority of politically conscious Spaniards, the military had little alternative but to accept it.

Juan Carlos played the major role in managing the army, together with the new minister of defense, Lieutenant General Manuel Gutiérrez Mellado. The young king had been educated as a regular officer, was identified with the military, and maintained close personal contacts with them. He also did not shrink from punishing or placing in retirement the rare general who publicly spoke out of line. In handling the military as in promoting the transformation of government, the initiative of the king was crucial. Juan Carlos fully merited the esteem in which he was held by most of the public.

Democratization also meant the transformation of Spain's relationship with the rest of the Western world. The twenty-year pact with the United States was officially upgraded to a bilateral five-year treaty in 1976, and negotiations proceeded for Spain's entry into the European Common Market. What was less likely, however, was any early entrance of Spain into the North Atlantic Treaty Organization (NATO), given the opposition above all of the Spanish left.

The democratization was finally completed on the national level by the holding of new elections in March and April 1979. To the surprise of many, the UCD slightly increased its plurality in the new parliamentary elections, winning 35.5 percent of the popular vote and 47.7 percent of the seats. The socialists declined slightly, while the right dwindled to less than 6 percent of the popular vote, and the Communists increased to approximately 11 percent. This relative victory for the center was clouded somewhat, however, by the outcome of Spain's first free municipal elections in more than forty years. In the balloting for municipal councilors that took place in early April 1979, the UCD won many more seats than any other party, but they were concentrated in the more conservative smaller towns and cities of central and northern Spain. Socialists and Communists predominated in large cities and industrial areas, and a subsequent electoral pact between the two main Marxist parties would enable them to appoint the mayors of most of the larger cities of Spain.

Four years after the death of Franco, Spain had achieved functional democracy and also reasonably stable government. Economic investment was growing and inflation somewhat moderating. Though the demands of labor would continue to be vigorous, the nation's economy was in better condition than most had expected several years earlier. Regional autonomy was also being negotiated for Spain's largest special region, Catalonia.

Only one major domestic problem of crucial dimensions remained unsolved—the defiance of Basque nationalism. A major police crackdown at the beginning of 1979 momentarily reduced the rate of terrorism, but by the spring of that year it had rebounded to a very high level once more. The intractable nature of the Basque problem was due not merely or even primarily to the incidence of terrorism but to the absence of terms and conditions for a creative political solution. Opinion within the three Basque provinces was completely fragmented between the Spanish left (Socialists), the Spanish center-right (the UCD), and the Basque nationalists proper. Among the 50 percent or so of the Basque population that voted for nationalists, there was further division between the less radical middle-class majority (the Basque Nationalist party—PNV) and the revolutionaries (Herri Batasuna), whose support increased dramatically in 1979. The nationalists would not accept a moderate Catalan-type compromise but insisted on terms of semi-independence. This was not a feasible solution, since nearly half the population of the Basque country is not Basque but consists of immigrants from other parts of Spain who support self-government but not radical Basquization. The Basque economy is thoroughly interconnected with the rest of the Spanish economy and comprises a major part of Spanish industry. Independence is not a practical possibility even if it were acceptable to most Spanish political groups, which it is not. Practically the only veto on which the military would still insist would be cast against any reduction of Spain's territorial integrity. The terms of a creative solution for the Basque problem were therefore not in sight as of mid-1979.

This scarcely detracted from the magnitude of the Spanish achievement of 1976–79. One of the world's oldest and most stable dictatorships had been thoroughly transformed from the inside out, with no serious disorder and a minimum of bloodshed, nearly all of which came from the revolutionary left and not from the government or even the remnants of the old regime. The extent of this achievement and the cooperation and civic maturity demonstrated by most of Spain's political forces created a mood of hope and optimism for the difficult decade ahead.

Shaping the Constitution
ANTONIO LÓPEZ PINA

─────── It is not easy to write a chapter that does justice to the complex and disorderly process that shaped the Spanish constitution. The Law for Political Reform (1976) and the Electoral Law created a new Cortes, consisting of a Chamber of Deputies and a Senate to serve as both legislature and constituent assembly. This meant that the constitutional debate took place first in committee and then in plenary session in each chamber. The process began when a draft constitution was submitted by the Constitutional Commission of the Chamber of Deputies in August 1977 and ended after the Senate debates and the work of the joint conference committee of both houses were completed. The final document was produced in October 1978.[1]

The debates in committee and in plenary sessions were in some respects irrelevant. Agreement was often reached privately by the leaders, and the vote in the Cortes simply formalized their decisions. The speeches in the Cortes were designed to sell the decisions to the public or to score debating points within parliamentary groups or parties. Occasionally they expressed little more than reactions to current events.

Moreover, in private and in public the parliamentary parties repeatedly accused each other of breaking previous understandings—and then acted as if they themselves therefore were no longer bound by these understandings or even by the logic of their own proposals. The phrase "Spanish labyrinth," coined by Gerald Brenan, to describe early twentieth-century Spain, also conveys the chaotic character of the constitutional writing process in the 1970s.

My purpose in this chapter is to identify the principal issues debated in the constituent Cortes and to analyze them within a political and theoretical framework. Elected to the Senate in 1977 for the Spanish Socialist Workers' party (PSOE), I was an active participant in the writing of the constitution. I have tried to write objectively and accurately; nevertheless, the reader should regard the essay more as a personal recollection than as a systematic scientific reconstruction of reality.[2]

The Issues

The Objective: Democracy   The party system that emerged after the Franco dictatorship included many parties with significantly different programs.[3] Many observers viewed the PSOE, with its history of opposition to Franco, as the only party capable of ensuring the democratic legitimacy of the constitutional process and the new regime. From the death of Franco in November 1975 to the ratification of the constitution in December 1978, the PSOE led the minority, prodding the conservative government of the Union of the Democratic Center (UCD) toward a more liberal constitution.

As early as April 1976, Felipe González, the secretary general of the PSOE, had said: "In a process of attaining a democratic breakthrough, the first demand must be freedom and basic liberties for all. . . . once these are granted, a constituent process must begin."[4] In December of the same year the PSOE proposed a "constitutional compromise": a formalized agreement between the main political parties, the aim of which would be to secure a democratic constitution that retained no trace of autocracy but guaranteed equal opportunity for all democratic groups.[5] By July 1977 the constituent Cortes was in session, and González thanked the government for sending to the Cortes a constitutional draft that had been prepared with the help of distinguished specialists in public law. At the same time he insisted that "the parties must do more than merely offer comments: the parliamentary parties must be active participants in the elaboration of the constitution."[6]

Catalan Deputy Miguel Roca Junyent stressed:

> The originality of the Spanish process consists precisely in the fact that we will achieve a breakthrough by means of convoking a constituent assembly, and not the reverse. We have not obtained a constitution through some breach in the status quo, but rather, through a constitutional process we have achieved a reform and, in a certain sense, a revolution—all at the same time. If the Nationalist Uprising of 1936 represented the negation of all of the institutions at odds with the values that General Franco sought to restore, the same method—a break with the past—has been used to recover a political order of liberty and democracy.[7]

Except for the Basque nationalists, all the parliamentary parties backed a strategy of consensus; that is, they supported drafting a constitution that would make possible the implementation of any party's programs. The consensus evolved from a series of basic agreements: the desire to eliminate the centralized unitary state while preserving a sense of national unity; the acceptance of the rule of law; the recognition that the people should ultimately be sovereign; the creation of a representative democracy with a bicameral legislature; and the acceptance of a monarchy.

"Consensus," as Roca said, "means accepting ambiguity . . . the kind of ambiguity that opens the way for any democratic party to rule without creating a dangerous constitutional crisis."[8] PSOE Deputy Joan Reventos asserted that the one necessary quality of the constitution was that it should "permit a legal transition to socialism."[9] Less inclined toward conciliation, consensus, and ambiguity, Manuel Fraga Iribarne of the Popular Alliance (AP) argued for a constitution that asserted that the society should be based on the market economy and oppose any language that could justify the development of the class struggle.[10]

The only serious discordant note came from two Basque congressmen, Javier Arzallus of the Basque Nationalist party (PNV) and Francisco Letamendía of the Euzkadi Left (EE), who dissented from the consensual strategy. Arzallus revived the old Basque idea of the *pacto foral* when he emphasized that the Basques preferred to see the Crown as "a point of confluence and a bridge between free peoples who agree to restrict their sovereignty."[11] Letamendía, for his part, called for outright Basque independence, rejecting the legitimacy of any constitution that failed to recognize the right of self-determination.[12]

The Modern State, Constitutional Government, and Society Spain's transition was a counterpoint of reform and *ruptura*. There was a deliberate break with the past, but one arrived at by consent and consultation. Its aim was democracy under a constitution that would permit the transfer of the control of government by free elections. This was the first item on the agenda. But transcending this concern was a more fundamental problem: how to frame the relationship between state and society.

The constitution and the new regime would operate in a society that was the product of complex historical processes. The nineteenth-century bourgeois revolution in Spain produced a civil society at odds with itself, divided by interest groups that were difficult to reconcile. Elsewhere in Europe—France is the prototype—bourgeois revolutions followed the sequence outlined by Gramsci: the hegemony of the bourgeoisie (over the other classes) was transformed into the cultural and moral direction of civil society, before it actually became coercive political control—exemplified by the repressive apparatus of the state. In Spain, however, the bourgeoisie assumed political control of the state without having previously consolidated its cultural and moral hegemony.

Born at a time of general economic depression following a premature plunge into industrialization, the liberal Spanish state of the nineteenth century espoused an agrarian policy that the people justly perceived as a swindle. As a result, the first liberal state failed to establish its legitimacy in Spain. From

1808 to 1939, constitutional government and civil order were repeatedly disrupted. Still there were extended periods of peace under a constitution, at least tacitly accepted by a majority of the citizens. The success of the government's performance, however, was conditioned both by the political and historical circumstances and by personal memories of earlier civil warfare. In times of civil peace, the people accepted the existing government as a fact of life; they obeyed the laws without granting them moral legitimacy. The *marais*—the *masas neutras*, the "silent majority"—tended to see authority as an annoying but necessary evil for the protection of the private sphere and the underpinnings in the self-interest of the family.

The great majority of Spaniards still regard the state as arbitrary and unfriendly. Paradoxically, this state with which nobody identifies himself is acknowledged as a powerful sovereign by nearly all citizens, who alternate between ignominious submission and impossible demands. After a century and a half of liberal constitutionalism, most Spaniards still feel more like subjects than citizens and seek to use the state to further their own private, sometimes excessive and irresponsible interests. The state has at the very end been converted into the necessary reference for all the demands for reform, all the lost opportunities, all the situations of impotence, and all the frustrations of the past.

The Spanish state's position could not be more difficult: in a capitalist society with low industrial growth and great inequality in wealth, the liberal state must reconcile the conflicting interests. This necessity imposes on it a reformist mission, but since the internal dynamic of power in society is determined at all decisive moments by the *gran burguesía's* hegemonic position, the state is incapable of ensuring its reformist mission.

All social classes make demands on the state; none wholeheartedly backs it. Only some professional elites identify totally with the state. A strong concern with inequality and social injustice reinforces a more general alienation from those wielding political power. The state, the political regime, and the government merge in the popular mind. Government, in particular, seems to most Spaniards to be an offshoot of the state, both oppressive and protective. This means that for most Spaniards the government (defined as the arbitrary will of those who rule) is all, and the state (defined as public action under law, directed toward the survival and development of civil society) is almost nothing.

Finally, the political mission of the state has usually had a religious foundation. Moral values in Spain are defined by the criteria and orientations of the Catholic church. Lacking an independent moral foundation, the state has become the enforcing arm for the church, punishing transgressions against Catholic morality.

The constituent Cortes set out to draft a charter to break the legal and political framework that existed under Franco and resume the tradition interrupted by the Civil War in 1936. In addition, the constitution needed to be amenable to both conservative and progressive interpretations. Moreover, the constituent parliament also faced the challenge of developing a secular state—up to that point weak and unsatisfactorily grounded—and of bonding that state to a society itself in need of structural transformation. Only a powerful and dynamic state founded on the principles enunciated by the constituent Cortes would make sense out of post-Franco Spain and set it on a new course.

Structural and Subjective Factors The strength and effectiveness of the political parties and the interplay of personalities on the Constitutional Commission conditioned the constitutional debates.[13] Miguel Herrero de Miñon and Jose Pedro Pérez Llorca were the principal UCD spokesmen during the drafting of the constitution. Skilled professionals with prestigious qualifications and competence in the areas of theory of the state and constitutional law, they often seemed more preoccupied with erudition and niceties of phrasing than with the historical and institutional connotations of their ideas.

Jordi Solé-Tura represented the Spanish Communist party (PCE) on the Constitutional Commission of the Chamber of Deputies. A professor of political theory and constitutional law, Solé-Tura appeared constrained because of the return of Communist Secretary General Santiago Carrillo to Spain in 1976. No other cause explains his silence when the PCE showed itself willing to sacrifice its doctrinal heritage and even the class interests it claimed to defend on a variety of issues. Nonetheless, he participated competently in the work of the commission.

The spokesman for the Popular Alliance was Manuel Fraga. For many Spaniards, Fraga was the embodiment of Francoism and the extreme right, the epitome of a conservative, authoritarian leader. Although many did not consider Fraga a democrat, yet most recognized his stature as a statesman. This quality distinguished him from many other members of the Constitutional Commission of the Chamber of Deputies.

The Catalan and Basque nationalists sent strong personalities to the commission. Both showed great competence and eloquence in the discussions. Roca, an intelligent, upper-class Catalan, played a leading role in the behind-the-scenes negotiations. Arzallus, a former Jesuit, possessed the zeal of the convert, and his speeches were sometimes impassioned to the point of demagoguery.

Speaking for socialism were Enrique Tierno Galván and Gregorio Peces-Barba. For decades Tierno Galván had been one of the most notable intellectuals in Spain and one of the most constant opponents of Francoism. On the commission he was politically crippled by the weak parliamentary position of his People's Socialist party, which held only 6 of 350 seats, and by his badly strained relations with the leading party on the left, the PSOE.[14] Peces-Barba, a lawyer and a Catholic who had gained fame as a human rights advocate during the last years of Franco's rule, brought to the debates a perspective that emphasized the rule of law (*estado de derecho*) and a conception of justice that drew on Catholic doctrine as well as on his legal experience.[15] Finally, we must mention the key role played in the decisive phases of the negotiations by two deputies, Alfonso Guerra (PSOE) and Fernando Abril Martorell (UCD), and by the Senate majority and minority leaders, Antonio Jiménez Blanco and Francisco Ramos Fernández-Torrecillas.

Although at this point we might be tempted to consider the intellectual influences on leading members of parliament and on specific sections of the constitution, in my opinion, this would not take us very far. True, Fraga counted Carl Schmitt as an intellectual mentor; Herrero de Miñon liked to introduce himself as heir to the conservative theory of monarchy; Jordi Solé-Tura had been inspired in important ways by the writings of Antonio Gramsci; and the PSOE felt a close identification with certain important working-class political traditions, notably the experience of the Second Spanish Republic (1931–36). The post-World War II constitutional developments and experience in Italy, the Federal Republic of Germany, and the French Fifth Republic also exerted important influences on the work of the Constitutional Commission. Nevertheless, my personal experiences in the constituent Cortes lead me to conclude that, in Spain as in other Mediterranean societies, the personality of politicians played an exceptional role that serves as a good guide to why and how important decisions were made.

Political Theory and the Constitution: The Dogmatic Aspect

The theoretical base of the new regime was bound to be a synthesis of many disparate elements. It could not have been otherwise, considering the weight of the past and the conflicting positions of the parties involved. We have all the more reason, then, to distinguish clearly between the dogmatic aspect of the constitution (dealing with issues such as the form of government, the problem of sovereignty, the territorial organization of the state, church-state relations, and the economic system) and the organic aspect (legislative power, relations between the executive and parliament, and the like).

Drafting the constitution occurred on various fronts. In the parliamentary debates there was a constant clash among three fundamentally different conceptions of the constitution: the rationalist view, which insists that the constitution establish norms with general validity; the traditional view, which holds it to be the fruit of a historical tradition; and the sociological view, associated with Ferdinand Lassalle's notion of the *Realverfassung*, which is that the constitution should reflect the actual power relations in society. On the most significant issues, the final document was a victory of the traditionalist and sociological views.

Considerations of space lead me to limit my discussion of these issues to the five mentioned earlier: form of government, sovereignty, the territorial organization of the state, church-state relations, and the definition of the economic system.

Form of Government Article 1.3 of the Spanish constitution reads: "The political form of the Spanish state is that of parliamentary monarchy."[16] The concept of parliamentary monarchy was supported by most groups in the Cortes—including the PSOE. This was a painful concession for the Socialists. From the liberal revolution of 1868 onward, "monarchy" and "republic" have not been just names for different forms of government in Spain: they have represented contradictory, antagonistic poles within the political culture. "Republic" has meant individual liberties and political rights, but also social revolution. The word conjured up all the myths of revolutionary liberation—land redistribution to benefit the agricultural proletariat, radical federalism with self-determination for peripheral nationalist minorities, a civil state associated with the anticlerical factions of the bourgeoisie and the working class, and so on. "Monarchy" symbolized the negation of liberating change. As Luis Gómez Llorente, speaking for the Socialist parliamentary group said, "In Spain, freedom and democracy came to have one name and one name only: republic."[17]

In return for the Socialists' acceptance of the monarchy, the UCD modified its positions including even those involving the Crown. First, the new monarchy would be different from the historical monarchy. During the constitutional debates in the Senate, as spokesman for the PSOE parliamentary group there, I said:

> The new democratic monarchy that this constituent Parliament is to create cannot but accept popular sovereignty as its ultimate reference. We Socialists will accept the monarchy, but only a parliamentary monarchy that assumes popular sovereignty, not one that questions the absolute primacy of the popular will. Nationalizing the Crown, an idea implicit in the concept of parliamentary monarchy, is the best way we have to safeguard popular sovereignty as the ultimate source of legitimacy.[18]

The second important concession made to the PSOE position on this score was that under the constitution the Crown would not function as the supreme executive but would play a purely symbolic role.

Sovereignty With the issue of parliamentary monarchy resolved, it followed that the constitution should recognize the principle of popular sovereignty.

Article 1.2 states, "National sovereignty is vested in the Spanish people, from whom emanate the powers of the state." This statement was in line with the wishes of all the democratic parties and with the goal Prime Minister Adolfo Suárez had enunciated in the Law for Political Reform in 1976.[19] The minutes of the debates in the constituent Cortes confirm the breadth of the consensus on this issue.

However much speculation there might have been about it, the constitution never considered the armed forces as an enclave immune to the principle of popular sovereignty. By no stretch of the imagination are they granted parallel sovereignty by our constitution. Some have cited article 8 (its text reads: "The armed forces, comprising the army, the navy, the air force, have as their mission the guaranteeing of the sovereignty and independence of Spain and of defending its territorial integrity and the constitutional order."); and article 62 ("The King is . . . the commander in chief of the Armed Forces.") in support of their view that a military coup could be constitutional. This is an absurd argument. The laws are unequivocal in this regard. Article 34 of the Royal Decrees for the Armed Forces, for example, declares that "the obligation a member of the armed forces has to follow the orders of a superior has its limit when the orders involve the execution of acts which are manifestly contrary to the laws and uses of war, or particularly when they constitute a crime against the constitution." Moreover, article 26 requires "every military man [to] know and obey exactly the obligations contained in the constitution." It should also be stressed that the aforementioned article 8 does not stand alone in the constitution, but in the context established by article 97. According to the latter, "The Government directs domestic and foreign policy, civil and military administration as well as the defense of the State." This formulation should remove whatever doubt might exist as to the government's powers to direct the armed forces. Only the government can decide in favor of a military intervention to defend the constitutional order. Such a decision can occur only within the boundaries foreseen by article 116: a "state of siege" can be declared and the armed forces used in defense of the constitutional order only when directed by the government and under the terms fixed by the Cortes. The armed forces are not an exception to the constitution, and they are subject to the guiding principle expressed in article 9.1: "The citizenry and the public powers are subject to the constitution and to the rest of the judicial structures."

The Territorial Organization of the State Article 2 states that "the constitution is based on the indissoluble unity of the Spanish nation, the common and indivisible country of all Spaniards, and recognizes and guarantees the right to self-government of the nationalities and regions of which it is composed and solidarity among them all." This article tries to bridge the gap between viewpoints of those who defend centralism and those who insist on the right of regional areas to secede. Article 2 not only guarantees the right of regional self-government, but goes a step farther in recognizing Catalonia, the Basque country, and Galicia as "nationalities"—an innovation that is carefully balanced by the principles of interregional solidarity and of national indissolubility. This was a core issue in the constitutional debates. The Cortes accepted the concept of nationalities in the hope of ending once and for all longstanding historical feuds and of ultimately integrating the various regions.

During the sessions of the Senate Constitution Committee, the Basque Nationalist parliamentary group proposed an amendment guaranteeing "the historical rights of the *foral* territories, whose integration and modernization [would] proceed by agreement between the representative institutions of those territories and the government."[20] This demand was presented as a condition for the integration of the Basque provinces into the Spanish state. The Basque nationalists wanted more than a conciliatory gesture: the PNV sought a historical-traditional constitution that recognized the Basque right to self-government and would take precedence over the principle of national sovereignty.[21]

The PNV was opposed to the consensual text that had been agreed to by the other parliamentary groups and presented its own version of the constitution in the form of an amendment. The Basque document showed how irreducible the conflict was between the national sovereignty and the historical rights to which the Basque nationalists laid claim, as well as the failure of the conciliatory approach adopted toward the PNV by Centrists, Socialists, and Communists. Later it would become evident that no concession—except the recognition of a fictive historical constitution and the defense of spurious economic privileges and political overbidding, which are the essence of nationalist politics—could dissuade the nationalist forces from their centrifugal course.

The historical-traditional approach could offer no solution to contemporary Spanish problems. On the contrary, the nationalist belligerence has distorted our sense of tradition: rather than unifying Spain's political culture, tradition has become divisive. The past and traditional projects themselves are a source of conflict, and identification with some aspect of the past has come to mean turning our backs on the possibility of coexistence. This grows out of the fact that there is not just one tradition in Spain, but many and that none is accepted or acceptable as the one authentic interpretation of our heritage. Our political culture and history have been so fragmented that no single piece of the puzzle can, at this point in history, claim unique and general validity.

The version of article 2 formulated by the majority in the Cortes nevertheless constituted a break with the rationalist-normative constitutional scheme. As such, it may jeopardize the structure of parliamentary monarchy and the supremacy of popular sovereignty.[22]

Church and State Church-state relations had been a major issue in the debates of the constituent Cortes of the Second Republic (1931–36). Although it was a less important issue in the more recent constitutional debates, strains over this question nevertheless posed an additional challenge to the emerging parliamentary monarchy.

Article 16 guarantees freedom of religion and worship. It goes on: "There shall be no state religion. The public authorities shall take the religious beliefs of Spanish society into account and shall maintain the consequent relations of cooperation with the Catholic church and the other confessions." The initial draft of article 16 presented by the Constitutional Committee in early January 1978 had made no explicit mention of the Catholic church. This version had Socialist support; and, as the PSOE parliamentary spokesman said at the time: "Never in our history has the delicate problem posed by freedom of religion and worship been approached in a more favorable context and been resolved as well as in the draft bill of 5 January." By the time the final version was approved in April, the text had been modified, introducing what the Socialist spokesman now called "a certain 'hidden' state confessionality, a residue of privilege, which we cannot but consider unacceptable."[23]

If during the debates on the nationalities question the historical-traditional approach to the constitution clashed with the rationalist-normative view on the church and state issue as well as on the role of the armed forces, it was the sociological approach, emphasizing power, that raised problems. The Catholic church must have exerted considerable pressure on the UCD for the government to reverse its initial decision to accept the 5 January version. As a result, the idea of equality among religious faiths fell by the wayside, and the rather promising but incipient secularization of Spanish society suffered a serious reversal. The UCD and the PSOE, meanwhile, engaged in a heated debate over the role of the Catholic church in the educational system as defined in article 27.[24] The real issue of the debate was not only the principle of freedom of education—a right never questioned by the Socialists—but whether and under what conditions the church would continue to receive the 40 billion pesetas from the public coffers for the costs of private education.

The Economic Order The clauses regulating the economic order generated as much controversy among the parliamentary parties as any of the others we have mentioned. The final compromise could hardly be more ambiguous, with both free-market and planned systems (in theory quite distinct) given explicit recognition.

Article 38 of the constitution says, "Free enterprise is recognized within the framework of a market economy. The public authorities shall guarantee and protect its exercise and the safeguarding of productivity in accordance with the demands of the economy in general and, as the case may be, of its planning." The market is seen as coordinating decentralized decisions through the instrument of prices, with competition as its watchdog. The market economy is further recognized in article 53.1, which commits the public institutions to protect the rights of individuals. Legislation that infringed those rights and liberties may be declared unconstitutional under article 161.

Meanwhile, article 128.2 recognizes "public initiative in economic activity. Essential resources or services may be restricted by law to the public sector, especially in the case of monopolies. Likewise, intervention in companies may be decided upon when the public interest so demands." Article 131 also notes that the "state, through the law, shall be able to plan general economic activity in order to meet collective needs, balance and harmonize regional and sectorial development, and stimulate the growth of income and wealth and its more equitable distribution." In other words, the legislature can choose a market economy model or one that inclines more to a centrally planned economy. Both are constitutional.

Some have contended that articles 128 and 131 contradict and invalidate the recognition that article 38 extends to private enterprise and the market economy. Some students of the constitution see its provisions on economic matters and on the role the state can play in them as so vague that future legislators will have to establish how far and under what circumstances the state may act.

In any case, limits do apply to what can be done under this constitution. Article 38, for example, guarantees free enterprise "within the framework of a market economy," but it also suggests that market and planned systems are complementary. Moreover, article 33 recognizes private property and thus leaves open only the possibility of "indicative" planning.

Various members of the Constitutional Commission submitted statements proposing that the economic provisions of the constitution should allow the adoption of any type of economic policy that would clarify the issue. Politically and juridically, the UCD's acceptance of article 131 represented the Centrists' decision to extend a rhetorical hand to the PSOE—it was not endorsement of an alternative to the market economy. If there are going to be limits on planning, however, they will be imposed by political and economic reality. Articles 131 and 128.2, after all, do not exist in a vacuum. They are directly related to article 9.2, which states: "It is incumbent on the public authorities to promote conditions which allow for the liberty and equality of the individual and of the groups to which he belongs to be real and effective, to remove the obstacles which prevent or hinder their full enjoyment, and to facilitate the participation of all citizens in political, economic, cultural, and social life." Here, I should stress that the historical alienation between state and society remains a burden for the parliamentary monarchy. Fortunately, though, the constitution offers the necessary instruments for changes should they become necessary.

The controversy over the market system and state planning was only one of many economic controversies that arose during the constitutional debates. The Spanish bourgeoisie tried its best to enshrine its privileges in the constitution. They tried to include guarantees in the constitution for private property, inheritance, business associations, and the lockout. Yet, at least one qualified spokesman argued against the workers' right to strike, since this would implicitly legitimate political strikes.[25] In the final version, "the right to private property and inheritance" is recognized, with the condition that "the social function of these rights shall determine their content, in accordance with the law" and that "no one may be deprived of his property and rights except on justified grounds of serving the public utility or social interest . . . in return for proper compensation in accordance with the provisions of the law" (article 33). The right to strike was also granted—without any conditioning limitations— and the lockout provision was defeated.

The debate over the economic system revealed the balance of forces in the Cortes. Although the PSOE could not impose its views, no important decision could be adopted without Socialist support. This reflected not the numerical strength of the party, but its symbolic weight. The Socialists were in a position to give the monarchy its democratic credentials: those who wielded economic power in the society again and again had to face up to the legitimating power the PSOE had. The Socialists, however, could do no more than ensure that the new phase of Spain's history would not begin with the adoption of a conservative constitution that tilted the balance against them. In the final analysis— and here I think I speak objectively—the results reflect the legitimation of established wealth and power on the one hand but, on the other, the final product can be interpreted as a moral victory for the PSOE.

The outcome of the debates on the major constitutional issues tells a great deal about the relationship between constitution and society in Spain. When Theophile Gautier visited Spain in 1840, he saw a street sign reading "Constitution Square" and commented: "This is what a constitution is in Spain—a lump of plaster splashed on granite." Today we might put it another way: the rationality embodied in a constitution is profoundly at odds with the "real" Spain, which refuses to be harnessed either to a sociological constitution or to a more or less distorted historical-traditional one. This "real" Spain, with its dramatic inequalities, resists laws of general applicability; it is intolerant of equality and openly rebels against civility and reason. Thus we have seen how the drive toward rationality and secularization in the shaping of the constitution ends in the nationalization of the Crown and its halfhearted proclamation of national sovereignty. Nationalist groups, the armed forces, the church, and the economic and financial powers successfully resisted the original thrust toward modernization and leveling reform.

Political Theory and the Constitution: The Organic Aspect

In our examination of the dogmatic aspect, we noted tensions between rationalist-normative, historical-traditional, and sociological conceptions of the constitution. When it came to the organic aspect of the charter, however, the lines of conflict were less clear-cut. Alliances were formed and dissolved on the basis not so much of ideological principle as of tactical considerations. This applied to the discussion about, for example, the electoral system, the basis for districting, the powers of the Senate, the motion of censure, the definition of legislative competence, and so on.

Representation and Plebiscites The parliamentary monarchy defined in the constitution is a representative democracy with a few plebiscitary features.[26] Article 1.3 recognizes parliament's central role. The powers of the legislature are more fully defined in Title III, dealing with the Cortes, and Title V, where government-parliament relations are discussed. Article 6 grants constitutional recognition to political parties: "The political parties are the expression of political pluralism, cooperate in the formation and expression of the people, and are a basic instrument for political participation. Their creation and the exercise of their activity are free insofar as they are compatible with respect for the constitution and the law. Their internal structure and operation must be democratic."

The Spanish people are represented in the Cortes, which consists of a Chamber of Deputies and a Senate. This parliament's essential functions are the exercise of legislative power, the approval of budgets, and the control of government action (article 66). The Senate is the chamber based on territorial representation (article 69).

A proportional electoral system is used for the Chamber of Deputies (article 68), a plurality system for the Senate. In both cases, the electoral district is the province (article 68). For the Senate elections, however, the "autonomous communities" will each designate one senator and an additional senator for every million citizens (article 69.5). Any change in provincial boundaries must be approved by parliament through an organic law, requiring an absolute majority of the parliament in a final vote on the entire proposal (articles 141 and 81.2).

A complicated series of negotiations led to the formulas adopted. The UCD first proposed that the Senate be coequal with the Chamber of Deputies and be in a position to block the initiatives of the lower chamber. As a territorial body, the Senate would overrepresent rural and low-density areas. The left, federalist in theory, was always wary of the potential conservatism of the Senate. It contended, not without foundation, that the more progressive legislation approved by the Chamber would founder in such a Senate, ultimately rendering impotent any leftist government with a majority in the Chamber of Deputies. The left became so obsessed with this idea that, even after the UCD granted certain concessions on the electoral system for the Senate (article 69.5), it refused to agree to granting the Senate any significant power.[27] In the end, the most ambitious theoretical defense of the Senate would have little practical effect, given the left's fixation with the menace of the Senate and its lack of sensitivity to the potential of the institution as an instrument for the political integration of minorities.[28]

I have argued elsewhere that neither a proportional electoral system nor a plurality-based electoral system has more than an incidental effect on the party system and party alignments.[29] By contrast, the dimensions of the electoral district can directly influence the party spectrum. In particular, the intermediate provincial districts inhibit manipulation by political bosses and local notables and moderate—depending on the number of seats at stake—the effects of pure proportionality. The choice of the province as the electoral unit and the strong defense of its boundaries in article 141 give stability to the party system.

According to article 108, the government (in the parliamentary sense, the executive) is politically responsible to the Chamber of Deputies. The government and each of its members are subject to questions put by both the Chamber and the Senate (article 111). The prime minister may request a vote of confidence from the Chamber (article 112), and an absolute majority of the Chamber may censure the government (article 113). That motion "must be proposed by at least one-tenth of the deputies and must include the name of a candidate to fill the office of Prime Minister." What is even more significant is the provision in article 115: "1. The Prime Minister, after deliberation by the Council of Ministers, and under his own exclusive responsibility, may propose the dissolution of the Chamber, the Senate, or the whole Parliament, which shall be decreed by the King. The decree of dissolution shall set the date of the elections."

The plebiscitary component of the constitution is found in article 92: "1. Political decisions of special importance may be submitted to all citizens in the consultative referendum. 2. The referendum shall be called by the King at the proposal of the Prime Minister after authorization by the Chamber of Deputies."

The representative and plebiscitary aspects of the constitution are decisively conditioned by the nature of the Spanish party system. Given the internal structure and discipline of the most important parties, all decisions pass through a "representative filter." In this context, it may be worth mentioning the different opinions the larger political parties expressed on the "constructive motion of censure." This procedural rule, adopted by the UCD and the PSOE over the objections of the AP and the PCE, was presented to the public as a tool for stabilizing the government. As such it has merit, but the rule also discriminates against the smaller parties. Although this certainly stabilizes the government, it also favored both leading parties, the UCD and the PSOE.

Legislative Power In the area of legislative powers, a head-on collision between the UCD and the other parties developed. The UCD proposal would have given the executive branch broad decree-law powers. The only exception was the reserve clause. But the proposal as presented had too much in common with Francoist doctrine and style of government to be acceptable to the opposition.

In the end the UCD accepted the opposition's point of view, but through article 87 it retained, for the government as well as the Chamber of Deputies and the Senate, the power to initiate legislation. The government may exercise the regulatory power in accordance with the constitution and the laws. The delegation of legislative power is carefully checked (article 82); thus the rulemaking power does not mean uncontrolled prerogatives for the government. Even though the government has the advantage of majority support, legislative power ultimately resides in the parliament. Since 1978 the Cortes has developed its parliamentary style more along German lines; the Chamber of Deputies wields its own political weight and forces the government to take it seriously. It has played a much more vigorous role than the French National Assembly or the British Parliament, controlled as they are by the government or the cabinet.

On the whole, the constitutional provisions were designed to enhance stability. Achieving stability, however, depends largely on the working of the party system. Unless the party system performs in a satisfactory fashion, the constitution could actually reinforce the authoritarian habits of a conservative government and thus stimulate alienation and centrifugal tendencies in the country.

The electoral system and the constructive motion of censure grew out of the alliance between the UCD and the PSOE with the anticipated effect that their alternation in power would be the rule. This arrangement, which was of course opposed by the other parties, was expected to have a stabilizing influence on the party system. The PSOE, aligned with the minorities, played a major role in determining the rules for electing senators.[30]

During the debate over the powers of the Senate, the UCD gave in to the Socialists on the issue of making the upper chamber a coequal legislative body. The Senate was not made stronger probably because the most important political figures sat in the Chamber of Deputies and they showed little interest in letting power slip through their fingers. Because the regulation of legislative power would directly influence the structure of the parliamentary system, the

UCD's effort to take away or limit the control of legislative power prompted the other parties in the parliament to close ranks.

In general, the parties were very sensitive to the consequences any given decision would have on their powers. This reaction is particularly understandable in the Spanish political context, where for the left there are no legitimate or legitimating forces above and beyond the parties. The legitimacy of the political regime and its institutions has always had a vicarious character in Spain. During the Second Republic and even today, many workers, for example, feel that they are represented not by regime institutions but by the PSOE.[31] The principal interest groups—the church, the armed forces, and the political parties—have long been important for legitimating and defining the political situation, and the relationship is such that it is unlikely that any regime in Spain could rid itself of its dependency on those groups.

The Constitution in Practice

The constitution extended the rule of law to the daily exercise of politics. Among the elites, the parliamentary monarchy enjoys a legitimacy it had never previously known. Financial and business circles required some time to adjust to the constitutional and legal limitations on property or private enterprise and to recognize trade unions as legitimate mediators in labor-management disputes. Agreements signed by labor, management, and the government since 1977—among them the Moncloa Pacts of 1977, the Basic Interconfederal Accord (ABI) in 1979, the Framework Interconfederal Accord (AMI) in 1980, the National Accord on Employment (ANE) in 1981, and the Economic and Social Accord (AES) in 1984—have persuaded businessmen that workers' demands are moderate and that business can continue to make a profit under the new industrial relations system. The situation evolved so favorably that when the Socialist government expropriated the holding company known as RUMASA, neither the banks nor the Spanish Confederation of Employer Organizations (CEOE) challenged the constitutionality of the move. The tension between propertied interests and the labor sector, which in Spain has historically been held responsible for the breakdown of regimes and for civil wars, on this occasion led only to an appeal to the Constitutional Court. In December 1983 the court ruled that the expropriation had been legal.

First under the UCD government and since 1982 under the Socialists, the parliamentary regime has successfully carried forward a politics of depolarization. As a result, the institutions associated with the parliamentary monarchy are so widely recognized as legitimate at the elite level, that not even high unemployment can diminish their standing. Never before in modern Spain has support for such a regime been more widespread, and ideological and social resistance to it is limited. Nor should this be surprising since trade unions have never enjoyed such complete recognition; liberties have never been so fully guaranteed; and—with the Socialists in power—leaders of banks, business, the church, and the military have had much reason for satisfaction.

Only nationalist forces in Catalonia and the Basque country vacillate in their support of the constitution. Self-rule (*estado de las automonías*), originally conceived as a system to encourage decentralization and to coordinate territorial administration, has instead tremendously increased public expenditures at a time of economic contraction; it has encouraged unrealistic expectations while frustrating legitimate popular demands for social services; and it has continually fed conflict and stimulated dissension. A relatively narrow legal question—how to distribute resources—has been distorted by partisan politics, by class interests, and by the irredentist (and even chiliastic) claims of some nationalist forces.

Although within the judicial system, the state security apparatus, and the bureaucracy and among some officers in the armed forces, some strategically located groups do look at the past with nostalgia and to the future with anger, Spain is nevertheless daily observing a deepening acceptance of the constitution. This would not have been possible without the strong support of three institutions: the Cortes, the Constitutional Court, and the Crown.

Under the UCD government, the PSOE headed the parliamentary opposition, and its activities not only redounded to the credit of Socialist leaders, but also strengthened democracy and its institutions. The February 1981 coup attempt only reinforced and encouraged public identification with and participation in democracy.

For the people who rarely, if ever, had occasion to identify with the agencies of justice, the Constitutional Tribunal strengthened their confidence in the law. Judicial decisions on a wide range of subjects—education and divorce, the Organic Law for the Harmonization of the Autonomy Process (LOAPA), and the expropriation of the RUMASA holding company—have restored faith in justice to many citizens.

Finally, the Crown has played a decisive role in the transition from dictatorship to democracy. The Crown accepted the way the constitution *socialized* its historical prerogatives, and the king played a key part in frustrating the February 1981 coup attempt. Less understood and appreciated has been the contribution the king and the royal family have made to the civility of a heterogeneous, disarticulated, and conflict-ridden society by their exemplary acceptance of the constitution.

With the exception of the nationalist problem, the Spanish citizen can contemplate with satisfaction how the constitution has been accepted since its proclamation in December 1978. But it is precisely here, where the reach of the law ends and where only effective government can grant legitimacy to the political class, that parliamentary government confronts the danger of an alienated citizenry.

Although the relatively favorable present situation has strengthened us in our task, Spain must not be seduced into disregarding or underestimating those challenges that are pending, especially those that tear at the nation's social fabric. Even as the condition of those at the bottom of the economic level has improved, the already extreme inequality between the rich and the poor has increased significantly in the past few years: the already favored have accumulated greater wealth and capital benefits during a period of high unemployment. Moreover, although neither the existence of terrorism nor the plagues of unemployment and drug addiction can be blamed primarily on the government, the increased insecurity of persons and property has prevented freedom from becoming a day-to-day reality in contemporary Spain.

In spite of significant progress, Spanish society is still plagued by conflicts over tradition, class, authoritarianism, secularization, and civility; therefore, if Spain is to acquire true modernity, it needs a firm hand at the rudder of the government. Greater still is the challenge for the Socialists to assist the many people still living in deprived conditions. Important political advances have not been matched in the social areas. These are the challenges the Socialist government faces as it seeks to deepen support for the constitution.

Even so, what Spain has achieved during the brief reign of the parliamentary monarchy has been so promising that, if these achievements are followed by effective solutions to the citizenry's social needs, they should strengthen popular "constitutional sentiment" in favor of the political order. The daily improvement in material goods and services as well as the guarantee of more complete freedom in the country may well lead the society to discard its historical traumas and to incorporate itself, through a long-term project of self-emancipation, into the destinies of Western Europe.

Electoral Rules and Candidate Selection
JORGE DE ESTEBAN AND LUIS LÓPEZ GUERRA

Nothing has intrigued me in political reporting, anywhere at any time, as much as this process of transfer of power. — Theodore H. White, In Search of History

The Transition to Democracy

———After forty years under a dictatorship of fascist origin, Spain effected a smooth transition to democracy and adopted one of the world's most progressive constitutions. What will disappoint students of transfers of power, however, is that Spain's experience yields up no magic formula for transforming dictatorships into democracies.[1] On the contrary, the Spanish recipe is almost certainly not exportable. Only in a country whose cultural history had been identical with Spain's in the last forty years—one that had passed from underdevelopment to a position of considerable economic and industrial power— could the Spanish way to democracy be repeated. Spain's rapid modernization was brought about by a dictatorship that, though it denied all political liberties and fundamental rights, allowed and stimulated economic development. Theoretically the evolution might have taken another course, but in fact what needs to be clearly understood is that political modernization in Spain was possible only *after* economic modernization.[2]

Let us look more closely at the reasons for Spain's easy political transition. It seems to have come about as a result of four other changes of different types.[3] First, a generational change: forty years had passed since the Civil War, and a majority of the Spanish population no longer remembered any government except Franco's.[4] This generational change had removed one of the most important obstacles to any rejection of General Franco's dictatorship: memories of the Civil War, which had paralyzed most of the postwar population. The young people had expelled those memories and had adopted attitudes orienting them toward the democratic political models of the West.

The second important change in Spain in the last few years of the Franco regime was an acceleration of economic growth. This had profoundly restructured Spanish society. Spain's passage from an agricultural economy and a traditional social structure characterized by great inequalities to a modern economy ranking it among the twelve economic powers of the world was due to an influx of foreign money resulting from an emigrant labor force, tourism, and foreign capital investment. This process created a large middle class and strengthened a modern working class, as well as modernizing attitudes and mores in every area from religion to sex. The important new fact about political attitudes was the people's desire to participate in all processes affecting the collective life.

Third, there had been institutional change, in four fundamental and traditionally reactionary areas: the crown, the large landowners, the church, and the army. For diverse reasons, all these had undergone radical change in their political orientation. The key factor—indeed, the driving force, of Spain's democratic transition—was the progressive attitude adopted by King Juan Carlos I from the very moment of his coronation, after Franco's death in November 1975. The large landowners lost economic power to a new managerial class that accepted the modes of modern capitalism and a democratic political system. The Catholic church, for its part, had no choice but to accept the message of the Second Vatican Council as well as the new realities of an increasingly secular society; it began to disengage itself from the civil power. Finally, the army came to the realization that it had to evolve toward strict professionalism and political neutrality. All these developments were essential in the transition from dictatorship to democracy.

Fourth, a similar change had taken place in the ruling class. In the last years of the Franco regime, a liberalizing sector was already visible within the political elite, and the assassination of Prime Minister Luis Carrero Blanco—who had been groomed to ensure the continuity of the Francoist system—in December 1973 accelerated the liberalization of the ruling class. The demands of the Spanish people for modernization of the political system, pressure from abroad (more clearly felt after the fall of the Greek and Portuguese dictatorships), and a sense of self-preservation all joined to convince the more dynamic elements of the ruling class that conversion to democracy was preferable to going against the grain and defending a regime that was fighting for its life.

The discrepancy between Spain's economic progress and its political backwardness became increasingly evident as these changes occurred. At the time of General Franco's death, the necessary conditions for the adoption of a democratic system were present, and the vast majority of the population desired change. What remained was to choose a road to this end that could be taken without causing undue social stress.

One could argue that, in terms of classes and not of individuals, no transfer of power occurred. In the final analysis the same class, virtually the same people, who had ruled Spain under Franco ruled it still. But for the political scientist what counts is the change from personal power, typical of authoritarian regimes,[5] to polyarchy, to use Robert Dahl's term, where the centers of power are plural;[6] and, most important, that power ceased to be a personal patrimony and became something channeled through periodic elections in which political parties aspiring to govern compete. One can aver, therefore, that Spain was transformed into a Western democracy through a particular transitional process, knowledge of which must underlie any discussion of the principal subject of this chapter: the characteristics of Spain's electoral legislation and the process of candidate selection within the political parties.

Electoral Legislation

When analyzing the electoral legislation indispensable to Spain's democratic restoration, we must bear in mind that political change was brought about by the Francoist ruling class under pressure from opposition groups. It followed a compromise strategy with three clearly differentiated phases.

After General Franco's death in November 1975, the new Spanish monarch named Carlos Arias Navarro—already leader of the last government under Franco—prime minister. Arias tried to maintain an ambiguous political stance while patching up the institutions inherited from the dictatorship. It became increasingly clear, however, that a significant part of the Spanish people demanded a profound democratization of the political institutions of the country; this meant first dismantling the old regime, then creating a modern state along the lines of the Western democracies. In one way or another, this desire was shared by all social and political groups except small extremist factions of the left and right.

On 3 July 1976, the king took the initiative and, after asking for the resignation of Arias Navarro, named Adolfo Suárez, then secretary general of the National Movement, prime minister. This appointment caused general amazement, but the pessimistic forecasts about its prospects were soon dispelled. On 16 July 1976, the new Suárez government formulated a program that called for general elections in just under a year, on 30 June 1977.

The task at hand would require the utmost skill: to pass from authoritarian institutions to potentially democratic ones without violating Spain's Fundamental Law.[7] Briefly, it was a question of striking a compromise so as to avoid a confrontation between the conservative forces, especially the armed forces, and the progressive opposition, which demanded the immediate convocation of a constitutional assembly.

The first step—perfectly consistent with Francoist law—was to call a national referendum to approve a new Fundamental Law, the Law for Political Reform. The purpose of this law was to make possible the calling of national parliamentary elections; it provided for universal suffrage, the secret ballot, and a bicameral parliament called the Cortes composed of a Chamber of Deputies and a Senate. This was the beginning of the restoration of democracy in Spain. In the area of electoral legislation, it hinged on three compromises.

The Provisions of the Law for Political Reform.

It was clear that the credibility of the democratic restoration in Spain would depend above all on the adoption of electoral laws allowing all opposition parties to participate in the electoral process. From the outset this proved difficult to realize within the framework of the Francoist Fundamental Laws. The Francoist Cortes, in an unusual gesture of political hara-kiri, would have to approve a Fundamental Law designed to bring about its own demise, and many doubted the integrity of electoral rules conceived under such conditions. Nonetheless, an important group within the Francoist Cortes, which later became the Popular Alliance party (AP), demanded that the Law for Political Reform stipulate the basic principles of the soon-to-be-drafted electoral law as a security measure. The Suárez government had no recourse but to accept this compromise. The guidelines contained in the law can be summarized as follows.

A bicameral legislature. A bicameral system was adopted for the future parliament, for reasons that are not always mentioned. On the one hand, bicameralism was a link with Spanish constitutional tradition. All of Spain's constitutions except the 1812 (Cádiz) constitution and the Republican constitution of 1931 had provided for two houses of parliament. In addition, it was thought that a single house elected by universal suffrage might prove a dangerous inducement to radicalism; a second house, more conservative because of its mode of selection, would serve as a brake, forcing the first to move slowly.

It was presumed (though not officially stated) that this parliament would become the constituent assembly, a unique phenomenon in comparative constitutional law:[8] there does not seem to have been any precedent for a bicameral constituent assembly in world history. It might turn out to be unworkable or to produce excessively conservative results.[9]

Universal suffrage The Law for Political Reform stipulated that the suffrage would be universal, direct, equal, and secret, as is characteristic of Western democracies. This signified a break with the Francoist corporative voting system, which had excluded the great majority of the Spanish population from the electoral process.[10] The voting age, however, was set at twenty-one, in accordance with the desire of many important sectors of public opinion.[11] This was another concession to the Francoist elements, which were suspicious of allowing young voters into the political arena.

Table 3.1 Chamber and Senate Seats and Population per Seat, by Province

	Chamber of Deputies		Senate	
Province	Number of seats	Population per seat	Number of seats	Population per seats
Alava	4	59,360	4	59,360
Albacete	4	82,851	4	82,851
Alicante	9	116,872	4	262,963
Almería	5	77,687	4	97,109
Avila	3	64,155	4	48,166
Badajoz	7	91,550	4	160,212
Balearic Islands	6	105,502	5	126,603
Barcelona	33	134,105	4	1,106,368
Burgos	4	87,353	4	87,353
Cáceres	5	85,133	4	106,416
Cádiz	8	119,041	4	238,082
Castellón	4	102,788	4	102,788
Ciudad-Real	5	96,242	4	120,303
Córdoba	7	102,429	4	179,251
Coruña (La)	9	115,875	4	260,720
Cuenca	4	55,576	4	55,576
Gerona	5	88,361	4	110,451
Granada	7	105,292	4	184,261
Guadalajara	3	46,504	4	34,878
Guipúzcoa	7	97,502	4	170,629
Huelva	5	80,594	4	100,743
Huesca	3	72,106	4	54,080
Jaén	7	92,217	4	161,381
León	6	87,749	4	131,623
Lérida	4	87,321	4	87,321
Lagroño	4	60,184	4	60,184
Lugo	5	83,283	4	104,103
Madrid	32	136,422	4	1,091,376
Málaga	8	114,427	4	228,855
Murcia	8	110,167	4	220,335
Navarre	5	96,773	4	120,966
Orense	5	87,042	4	108,802
Oviedo	10	109,681	4	274,202
Palencia	3	62,236	4	46,677
Palmas (Las)	6	111,964	5	134,357
Pontevedra	8	103,001	4	207,203
Salamanca	4	87,465	4	87,465
Santa Cruz de Tenerife	7	98,136	5	137,391

Table 3.1 continued.

	Chamber of Deputies		Senate	
Province	Number of seats	Population per seat	Number of seats	Population per seats
Santander	5	98,627	4	123,284
Segovia	3	50,400	4	37,800
Seville	12	114,628	4	343,885
Tarragona	6	80,618	4	120,927
Teruel	3	52,196	4	39,147
Toledo	5	92,817	4	116,059
Valencia	15	126,736	4	475,260
Valladolid	5	89,295	4	111,618
Vizcaya	10	115,110	4	287,775
Zamora	4	57,696	4	57,696
Zaragoza	8	99,678	4	199,357
Ceuta	1	67,077	2	33,538
Melilla	1	60,191	2	30,095

Source: P. Perez Tremps, "La ley para la reforma política," *Revista de la Facultad de Derecho de la Universidad Complutense,* 54 (1978):157–158.

The electoral system. Electoral systems are dear to politicians, since many see in them ways of giving greater or lesser advantage to particular parties. This commonly held belief, highly questionable from a scientific standpoint,[12] held sway at the time of the adoption of the Law for Political Reform. The conservative Francoist elements, who only grudgingly accepted the principle of elections in the first place, insisted on the adoption of the plurality system, which they believed would favor the conservative parties.[13] The opposition and other currents of public opinion felt, however—both because it seemed more democratic and because the Cortes would also be a constituent assembly—that there should also be proportional representation. The result was a Solomonic solution: proportional representation for the Chamber of Deputies and a plurality system for the Senate.

The Chamber of Deputies The lower house would have 350 members. Mechanisms designed to reduce fragmentation would be built into the electoral system; and the province would be the voting district, with a stipulated minimum number of representatives (see table 3.1).

Though the government was able to obtain the adoption of the proportional system for the election of representatives, it had to agree to limit their number to 350, which it considered low for a population of 35 million. In the second place, the proportional system was checked by some of the measures ostensibly intended to discourage fragmentation but whose real purpose was to prevent the entry of radical minority parties. Finally, the adoption of Spain's administrative unit, the province, as the electoral district undoubtedly reflected a right-wing strategy, since the majority of the provinces are rural and traditionally conservative. This would work against the parties of the left, which have their power base in the more populous, industrial provinces. On the other hand, the choice of the province as the electoral district eliminated the need to establish new voting districts and with it the problem of gerrymandering.[14]

The Senate The upper house was to be composed of 207 senators, four from each of the fifty provinces (five for each island province), two from Ceuta, and two from Melilla.[15] In addition, the king could appoint a number of senators not to exceed one-fifth of the total number elected. As we have seen, the plurality system was expected to produce a more conservative group than the proportional representation adopted for the Chamber of Deputies.

All these principles, as part of the Fundamental Law approved by national referendum in December 1976, were to weigh heavily at the time the electoral law was drafted since they had constitutional status and were therefore to be respected in the transition process.

The Decree of 18 March 1977 Dealing with Electoral Procedures

The stipulations of the Law for Political Reform left little room for new electoral guidelines. Still, some important questions about the future electoral system remained; the Francoist Cortes was dissolved after the referendum, and authority to establish electoral norms passed to the Suárez government, as provided in the new law. Meanwhile, an opposition was emerging, whose leaders would have to be consulted on any matter as essential as electoral legislation if a democratic restoration with widespread popular support were to be achieved. Thus, a commission of ten representatives of the opposition parties met repeatedly with the government.[16] Though few decisions regarding electoral procedures were reached at these meetings, some were important [17] — and the symbolic value of consultation was significant. The final electoral decree was promulgated on 18 March 1977. The rules under which the elections of 15 June 1977 and 1 March 1979 were conducted are essentially those contained in this decree. We will confine our attention here to its most important provisions.

Electoral qualifications: candidate and voter. Article 2 of the 1977 decree defines the electorate as "all those Spaniards who are of voting age, included in the census, and who are in full exercise of their civil and political rights." In the elections of 15 June 1977 the voting age of twenty-one, established by the Law for Political Reform, was maintained.

Inclusion in the census took the place of prior voter registration, as it does in many European countries. This requirement caused many problems, which were due to the mistakes of the census in many townships. Article 18 of the decree establishes an alternative course of action for anyone otherwise eligible who is excluded from the census.

The important point is that full possession of civil and political rights was required in order to vote. This requirement had special significance in Spain, where, for the first time in its modern history, democracy did not bring the prosecution of any political group. With the exception of groups whose political expression was terrorism, all Spaniards could claim full civil and political rights. Former exiles and Francoist functionaries alike saw their right to vote recognized.[18]

Partly in response to pressure from opposition groups, the decree specified that all Spaniards save those who currently held political office were eligible to seek election. Article 4 presented a comprehensive list of categories excluded so as to avoid the improper exercise of official influence by the candidates in a country whose only known politicians belonged to the previous regime. The list of those disqualified was long, from cabinet ministers down to local officials.[19] Not included, however, were the prime minister, the president of the Cortes, and the members of the Council of the Realm. The omission of the first, especially, was cause for much controversy since it directly benefited Suárez, who could (and did) avail himself of his role in the transition to ensure his own election.

Last, we should mention the stipulations of the decree with regard to incompatibility of offices, which was dealt with less severely. Members of the executive branch, subdirectors, or directors general could by this decree, also hold the office of deputy or senator. These compatibility provisos are in keeping with the practice of all parliamentary governments.[20] Nonetheless, in Spain this tendency could be dangerous, since during the previous regime executive and judicial powers had been held by the same people.[21]

Electoral administration   One of the greatest difficulties encountered as the elections approached was the absence of an administrative structure. An electoral structure had to be created *ab nihilo* in order to hold elections that could not be considered manipulated by the government.

It was decided to adopt an electoral organization based on "juntas," comparable to the one set out in the Spanish Electoral Law of 1907. These were to operate on three levels: a Central Electoral Junta with its headquarters in Madrid, provincial juntas with headquarters in each of the fifty provinces, and local juntas with headquarters in the judicial jurisdictions. These juntas were formed by members of the judiciary, magistrates, and judges, representatives of bodies such as bar associations and schools of law, and (except at the local level) representatives of the parties and coalitions running in the elections. It was thought that such people would be the most appropriate to ensure impartiality.

The juntas, especially the Central Electoral Junta, were to administer the entire electoral process, beginning with voter registration and including the setting up and safeguarding of polling places and adjudication of conflicts or points of law.

Lists of candidates and the electoral system of both houses. The decree of 1977 stipulates three types of groups that may nominate candidates for Chamber of Deputies and Senate elections: associations or federations registered with the Ministry of the Interior, coalitions formed from such groups or for electoral purposes, and voters' groups. These provisions shed further light on the peculiar process of the restoration of democracy in Spain.

A few months before the elections of 15 June 1977, all political parties were illegal. The need for a procedure to legalize the various political groups that were to take part in the elections was urgent, for only if the parties were seen to be truly free could the Suárez government establish its democratic credibility. The main problem was whether the Communist party and other Marxist-Leninist parties would be granted official recognition. During the months of March and April, the "establishment" applied great pressure to prevent the legalization of the Communists. Faced with the threat of a boycott of the elections by the parties of the left, however, the Suárez government recognized the legitimacy of the Communist party two months before the elections.[22] Other leftist political parties of diverse tendencies were not able to obtain recognition, but some were able to offer candidates as voters' groups, since the decree, as we have seen, provided for such cases.

The election of deputies The proportional system in effect for the election of the Chamber of Deputies requires the parties, coalitions, or voter groups to draw up slates of candidates at the district level. The lists include as many candidates as there are seats available in the corresponding voting district. The minimum number of representatives was set at two by the electoral decree, with an additional representative for each 144,500 inhabitants or fraction larger than 70,000. This meant that there would be a great inequality in the number of votes a candidate needed to win election in each of the various provinces. While in Soria a candidate could be elected with 34,639 votes, in Barcelona a minimum of 134,105 votes was needed (see table 3.1).

In the second place, the decree stipulates that the lists of candidates should be "definitive," which means that the order of candidates cannot be altered nor can new candidates be added. This system was adopted both to simplify matters and to encourage the development of fewer, more defined parties.

In the third place, the decree established, within the parameters of the proportional system already adopted under the Law for Political Reform, the d'Hondt highest-average system of translating votes into seats. This method, invented by a Belgian mathematician, obviates certain inequities of proportional representation, although it obviously favors the large parties to the detriment of the small and thus may be criticized from the viewpoint of strict electoral justice.[23] Still, it was justifiable in Spain's predemocratic environment, where large parties were nonexistent. In fact, political fragmentation was extreme; more than two hundred political groups had sprung up. The electoral legislation was designed to promote a system of strong and stable parties, deemed essential if democratic government were to take hold. A further provision designed to discourage fragmentation in the Chamber of Deputies was the requirement that a party win a minimum of 3 percent of the votes in at least one district in order to obtain parliamentary representation there. (This measure, stipulated in the Law for Political Reform, did not actually prevent any party of coalition from obtaining a seat in either 1977 or 1979.)

The election of senators   As we have seen, the Law for Political Reform established the number of senators at 207, four per province (again excluding the North African enclaves, Ceuta, and Melilla). Just as for the Chamber of Deputies, associations and federations, coalitions, and voter groups may propose candidates for election. Since senators were elected by plurality vote, the parties did not generally present lists;[24] indeed, the system encouraged the participation of independent candidates. Although there were four Senate seats to be filled for each province, the voter voted for a maximum of three candidates. It was believed that this arrangement would promote the representation of minorities.[25] It was, therefore, a plurality system with proportional characteristics designed to lessen the chances of serious overrepresentation of one party. The equal representation of provinces favored the rural provinces, which tend to be more politically conservative than the more populous industrial provinces.[26]

The electoral campaign   The decree set the duration of an electoral campaign at twenty-one days. It acknowledged the principle of parity among the candidates, although in the elections of 15 June 1977 the government candidate enjoyed a clear advantage, and some parties were barred from participation since they had not yet been legalized.

The decree provided for a committee to administer party broadcasts on the state radio and television networks, composed of members of the various parties. These media were still in government hands in 1977, but they were quite unregulated and made arbitrary use of their authority despite the complementary guidelines that the government was obliged to publish during both elections.

Given the Spanish situation, state subsidies to the parties could not be geared to the parties' strength before the elections. Therefore, the decree stipulated a system of a posteriori funding: the state promised to disburse 1 million pesetas for each parliamentary seat obtained and an additional forty-five pesetas for each vote received by each candidate to the Chamber of Deputies, fifteen pesetas for each vote obtained by a candidate elected to the Senate. Though this system was reasonable under the circumstances, the fact is that the parties of the right were more able to obtain credit from banks than the parties of the left, which had to limit themselves, in many cases, to the limited sums they could raise.

Procedures and guarantees of the electoral process   Each electoral district (that is, each province) is divided into precincts (*secciones*) of no more than 2,000 voters or fewer than 500. Each precinct, according to the number of voters, is divided into electoral tables (*mesas electorales*), composed of a president, two assistants, and representatives of the political parties.

This organization, as can be readily seen, did not differ greatly from that of other countries. There was a fundamental difference, however, with respect to the vote count. According to the decree (which often follows the 1907 Spanish electoral law, designed for a radically different set of circumstances), the provincial juntas, once the returns from all the sections are in, announce the winners after reading aloud all returns. Were it followed to the letter, this would have meant that in provinces such as Madrid or Barcelona the results would not be known for months. As far as appeals were concerned, the decree states that these may be brought before the administrative section of the Supreme Court.[27]

The Constitution of 1978

The Spanish parliament elected on 15 June 1977 immediately confronted one essential task: to write a constitution that would serve as the basis for a new democratic state. The fact that these elections, the first in forty years, had been conducted in conformity with the Fundamental Laws of Francoist Spain did not mean, obviously, that those laws had to be maintained. On the contrary, all political groups and the king himself[28] agreed that there was an immediate need for the adoption of a democratic constitution. This would be the ninth Spanish constitution in 170 years, and it was hoped that it would be accepted by a majority of Spaniards, as the previous documents had not. Those constitutions, of course, had all been highly partisan documents that had tried to impose particular ideologies upon the nation.[29]

After nearly a year and a half of deliberations within and outside the Cortes, the definitive text of the new constitution was approved by national referendum on 6 December 1978. Without entering into great detail, let us look at two aspects of this constitution.[30] In the first place, it is one of the most democratic constitutions in the West today. Though not entirely original,[31] it has the merit of granting a broad range of rights and liberties, with their corresponding safeguards, that will permit the Spanish people to participate in government at various levels. The virtue of this constitution is heightened by the fact that it was drafted with the participation of the majority of the political forces of the country, a circumstance heretofore unknown in Spanish constitutional history.[32] This is particularly noteworthy with respect to the electoral procedures it stipulates, which, in accordance with article 81, will eventually be complemented by an Organic Electoral Law.[33]

According to its preamble, the Spanish constitution reflects an advanced democratic society, based on citizen participation. As a result, the constitution addresses various aspects of electoral participation, in some cases confirming, in others modifying, what had been established by the Law for Political Reform and by the 1977 decree. Most important, it recognizes political parties, broadens political participation, and establishes bicameralism.

Recognition of political parties. Article 6 of the constitution recognizes the political parties as the expression of the political pluralism upon which Spanish democracy is based. Their role is to shape and express the popular will, and they are considered instruments of political participation. Moreover, their formation and activities are not restricted, provided that they respect the constitution and the law and that their internal structure, as well as their activities, be democratic. This stipulation aligns Spain with the modern tendency toward the constitutionalization of political parties, but above all it definitively legitimizes their existence. At the beginning of the Spanish transition, political parties were still illegal, and as a result neither the Law for Political Reform nor the 1977 decree included a strict definition of political parties. The future electoral law, therefore, should deal with them explicitly.

Broadening of political participation. The constitution not only recognizes the right of citizens to participate in public affairs, either directly or through periodic elections (article 23), it goes on to state that it is a duty of public authorities to facilitate this participation (article 9.2). With respect to elections, this stipulation has three concrete repercussions.

First, article 12 of the constitution lowers the legal age of majority in all respects, and therefore the voting age, from twenty-one to eighteen.[34] Eighteen is also recognized as the minimum age for election to the Chamber of Deputies and the Senate. Unlike most other countries, Spain does not set a higher minimum age for election to the legislature or to the upper house.

Second, in consonance with the recognition of the indispensable function of political parties, article 20.3 establishes parliamentary control of all state mass media,[35] as well as the obligation of public authorities to facilitate access to the media by significant social and political groups.

Last, article 68.5 indicates that the state recognizes the right to vote of Spanish citizens residing abroad and will facilitate their electoral participation. This is an important provision if one bears in mind that in 1978 there were nearly 2 million Spanish citizens working abroad and that it had proved difficult for them to participate in the referendum and the 1977 election.

The bicameral parliamentary system The constitution maintains the bicameral system adopted by the Law for Political Reform—a Chamber of Deputies and a Senate—although it curtails the powers of the upper house. Likewise, it maintains the province as the electoral district, as well as the proportional representation stipulated for the Chamber of Deputies by the Law for Political Reform. It does not specify an electoral system for the Senate, deferring this matter to future electoral legislation. With respect to the composition of both houses, the constitution makes some changes. It establishes a minimum of 300 and a maximum of 400 deputies, instead of the 350 specified in the Law for Political Reform. The Senate, considered the house of territorial representation, seats four senators from each province, plus those specified for the island provinces and Ceuta and Melilla. In addition, each "autonomous community" set up as provided in chapter III would receive one senator, plus one for each 1 million inhabitants. Finally, article 70 of the constitution enumerates the most important cases of incompatibility and ineligibility that the future electoral legislation should consider.

The Candidate Selection Process

The Importance of Candidate Selection

Under the electoral laws governing the 1977 and 1979 elections, voting for the lower house of the Cortes was by party list; the voter was denied the option of deleting or adding names or altering their order. Seats were allocated to each party in a province according to the votes it received, then assigned to the candidates in the order in which their names were listed. Thus, if a party obtained three seats in a province, the first three candidates on the list became deputies. As a result, a candidate's chances of being elected depended on his position in the party list, which was decided by the party leadership. For this reason, drawing up the list was a hectic process, where the political future of the candidates was at stake. Once the list was established, each candidate's fate was sealed: the voters would determine the outcome only by their choice of party.

The situation was different in the Senate elections, where votes could be split. Election depended not on inclusion in a "good" position on a party list but on personal prestige and vote-getting appeal. For this reason, competition for selection centered on the Chamber of Deputies lists—all the more in 1979 after the powers of the Senate had been reduced by the new constitution.

This discussion will focus on the candidate selection process in 1979, since the events of 1977, before the parties had taken shape, were atypical. A brief analysis of candidate selection in 1977, however, will facilitate an understanding of later developments.

A Precedent: The 1977 Elections

By the beginning of 1977, it was clear that a general election would take place, but Spanish political life was still extremely confused. Most of the parties on the left were not yet legal,[36] and in the center the multiplicity of parties was extreme, at both the national and regional levels. Only the right-wing parties, under the label Popular Alliance and led by former minister Manuel Fraga Iribarne, showed a united front.[37]

On the left, as long as the government made no move to legalize the Spanish Communist party (PCE), the several socialist parties remained diffident, unwilling to collaborate too soon with the reformist policies of Adolfo Suárez. In addition, the socialist parties were deeply divided. At the beginning of 1977 there were three main socialist organizations:

1. The Spanish Socialist Workers' party (PSOE), the oldest and best organized, backed by the Second Socialist International and by the powerful German Socialist party (SPD). The PSOE was slowly absorbing the remnants of a splinter party, the "historical" PSOE (PSOE-h), which had split off in 1972.

2. The Popular Socialist party (PSP), formed mainly by intellectuals and university professors, followers of Professor Enrique Tierno Galván, and centered in Madrid.

3. The Federation of Socialist Parties (FPS), formed by socialist parties of regional scope and with a certain federalist ideology, among them the Madrid Socialist Convergence (CSM); the Socialist party of Valencia (PSPV), and the Socialist party of Andalusia (PSA).

In the center, liberals, social democrats, and Christian democrats founded numerous tiny organizations. Some pretended to national scope—including the Democratic Left (ID), directed by Joaquín Ruiz Giménez, and the People's party, directed by José María de Areilza and Pío Cabanillas. Others were regional, such as AREX in Estremadura and the Independent Galician party (PGI) in Galicia. The regionalist parties of the Basque country and Catalonia were also divided. The old and powerful Basque Nationalist party (PNV) remained the main moderate force. But to the left of the PNV, the patriotic or *abertzale* ultranationalistic parties were a confused lot, some of which eventually formed a loose confederation called the Socialist Patriotic Coordination (KAS). In Catalonia the situation was no better. Apart from the Marxists (that is, the Communists, still illegal, under the label Unified Socialist party of Catalonia, PSUC), and the Socialists, under the name Catalan Socialist party (PSC), the center-left was occupied by many groups, notably the Democratic Convergence of Catalonia (CDC), the Democratic Left of Catalonia (EDC), the Republican Left of Catalonia (ERC), and a moderate splinter group of the PSC, called PSC (Reagrupment).

Most of the center parties were loose coalitions of local notables without significant membership. Indeed, Spain's emerging democracy faced a grave danger: that in the forthcoming elections the voters would be presented not with a few clear-cut alternatives, but with a plethora of candidates backed by weak organizations. The menace was particularly acute for the forces of the center, which faced a united front on the right, the Popular Alliance, as well as the growing mass parties of the Marxist left.[38]

In March 1977 the political forces began to regroup. The royal decree established the format for the elections, and the government proceeded to legalize the Communist party, removing the most important roadblock to endorsement of the elections by the left. It was already clear that elections would take place and that they would be competitive. Political forces that remained divided would stand little chance against unified parties and coalitions.

Thus, in a matter of weeks, a few coalitions took the place of the previous multiparty system. The Democratic Center, an alliance of moderate parties formed around the Popular party, which had been launched back in January, was strengthened as further groups joined and parties already supporting it merged. The Democratic Center won the clear support of the government when its former leader José María de Areilza was forced to withdraw in favor of Adolfo Suárez. By the end of April it had become the Union of the Democratic Center (UCD), and it looked like a "government" coalition.[39]

On the Socialist side a similar process was taking place. The PSOE was able not only to attract members of the PSOE-h but also to merge with several regional socialist parties belonging to the FPS; these included the Madrid Socialist Convergence and the Socialist party of Murcia. In Catalonia the PSOE formed an electoral coalition with the PSC, and negotiations started toward a merger of the two parties. As a result, the other Socialist parties were forced to unite. The PSP and the remnants of the Federation of Socialist Parties formed a coalition called Socialist Unity. Two weak groups, the PSOE-h and the Social Democratic party of Spain (PSDE), formed a coalition under the name Social Democratic Alliance (ASD).

The regionalist parties followed the same pattern. In the Basque country many of the leftist patriotic parties joined to form the Euzkadi Left (EE). In

Catalonia the regionalist parties grouped themselves into two main coalitions: the Democratic Pact for Catalonia (PDC) and the Catalan Left (EC).[40]

The parties not included in these coalitions by the end of April tried desperately to integrate themselves in some kind of unified organization. Thus, the Christian democrats not included in the UCD formed the Christian Democratic Team (EDC) with close ties to the PNV and the Union of the Center and Christian Democracy of Catalonia (UCDCC). The parties to the left of the PCE formed a number of coalitions (CUP, FUT, FDI, and so on), which had to run under other labels or as independents since these parties had not yet been legalized.

The process of consolidation affected the business of candidate selection. Most of the parties either were too new to have a consolidated membership or had too recently come out "in the open" to be able to consider election of candidates by the party membership. As a result, most of the candidate lists were the product of dealings between party heads or hurried decisions by party leaders. It may be enough to remember that the deadline for presenting candidates was 8 May while the Catalan Communist party, the PSUC, was legalized only on 3 May and its parent party, the PCE, on 9 April.

But even in parties that had more time, candidate selection had to be left up to the leadership. This was mainly a result of coalition politics: the electoral lists would necessarily be negotiated between groups. Thus the PSOE lists reflected compromises with allies like the CSM in Madrid and the PSC in Catalonia.[41]

This process was most visible in the Union of the Democratic Center. By the middle of April, the minister of public works, Leopoldo Calvo Sotelo, had resigned his office to devote himself to the task of organizing the UCD coalition and of selecting adequate candidates for the provincial lists. His task was not only to distribute places among the coalition parties but also to find proper places for the "independents," the followers and friends of Adolfo Suárez who did not belong to any party and who, in many cases, had notorious Francoist pasts.[42] Despite Calvo Sotelo's effective performance, several of the coalition parties protested the invasion of Suárez men, and a couple of parties (the Liberal party and the Popular Progressive party) dropped out of the UCD.[43] In many provinces where the UCD was not adequately organized, the civil governors, provincial administrators named by the interior minister, were charged with the task of selecting the UCD candidates.[44]

Selection of Senate candidates also proceeded on the basis of alliances, the party leaders playing the key role. At the beginning of April the PSOE, by means of its Federal Committee, invited "all democratic parties" (that is, excluding the Popular Alliance) to join with it in forming a common list in all provinces, which would include distinguished intellectuals and public figures who were independents.[45] This was the origin of a series of integrated Senate lists on which Socialists, Christian democrats of the EDC, and independents all figured. Bearing labels like Senators for Democracy or Agreement of the Catalans, these lists were supported, in many cases, by the Communist party.[46]

The 1979 Elections

By the time of the 1979 elections, the situation had changed. The main parties were already consolidated. Since its First Congress, the UCD had become a unified party with strong leadership. The PSOE was the only socialist party at the national level, and its leadership seemed to have fallen to the so-called Seville-Euzkadi Axis. Thus candidate selection was no longer a process of negotiation between coalition partners. Only the partners of the right, whose position was weak, and some regional parties had to look for alliances to have any chance of getting their candidates elected. The only national coalition of any importance (apart from the extreme right coalition, the National Union) was the Democratic Coalition (CD), formed by the right-of-center Popular Alliance, Liberal Citizens' Action (ACL), and the new Progressive Democratic party (PDP).

In 1979 candidate selection in the major parties (UCD, PSOE, PCE, PNV) was a matter not of interparty dealings but of intraparty processes, which shed much light on the nature of each party. Let us briefly review the general characteristics of the candidates, then explain at greater length the selection process in the main parties.

General characteristics The 1979 elections witnessed an explosion in the number of candidates. Under Spanish law candidates can be presented by political parties, party coalitions, and voter groups. Since 1977 many parties had merged, but many new parties had been legalized. Even though the number of registered parties was not much higher in 1979 than in 1977 (204 versus 194), the number of "real" parties—that is, organizations with a sizable membership, a distinct ideology, and any promise of durability—had grown, mainly on the left. No fewer than forty-three parties ran in the 1979 elections, alone or in coalitions, but only six ran in all provinces: UDC, PSOE, PCE, the Spanish Labor party (PTE), the Workers' Revolutionary Organization (ORT), and the CD coalition.[47] As a result, the total number of candidates running for the Chamber of Deputies and the Senate increased from about 5,000 in 1977 to nearly 8,500 in 1979.

There were several reasons for this increase. One was the simple passage of time: between 1977 and 1979 many political parties had managed to organize sufficiently at the provincial level to be able to present candidates in most of the provinces. Another was the incentive of the municipal elections that would take place a month after the parliamentary elections. The parties wanted to test their candidates and to give them some publicity. Under the legal norms of 1977, to be applied provisionally in 1979, radio and television time had to be

Table 3.2 Cortes Incumbents in the 1979 Election

	Incumbents running in 1979		Incumbents not running in 1979	
Party	Deputies	Senators	Deputies	Senators
UCD	113	62	53	43
PSOE	88	48	31	18
PCE	16	6	3	0
AP (CD)	9	8	9	0
PNV	7	4	0	0
PDC	8	0	4	0
Other	10	10	0	0

Source: El País, "Recapitulaciones Electorales," 21 February 1979.

provided gratis to all parties presenting candidates in a certain number of provinces, regardless of how well they had done (if they had run) in the 1977 elections. A powerful propaganda machine was thus made available at no cost, and many small groups with no chance of electing candidates rushed to present lists in enough provinces to entitle them to radio and television exposure. The government's attempt to restrict the use of radio and television was defeated by the Central Electoral Junta. Candidates and "parties" sprouted like mushrooms, some of them—like the Freedom of Expression Union (ULE), formed by newsmen of the state press, who were threatened with unemployment[48]—running only in order to obtain free television time. The absence of mixed coalitions for the Senate along lines of the Senators for Democracy or the Agreement of the Catalans was an important sign of political change since 1977. The PSOE in particular decided not to join forces with Communist or Communist-sponsored candidates in order to highlight its identity as an "alternative."

Another sign of change was the general turnover in the political personnel. Many of those nominated in 1977 had been compromise candidates, who were no longer necessary in 1979 or now no longer responded to the prevailing tendencies within their parties (see table 3.2).

Turnover was particularly high in the UCD, where fifty-three of 165 incumbent deputies (32 percent) were not renominated in 1979. Similarly, the PSOE dropped many of the candidates it had drawn from the PSOE-h in 1977. But the PCE, the PNV, and the Catalonian Convergence and Union (CIU) did not risk backing new names where old ones had succeeded. Except in the badly disrupted AP, the candidate turnover rate was generally proportional to the number of seats held in the 1977 Cortes.

The number of women on the electoral lists increased somewhat over 1977, but the increase was due to the presence of small ultraleftist parties with no

Table 3.3 Women Candidates and Total Seats Won, Chamber of Deputies Elections, by Party 1979

Party	Women candidates	Total seats
MC–OIC	127	0
ORT	101	0
LCR	81	0
PTE	66	0
OCE–BR	66	0
UN	62	1
CD	57	9
PCE	57	23
IR	51	0
Carlist party	47	0
PCT	47	0
PSOE	46	121
UC	46	0
UCD	40	168

Source: *Cambio 16*, 18 February 1979.
Note: Regional and very minor parties excluded.

chance of winning any seats. The number of women candidates presented by the parties seems to be inversely proportional to their chances of winning (see table 3.3 and 3.4). The stronger parties, like the PSOE and UCD, did not significantly increase the number of women candidates, and even the parties making a show of feminism, placed most of their female candidates so low on their lists that their chances of being elected were practically nil. Feminist movements and publications charged that clear discrimination against women was the explanation for this state of affairs, and some women deputies elected in 1977 protested and eventually resigned their seats, allegedly in protest against the machismo of their parties. The socialist deputy for Madrid, Carlota Bustelo, was one of these.[49]

The Communist party and the Democratic Coalition In the PCE, candidate selection seems to have been strongly influenced by the principle of centralism; if there were conflicts, they were not reported in the press. According to the PCE bylaws, candidate lists originate at the provincial level through a process involving the local organizations of the party. The provincial committees forward their proposals to the Central Committee, which can modify them. In 1979, however, "lack of time" prevented the local organizations from participating. Even so, conflict seems to have been less than in other parties.[50]

Four major considerations appear to have guided the PCE leaders' choices. First, incumbency: only three incumbents were dropped—one of them, Dolores

Ibárruri, from Asturias, for reasons of age and the others for similar reasons. Second, the PCE tried to improve its image by including independents where possible (such as Joan Benet in the Communist-sponsored independent list for the Senate in Barcelona or Lorenzo Martín Retorillo in Zaragoza). Third, candidates from other parties on the left were included, notably Juana Doña in Madrid (former candidate for the Workers' Revolutionary Organization) and José Alonso (former PSP senator). Finally, the PCE decided to play the union card, including many members of the *Comisiones Obreras* (Workers' Commissions), the unions controlled by the PCE.[51]

The Democratic Coalition drew up its candidate lists by a process very similar to that followed in 1977—essentially, agreement between party leaders. Since the three allied parties (ACL, AP, PDP) were "cadre parties" without mass memberships, they did not face serious difficulties in reaching agreement. In most provinces the AP component was the only one with any organization and tended to dominate the lists. In any case, the Democratic Coalition tried to shed its "fascist" image by stressing its alliance with liberal ACL and its leader Areilza, as well as including in almost all provinces some token women and student candidates. On the other hand, the exclusion of several AP members who were considered too Francoist precipitated clashes,[52] and several local AP and ACL organizations refused to collaborate in the campaign on ideological grounds.[53]

The major parties: the UCD At the time of the 1979 elections the Union of the Democratic Center was no longer the loose confederation it had been in 1977, hurriedly pieced together under the leadership of the head of the government to stop the advance of the Socialists and Communists on the left and the Popular Alliance on the right. After the 1977 elections the UCD had developed into a unified party. In December 1977 the highest organ of the UCD, the Political Council, formally requested the dissolution of all the parties it em-

Table 3.4 Candidates and Winners, by Sex, National Elections of 1977 and 1979

	Chamber of Deputies		Senate	
	1977	1979	1977	1979
Candidates				
Women	645	1,290	51	119
Men	4,047	5,706	894	1,330
Total	4,692	6,996	945	1,449
Winners				
Women	21	19	4	6
Men	329	331	203	201

Source: *Cambio 16*, 16 February 1979, and personal data.

braced and their merger in a unified party. In April 1978 during the First Congress of the UCD, the organization was consolidated. The unified party was led by an Executive Committee headed by the party leader with the assistance of a secretary general.[54]

Adolfo Suárez's leadership of the UCD centralized power within the party in a way that gave the Madrid headquarters decisive importance when it came to selecting candidates in January 1979. Under the party rules, a provincial committee in each province would draw up, with the help of local party organizations, a proposed list of candidates, which could be altered by the executive in Madrid. In reality, however, the process seems to have been just the opposite: lists were compiled in Madrid and then sent to the provincial organizations.[55] The provincial committees' proposals usually reflected the desires of the central leadership. The lists were then studied by an electoral committee formed by Suárez and five close friends,[56] which forwarded definitive lists to the provincial organizations.

In some provinces there was clear and definite resistance to the orders from Madrid. In other places, like the capital, the lists remained secret up to the very moment of their official submission.[57] Finally, in some provinces last-minute changes were needed. But, in general, candidate selection was a Madrid affair, the officials at party headquarters taking into account the peculiar conditions of each province. Given Suárez's power within the party, only in a few cases, as we will see, were there open conflicts between provincial organizations and the party leadership.

The criteria followed by Suárez and his close group of friends in selecting the candidates varied. Personal loyalty to the prime minister seems to have been the main factor. The ideological families within the UCD, descendants of the parties that had joined the coalition in 1977, had very little voice in the proceedings. Indeed, one of the party leaders' objectives seems to have been precisely to break up the ideological identifications of former Christian democrats, liberals, and social democrats in favor of a looser differentiation between conservatives and progressives in the party.

Second, Suárez wanted to get rid of all the deadwood inherited from the 1977 compromises and to eliminate from the lists those deputies that had proved themselves either an ideological nuisance or, on the contrary, not active or energetic enough.[58] Thus Suárez ordered a performance report to be drawn up on each of the deputies elected in 1977, based on attendance at parliamentary sessions, committee hearings, and so on.

Third, an important problem had to be considered. The new Spanish constitution established a series of ineligibilities, incorporating those provisionally established by the royal decree of March 1977. Civil servants, for example, were ineligible for Parliament. Thus, a number of government officials found themselves confronted with a choice between remaining in their offices and resigning in the hope of being nominated. At the beginning of January 1979 it was clear that many UCD officeholders were in favor of resigning, and the government faced the prospect of a wave of resignations that could lead to an administrative vacuum.[59] Suárez and the top UCD leadership decided that the administrative and parliamentary spheres should be considered separate and the number of resignations kept to a minimum. This meant that, apart from the ministers—who were allowed by law to run as candidates—UCD personnel in administrative posts should give up the hope of becoming candidates, with a few exceptions.[60]

Once these criteria were established, the question remained where to allocate the main candidates, those that would head the UCD's provincial lists. The Madrid list was generally considered most desirable, both because of the national visibility it would bring and because as many as eleven or twelve Madrid seats were considered safe. The policy employed, however, was to send the most prominent UCD leaders out of the capital, reserving the Madrid list for lesser-known figures.

The reason for this was twofold. First, Suárez did not want to run members of the progressive wing of the UCD in Madrid. One of these was Francisco Fernández Ordoñez, minister of finance; a policy of placing all ministers on provincial lists was a way to avoid singling him out and sparking conflict. In addition, the presence of a strong conservative CD list, headed by Fraga Iribarne, Areilza, and Alfonso Osorio, forced Suárez to present a conservative list in the capital.[61]

Second, the government wanted the UCD to be able to put up a good fight in the provinces against the PSOE. To the top UCD leadership it seemed wise to head the party's provincial lists with politicians who were well known to the electorate thanks to their positions as ministers and their constant television exposure, which increased just before the campaign.[62]

The UCD's highly centralized candidate selection process provoked some clashes with provincial organizations of the party. The most widely reported of these occurred in Galicia, a region that has traditionally been controlled by political machines. The bosses (*caciques*) had been able to ensure the UCD and conservative forces in general a phenomenal success rate in the 1977 elections, and in 1979 they were not ready to turn control of the lists over to Madrid without resistance.[63]

In the Galician province of Orense, Madrid tried to impose a list led by Luis González Seara, of the progressive social democratic wing of the UCD. The highly conservative local establishment reacted, and the provincial boss, Eulogio Gómez Franqueira (head of both the UTECO corporation and the powerful Caja de Ahorros, the provincial savings and credit institution) presented a counterlist headed by the conservative minister Pío Cabanillas, with himself in second place. Madrid dared not oppose the move, and González Seara, number three on the local list, chose to renounce his candidacy in Orense.

Another place was sought for González Seara in another Galician province, Pontevedra. But here too, local resistance was strong. The provincial committee had already drawn up a list headed by two local notables, the undersecretary of fisheries, Victor Moro, and the Galician autonomist José Rivas Fontán. The latter was unacceptable to the Madrid UCD executive because of his radical autonomist leanings, and an offensive was mounted against him. At Madrid's request, several local UCD militants organized supporters to deluge headquarters with telegrams protesting the inclusion of Rivas in the provincial UCD list. Madrid felt its position to be strong enough that it continued to press its own list, headed by Seara, and to exclude Rivas completely.

The storm was immediate. Charging the UCD central leadership with anti-Galician prejudice, Rivas launched a campaign in the regional and national newspapers. The second candidate on the list, Victor Moro, resigned in solidarity with Rivas, and no fewer than fifteen local UCD committees in Pontevedra resigned as well. At the same time, Madrid's candidate, González Seara, was the object of strong attacks within the Galician UCD. The top leadership feared internal divisions severe enough to threaten the party's strength in Pontevedra, and the UCD general secretary Rafael Arias Salgado, was sent there to calm tempers and offer compensation to the losers, promising to include them in the lists for the forthcoming municipal elections.

In La Coruña, also in Galicia, the Madrid leadership had to intervene to prevent internal feuds from doing serious damage. The head of the La Coruña UCD, José Luis Meilán Gil, of conservative and Francoist origins, tried to purge the social democratic wing of the party, expelling from the UCD lists Antonio Vázquez Guillén and Perfecto Yebra, both social democrats. Madrid's intervention in this case was successful, preventing an exclusion that might have sparked new conflict.

Finally, in the Galician province of Lugo the Madrid leadership found itself in confrontation with Antonio Rosón, the powerful boss of the provincial UCD and president of the Galician administrative junta. Madrid wanted to place Manuel Otero Novas in the first slot on the provincial list. Rosón, who wanted the place for himself, gave way, but only on several conditions: numbers two, three, and four went to Rosón men, and the Senate list, headed by Rosón, was completed with two more of his supporters. In addition, the UCD leadership had to cede certain powers to the Galician junta, of which Rosón was president.

The major parties: the PSOE   The course of candidate selection in the PSOE in 1979 was very largely determined by ideological struggles between the radical Marxist wing of the party and the moderate social democratic leadership.[64] The consolidation of the PSOE as the only significant socialist party at the national level made it possible for the leadership to try to do without the more radical sections of the party.

To this end, the leadership used the internal regulations of the party.[65] In January 1979 the highest organ of the PSOE, the Federal Committee, issued a bylaw regulating candidate selection. In each province a provincial committee would draw up a tentative list composed of twice the required number of candidates. A Federal List Committee (elected by the Federal Committee) would pare these down and propose final lists to be approved (in some cases, modified) by the Federal Committee. In some provinces a further step would be introduced: the tentative provincial list would have to be approved by a regional committee, a body intermediate between the provincial and the federal committees. The leadership could significantly affect the outcome through both the Federal List Committee and the Federal Committee, but it could also influence the initial proposals informally by exploiting its contacts within the provincial organization.

Even so, problems arose in many provinces, centering mainly on the figure of Alfonso Guerra, the party's campaign manager. In the first phase, some provincial and regional committees started by "killing" the informal proposals emanating from the central leadership: such as the case of Alonso Puerta, who was excluded by the regional committee from the Madrid list.[66] But the strongest reaction came after the lists endorsed by the Federal Committee were made public. The PSOE leadership justified them by quoting as guidelines for candidate selection the need to include technicians and experts who would show that the PSOE was really an "alternative to the government," as well as some candidates who were expected to run in the upcoming local elections, in order to give them publicity.[67] But many of the PSOE rank and file and defeated aspirants to candidacy interpreted the lists as a maneuver of the party leaders to purge the left wing. As a matter of fact, 62 percent of the candidates had already run in 1977; but no fewer than thirty-one incumbent deputies were excluded.

The reaction was immediate. Some provincial branches of the General Workers' Union (UGT), the Socialist union, claimed that UGT leaders had been forgotten or relegated to the bottom places on the lists, where they would have no chance of being elected.[68] But protest developed mainly in the provincial organizations of the PSOE itself. Like the UCD leaders, those of the PSOE were unsympathetic to the movement for Galician autonomy, and the Galician organizations of the PSOE resented the Federal Committee's alterations to the lists prepared by three of the four Galician provinces. Furthermore, in the definitive lists names such as Modesto Seara, general secretary of the party in Galicia, and Remigio Fortes Bouzán, who had received national publicity over his expulsion from the army after he was accused of belonging to the

Democratic Military Union, had been left out.[69] The excluded candidates organized an assembly of party militants and decided to leave the PSOE and to found a new Galician Socialist party. Some of the local organizations decided to dissolve, and some party militants were expelled.[70]

Unrest was widespread in other areas, too. In Aragon the left wing protested that the provincial list was composed almost exclusively of social democrats.[71] In Seville, de facto capital of Andalusia, the UGT protested the presence of a social democrat, Luis Yañez, in second place on the PSOE list, while the two main leaders of the UGT were consigned to "bad" places. In Badajoz, in Estremadura, the regional secretary left the party in protest. Similar incidents were precipitated in Jaén by the inclusion in the provincial list of social democratic economist Miguel Boyer (excluded previously from the Madrid list by the regional committee). Other conflict-ridden places were Guadalajara, Málaga, Salamanca, Barcelona, and Murcia. But the top leadership of the party retained the upper hand, dismissing the complaints as inevitable in any party that attempted to achieve internal democracy.[72]

In conclusion, the large number of candidates and the differences among the parties made it difficult to generalize about either the process of candidate selection or the kinds of people chosen to run. The most one can say is probably that, as a result of the development of the parties since 1977, the elections of 1979 saw more candidates belonging to the bureaucracy of the parties and fewer chosen for their personal renown. Perhaps this deprived the Spanish parliament of some forceful personalities, but it certainly increased the discipline and uniformity of the parliamentary groups and their dependence on the parliamentary and party leadership.

The Transition from Below: Public Opinion Among the Spanish Population from 1977 to 1979

JOSÉ IGNACIO WERT ORTEGA

This chapter deals with the climate of opinion in Spain during the core of the "transition years"—the twenty months from the first general election in June 1977 to the first election under constitutional rule in March 1979. From a formal vantage point, this is the period in which the crucial step in Spain's process toward democracy took place—the drafting, approval, and popular ratification of a new constitution. Approval of the constitution in December 1978 opened the door to elections in 1979 through implementation of one of the constitution's transitory provisions.[1]

In addition to the constitutional process, other political events and issues attracted public attention throughout the period, among them the signing of the Moncloa Agreements[2] the first step in the process of devolution in the Basque country and Catalonia;[3] the passing of a fully inclusive Amnesty Act;[4] the continuing deterioration of public order and the increase of terrorist activities, mainly in the Basque country;[5] free industrial (trade union) elections;[6] and the emergence of action against the democratic process among sectors of the armed forces.[7]

The Inheritance: "Frozen" Political Attitudes and How They Thawed

To place the discussion in context, I begin with a brief examination of the evidence on the political attitudes of Spaniards at the end of the Franco regime[8] and the beginning of the transition.[9] Some conclusions can be drawn from the data:

1. Democracy was seen by most of the Spanish people as a "natural" development after Franco's passing. Only a small proportion of the population seriously believed in the survival of the regime. The political orientations of

Table 4.1 Attitudes on "Democratic" versus "Authoritarian" Principles of Government, 1966–1976 (percent)

Attitude	1966	1974	1976
Important decisions should be taken by an outstanding man	11	18	8
Important decisions should be taken by representatives elected by the people	35	60	78
Don't know; no answer	54	22	14

Source: Data for 1966 and 1976 come from surveys by the Instituto de la Opinión Pública; those from 1974 come from a survey by Consulta and were published by *Cambio 16*, 3 June 1974. Reproduced from Rafael López-Pintor, "El estado de la opinión pública," p. 20.

the citizens, though reflecting the traces of a long authoritarian period, showed nevertheless a pattern of progressive accommodation to the anticipated democratic future. This pattern appeared clearly in the evolution of the acceptance of the democratic principle of government between 1966 and 1976; in those ten years the percentage of the adult population accepting the principle rose from 35 to 78 percent (see table 4.1).

2. In the immediate aftermath of Franco's death, the attitudes of a majority of the population favored democratic evolution of the regime. Not only was democracy as a theoretical principle acceptable to most Spaniards, but the substantial implications of that principle had by then won widespread support (see table 4.2).

3. Nevertheless, the transition itself was anticipated by a majority as a harsh and frightful experience, a sort of ordeal. Even though their fears were somewhat nebulous, there is a consistent evidence of anxiety about the future on the eve of Franco's death and in its immediate aftermath. Only after the appointment of Adolfo Suárez as prime minister in July 1976 and the announcement of political reform did the climate of opinion change (see table 4.3).

4. In this context the government's path toward democracy had massive support. One month before the passing in the Francoist Cortes of the Law for Political Reform (November 1976), a clear majority (58 percent) anticipated that the bill would be passed, and only a small proportion (6 percent) thought it would not.[10] In a survey conducted in the days after the referendum for the popular ratification of the bill,[11] those voting "yes" gave as the main reason for their approval that "it was the best thing to do" (29 percent) and that "there is need for change and democracy" (29 percent).[12] The balance between "active" supporters of the reform process (those saying "there is need for change and democracy") and "passive" followers of the government's lead (those saying "it was the best thing to do") illustrates the particular combination of factors that made possible the transition and the way it was carried out. The strategists of

the reform took advantage simultaneously of those remainders of legitimacy that gave the government credit for any initiatives and of the trend toward democratic ideas in significant sectors of the population.

In summary, the years preceding and following Franco's death were, in the opinion of the public, times of "resurrection or reemergence of the civil society."[13] The many factors contributing to that reemergence (social, economic, and cultural) cannot be discussed here in detail, but an attitudinal ground for democracy was not created overnight by a "miraculous conversion," but rather

Table 4.2 Attitudes on the Desirability of Democracy in the Aftermath of Franco's Death, May and December 1975 (percent)

Attitude	Percent
December 1975 (national survey)	
Would like the king to:	
Grant more freedom of speech	72
Grant universal suffrage	70
Grant more regional autonomy	61
Grant amnesty	61
Grant more political freedom	58
Follow more democratic policies than previously existed	58
May 1975 (sample of seven large cities)	
The system should evolve toward a democracy of the Western kind	74
This evolution is not possible without reforming the Fundamental Laws	60

Sources: Data for December come from a survey carried out by Consulta and published by *Cambio 16* (1 December 1975); those for May come from a survey by Metra 6 and were published by *Informaciones* (31 May 1975). Table reproduced from Rafael López-Pintor, "Transition toward Democracy in Spain: Opinion Mood and Elite Behavior," *Working Papers*, no. 80 (Washington, D.C.: The Wilson Center, 1981).

Table 4.3 Attitudes toward the Future, March 1975–January 1976 (percent)

Attitude with which people look at the future	March 1975	June 1975	January 1976
With worry	58	57	54
With tranquility	39	31	34
Don't know; no anwer	3	12	12

Source: Surveys from the Instituto de la Opinión Pública, reproduced from López-Pintor, "Transition toward Democracy in Spain."

developed over the years and crystallized when the political conditions made it possible.

The Shaping of the Political Map in the 1977 Election

The results of the 1977 election have often been read in both academic and journalistic literature as a verification of certain basic trends in public opinion:

1. The massive participation (81.2 percent of the eligible voters) demonstrated a reemergence of political interest and a willingness to be "reincorporated" into politics.

2. The low vote for those parties claiming—overtly or implicitly—any allegiance to the Franco regime verified the volatilization of support for authoritarian rule only twenty months after the death of the regime's "Founding Father."[14]

3. The concentration of the vote in two political groups—the sum of votes for the Union of the Democratic Center (UCD) and the Spanish Socialist Workers party (PSOE)—was more than 60 percent of the total despite more than a hundred contending parties and coalitions, was seen as a symbol of political maturity on the part of the people, who efficiently rationalized their political preferences. This seems especially relevant since the main campaign tools—above all, free television time—were available to all parties.

4. Despite that concentration, the emerging system had the characteristics of "polarized pluralism" (in Sartori's terms) rather than "bipolar" ones. Even though not all the features of such a system could be identified in the Spanish party system arising from the 1977 election, it fit better in that category than in any other. The regional cleavages and their electoral implications were crucial for that characterization.[15]

5. The electoral returns reflected both some continuity and some change since the last electoral experience of the Second Republic. The paramount changes in social and economic structures that took place from 1936 to 1977 did not completely eliminate the old political alignments, and traces of old loyalties were still found in 1977. Table 4.4 illustrates this fact, even though in most cases the parties were not identical.

6. Among the "national" parties that won seats in Parliament, there was a tight balance between right and center on the one side and left on the other.[16] The split of the socialists in two contending parties (the PSOE and the Popular Socialist party, PSP), together with some features of the electoral system, gave some advantage to the UCD, which won almost half the seats (47.1 percent) with a much more modest share of the vote (35.1 percent).

7. The regional parties won significant numbers of votes in the Basque country and in Catalonia. In the Basque country, the Basque Nationalist party (PNV), having a rather radical platform on the devolution issue and a much

Table 4.4 Correlations between Right or Left Vote, by Province, February 1936 and June 1977

Vote in 1936	Vote in 1977	Correlation
CEDA	UCD	.46
Popular Front	PSOE and PCE	.65
PSOE	PSOE	.54

Source: Maravall, "Transición a la democracia," p. 87.

more moderate stance on socioeconomic ones, captured 28 percent of the vote and became the foremost party at the regional level. Other nationalist coalitions (both moderate and revolutionary) received nearly 20 percent of the vote, though they won only one seat in the Cortes. In Catalonia two moderate nationalistic parties, the Democratic Pact for Catalonia (PDC) and the Democratic Union of Catalonia, together won 24 percent of the vote. A leftist nationalist party, the Republican Left of Catalonia, captured an additional 5 percent. The strength of other nationalist parties was insignificant, even in regions with some historical experience of self-government, such as Galicia.

In summary, the results of the 1977 election ratified the alignment of a substantial proportion of the Spanish public on the side of democracy and moderation. They also reflected the political consequences of the modernization process that had been taking place since the early 1960s, as well as the persistence of cleavages that had characterized the political arena in earlier democratic experiences.

Governing by Consensus: From the Moncloa Agreements to the Constitution

The period from June 1977 to December 1978 has been described as one of political pact and agreement. The term "consensus" appeared frequently on the front pages of the newspapers and was often used in the speeches of the leaders. A majority of the relevant political actors had in fact some interest in achieving consensus.

For the government and its party, the UCD, the consensus was a natural development of the strategy acted on before the election: after the success of the political reform, an agreement was needed to rebuild the fabric of the state without major disruptions. Moreover, without an absolute majority in parliament, pacts and transactions were a requirement of day-to-day politics.[17]

For the main opposition party, the PSOE, consensus was seen as a tool to win social power and legitimacy. Although the Socialists had a remarkable electoral success in June 1977, their political power was limited, given the absence of representative institutions other than parliament.[18] Receiving nearly 30 percent of the votes at the national level could mean little in real influence, since the party was out of government and local government was still unrepresentative. The aim of the PSOE was both to gain a voice in the definition of the political process without formal involvement in government and to push the government to take initiatives that could expand the field of influence of the party (such as local elections and industrial elections).

As for the Spanish Communist party (PCE), any chance of participation would be welcomed by a party still facing a deep problem of legitimation after forty years as the scapegoat for the regime. The secretary general, Santiago Carrillo, asked for a government of national concentration, and this became a slogan of the Communists during the transition process.

Among the national parties, only the neo-Francoist Popular Alliance (AP), under the strong leadership of Manuel Fraga, was reluctant to take part in agreements or transactions that could erode the image of strong opposition the party was trying to convey.[19] The AP remained the only national party that refused to sign the political segment of the Moncloa Agreements and that abstained in the vote on the constitution in parliament.

Of course, the consensual approach involved in various degrees other political forces (such as the moderate nationalist parties) as well as some other relevant social actors (trade unions, business organizations, etc.).[20]

The two most visible results of the consensual period were the Moncloa Agreements and the constitution. The former constituted an extensive agreement on policy orientations for the preconstitutional period, that is, an agreement on the political agenda and the guidelines for action. The agreements covered a broad variety of fields—political development and civil rights, employment policy, labor relations, tax reform, administrative reform.[21] Shortly after the agreements were signed, mutual charges of lack of commitment began to circulate between the government and the opposition. Given the nature of the agreements and their extensiveness, their fulfillment would obviously be a matter for argument. But two different attitudes emerged in the main opposition parties. While the PSOE tended toward keeping a distance from the agreements and therefore from the government, the PCE urged that the agreements be made more extensive and deeper. The reasons for these different attitudes need no elaborate explanation: while the socialists were confident of their chances of reaching the government "through the front door" in the next election, the communists knew that they could enter government only "through the back door" of a political compromise.

Popular reactions to the Moncloa Agreements were somewhat contradictory. Among the social sectors most directly concerned with the economic outcome of the pacts, evaluations—as table 4.5 illustrates—were correlated with occupational status: the higher the status, the more positive the judgment about the agreements. These evaluations most likely reflected different aware-

Table 4.5 Evaluation of the Moncloa Agreements among Technicians, Clerks, and Manual Workers, April–May 1978 (percent)

Evaluation	Technicians	Clerks	Manual Workers
Reasonable	55.6	38.2	2.54
Useless	33.8	33.8	35.9
Don't know; no answer	10.6	27.9	38.7
N	212	499	3,443

Source: Survey conducted by EMOPUBLICA, in April–May 1978; sample of 4,154 workers in the industrial sector. Adapted from Perez Diaz, *Clase obrera partidos y sindicatos.*

Table 4.6 Opinions on the Economic Measures of the Moncloa Agreements, January 1978 (percent)

Opinion	Limitation on salary demands		Tax reform		Liberalization of the labor market	
Fully approve	8	25	18	38	7	20
Mostly approve	17		20		13	
Mostly disapprove	19	32	7	11	14	36
Fully disapprove	13		4		22	
Don't know	37		45		38	
No answer	5		6		6	
Total	100		10		100	

Source: Survey conducted by the Center for Sociological Studies in January 1978. National sample of 5,653 persons of voting age.

ness of the economic crisis in the different strata. The reluctance of manual workers to agree on policies of austerity was probably related to fears about the consequences for their economic position. As López-Pintor has demonstrated, average wages and salaries consistently rose faster than inflation in the years of political transition (1974 to 1979), in contrast to the experience of most Western countries.[22]

This hypothesis is supported by the data shown in table 4.6. The only aspect of the agreements for which approval was higher than disapproval among the population as a whole was "tax reform." More people disapproved than approved the limitation on salary demands and the liberalization of the labor market, accustomed as they were to increases in their wages that were higher than the inflation rate and to stability in their jobs. Approval of "tax reform" may well be explained by the persistence of egalitarian values among many sectors of the population as well as by the lack of understanding as to what the effects of tax reform would be on their individual economic positions.[23]

The most important political expression of the consensual climate was the constitutional process, from the first meeting of the drafting subcommittee of the Parliament in September 1977 to the publication of the law at the end of December 1978.[24] During this period, there were times of peace and times of battle among the main parties fostering the process, the UCD and the PSOE. The most serious crisis came when the Socialists withdrew from the drafting subcommittee, claiming that the UCD was imposing a "reactionary" approach in topics such as education and relations with the Catholic church. The withdrawal appears now to have been a "tactical maneuver" by the Socialists to call attention to the limits of compromises they were ready to accept.[25] It was basically aimed at stopping the left-wingers of the party, who were criticizing the absence of the traditional slogans—anticlericalism, republicanism—in the constitutional consensus. The basic agreement was soon restored, and a spirit of compromise between Centrists and Socialists dominated the political scene. Disputes emerged nevertheless in later stages of the drafting process (both in the Chamber of Deputies and in the Senate), but the political will to reach a consensus helped to find suitable formulas of compromise in the most divisive issues. Agreements were reached outside parliament in a series of dinners between the heads of the UCD and of the PSOE. These "restaurant agreements" were bitterly criticized by the press and the minor parties. There were complaints that the compromises between the two main parties were contemptuous of the sovereignty of parliament and contributed to the indifference of public opinion toward the constitution. In my opinion, these attacks were basically unjustified. First, because given the publicity of the discussion in parliament, it was almost impossible for the major parties to arrive at agreements on the most divisive issues without losing face before their constituencies; and second, the assumed indifference of public opinion had nothing to do with where the constitution was agreed upon but, rather, was caused by the technical complexity of both the approval process and the content of the draft.

Probably the main question that remains is whether in fact there was as much public indifference as alleged. For if it is true that the process took place in the absence of either enthusiasm or popular confrontation, it is also true that the Spanish public was quietly aligned in favor of a Fundamental Law that could modernize the political system. Table 4.7 reports the attitudes of the population toward significant modernizing elements of the constitution. It illustrates that (1) most Spaniards were in favor of the "progressive" solution to the issues and (2) the society was seen by the public as slightly more backward than it really was. In fact, the percentage of people who personally agreed with the modernizing attitude on each issue exceeded the percentage of those who thought that most Spaniards would agree.

After the constitution was passed by both chambers in October 1978, the government called a referendum on 6 December for the ratification of the Fundamental Law as ordered in the Law of Political Reform.[26] The govern-

Table 4.7 Attitudes toward Modernizing Policies, July 1978 (percent)

Issue	Think most Spaniards will support	Personally support	Think most Spaniards will reject	Personally reject	Don't know Most Spaniards	Don't know Self
Lowering of voting age to eighteen years	70	74	19	22	11	4
Legalization of divorce	57	67	28	29	15	5
Abolition of death penalty	66	74	19	20	16	5
Legalization of contraception and adultery	56	63	24	27	20	10
Legalization of conscientious objection	58	69	14	13	28	19

Source: Survey conducted by Metra-6 in July 1978; national sample of 1,184 persons of voting age.

Table 4.8 Knowledge about the Constitution, October-December 1978 (percent)

Question: Do you consider yourself sufficiently informed about the contents of the constitution?

	Yes	No	Don't know	No answer	N
October 1978	24	58	18	1	1,196
October 1978	26	56	17	1	1,169
November 1978	30	57	13	1	1,189
November 1978	40	48	10	1	1,189
November 1978	51	40	8	1	1,199
December 1978	57	34	8	0	1,196

Source: Surveys conducted by the Center for Sociological Research during the two months preceding the referendum.

ment and the parties aligned in favor of the text strongly campaigned for the "yes" vote. Of the main parties, only the rightist Popular Alliance (AP) and the Basque Nationalist party (PNV) were exceptions to the dominant stream of support for the constitution. The PNV openly campaigned for abstention in the Basque country; the AP did not campaign at all and left the vote to the individual decision of the party's members and sympathizers.

Table 4.9 Voting Intentions in the Constitutional Referendum, July–December 1978 (percent)

	In favor	Against	Don't know; no answer	N
July 1978	36	2	61	1,200
September 1978	33	3	65	1,178
September 1978	34	5	61	1,184
October 1978	36	4	60	1,196
October 1978	36	6	57	1,169
November 1978	40	5	55	1,189
November 1978	39	5	57	1,183
November 1978	50	5	46	1,199
December 1978	52	5	43	1,196

Source: Surveys conducted by the Center for Sociological Research during the six months preceding the referendum.

The public opinion data (table 4.8) suggest that the campaign was relatively successful in interesting the population in the constitution even when it did not arouse the enthusiasm some had expected. Although the percentage of those who considered themselves "sufficiently informed" is barely reliable as a measure of real information, its growth throughout the campaign attests at least to an emergence of interest in the law.

Probably the most important aspect in which the campaign can be said to have been relatively successful concerns voting intentions. As table 4.9 shows, these were quite stable from June 1978 to the beginning of the referendum campaign in November. In the three-week campaign the percentage of "decided supporters" of the constitution rose from 39 to 52 percent. That does not seem a bad score given the circumstances, that is, the absence of a partisan conflict about the issue.

The results of the referendum confirmed the survey predictions. Although the rate of participation was almost ten points below that for the referendum of 1976, this was the third time Spaniards had been called to the polls in less than two years, and there was little or no doubt about the result of the referendum.[27] The ratio of "yes" to "no" votes (more than ten to one) was the highest for any modern constitution ratified by popular vote.[28] Given the paramountcy of the change from the Francoist Fundamental Law embodied in the constitution, the high degree of consensus on the constitution should be regarded as a relative success rather than, as it usually was, as a relative failure. Only in the Basque provinces were the returns significantly different—although the "yes" votes were much higher than the "no," blank, and null votes—from the results in the rest of the country. The failure of the PNV to join the "constitutional coalition" determined the lesser support the constitution won in that region. The ambivalence of the most significant Basque forces toward the constitution remains a major problem for the stability of democracy in Spain.[29]

Seen in retrospect, the consensual period does not seem to deserve the vitriolic judgments it suffered from an influential sector of the media. There is no evidence that consensus led to disenchantment, as has been argued.[30] Rather it appears that consensus was the logical consequence of the model of transition that had been adopted.

The Basic Alignments: Change and Stability

Spaniards lived the transition process in the midst of fundamental contradictions. The economic situation was worse than five or six years before, and the consequences of the crisis for individuals began to appear in the very moment of political transition. At the same time terrorism and delinquency considerably increased.[31] The political change, however—both its essence and its process—accorded rather well with the aspirations of the population. As the blossoming of democracy coincided with the deterioration of economic conditions and public order, perceptions of the political situation were negatively influenced by those conditions. Politicians used their best rhetorical weapons to demonstrate the "innocence" of the political change in the worsening of everyday life. And they partially succeeded: as tables 4.10 and 4.11 show, at the end of the transition there was more than acceptable support for democ-

Table 4.10 Popular Support for Democracy, November 1980 (percent)

Democracy is better than any other regime	49
In some cases a dictatorship may be better	9
Any other regime is better than democracy	1
The kind of regime does not matter to ordinary people	8
Don't know; no answer	33

Source: Poll conducted by the Center for Sociological Research in November 1980; national sample of 4,515 persons of voting age.

Table 4.11 Perception of Effectiveness of Democracy, September 1979 (percent)

Democracy helps to solve the real problems	34
Democracy is irrelevant to solving the real problems	27
The real problems will get worse under democracy	21
Don't know; no answer	19

Source: Poll conducted by the Center for Sociological Research in September 1979; national sample of 1,175 persons of voting age. Adapted from Maravall, "La alternativa socialista."

84   The Transition from Below

Table 4.12 Evaluation of the Present and Future Political Situation, June 1978 (percent)

Evaluation	1978	Future
Very good	2	5
Fairly good	20	35
Unsatisfactory	39	18
Fairly bad	13	7
Very bad	4	2
Don't know	19	31
No answer	3	2
Total	100	100

Source: Survey of 1,180 persons of voting age conducted by the Center for Sociological Research in June 1978, one year after the first general election.

Table 4.13 Perception of Change in Political Situation, October 1978 (percent)

Question: Do you think the political situation has gotten better, worse, or remained the same as in the past?

Better	19
Worse	19
The same	33
Don't know	26
No answer	2
Total	100

Source: Survey conducted by the Center for Sociological Research in October 1978, national sample of 1,183 persons of voting age.

racy as a principle, and attitudes on the effectiveness of the system were not predominantly negative.

Nevertheless, when we pass from a general and abstract evaluation of democracy to an evaluation of the political situation in 1978 and prospects for the future, the picture becomes less clear. Table 4.12 reflects a rather negative view, in sharp contrast with the data of two years before, at the beginning of the transition. Although in December 1976, immediately after the Law for Political Reform was passed, 52 percent of the population evaluated the political situation as "very good" or "good,"[32] one year after the first election the positive evaluations decreased to 22 percent. Behind this change in perceptions lay an obvious influence of the economic malaise and the deterioration of public order. Nevertheless, the negative perceptions did not carry over to the immediate future: 40 percent expected political conditions to be good or very good while 9 percent expected them to be fairly or very bad. In fact, pessimism about the ability of the system to overcome the difficulties emerged later.[33] The 1978 situation was perceived not in the dramatic terms some have argued but, rather, with a mixture of worry and hope.

That combination appears when we look at the perception of the change in the political situation. Even though the indication is somewhat vague and cannot be understood as a general judgment on the transition, it illustrates the climate of those days as a blend of worry and hope (see table 4.13). There was a tight balance between those who thought the situation had changed for the better and those who thought it had changed for the worse. Even more important, less than 40 percent were able to evaluate the change.

Political alignments, in the sense of party preference and the popularity of the main political leaders, changed very little during the years we are considering. An impressive number of surveys on voting intentions were taken during this period.[34] Tables 4.14 and 4.15 summarize the results of a series of polls on voting intentions taken by the Center for Sociological Studies during 1978 and early 1979. The general pattern that emerges is one of basic stability in the preferences for the three main parties since the 1977 election. Although

Table 4.14 Voting Intentions for the General Elections, September 1977–February 1979 (percent)

	UCD	PSOE	PCE	AP	Don't know; no answer	N
September 1977	23	29	5	6	32	1,182
January 1978	19	23	6	3	44	5,651
July 1978	20	25	6	3	38	1,180
September 1978	22	24	6	5	32	1,184
October 1978	24	26	6	4	35	1,196
October 1978	20	17	4	4	46	1,190
November 1978	22	23	5	5	37	1,169
November 1978	27	22	4	3	36	1,189
November 1978	24	23	4	3	35	1,183
November–December 1978	25	24	5	3	35	1,199
December 1978	26	23	5	6	32	1,196
December 1978	27	22	4	4	34	987
January 1979	24	28	6	3	31	1,188
January 1979	27	23	5	3	35	1,170
January 1979	25	23	4	3	36	1,188
February 1979	23	21	5	3	42	24,395

Source: Polls conducted by the Center for Sociological Research from September 1977 to February 1979; all national samples of persons of voting age.

Table 4.15 Voting Intentions for the Local Elections, August 1978–January 1979 (percent)

	UCD	PSOE	PCE	AP	Don't know; no answer	N
August 1978	17	33	8	3	33	1,199
September 1978	16	20	5	3	53	1,184
September 1978	14	27	9	5	39	1,216
October 1978	19	21	5	3	45	1,196
October 1978	17	21	4	4	48	1,169
November 1978	20	18	5	2	48	1,189
November 1978	18	21	4	2	49	1,183
November 1978	19	21	5	3	47	1,199
November–December 1978	21	19	5	5	43	1,196
December 1978	21	20	4	3	46	1,184
January 1979	19	22	6	2	45	1,188
January 1979	18	19	4	3	52	1,170
January 1979	18	18	3	3	54	1,188

Source: Polls conducted by the Center for Sociological Research from August 1978 to January 1979; all national samples of persons of voting age.

support for the AP remained fairly constant, it was significantly lower than the electoral results for the party in 1977. The 1979 returns confirmed these predictions. The UCD, PSOE, and PCE remained more or less the same, whereas the AP—in 1979 under the name Democratic Coalition (CD)—lost substantial support. In two ways voting intentions for local elections differed from those for general elections. One was the higher proportion of undecided voters, the other the broader support for parties of the left. Both were confirmed in the local elections of 4 April: higher indecision meant higher abstention, and the left, especially the socialists, won more votes, mainly in the largest cities.[35]

The same pattern of stability can be found in the evaluation of the main political leaders (see table 4.16). Adolfo Suárez, the prime minister, and Felipe González, the Socialist leader, continued to be the most popular, with similar levels of public acceptance, while Manuel Fraga and Santiago Carrillo remained considerably behind.

In the more general political alignments—self-placement on a left-right scale—there was no significant change (see table 4.17). The most important change had taken place in the earlier stages of the political transition, when the very meaning of the terms "left" and "right" was restored.[36]

In conclusion, the twenty months between the elections of 1977 and those of 1979 were times of some ambiguity and contradiction in public opinion. Support for democracy in the abstract was consolidated, but the satisfaction with day-to-day conditions was eroded, basically because of deterioration of the economy and of public order. In political alignments, stability predominated over change, and the electoral returns of 1979 confirmed that trend in public opinion. In the relation of people to the political system, there was a wait-and-see attitude. Neither criticism of nor enthusiasm for the political system can be found in the attitudes of the Spanish population during those days. And—if one compares this "low profile" reaction with the experiences of previous democratic periods in Spain—it seems legitimate to say this was the best that could have happened.

Table 4.16 Evaluation of Major Political Leaders, 1978 (Mean score on a scale ranging from 0 to 10)

Party Leader	January 1978	July 1978	October 1978	December 1978
Manuel Fraga (AP, right)	3.6	4.2	4.2	3.9
Adolfo Suarez (UCD, center)	6.1	5.9	6.4	6.2
Felipe González (PSOE, socialist)	6.2	5.9	5.7	5.8
Santiago Carrillo (PCE, communist)	4.5	4.5	4.0	4.0
N	5,651	5,348	1,183	5,712

Source: Polls conducted by the Center for Sociological Research, national sample of persons of voting age.

Table 4.17 Self-Placement on the Left-Right Dimension, July 1978 and July 1979 (percent)

Self-Placement	July 1978	July 1979
1	3	4
2	5	5
3	15	15
4	17	17
5	21	17
6	12	13
7	6	5
8	4	5
9	1	1
10	1	1
Don't know; no answer	14	18
Mean self-placement	4.68	4.78
N	5,898	5,499

Source: Opinion surveys carried out by DATA S.A.; national samples of persons of voting age. Adapted from Linz et al., *Informe sociológico*, p. 372.
Note: Scale ranges from 1, the furthest left, to 10, the furthest right.

The Democratic Center and Christian Democracy
in the Elections of 1977 and 1979
JAVIER TUSELL GÓMEZ

———This chapter describes the evolution of the political center in the first years of Spain's democracy. Its two chief protagonists—the Christian Democratic Team and the Union of the Democratic Center—met very different fates at the polls. Despite high hopes, the former was wiped out in the general election of 1977, while the latter made a strong showing and consolidated its position and became the most successful electoral force in Spain in 1979. For both, the story begins with the moderate opposition that grew up inside the dictatorship and with the surprising collaboration between Francoists and anti-Francoists that made the transition to democracy possible.

Francoism and the Moderate Opposition

During the Civil War of 1936-39, the Nationalists received support from Hitler's Germany and Mussolini's Italy. Nevertheless, the government they eventually set up was in many respects more like a traditional dictatorship than it was like either of its allies. After the Second World War the Franco regime stripped off the fascist attributes thrust upon it by circumstance and described itself as an "organic democracy." Instead of being represented by a democratic political party, the citizen was represented by the "organisms" in which he lived "naturally"—the family, the municipality, the trade union. Indeed, as Juan Linz has shown, by the 1950s Franco's Spain had become a paradigm of the authoritarian regime, not democratic, of course, but never truly fascist. Unlike fascist regimes, it had no definite ideology, and it did not attempt to mobilize the masses for political ends. On the contrary, it encouraged demobilization and allowed an element of pluralism, which, though limited to those denoted as "families" of the regime and therefore nothing like democratic pluralism, had never existed in a fascist country. The regime was prepared to tolerate internal dissent on condition that the supreme leadership of General Franco remain unchallenged. As time passed, tolerance was extended even to certain opponents of the regime.[1]

These made up the moderate, or democratic, opposition, as distinct from those elements who sought to alter the socioeconomic organization of society, espoused violent means, or rejected democratic institutions. Some members of this moderate opposition were former Republicans and Socialists; others, however, had supported Franco during the Civil War and had espoused democratic views only when the regime had been converted into a personal dictatorship. As the old Republicans died off, the moderate opposition became more active and capable and eventually turned into a powerful political force.

Those within the moderate opposition who had once been Francoists could trace their origins to the views of Don Juan de Borbón, son and heir of Alfonso XIII. By 1943 Spain had already been converted into a personal dictatorship, and Don Juan had come to oppose it: though not originally democrats, he and his followers eventually became decided partisans of democracy. Above all, however, they wanted peace and were willing to work with their old enemies to achieve it. Even so, by 1949 Don Juan de Borbón's chances of succeeding Franco had shrunk to nil.

Starting in 1956, small political groups parallel to the major parties of the Western European democracies began to appear.[2] These groups were notable not for their size (they were very small) or their chances of making the Franco regime more like the Western European democracies (which were remote). Their function was to exist and to be known to exist; therefore, except on those rare occasions when their activities attracted any public attention, they were not persecuted. In view of its incapacity to offer an alternative to the Francoist system, this opposition led a peculiar life, substituting cultural for political action, often absorbed in its own internal debates and factional splits.

Meanwhile, within the Franco regime, a slow but important change was taking place. Originally the political elite had been made up of individuals drawn from the Second Republic's rightist parties. Although Franco had combined them in such a manner as to make it impossible to say he had favored any one sector, still, individuals remembered their own political antecedents. With the passage of time this sense of their origins became blurred, and the politicians adopted the ways of technocracy. The youngest were, besides, models of pragmatism; many of them, ignorant of the original ideology of the regime, were simply administrators with a vague desire that Francoism "open itself" (the phrase was key for this group) to institutions more akin to those of Western Europe.

From the beginning there was occasional contact between the political elite and the opposition. Through the 1960s contact increased as it became more and more evident that the regime would not outlive Franco and that the younger generations showed a growing dislike of Francoism. Although the opposition groups did not grow significantly in membership, they became more active.

Of the modern anti-Franco elements, the Christian Democratic movement might have been thought most likely to become a mass party, but in the second half of the 1960s it suffered some serious setbacks. In 1966 the two small Christian Democratic groups, after a vain attempt to unite, each split again. The leader of one group, Manuel Giménez Fernández died at the end of the decade, and his followers regrouped around Joaquín Ruiz Giménez, Franco's minister of education until 1956, when his liberalizing tendencies had collided with Falangist policy. By the beginning of the 1970s, Ruiz Giménez was associated with the journal *Cuadernos para el Diálogo* and had united behind him a good part of the young intelligentsia. Partly because of his personality, however, this group did not become the nucleus of a Christian Democratic party but developed in different directions. While some of its members would remain faithful to Christian Democracy and others would actually join the Franco regime, a significant number of the *Cuadernos para el Diálogo* group moved from Christian Democracy to Christian progressivism and ultimately to socialism or more radical solutions. A clear sign of this evolution was the attitude *Cuadernos* adopted toward the Chilean coup d'état against Chilean president Salvador Allende: the journal's contributors accused Christian Democracy of becoming an ally of dictatorship. Henceforth, *Cuadernos* would serve as a meeting point for the anti-Francoist opposition, including the most extreme groups.

With hindsight, one can say that by the 1970s Spanish politics had come to revolve around three alternative positions: acceptance of the fundamental characteristics of the Franco regime; belief that a legal, reformist transformation was possible; and unequivocal opposition to the regime and insistence on "rupture" with the past. But even those who held the first view sought change, and the boundaries between the two others were not always clear.

The Case for a Legal Transition The history of Tácito illustrates the convolutions of Spanish politics in this period. Early in 1973 a group of Catholic professionals and intellectuals associated with the Asociación Católica de Propagandistas came together for purposes of political discussion. Many of them were high government officials, and some (such as Fernando Alvarez de Miranda, Juan Antonio Ortega Díaz Ambrona, Iñigo Cavero, and Oscar Alzaga) had ties with the Christian democratic opposition. Starting in June, they published their views under the collective pseudonym Tácito. Their articles appeared in *Ya* and the regional papers of Editorial Católica, a publisher associated with the right during the Second Republic. The *Ya* articles were widely read. At this time the defining characteristics of Tácito were its members' will to act in common, their advocacy of Spain's integration into Europe, and their support for international declarations on human rights. They were also explicitly committed to lawful action.

The Tácitos, as the group came to be called, maintained that the succession of the head of state could be resolved within the existing legal structure. They welcomed the nomination of Luis Carrero Blanco as deputy prime minister, and some accepted administrative posts in the government of Carlos Arias Navarro, Franco's last prime minister. These Tácitos played a very important role in drafting a speech Arias delivered on 12 February 1974, which revived the hopes of those who believed substantial change in the structure of Francoism would be possible. But these hopes were disappointed; with the progressive hardening of the Arias government, some of the Tácitos resigned, and in October 1974 in an article published, as always, in *Ya*, Tácito lamented the turn things were taking.

The hardening of the regime divided Tácito over tactics. By January 1975 a split had emerged between those who preferred contacts with clear opponents of Francoism (Alvarez de Miranda, Cavero) and those who were prepared to accept the Statute of Political Associations (Alfonso Osorio, Andrés Reguera Guajardo, and Eduardo Carriles), under which they would eventually form a Christian democratic group called the Spanish Democratic Union. Those who continued to use the label Tácito rejected the option of forming a political party and even the idea of political action; for the most part, they cooperated with Manuel Fraga Iribarne in the founding of the research-oriented Federación de Estudios Independientes (FEDISA). At the time there was little Tácito could have done. Late in October 1975 an article entitled "The Successors" written by Ortega and published under the usual pseudonym openly advocated "democratic monarchy" after Franco. "The government ought to resign," it said, "and the people become protagonists." The author was brought to trial, and eighteen people associated with the work of the group publicly declared their solidarity with him.

General Franco died on 20 November 1975, and his last prime minister, Arias Navarro, became the first prime minister of the monarchy, naming the former Tácito member Alfonso Osorio to his cabinet. At the beginning of 1976 the Tácitos declared their support for the "democratic center," which they saw as essentially Christian and still "excessively fragmented and divided"; they were obviously courting the small clandestine Christian Democratic groups. About this time a leading Tácito, José Luis Alvarez, announced the formation of another party, which he promised would not collaborate with Democratic Coordination, the umbrella organization of the opposition created in April

1976, which included the Communists. The Tácitos already foresaw the necessity of a coalition of social democrats, Christian Democrats, and independents in the elections that would eventually be held.[3]

The Case for a Break with the Past: The EDC What happened, meanwhile, among those who did not believe reform to be possible within Francoist legality? The Christian Democrats, of course, had an advantage over the official Catholic groups that had collaborated with Francoism, namely, international recognition. From 1965 on, Spanish groups were represented in the European Christian Democratic Union, and in the 1970s a number of them began to act collectively as the Christian Democratic Team of the Spanish state (EDC).[4] At three meetings held in Montserrat, Valencia, and Madrid, the EDC approved a number of documents. The third session, held in January 1976 after Franco's death, was public and included a meeting for which authorization had never been sought. They endorsed a federal structure for the Spanish state and democratic liberties, though without recommending to the government a means of achieving them. The EDC advocated a break with the past: "the peaceful replacement of the present regime by another that would give rise to the democratic organization of the Spanish state."

In a memorandum submitted to the king in April 1976, the leader of the more conservative FPD, José María Gil Robles, argued that holding back would be fatal for the monarchy. The king must take the lead in the transition. His duty was to name a government untainted by Francoism, which would hold a "referendum of democratic arbitration" to authorize the direct election of a constituent Cortes under universal suffrage, the secret ballot, and proportional representation. At the same time, by decree, this government would begin to legislate on fundamental rights, amnesty for political prisoners, and the legalization of political parties. Assuming the referendum results were favorable, the government would also draft an electoral law, suspend the law of public order, and dissolve the old Cortes. This sequence would have allowed for a smooth transition, never broken by a power vacuum. The course that events actually took was much more tortuous. The weaknesses of Gil Robles's proposal could be that it provided inadequate protection against either a regression to dictatorship or the elimination of the monarchy.

Meanwhile, thanks to the atmosphere of tolerance that came into being under the Arias government, the two most important Christian democratic groups held congresses in April 1976. These were expected to define the programs of the Popular Democratic Federation (FPD) and the Democratic Left (ID), to establish unity between them, and to formulate consistent positions regarding Democratic Coordination, the association of all the anti-Francoist groups that had appeared in the middle of the month. These two congresses—the FPD's in Segovia and the ID's in the Escorial—were preceded by vigorous discussion. The principal issue was the desire of a group within Ruiz Giménez's party to create a much broader party than had existed up to then—and consequently to reject a link with Democratic Coordination, in which the extreme left participated. This "autonomous wing" within ID had contacts with the Tácitos and actually included Alvarez de Miranda, Cavero, and Ortega. Others in the ID would have preferred the party to adopt more leftist positions on issues like worker control, and above all, to collaborate with all the opposition; Ruiz Giménez himself, long considered the personification of the opposition, tended toward this view.

The two congresses had an unexpected finale. Despite the opposition of Gil Robles, the FPD decided to join Democratic Coordination, perhaps to make union with Ruiz Giménez's group more feasible. The ID congress approved some rather stiff conditions for joining Democratic Coordination: that all parties wishing to join, including regional ones, be permitted to do so; that they renounce violence; that the organization be dissolved when elections were called; and that, above all, member parties give up their right of veto. Even so, the "autonomous wing" split off, in the belief that by entering Democratic Coordination they would have ruined their chances of organizing a truly mass party. It is probable, too, that the autonomous wing expected a tie with coordination to divide the Christian Democrats—as it did, in the long run. The autonomous wing adopted the label Christian Democratic Left (IDC).

Most political observers agreed that the Christian Democrats were the moderates most likely to do well in elections, but there were other moderate elements as well. In the 1970s liberal groups had appeared, most of them very small and held together primarily by personal leadership. Perhaps the most active of these was the Federation of Democratic and Liberal Parties (FPDL), founded in mid-1974 by Joaquín Garrigues and Antonio Fontán. Businessmen played an important role in its activities. Enrique Larroque's Liberal party (PL) and the Popular Democratic party inspired by Ignacio Camuñas appeared about the same time. Camuñas and Garrigues came to represent a new liberalism that had nothing to do with the regime on whose fringes it had grown up; this differentiated them from the liberal tradition of opposition to Francoism, which harked back to Joaquín Satrústegui and his Spanish Union (UE) in the 1950s, and from Larroque, whose party had originated in the liberal sectors of the regime. In August 1976 a Liberal Alliance was created between the FPDL, the UE, and the PL, with a united secretariat, which publicly espoused the 1947 and 1967 manifestoes of the Liberal International, but it failed to achieve any real effectiveness.[5]

There was also a social democratic tradition, which Dionisio Ridruejo drew upon in forming his Social Party of Democratic Action. Ridruejo had played a decisive part in the opposition in the 1960s inside and outside Spain; his followers, though few, were men of intellectual prestige. The group took on the structure of a party only in October 1974, when it assumed the name Spanish Social Democratic Union (USDE). It drew its support from the friends of Dionisio Ridruejo, on the one hand, and those of Antonio García López, an old PSOE leader, on the other. Ridruejo's death in the summer of 1975 was a turning point: thereafter García López would move the group toward the center-left in cooperation with other longtime Socialists, but it would fail to attract many votes.[6]

Suárez and the Blooming of the Centrist Groups

Let us turn now to Prime Minister Adolfo Suárez, whose actions and personality decisively shaped the Union of the Democratic Center (UCD).

The first government appointed by the king was presided over by Franco's last prime minister. Probably the king had no choice but to allow Arias to remain at his post, given the likelihood that any alternative promoted by the Council of the Kingdom would be worse still. Arias's actions were halting and confused; he seemed unable to forget his Francoist loyalties or to formulate any coherent program for the future. During his months in office, a degree of tolerance was instituted, but he finally resigned, probably at the king's request.

The selection of Suárez to succeed him came as a total surprise to most political observers. No one thought of Suárez as having played a part in great decisions, and no one thought it opportune that a minister and general secretary of the Falangist party should lead the country to democracy. The choice had its logic, however. In the first place, by choosing a younger man, Juan Carlos freed himself from the tutelage of advisers and of his father; second, Suárez had tactfully demonstrated to the Cortes his ability to lead. In the months that followed, Suárez would demonstrate his capacities as a leader. Criticized for his supposed lack of intellectual stature, he nevertheless acquitted himself well during the delicate transition to democracy. Though the product of a regime that had abominated democratic values, he was sufficiently pragmatic to grasp the need for peaceful change. It was time to take the drama out of politics, Suárez said, and concentrate on the normal concerns of the man in the street.

Suárez represented a sharp change from Arias, as the country soon realized. He moved decisively and fast. His plan for reform, whatever its shortcomings, made it possible to hope that the country could legally arrive at democracy. What is more, Suárez knew how to get it approved in the Cortes without substantial modifications and without the most conservative deputies' feeling it had been forced upon them. His relations with the opposition, while not always cordial, were much more correct that Arias's. Suárez talked with the opposition and saw to it that the moderates would resist sweeping condemnations of his government.[7] What criticism there was of the new prime minister in the months that followed tended to stress his supposed inability to keep abreast of events. On the legalization of the Communist party in April 1977, for example, he gave the impression that a decision had been forced upon him—though some believe that, had the legalization occurred differently, it might well have backfired.

Most important, a clear majority of the Spanish people approved of the course charted by Suárez. In December 1976, 77.7 percent of those eligible voted in the referendum on the Law for Political Reform, despite the fact that the Socialist and Communist parties had campaigned for abstention. The "no" vote was scarcely 2 percent and seems to have come from sectors of the traditional middle class that were losing ground. As for the "yes" vote—highest in the nonautonomist, Catholic, rural areas and among the urban middle class—it gives us a clear cross section of support for Suárez's reform. The future UCD electorate had already taken shape.

A year after this referendum, at the end of 1977, Suárez's popularity remained high: according to an opinion poll, he was the best-known politician in Spain and the one perceived as the most capable of solving a whole series of problems—prices, public order, unemployment, strikes, and the inauguration of democracy.[8] It is significant that Suárez's lead was largest on the matter of democracy: 38 percent of those polled did not respond, but 45.4 percent named Suárez, while Felipe González garnered 5.9 percent, José María de Areilza 4.2 percent, Fraga 2.5 percent, and Ruiz Giménez 2.2 percent. These figures should be borne in mind when we come to Suárez's role in shaping the UCD.

Another poll suggested that the politicization of the Spaniards was advancing very slowly. In December 1976, 45 percent of Spaniards were still unable to name any political party, and by March the figure had dropped only nine points. Just before the referendum, most Spaniards seemed perplexed about their choice.[9] The moderate opposition, as we have seen, was receptive to Suárez's reforms but never enthusiastic about the 1976 referendum. Given that the "yes" vote would be overwhelming, many people did not bother to vote. Yet the referendum was a turning point: from that point on, moderates found a more congenial spokesman in the government than in the opposition. Of the moderates, only the Democratic Left participated in Democratic Coordination—often to oppose its positions from the inside. Indeed, Democratic Coordination lost its appeal the moment reform and peaceful evolution within a legal framework were seen to be real possibilities. When negotiations with the government finally began, it was not Democratic Coordination but a delegation from the moderate opposition that spoke for the forces outside the government.

The Creation of the Popular Party When the Democratic Left split, the group that formed the Christian Democratic Left sought support not from the leftist opposition but from reformists identified with European Christian Democracy. This approach was similar to that of the Tácito group. It was foiled when some key figures decided to enter the government Suárez formed in July. Fraga, Areilza, and Garrigues refused to cooperate with Suárez, but the old Tácito Alfonso Osorio accepted the post of deputy prime minister and was the key figure in the selection of several ministers. Reguera Guajardo, Carriles, Enrique de la Mata, Landelino Lavilla, and Marcelino Oreja joined the government; they all could be considered sympathetic to European Christian Democracy. The first three, like Osorio, were members of the Spanish Democratic Union (UDE), and the last two were prominent Tácitos. Osorio also tried unsuccessfully to appoint Alvarez de Miranda, the best-known figure of the Christian Democratic Left, to the post of minister of education. In any event, from this time on there was frequent contact between Osorio and the Christian Democrats. Osorio tried directly and indirectly to interest Gil Robles in a Christian Democratic movement that would include both collaborators and noncollaborators with Francoism—but to no avail.

The original impetus toward the formation of the Popular party (PP) came from Christian Democratic groups. In effect, from the time of the schism in the Democratic Left, the group that wanted to adopt the label "Christian Democrats" also wanted to create a vigorous mass party that would be recognized by international Christian Democracy. During the middle months of 1976 there were conversations on this subject between members of the IDC, the Tácitos, and the FEDISA groups. They agreed to call the new group the Popular party or Popular Democratic party, a formula used by Christian Democrats elsewhere in Europe. The talks proceeded slowly. One of the many points of contention was the inclusion of Pío Cabanillas, a Francoist minister who had been dismissed for his liberal attitudes.

Finally, in September 1976, there was a break between those who insisted upon the Christian Democratic identity of the new party and those who sought a more inclusive, less ideologically specific formula. The first group, composed mostly of the IDC militants, became the Popular Christian Democratic party (PPDC).[10] Its prospects were poor, for, although its goal was to build up a great Christian Democratic electorate, it lacked the international recognition of the FPD and the ID. At the same time it participated in the electoral committee of the Christian Democratic Team, but it also joined with the UDE in approaching the Christian Democratic International. By the end of 1976, all hope for international recognition had disappeared as a result of the indecision of Ruiz Giménez, the rebuff of Gil Robles, and the Basque nationalists' rejection of a joint electoral campaign. As a result, the PPDC finally came around to the idea of the broad electoral alliance.

The second, less ideological group founded the Popular party in December

1976. The Tácitos and also Ortega of the IDC played a leading part in this project, but the Christian Democratic element was diluted almost immediately. At its First Congress, the Popular party adopted a manifesto that declared the party "open to liberal Christian Democrats, social democrats, and independents." Above all, the leadership itself was not specifically Christian Democratic. The presidency was conferred upon Pío Cabanillas and the vice presidency upon José María de Areilza, who had joined the effort only at the last moment; however, with the exception of the social democrat José Pedro Pérez Llorca, the rest of the executive officers were people of Christian Democratic background. The Popular party declared its opposition to both an "exclusive right and a dogmatically Marxist left." It rejected traditional liberalism, Marxist socialism, and religious confessionalism in political life but espoused freedom, social reform, and Christian ethics. On the occasion of the constitutional referendum, the Popular party openly recommended a "yes" vote (which none of the other opposition parties did) and at the same time called for the legalization of the Communist party. Unlike other small political groups, the Popular party very soon began an active campaign, in which Areilza played the principal role. With the exception of some Christian Democratic groups, it was the only party with sufficient resources for a serious propaganda effort. But it shared with all the small centrist parties the tendency to fragment. Areilza, a fine orator and a person of great prestige among moderates, was doomed to a secondary position partly because he was seen as too ambitious; he hoped to be prime minister some day. Pío Cabanillas, too, was the center of rivalries and conflicts, which, however, barely reached public notice.

This long enumeration of the small centrist groups could give an exaggerated impression of the fragmentation and incoherence of the country's political center. In reality all these groups had a great deal in common, and the differences between their programs were often minimal. None of those affiliated with any of these tiny parties would have opposed Christian values, the principles of liberal democracy, or social reformism. The biographical similarities of their leaders, their cooperative publishing ventures (like *Cuadernos para el Diálogo* and *Discusión*), and the common social origins of their supporters all suggested the possibility of an electoral alliance.

Origins and Development of the Democratic Center

The Democratic Center was brought into being in the last days of 1976 and the first days of 1977. It was the creation of the moderate democratic opposition to Francoism and the reformist collaborators with Francoism of whom we have already spoken. Two factors help explain this event: first and most important, the appearance in late 1976 of a well-organized party on the right, the Popular Alliance (AP), which seemed to have some chance of doing well at the polls; and, second, the imminence, once the referendum was past, of Spain's first elections in forty years.

The first attempts to create a great electoral coalition capable of defeating the Popular Alliance were led by opponents of Francoism. Ruiz Giménez was the first to bring social democrats and Christian Democrats together. This initial meeting was followed by another two in January in the offices of Ignacio Camuñas's Popular Democratic party, at which the liberals and the Popular party joined the dialogue. At this point, one sector of the moderate opposition was still reticent about creating any electoral alliance; yet the idea would triumph quickly.[11]

On 20 January the press announced that the UDE and the Popular party had federated and that the latter had established an electoral alliance with the Popular Democratic party and Garrigues's Federation of Democratic and Liberal Parties to be known as the Democratic Center. The Popular party thus served to bind together reformist Francoism and the moderate opposition, but it did not dominate the alliance. The liberals conditioned their cooperation to the extension of the alliance to other sectors, and the Popular Christian Democratic party quickly joined, as did a part of Francisco Fernández Ordoñez's Social Democratic Federation. Whether the two Christian Democratic parties recognized by the Christian Democratic International would join remained uncertain. Curiously, collaboration between the PPDC and the Democratic Center seemed more of a hindrance than a help in the attempt to establish electoral unity. While Ruiz Giménez had strong reservations about groups like the UDC and the Popular party because of their conservative character, Gil Robles's opposition was grounded in his Francoist origins. An old leader of the Spanish Confederation of Autonomous Rightist Groups (CEDA), Gil Robles spoke with contempt of the "swarm of new democrats" eager to jump on the centrist bandwagon.[12]

In spite of the Christian Democrats' refusal to join, the Democratic Center prospered in January and February 1976. The opinion polls placed it comfortably ahead, and the press expressed no opposition. A liberal Madrid daily defined the center as a "complex mixture of the civilized right, opposition to Francoism, ex-Francoism, and progressive liberalism," and predicted that it would either turn into a major electoral force or fail to live up to its promise.[13] In early February Miguel Boyer, an outstanding economist and the drafter of the economic program of the Spanish Socialist Workers' party (PSOE), announced that he was joining the Democratic Center. He had "lost hope," he said, "that his party could contain a social democratic wing," so committed was it to an "archaic" Marxism "more extreme than that of the French Socialist party or the Italian Communist party."

Soon, however, difficulties emerged. The first sprang from internal differences. The UDE was the member of the coalition with the most decidedly Francoist origins, and when the electoral lists were planned, some of its most eminent members were relegated to second place. On 23 February the UDE declared that it had broken with the Popular party over differences on education and family issues; in fact, the problems were personal, for the UDE was at odds not only with the Popular party but with the rest of the coalition as well. A second problem facing the Democratic Center was that it did not encompass all the centrist groups, and even those that did belong acted at times with absolute independence. For weeks, social democrats, liberals, and Gil Robles's Christian Democrats studied the possibility of creating a "constitutional bloc." In mid-March two liberal sections of the Democratic Center met with their European counterparts and issued statements independent of the coalition.

Finally, the third most serious problem was the Democratic Center's relationship with the government and Suárez. Despite the initial distance between them, as time passed, the similarity between the proposals being put forward by Suárez and the Democratic Center became stronger and stronger. What is more, Suárez was a known leader and a sure vote winner, and the leaders of the Democratic Center counted on his support as well as on Areilza's power as a speaker. At the beginning of March, however, a new group appeared, the Independent Social Federation, formed of young deputies of Falangist origin who called themselves center-left. This group was sponsored by the interior minister, Rodolfo Martín Villa, and seemed likely to win the government's support even before the election campaign. Suárez denied this before the leaders of the Democratic Center; meanwhile, his unwillingness to allow Areilza to lead the Democratic Center was obvious.

The decisive event in the early history of the Democratic Center came in the second half of March: the departure of Areilza from the coalition. Areilza had risen quickly to the vice-presidency of the Popular party, and his personal popularity was great enough to make him Suárez's rival. Probably with reason, Suárez feared this competition. He was also skeptical about the Popular party's bid for mass appeal.

The initial attack on Areilza came on 19 March at a private dinner in the home of Popular party leader José Luis Ruiz Navarro. Apparently on instructions from Suárez, Alfonso Osorio, Suárez's deputy, broached the view that the political prominence of Areilza (who was not present) was incompatible with the leadership of Suárez. Four days later Suárez received Cabanillas and Areilza as leaders of the Popular party; at this meeting he expressed his reservations about the public activities of the party and announced his own decision to run in the elections. Nevertheless, the interview was cordial, and, though Suárez by this time was certain that he did not want Areilza's name on the Madrid list, an agreement seemed possible. As late as 24 March, some observers thought that Areilza would accept second place after Suárez on the

Democratic Center list. The following day, however, Areilza resigned from the vice-presidency of the Popular party and from public life. "I understand," he wrote, "that this definitive withdrawal of mine will simplify the position of the Popular party in the elections, in which, in any case, I do not wish to participate." If these words contain a hint of bitterness, it is also true that Areilza did not really consult with the executive of his party before making his decision—and that the Popular party had no choice but to cooperate with Suárez. Areilza had abandoned his party as much as it had abandoned him.

Whatever its motivation, Areilza's resignation damaged the Democratic Center's public image. Suárez later tried to recoup by persuading Areilza to run for the Senate in Madrid, and other Centrist leaders wanted to give him first place on the Chamber of Deputies list for Barcelona; the first offer may have seemed insincere, and the second arrived too late. In any case, the press was highly critical of Areilza's "expulsion." *ABC*, a conservative Madrid daily, condemned the secrecy of the operation, while *El País*, a progressive daily, demanded that Suárez himself withdraw: he should not be a candidate, it argued, in elections in which the "bureaucratic apparatus would weigh heavily" and in which his participation would give an unfair advantage to one side. Apart from giving the Democratic Center a bad name and leaving it open to the charge of excessive support from the government, Areilza's resignation undoubtedly cost the coalition votes it might have won from the Socialist electorate.[14]

Whether Suárez himself would run remained in doubt until the beginning of May. The leaders of the Democratic Center had no objection in principle to the prime minister's being a candidate; as the most prestigious politician in the country, he would bring distinction to the party's lists. A totally different question was whom Suárez might bring with him. Apparently the prime minister named three independents who might run on his ticket. Because of their Francoist origins, they were not acceptable to the Democratic Center, however, and its leaders vetoed their participation. For the moment both the candidates and the program remained uncertain, a dangerous situation in that it delayed presenting the electorate with a clear alternative. At a time when polls showed majority support for Suárez's candidacy, and even some leftist leaders expressing approval.

At least one serious question concerning the ultimate configuration of the Democratic Center remained: its ties with the Christian Democratic parties of Europe. On 13 March, to the great surprise of the media, Gil Robles resigned as president of the Popular Democratic Federation. The press speculated that he had been forced to retire because of his hard-line image, which impeded Christian Democratic unity, but both the press and the centrist leaders praised the resignation as an act of political courage on the part of an old Francoist unwilling to bend as far as some. With the way cleared at the end of March, the followers of Gil Robles and Ruiz Giménez joined forces again in the Federation of Christian Democrats (FDC). The latter became president, and the secretaryship fell to Gil Robles's son. The party would be governed by a political council in which each of the constituent organizations would be represented in proportion to its membership, although Ruiz Giménez's group would be predominant. The FDC invited other groups to join, though its leaders clearly intended to remain in control.

The UDE and the PPDC were the parties most directly affected by the Christian Democrats' new-found unity. At the beginning of April those two groups finally fused to form a new political party, the Christian Democratic party (PDC), with Fernando Alvarez de Miranda as president, and no fewer than four vice-presidents and three secretaries. They showed some interest in joining the FDC, but with the elections only two months off, the PDC finally opted to join the Democratic Center.

From the middle of April the electoral chances of the center turned on the talks between the leaders of the Christian Democratic party and the Democratic Center coalition. Suárez received the Christian Democratic leaders and indicated that he would be prepared to stand aside if his running in the election were an obstacle to unity. It is very possible that Suárez made this offer only after he was quite sure that the electoral law would permit him (though not his ministers) to be a candidate, but his desire to collaborate with Christian Democracy seems to have been sincere. He indirectly offered Ruiz Giménez the presidency of the Senate.

The negotiations over broadening the Democratic Center to include the Christian Democrats and other small centrist groups (liberals and social democrats) began on 15 April in Ruiz Giménez's office. From the beginning obstacles loomed. The Democratic Center wanted a nationwide alliance of the participating parties. Gil Robles wanted only limited alliances, given the expectation that the Christian Democrats would win abundant representation in their own right in many provinces. Besides, for the Senate elections they were disposed to collaborate with the Socialists, a matter in which Ruiz Giménez had great interest. Finally, Joaquín Satrústegui, leader of a small liberal party, demanded that the Popular party, which he accused of being excessively heterogeneous, disband. His own program spoke of including liberals, social democrats, and Christian Democrats. All these terms were unacceptable to the Democratic Center, and the negotiations that had begun under such favorable auspices gradually broke down. The press, which had announced the launching of a great coalition, in the end reported just another limited alliance.

The candidate lists were drawn up in late April and early May. On 21 April the FDC and the PSOE agreed on joint senatorial lists (including a few independents to guarantee their democratic character). On 24 April, Leopoldo Calvo Sotelo resigned his ministry to take part in the elections, and Suárez announced that he would run a few days later. Finally on 27 April, the FDC rejected alliance with the Democratic Center and chose to run as part of the Christian Democratic Team (EDC). Paradoxically, more than half the political council had voted in favor of alliance, as had the Ruiz Giménez group, but they failed to reach the required two-thirds majority.

Selection of the Candidates

By the end of April it was plain not only that Prime Minister Suárez would run but that he would be the final arbiter in drawing up the candidate lists for the Democratic Center. Under the circumstances this was a necessity; yet it posed serious problems for the alliance. It was practically impossible for some small groups with very few members and no program or popular appeal to accept Suárez's having the last word, and it would come under attack from his anti-Francoist adversaries. The prime minister would need the support of the most prestigious centrist leaders to stay the course.

On 3 May the Centrist leaders met, and Calvo Sotelo put before them several propositions: that some candidates clearly associated with the government would have to be included in the Democratic Center's list; that a series of small regional groups important to former Francoists be represented;[15] and that the Democratic Center should present itself to the electorate as moderate and non-Marxist, affiliated with broadly Christian Democratic, liberal, and social democratic views and committed to supporting Prime Minister Suárez in the next Cortes. None of these proposals was warmly received. Calvo Sotelo also called for changing the name of the alliance to Union of the Center, but in the end the word "union" was merely added to Democratic Center to indicate that a new political grouping had been formed.

The Union of the Democratic Center (UCD) was still not the united party the government had hoped would emerge. Its executive committee consisted of seven people—two from the government (Calvo Sotelo and Sánchez de León, once a significant figure in the government's domestic policy who had been in close contact with the civil governors) and the rest from the old alliance (Cabanillas, Garrigues, Alvarez de Miranda, Camuñas, and Fernández Ordoñez). In all they represented fourteen parties.

Government intervention might serve to mediate between the various centrist parties, but it did not solve the problem of the candidate lists, which caused more conflict within the UCD than in any other party in 1977. As a result, Calvo Sotelo was a constant target of criticism by former members of the Democratic Center. Only in regions where one component of the UCD was clearly predominant did the process run smoothly; this was true, for example, in Asturias, where the Christian Democratic party was the strongest member of the coalition. Elsewhere the triumph of one tendency prompted withdrawals and protests.[16] In some cases members of the government had the last word in drawing up the lists: Minister of the Interior Martín Villa in León, Deputy Prime Minister Osorio in Santander, and Suárez himself in Segovia and Avila. In general, it was candidates associated with the democratic opposition who tended to be displaced at the last minute; if they had done little enough to generate popular support for the coalition, they nevertheless had reason to protest the sudden appearance of unwanted allies relegating them to second place.

The cases of Madrid and Barcelona, the districts with the most deputies, illustrate the problems of candidate selection in the UCD. In Madrid the government decided the order of the candidates. When Calvo Sotelo read out the list of candidates to the coalition leaders, a split seemed on the point of developing. Fernández Ordoñez was especially indignant. Of the twelve slots the UCD could expect to win, eight had gone to men who had been members of the electoral coalition before Suárez had become leader, but they were clearly subordinated to Suárez. Not only did Suárez and Calvo Sotelo occupy the first two slots on the list, but the third went to Fanjul Sedeño, a former Francoist deputy who was expected to bring organizational support that never materialized. The ninth slot went to another old Francoist. Some thought this excessive, given the leftist tendencies of the Madrid electorate.

In Barcelona the candidate selection process was even more fiercely criticized. Here, by contrast with the rest of Spain, there was no tradition of democratic anti-Francoism that was not tied to regional nationalism; this had made it difficult for the forces of the democratic opposition to unite. Moreover, the reformist Francoists had never carried much weight for the simple reason that Francoism generally had not enjoyed great acceptance in Catalonia. In the end the civil governor played an important role in choosing the candidates, some of whom were little known and some of whom had had difficulty reaching understandings with other candidates.[17]

When the UCD's final lists were announced, a great uproar broke out. Much of the liberal and leftist press (though not the Communist) had severely criticized Suárez for running, but now his most outspoken critic was the Popular Alliance. The presence of so many former Francoists, meanwhile, brought strong protests from every sector of opinion; what was worse, the candidates in question did not speak up convincingly in their own defense. Others refused to participate in the campaign—or campaigned half-heartedly. Garrigues himself urged support for the UCD as the lesser evil, and an influential commentator said he would hold his nose and vote UCD.

The immediate reaction was a series of withdrawals from the Democratic Center. Enrique Larroque, leader of a liberal party, signaled his opposition to the UCD as constituted and retired from the elections, as did Antonio Senillosa, leader of the Popular Catalan party, and Juan García Madariaga, leader of the miniscule Progressive Liberal party. In La Coruña a rival democratic centrist list was formed alongside the official one by activists from Garrigues's group and the USDE, and independent lists sprang up elsewhere as well. Their most significant effect was probably to encourage attacks on the "party of Prime Minister Suárez" during the campaign. In fact, the independents were peripheral figures in Spanish politics, and their decision to remain on the sidelines instead of joining the coalition proved their political weakness. Their protest sprang less from real opposition to anything the UCD stood for than from a sense that they had been overlooked.

Background of the Candidates The average age of UCD candidates for the Chamber of Deputies in June 1977 was forty-three, for the Senate forty-eight. The average age of elected deputies was forty-four for the UCD, forty-three for the Socialists; however, only 35 percent of the elected UCD deputies, but 57 percent of the elected Socialists, were under forty. The Socialists, moreover, ran more very young candidates, as well as a number of longtime militants over sixty. The Centrist candidates tended to be the children of professionals and fairly high-ranking civil servants, as well as businessmen and journalists and a few intellectuals. Few came from lower-class or even lower middle-class backgrounds; whatever populist appeal the UCD had it derived from the image projected by its leader rather than from the social composition of its candidate lists. Figures released by the party during the campaign showed that its candidates included 138 lawyers, 34 doctors, 30 engineers, 30 businessmen, 14 economists, 9 chemists, 8 physicists, and 7 journalists.

It is difficult to quantify the Francoist dimension of the UCD lists. Fifty-one UCD Chamber of Deputies and Senate candidates had been deputies in Franco's time, and five had been ministers. (The Popular Alliance lists included seventy-nine former deputies, a dozen of whom had been ministers.) Twenty-five of these were running for the Chamber, and seventeen of them headed their lists. Of the seventeen, eleven were independents, and four came from the Popular party. The largest number of first places went to independents (39.8 percent in the Chamber, 51.7 percent in the Senate), followed by the Popular party (15.7 and 15.0 percent), the Christian Democratic party (11.4 and 9.5 percent), the Federation of Democratic and Liberal parties (11.4 and 5.4 percent), the Social Democratic party (5.8 and 6.1 percent), the Popular Democratic party (3.1 and 4.0 percent), and regional groups.

But these figures give only a rough indication of the degree to which the Center contained Francoists. Not all the independents were actually Suárez candidates; some were, in the strict sense, but others came from opposition groups that had chosen to side with the UCD for a variety of reasons. And none of the groups in the UCD were composed exclusively of people unconnected with the past regime. In Madrid the ratio of former Francoists to members of the opposition was four to nine, but in five of the seven provincial capitals of Andalusia the candidate at the head of the UCD list was a former Francoist deputy. Finally, one must bear in mind that many of the candidates were people who had had no particular position regarding the previous regime. It is hardly surprising that the voters were disconcerted by the range of candidates —from the most pragmatic (some said cynical) collaborators with Franco to passionate opponents of a regime they denounced as morally beyond the pale.

Another aspect of the UCD lists that should be mentioned was the provincial ties of the candidates. While leaders from Madrid occupied the first slot on many PSOE lists, in the UCD there was marked resistance to accepting candidates sent from Madrid. Thus, Iñigo Cavero, future minister of education and the number two leader of the Christian Democratic party, was obliged to renounce his candidacy in Navarre, which had been imposed by Madrid, and Salvador Sánchez Terán, a trusted associate of Suárez and another future minister, renounced the first place on the list for Salamanca, which passed to Jesús Espérabe de Arteaga, a former Francoist deputy who had been noted for his reformist stance in the last phase of Francoism. Finally, the proportion of women on the UCD list was low—8.4 percent in the Chamber and two percent in the Senate.

The UCD ran lists in every province except Guipúzcoa. By contrast, the Christian Democratic Team, which included the FDC, failed to cover a good number of provinces. In addition to Ceuta and Melilla, the EDC did not present candidates in one of the Galician provinces, in Teruel and Cáceres, in four provinces in Old Castile, and in three in New Castile. The weak presence in Castille is especially significant since Catholicism is strong in this region and Christian Democracy might have hoped to do well; the dearth of EDC candidates suggests that this was an urban group with little penetration even in areas where it might logically have hoped for support. In addition, the EDC made few electoral alliances.[18]

Candidates for the Senate We have deliberately left the Senate lists to the end of this section since certain features of the electoral law made the candidate selection process more confused for the Senate than for the Chamber of Deputies. Very broad, ideologically vague alliances were favored. For the UCD this held both advantages and disadvantages. On the one hand, the first-past-the-post system made it likely that in regions where the electorate remained fragmented the UCD would do well: with its national standing, it would win more than a proportionate share of the seats. On the other hand, the absence of a list system made it impossible to broaden the coalition's appeal by including independents. Though the UCD nominated a few independents for the Senate, most of its candidates were highly partisan. The UCD ran Senate candidates everywhere in Spain (though in a few provinces fewer than the three who could be elected). Candidate selection seems to have posed serious problems only in Soria, where a number of independents ran, and in Castellón, where there were four UCD candidates instead of the normal three, which would split the centrist vote.

Shortly before the campaign began, the Christian Democratic Team made an unexpected decision that had very important consequences. The Christian Democrats' natural allies for example included the Federation of Christian Democrats who were in the ranks of the Democratic Center, which had refused to ally itself with any group collaborating with Marxists. But the Christian Democrats had accepted support from socialists. In the end they preferred this allegiance to a tie with the Center. As a result, lists representing all the democratic opposition short of the UCD were mounted in some places, usually under the label Senators for Democracy. The group included socialists, independents, and liberals, as well as some Christian Democrats who had not run for the Chamber of Deputies because they lacked UCD support. These lists allowed the forces of the left to extend their appeal toward centrists dissatisfied with the UCD lists. There were Senators for Democracy lists in about twenty provinces: fewer than half included members of the Federation of Christian Democrats. In most of these districts, the chances of the left were poor. For the Christian Democrats this strategy posed the problem of links with the Spanish Communist party (PCE). The Communists, well aware that their chances were minimal in the Senate elections, were happy to go along with the formation of these Senators for Democracy lists, though in fact few party members figured among the candidates. (Much more numerous were so-called independents with stronger links to the Communist party than to any other group.) The FDC took as axiomatic that the role of the Communists should be minimal in these lists—and nonexistent in any that included Christian Democrats. In fact, in the vital province of Madrid, it was the Christian Democratic party that vetoed the inclusion of the Communist or pro-Communist candidate, with the result that the PCE ended up instructing its electorate to vote for two of the Senators for Democracy candidates (instead of the third, a Christian Democrat) and for a Popular Socialist party (PSP) candidate who was an important figure in the Workers' Commissions. In Asturias, on the other hand, the presence of a Communist candidate prompted the FDC to disavow its own candidate, who refused to abandon his position on the list (and was eventually elected).

In Catalonia and the Basque country the situation was different. In Catalonia the UCD's isolation from the centrist and rightist sectors prompted it to run its own list even though its chances were slim. For their part, both the Catalan Christian Democrats and the Socialists refused to run on lists that included Communists; the result was lists labeled Democracy in Catalonia that grouped Christian Democrats, socialists, and centrists. In the Basque country assorted socialists and nationalists mounted Senate lists labeled Autonomous

Front, in which no Christian Democrats participated. Finally, in the provinces where the FDC did not run on Senators for Democracy lists, it presented its own lists, with very little hope of success. Wherever it had not offered candidates for the Chamber of Deputies, it stayed out of the Senate race too.

The Election Campaign

The UCD's choice of candidates was hasty and imperfect, and so were its efforts to mount a campaign. To begin with, it was slow to announce a program. The policies a Centrist government would pursue became clear only late in the campaign, and even then they had to be pieced together from a series of documents. On 26 May the economic plan was published, on 30 May the cultural and social program, on 4 June a preliminary draft constitution, and not until 10 June, five days before the election, a *Manual for 22 Million Electors*, which summarized the Centrist philosophy. This sort of behavior would seem strange in an established Western European political party, but the UCD was no such thing: as late as 11 May it did not even boast a headquarters with telephones. What is more, many of its leaders had no idea of what was involved in a democratic election campaign. This lack of preparation was only partly made up for by financial resources superior to those of any other party but probably poorly used. A letter Suárez sent to every voter seems to have reached almost none.

A further damper on the UCD's campaign was that the party suffered the disadvantages of being in government and almost none of the advantages until the final stage. Instead of capitalizing on the contribution many of its leaders had made to political reform, it adopted an apprehensive, almost apologetic tone in asking for the people's votes. The Centrist candidates were instructed "not to show aggression toward other candidates." Attendance at the party's meetings scarcely ever exceeded one thousand, and even the major meeting in Madrid failed to attract the numbers its organizers had predicted. The party bent over backward not to make the campaign a great national commotion. It had been expected that Suárez's presence would count for a lot, but so did the lack of a real party organization capable of turning out supporters for rallies and lining up canvassers on election day.

The benefits of Suárez's position could be appreciated only in the final days. The prime minister had originally announced that he would not campaign, but this was too great a sacrifice for a coalition that saw him as its major hope.[19] At the beginning of June, Suárez began to participate, and by election day he had become the central figure. His television statement, in particular, was decisive. On the other hand, the UCD was criticized for excessive use of personality politics; one Madrid daily replaced the Centrist slogan "Vote Center, Vote Suárez" with "Vote Center, Vote Coexistence." Late in the campaign the UCD, which had at first assumed its greatest enemy to be the Popular Alliance, gently attacked the Socialists—with no effect on the result.

As the front-runner, the UCD was vigorously attacked by all the other parties. It did very little to defend itself. The Popular Alliance claimed that Suárez's commitment to reform was only "copied" from Fraga Iribarne; Socialists called the UCD the principal enemy and claimed that it would rig the elections and never produce a democratic constitution. But the most serious attacks—because they came from figures with greater influence over the centrist electorate—were those of centrists displaced from the Suárez coalition. Among these the most significant was Areilza, who, though not affiliated with any party, supported the Senators for Democracy. Areilza denounced the Popular Alliance and the UCD as the two great wings of Francoism, mysteriously in league.

The UCD could not respond with what would have been its most effective defense—a reply from those of its leaders who had originated in the democratic opposition; offended by the way the candidate lists had been drawn up, they were not inclined to speak out with real fervor. On the contrary, they were all too capable of noting in their articles that the Center had "no well-defined ideology" or advising a vote for the center as a matter of "common sense." Perhaps most revealing of all was Joaquín Garrigues's admission that the UCD had made innumerable mistakes and was obviously the worst choice open to the electorate "if all the others were excluded."

As for the Christian Democratic Team (EDC), its campaign was slow to take off and badly focused. Three fundamental errors were made. In the first place, the leaders' statements were almost always pitched to the left of their electorate's hopes. On matters like self-rule or federalism, they sounded more like a progressive Christian group along the lines of the Movement of Unitary Popular Action (MAPU) in Chile than like Christian Democrats. The inexperience of their leaders, of course, aggravated this problem. In the second place, the EDC did not seek, and did not know how, to capture the Catholic vote: though the mention of the word "Christian" in the party name was perfectly deliberate, the leaders seemed oblivious of the danger that other groups might snatch away the Catholic vote. Finally, the EDC devoted considerable effort to demonstrating that they were the Christian Democrats, recognized as such internationally, which was doubtless true but did not much interest the electorate. (For that matter, a time would come when the European Christian Democrats would wonder whether they had placed their confidence in those that most deserved it.)

In the end, there was not one Christian democratic campaign but two, corresponding to the personalities of the principal leaders. In his public pronouncements Gil Robles made a point of repudiating the Franco regime and endorsing a decided break with the past; he accused the center of not really

Table 5.1 Performance of Centrist Parties, Chamber of Deputies Election, 1977

Party	Popular Vote	Percentage of Electorate	Seats
Union of the Democratic Center (UCD)	6,310,151	34.4	165[a]
Christian Democratic Team (EDC)	250,904	1.4	0
Independent centrists	121,575	0.6	2
Social Reform, Popular Center, and other	—	0.5	0

Source: Preliminary returns based on the 97.34 percent of the votes that had been counted two days after polling day, released by the Ministry of the interior.
[a] 47.1 percent of the seats in the Chamber

wishing to produce a democratic constitution and of manipulating the elections. On the other hand, Ruiz Giménez neither attacked the left nor enraged the right; he would have been glad to campaign for the UCD. His speeches abounded with poetic and biblical allusions, and his tone was sometimes positively mystical. Ruiz Giménez alone made a considerable effort to reach the working class, but his chief audience was the Catholic middle class. He declared that he was not a Marxist but also that it was possible to be both a Marxist and a Christian.

The June 1977 Results

The results for the parties under study here are given in table 5.1.[20] Several points are of interest. Despite the weaknesses of its campaign, the UCD did quite well. It took almost as great a share of the votes as its strategists had aimed for. The creation of a broad electoral coalition, though no solution to the problem of governmental cohesion, had paid off generously in terms of seats. Ironically, the UCD was the main beneficiary of the electoral law—whose majority features had been adopted at the insistence of the Popular Alliance in the old Francoist Cortes, while the democratic opposition had fought for a proportional system. The Christian Democratic Team, on the other hand, suffered: it did not win a single seat despite its quarter of a million votes, except in Catalonia and the Basque country, where its vote was more nationalist than Christian Democrat.

The provincial distribution of the vote (see table 5.2) shows the EDC to have been a small minority party whose strength was spread fairly evenly across the country. Outside of Catalonia and Valencia, the EDC took between 1 and 3 percent—a range not easily explained by socioeconomic or cultural correlates of the vote. The fact that in four of the seven provinces of Andalusia (a traditionally leftist region) the vote did not reach 1 percent is, however, significant. It might also be significant that in the two most economically developed areas

Table 5.2 Performance of the Center Parties, Chamber of Deputies Election 15 June 1977, by Province (percent)

Province	UCD	EDC
Alava	30.9	2.7[a]
Albacete[b]	38.1	—
Alicante	36.0	1.4
Almería	49.8	3.0
Avila	68.3	4.5
Badajoz	46.5	0.9
Balearic Islands	51.0	1.8
Barcelona	15.2	5.4[c]
Burgos	45.7	1.6
Cáceres	55.3	—
Cádiz	27.3	1.2
Castellón	35.5	2.3
Ciudad-Real	41.1	—
Córdoba	32.6	0.8
La Coruña	49.5	2.8[d]
Cuenca	56.0	1.2
Gerona	18.2	5.4
Granada	43.4	0.8
Guadalajara	49.1	—
Guipúzcoa	—	4.9[a]
Huelva	47.9	1.3
Huesca	45.7	2.3
Jaén	33.1	1.6
León	51.0	—
Lérida	24.3	9.1
Logroño	41.2	0.7
Lugo	52.1	—
Madrid	32.0	1.5
Málaga	27.6	0.9
Murcia	40.8	1.9
Navarre	29.0	3.9[a]
Orense	62.0	2.0[d]
Oviedo	30.8	0.4
Palencia	50.7	—
Las Palmas[e]	66.2	—
Pontevedra	56.4	1.9[d]
Salamanca	56.4	2.7
Santa Cruz de Tenerife[f]	55.0	—
Santander	39.8	2.2
Segovia	57.5	—
Seville	32.5	0.9

Table 5.2 Continued.

Province	UCD	EDC
Soria[g]	58.9	—
Tarragona	27.8	5.5
Teruel	50.6	—
Toledo	38.6	—
Valencia	29.8	3.1
Valladolid	42.6	2.8
Vizcaya	16.3	1.0[a]
Zamora	45.8	3.2
Zaragoza[h]	31.7	
Ceuta	36.4	—
Melilla	56.6	—

Source: Institute for Political Studies, Department of Information and Documentation, *Partidos políticos y elecciones: Political parties and elections*, July 1977; General Directorate of Information Coordination, Division of Documentation and Analysis, *Elecciones al Congreso y al Senado*, 15 de Julio de 1977, Elections to the Chamber and Senate, 15 July 1977.
Dash (—): Party did not run.
[a] Figure refers to Basque Christian Democracy; Basque Nationalist Party (PNV) not included.
[b] In addition, the PSO-ID alliance obtained 7.2 percent.
[c] Includes 0.3 percent for the Christian Social Democracy of Catalonia.
[d] Figure refers to EDC-Social Democracy party alliance.
[e] In addition, the Popular party of the Canaries took 0.7 percent.
[f] In addition, the Popular party of the Canaries took 2.9 percent.
[g] In addition, the Christian Democratic Union took 2.1 percent.
[h] In addition, Christian Democracy of Aragon took 1.3 percent.

(the stretch from Catalonia to Valencia, and the Basque country) the EDC exceeded 3 percent in seven provinces.

In any event, the EDC did best in regions where nationalist sentiment was strong, where Catholics were numerous, where, for historical and cultural reasons, the Franco regime had never taken deep root, and where the UCD seemed excessively centrist (see figure 5.1). This was the case in Catalonia, the only region where the EDC obtained a seat (in Barcelona, running as the Democratic Union of Catalonia); its allies in the Catalan Center took another. In all four provinces of this region the EDC took more than 5 percent of the vote, and in one of them—Lérida, the agricultural province par excellence—it reached over 9 percent. An important factor in this relative victory was that the Catalan Christian Democrats, unlike their coreligionists in the EDC, did not adopt too leftist a posture in their electoral alliances. The case of the Valencia area was similar, although the percentage was much lower (only slightly above 3 percent) and the party had projected a much more authentically Christian

112   The Democratic Center and Christian Democracy in 1977 and 1979

Figure 5.1   The UCD Vote, by Province, June 1977

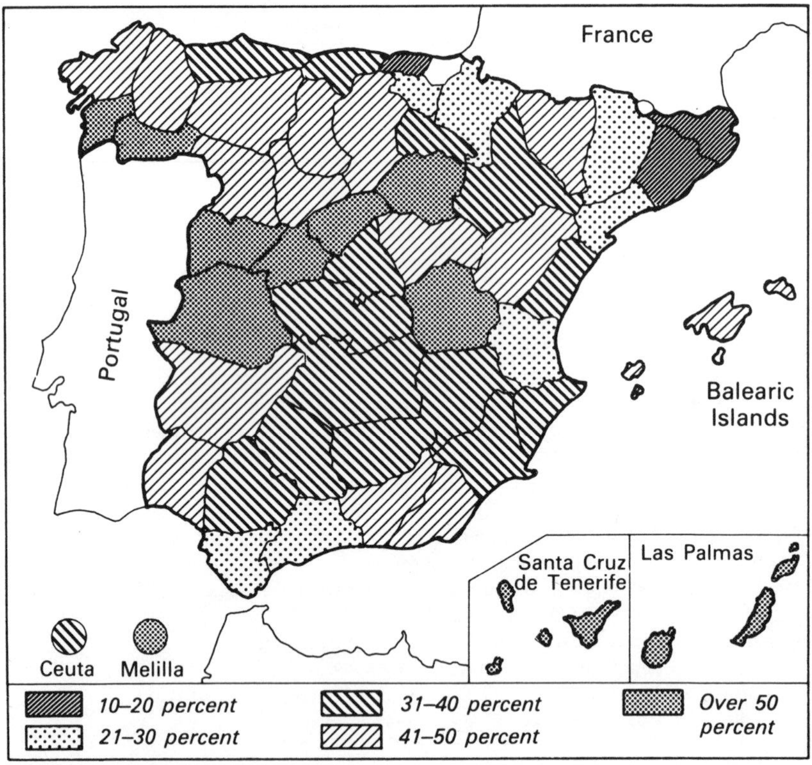

10–20 percent	31–40 percent	Over 50 percent
21–30 percent	41–50 percent	

Democratic image. The mistake in this region was probably the excessively nationalist character of the candidates. Finally, what probably explains the low percentage in the Basque country is competition from the Basque Nationalist party (PNV), which, though it did not run as such, could have been considered Christian Democratic by the electorate. The case of Guipúzcoa reveals the complementarity of the UCD and EDC lists: with the former not in the field, the EDC reached 4.9 percent of the votes. In Navarre the strong tradition of religious practice may also have influenced the results.

The UCD vote, too, was spread across the country: excluding the most nationalist regions, the UCD took between roughly 25 and 70 percent of the provincial vote. Nevertheless, unlike the EDC, the UCD had very specific geographical strongholds. Of the sixteen provinces of Castille and León, only two (Madrid, as the capital of the nation, and Santander, where the Popular Alliance was strong) gave it less than 40 percent of the vote, and six gave it more than 50 percent. In three of the four Galician provinces and in the three island provinces (Las Palmas, Santa Cruz de Tenerife, and the Balearic Islands), the UCD also took over 50 percent. The Centrist vote declined toward the south and the periphery of the country, dropping below 30 percent in the traditionally leftist (historically speaking, anarchist) provinces of Cádiz and Málaga and in Catalonia, the Basque country, and Navarre with their regional-nationalist orientation. Guipúzcoa, in the Basque country, was the only province where the UCD did not present candidates.

Even in the areas where regional nationalism is strong, the UCD was more than a peripheral force. In Catalonia the problems in candidate selection clearly cost it votes, but it still won between 15 and 18 percent of the vote in Barcelona and Gerona, over 23 percent in Lérida, and 27 percent in Tarragona; not surprisingly, it did best where Catalan consciousness was least developed. In the Basque country and Navarre, the UCD percentage was high in Alava, somewhat lower than hoped for in Navarre (where, however, the fragmentation of the vote allowed the UCD to win significant parliamentary representation), and low in Vizcaya. Broadly speaking, by comparison with the last democratic elections, held in 1936, the political system, had been "nationalized" in Catalonia: the UCD displaced any Catalanist right, and in two of the four provinces it ran ahead of the Catalanists of the Democratic Pact for Catalonia (PDC). On the other hand, in the Basque country the comparison with 1936 suggests a growth in nationalist sentiment not in terms of support for the nationalist party (which was actually beaten by the UCD in Alava and Navarre) but in terms of identification of the left with regional autonomy or federalism.

A comparison of the results of 1936 and 1977 is instructive in other areas. The correlation between the vote for right-wing Catholic organization CEDA in 1936 and for the UCD in 1977 was .46.[21] In all the provinces where the rightist coalition triumphed in 1936, the UCD list took the most votes in 1977—over 30 percent in every province except Navarre. Indeed, the correspondence is so close that it shows up even in quite limited and specific areas. In both years, Cáceres was more rightist than Badajoz in Estremadura, and Las Palmas was more rightist than Tenerife. The greatest difference between the electoral maps of 1936 and 1977 occurred in Galicia, where in 1936 the center-right vote was badly fragmented and the left carried several districts.

Another point worth examining is the fragmentation of the centrist vote. Before the election it seemed likely that a large number of centrist votes would be lost to an assortment of small groups without any real coherence. In fact, however, these groups' inability to mount serious campaigns and the Spaniards' wish to identify themselves with a meaningful political choice eliminated them along with the EDC. Only in two provinces did independent candidates achieve a significant poll: Castellón and Zaragoza each elected an independent deputy, with 12.7 percent and 8.4 percent respectively. In the rest of the country the fragmentation of the center vote was slight.[22] In general, where minor centrist

114   The Democratic Center and Christian Democracy in 1977 and 1979

Figure 5.2   The ECD Vote, by Province, June 1977

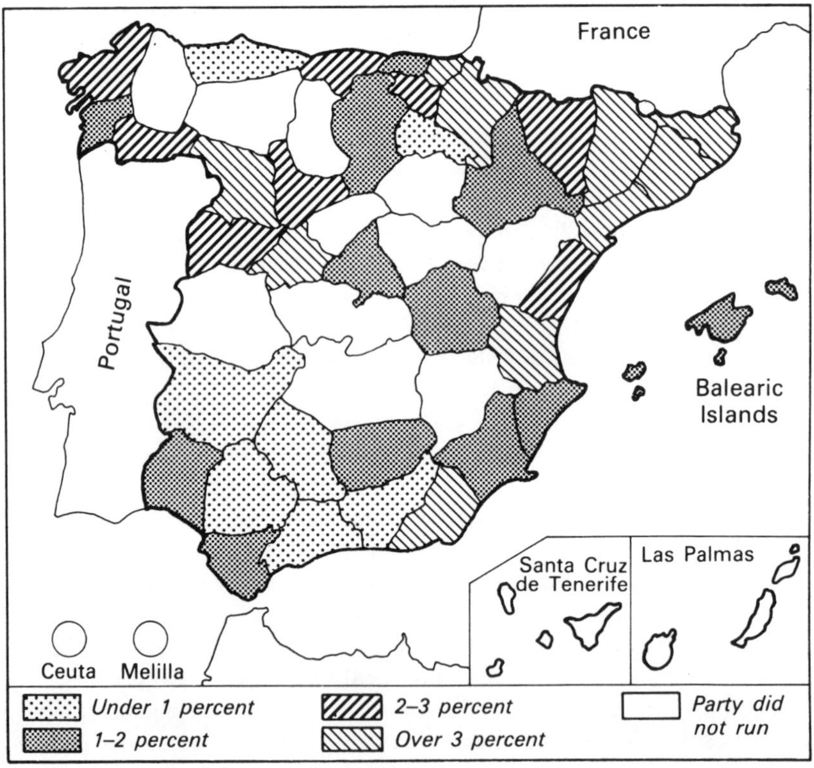

Under 1 percent
1–2 percent
2–3 percent
Over 3 percent
Party did not run

lists did at all well, the crucial factor was the candidates' local reputation—and even that never outweighed the voters' desire to support strong political organizations. In La Coruña the centrist Galician Democratic party decided not to identify itself with the UCD and was rewarded with a disastrous 0.3 percent of the vote. The Christian Democrats who ran as independents rather than on the EDC lists generally suffered a similar fate.

When it comes to social class, the Centrist vote remained strong in rural areas: the correlation was .63 (see figure 5.2). This was partly due to the habitual passivity of rural people; in Spain for the last forty years or longer, the rural sector identified itself with the government in power. In addition, this correlation is consistent with patterns elsewhere in Western Europe. In urban middle-class areas the UCD vote was high, as was the vote for the PSP and the AP. Clearly, however, the middle class was not the only group that supported the UCD. The best proof of this came from the province of Madrid.[23]

In the Madrid metropolitan area, the UCD bested the PCE in seventeen of the eighteen municipal districts, including those where the working-class component of the population was greatest. In those districts, the PSOE ran ahead of both the other two groups; and in a total of twelve of the eighteen districts, the UCD list took the most votes. Excluding the district where the PCE was ahead of the UCD (Mediodía), the Center's highest vote was more than one and a half times as great as its lowest. The Popular Alliance's best showing was more than ten times as high as its worst. While the seven districts where the Popular Alliance did best were those in which the PSOE and the PCE were weakest, the correlation was not so close in the case of the UCD. In the district of Salamanca, a traditional middle-class quarter of Madrid, the UCD won thirty-nine percent of the vote, but the AP still managed to take 30 percent. In no other district was the gap between them so small. An important part of the upper middle class, which had voted "no" in the referendum the previous December, continued to vote against the UCD.

In the provincial towns of Madrid victory went to the left, which managed to win over 50 percent of the vote in twenty-one of the twenty-three municipalities. Here again, the range of the Centrist vote was very small compared with the AP vote. Even where the left was strongest, however, the UCD obtained between 15 and 20 percent of the votes, while the AP took only about 3 percent.

All of this points to the interclass nature of the UCD vote. This is even more true of some European populist and Christian Democratic parties, but it was still an important feature of the centrist vote in Spain.

Finally, let us compare the election results of the UCD and the EDC in the Chamber of Deputies and Senate elections. The plurality system used for the upper house meant that, even if the UCD won fewer than 50 percent of the seats in the Chamber, it was likely to take a majority in the Senate, where, in addition, a number of senators named by the king were identified with the center. While the EDC did not obtain a single seat in the Chamber outside the Basque country and Catalonia, it took five Senate seats in the rest of Spain, in Badajoz, Cádiz, Madrid, Oviedo, and Santander. All these seats went to candidates running as Senators for Democracy or under some similar label, which attracted votes not only from Christian Democrats but also from the democratic left, Socialists, and sometimes Communists. In only one of these five constituencies (Madrid) did the Communist party instruct its members not to vote for the EDC but to support the PSP candidate, who was a member of the Workers' Commissions. In the other four the Communists supported the joint lists. In only one of the five constituencies (Santander) did the UCD list take more votes than any other.

A comparison between the votes obtained by the UCD in the Senate and Chamber elections is also instructive. Of course, with a complicated electoral system and an inexperienced electorate, the number of invalid votes was high. Part of the UCD electorate was probably dissatisfied with the candidates and therefore attracted to formulas like Senators for Democracy. In Madrid the centrist Senate list took 200,000 fewer votes than the Chamber list. There were few provinces where the Center's Senate list obtained more votes than its Chamber list. The reason for the difference could lie in the lesser percentage of the Centrist senatorial candidates, but it is interesting to point out that in at least three provinces (Almería, Jaén, and Santander) the UCD Senate list took roughly the same number of votes as the EDC list for the Chamber. A year before the elections the EDC had had high hopes of becoming a major pole of attraction in Spanish politics, but its sectarianism and sometimes its identification with the left had dealt it a fatal blow. Though the EDC's party support was widespread, it nowhere amounted to more than a symbolic minority. As to why it had sunk so low, opinions were divided.

By contrast, the UCD's election results demonstrated that, even though candidate selection had been rushed and directed from above and despite the obvious defects of the campaign, the coalition had responded to the desires of a significant part of Spanish society. The UCD was no state party; its predominance was not overwhelming, and it had come by its support in honest competition with other parties. After the election its major problem remained to define itself and to build up a coherent organization.

Toward the 1979 Elections

The Christian Democratic Team was wiped out in the June 1977 elections. Burdened by debts and defeat, it decided to dissolve, and each of its components rapidly joined other centrist political forces. Although a few deputies linked to Joaquín Ruiz Giménez quickly moved leftward, after the summer of 1977 most former EDC militants joined the ranks of the UCD, and the Christian Democrats in Catalonia and Valencia moved, perhaps more slowly, in the same direction. Ruiz Giménez himself was mentioned as a possible UCD Senate candidate in the 1979 elections. The Christian Democratic option seemed to have been swept away. Its old leader, José María Gil Robles, summed up his pessimistic view of the point things had reached in a book entitled *Un final de jornada*. Spain was in the hands of personalistic and authoritarian leaders; his own errors in the campaign had been failing to set up an effective organization and collaborating with a figure like Ruiz Giménez, whose program was more Christian progressive than Christian Democratic.[24]

In the end, the Christian Democratic option had been politically viable only for a few months, in late 1976 and early 1977. With its passing, the forces of the center came to identify themselves exclusively with the UCD. Between the general elections of 1977 and 1979, the direction of UCD's development was unequivocal. Yet the process was far from simple. A multitude of problems flowed from the exercise of power. The principal economic issues were addressed, but hardly solved, in the multiparty Moncloa Agreements, and writing the constitution proved a much lengthier process, much more fraught with conflict, than anyone had expected. The fragmentation of the Spanish political spectrum made complicated negotiations continually necessary. They dragged on till late 1978. To these could be added the persistent problem of terrorism and a growing preoccupation with the regional organization of the state. Although surveys showed most Spaniards to be in favor of centralization at the beginning of the transition, their attitudes quickly changed.

In the meantime, the UCD was developing as a political party. In late 1977 the small parties that had been part of the victorious coalition dissolved, and in January 1978 the leading sectors of the party, acting through a commission on which they had equal representation, issued a first *Ideological Document*, which drew heavily on the electoral propaganda of the previous summer. In October 1978 the UCD celebrated its First Congress and approved its *Ideological Principles and Model of Society* in preparation for the March 1979 elections.[25]

The possibility of calling elections so soon had been raised particularly by the opposition forces in the preceding months. It was a typical product of Spain's peculiar transition to democracy. In strictly legal terms, no dissolution of the Cortes was necessary. After all, the Cortes elected in June 1977 had never been formally designated a constituent assembly. What is more, there were important reasons for not calling new elections. Aside from the gravity of the political and economic situation, as the Catalan Jordi Pujol correctly predicted, the results of new elections would be very similar to those of June 1977. Nevertheless, it is likely that quite early on the prime minister considered the possibility of dissolution; at least on several occasions, his then closest collaborator, the deputy prime minister for economic affairs, Fernando Abril, said so. When, on the day the constitution was promulgated, Suárez finally announced his decision to dissolve the Cortes, the reason he gave was the need for greater political efficacy. Basically, he argued that the prospect of new elections would weigh more and more heavily on the government the longer they were postponed. Moreover, with the constitution approved, the transition had been completed, and new demands related to the economy, to public order, and to the devolution of power to the regions would surface. Undoubtedly these were important issues, but there may well have been others. Several months before, amid repeated demands from the opposition and especially the PSOE, Suárez had announced that municipal elections would be held after the constitution was approved. The left might well obtain more votes in local than in national elections, and this raised the possibility of a moral and political defeat for the center. Yet another consideration was the fact that the long, complicated constitutional negotiations had sometimes produced ambiguous compromises, which gave exceptional importance to the complementary laws that would flesh out the structure created by the constitution. Elections renewing the government's mandate would allow it to interpret the constitution along the lines the Centrists favored.

The call for elections in March 1979 raised the issue of political alliances. The groups on the right quickly sought to establish contact with one another. Their work on the constitution had brought the Popular Alliance close to the UCD, and the former now sought an electoral alliance. The government was probably never much interested; conservative leaders had interviews with three ministers, but there was little likelihood of agreement. Areilza, now CD leader, had come to favor a pact with the UCD. Indeed, he considered it an urgent necessity. In addition, part of the conservative press regarded the proposal with satisfaction,[26] and two Madrid deputies from the Christian Democratic faction of the UCD spoke up for it. Between fascism and the left, they claimed, there was an electoral space that was sufficiently coherent to be represented by a single force in the elections. By the second half of January, however, there was little talk of this possibility.

The important development leading up to the new elections was the evolution of the electorate after June 1977. That evolution shows what a gamble Suárez's decision was. Broadly speaking, the Spanish electorate became more politicized and more sympathetic to the left. Whereas 34 percent of the electorate had claimed in early 1977 that they knew nothing about politics, only 23 percent did so by late 1978. And politicization did not mean optimism about politics in Spain: on the contrary, 54 percent of those questioned thought the situation in all areas was getting worse every day, and only a tiny proportion valued the role of the Chamber of Deputies and the Senate very highly. Meanwhile, the country moved leftward: on a left-right scale of one to seven, Spain rated 4.12 in December 1976 and 3.56 in September 1977. The process continued in the subsequent months. According to survey evidence, in a very short span of time, basic political attitudes in Spain moved from a pattern similar to that in Germany to one slightly to the left of Italy's—and the Italian electorate is one of the most left-oriented in Europe. In the summer of 1978 a survey showed that one of three Spaniards was anticlerical and more than half were anti-Francoist. Attitudes toward Marxism and political self-definition had also changed in a direction unfavorable to the UCD. The proportion of Spaniards who described themselves as leftist had doubled, whereas the centrist component had shrunk by about one-third.

Other signs, however, were more favorable to the Union of the Democratic Center. First, in Senate by-elections held in May 1978 in Alicante and Asturias, two left-leaning provinces, turnout was low, particularly among the centrist electorate. This apparently contributed to the UCD defeat, but there was no evidence that the basic attitudes of the electorate had changed. Indeed, they seemed to have crystallized—which would suggest that in Spain, as in most other Western European countries, political attitudes were changing only very gradually. Second, there was the personal prestige of Suárez, the UCD's most important asset. Suárez was a very popular leader, whose personality appealed to the centrist electorate more than did the specifics of the UCD program. According to a survey taken in the summer of 1978, the Spaniards judged Suárez the least excitable and the most skillful, understanding, honest, and responsible Spanish political leader. Seventeen percent of those queried gave him complete approval; PSOE leader Felipe González had three points less. These two factors seemed to give the Centrist leaders grounds for cautious optimism.[27]

Candidate Selection From the moment the elections were called in January 1979, ultimate authority over the lists was placed in the hands of the prime minister and the leader of the UCD, Adolfo Suárez; as in the other Spanish parties, the leadership worked from proposals from the provinces. Given the absence of any commonly accepted procedure for obtaining the support of the local or provincial party when it came to fighting the election, candidate selection was bound to be fraught with conflict. A second difficulty lay in the fact that a good part of the Centrist elite was immersed in the tasks of public administration. The news of the forthcoming elections provoked a tide of resignations that was stemmed only when UCD leaders explicitly reminded the party that there were routes of access to a political career (including regional and local as well as national administrative office) other than election to Parliament. These same leaders stressed the need for deputies to dedicate themselves to their parliamentary tasks more seriously than they had up to that point. A report presented by the parliamentary leader of the UCD group in the Chamber of Deputies, Pérez Llorca, evaluating the parliamentary work of Centrist deputies apparently played an important role in the drawing of the lists.[28]

Another problem was the overlap between the legislative and municipal campaigns. Many potential candidates had to decide in which election to run —or whether to run in both. Running in the general election first would give a publicity boost to a municipal aspirant. The case that received the most attention and proved most difficult to resolve was that of the candidate for mayor of Madrid, José Luis Alvarez; in the end, despite objections within his own party, his name was entered on the Chamber list as well as the municipal list. Then there was the problem of where to place ministers running for the Chamber of Deputies. The district where a given minister had run in June 1977 was not always the logical choice in March 1979, but not all could be candidates in Madrid. In the end, since the ministers were well known to the public, after much deliberation they were placed at the head of lists throughout Spain. This policy was a product of the electoral system, which placed a premium on the voter appeal of the candidate at the head of the list in each province. Sometimes the ministers' provincial links were tenuous, but on the whole the policy gave good results. All of Suárez's ministers were candidates, but some high officials were denied the chance to run.[29]

A third but related difficulty was the diminished role of the Senate under the new constitution, which prompted some of the most dynamic senators to seek election to the Chamber of Deputies. In all, sixteen former senators were given attractive slots on the Chamber of Deputies lists. Among them were four senators named by the king and one minister, Rafael Calvo Ortega, who had been elected senator from Segovia. Antonio Fontán, president of the Senate, was given the third spot on the Madrid list. Fourth, there was a problem that would surface later, though it attracted little attention at the time: the requirement that every candidate sign an undated letter of resignation. As might be supposed, this disciplinary measure drew fire from most independent observers, some of whom even judged it unconstitutional.[30]

While the lists were being drawn up, disputes were frequent. The absence of an established procedure, the supremacy of Madrid, and the importance of personal connections were the overriding factors in most places, though ideological rivalries opposed Christian Democrats and social democrats in Asturias, and personal animosity played a part in the conflicts in Galicia, both in La Coruña and above all in Pontevedra, where a Madrid-based effort to get rid of the number three candidate led to the resignation of the man who headed the list. There were also conflicts in Estremadura and in Madrid, where the president of the provincial UCD resigned after being placed relatively low on the list; this led to the formation of a provisional administrative commission to conduct the campaign. And there was trouble in Granada and elsewhere. Overall, however, there was not an excessive shake-up of the centrist elite in 1979. A few former Centrist leaders such as Enrique de la Mata in Teruel and Alberto Oliart in Cáceres resumed their political careers to run on UCD lists, 109 incumbent deputies ran for reelection to the Chamber, and a dozen more ran for the Senate. Thus there was considerable stability. In the Senate 69 of the 115 candidates were running for reelection. Were we to try to generalize about the changes in the UCD's parliamentary leadership, we might say that in March 1979 it was those individuals who were most conservative, most closely tied to the previous regime, and, above all, most senior who did not run again. The median age of the parliamentary candidates was only thirty-seven. On the other hand, it was clear that there was no need this time around, as there had been in the first election after Franco's death, to include former Francoist deputies. These could be replaced by candidates more comfortable with the new political climate.[31]

The Electoral Campaign

Compared with the 1977 campaign, which had at least had the novelty of coming after a very long period without elections, the one in 1979 was dull. There were no mass meetings, by 1977 standards; in any case, these had never been the UCD's forte. The one UCD meeting that attracted large numbers of centrist sympathizers, held late in the campaign at an airport near Madrid, was as much a sports event as anything else. The Centrist campaign consisted mainly of small, poorly attended rallies. Nevertheless, there was the sense that on this occasion, in contrast to 1977, the UCD had the initiative. It had called the elections, and it was ready for them.

In presenting itself to the electorate, the UCD tried first to identify itself with the continuity of the state and the successful transition to democracy. That is why, until the final phase of the campaign, Prime Minister Suárez never attacked his principal opposition, the PSOE. His choice to launch the campaign with an address to the Council of Europe at Strasbourg, was clearly intended to associate him in the voters' minds with the highest and most permanent interests of the state.

Meanwhile, the UCD presented itself as the principal author of the transition from dictatorship to democracy. On 7 February 1979, *El País* carried an article by UCD Secretary General Rafael Arias Salgado, entitled "Promise Fulfilled," which made at greater length the same point as the party's principal slogans in this first phase: "Said and Done" and "Suárez Delivers." At this time, too, the party published a book containing the program approved at the UCD First Congress.[32] In the introduction Suárez spoke of the harmony brought to Spain by the constitution thanks to the efforts of the Center. Clearly, he claimed, the party "knew how to place the general interests of the country and the demands of democratic consolidation above the interests of the party." Credit for the transition belonged to the leadership of the Centrist party. The new elections, Suárez said, presupposed an important change in the political life of the country: the coalitions so necessary to the process of drawing up a constitution would have to give way to a sharper differentiation between the UCD and its adversaries. "Once the transition period has ended," Suárez said, "the UCD will be ready to fight (always respecting the freedom of others) to achieve that model of democratic society that flows from its ideological principles." This insistence on the democratic model of society would become an essential theme in the final phase of the campaign; meanwhile, the UCD promised its supporters a "new style" of government in exchange for their votes.

This new style, this consolidation, would be possible only if the UCD attained a sufficient number of votes to be able to govern alone. Of course, it was likely, given the nature of the party system, that the UCD would not receive an absolute majority of the votes; equally, thanks to the electoral system, a slight change in its vote could significantly reinforce its position in the Cortes. Fernando Abril, deputy prime minister, and Martín Villa, minister of the interior, speaking during the first phase of the electoral campaign, emphasized their hope that the UCD would obtain enough votes to govern alone. On the other hand, possibility of a coalition, especially an entente with the PSOE, was dismissed out of hand by Garrigues and others early in the campaign.

Responsibility for the party program was given to the secretary general and four others representing different tendencies in the UCD: Francisco Fernández Ordoñez for the Social Democrats, Landelino Lavilla for the Christian Democrats, Joaquín Garrigues for the Liberals, and Calvo Ortega for the independents linked directly to Suárez. The press announced the UCD program on 7 February 1979, with interpretations offered by each of the participants. Each put special emphasis on the aspects of the program that might directly motivate those sectors of the electorate he represented. Thus Landelino Lavilla insisted on the promise that effective measures would be taken to ensure the citizens' security and to defeat terrorism, to protect the family as the natural environment in which the human person could develop, and on both the right of education and the right of various social groups to establish centers of learning freely. For his part, Fernández Ordoñez stressed the fight against unemployment, the anti-inflationary policies of the government, and fiscal reform. Garrigues repudiated economic collectivism and affirmed the system of private initiative. Finally, Calvo Ortega made special mention of Spain's social problems, especially unemployment.

UCD leaders estimate that they spent about 850 million pesetas publicizing the party program—on 4,500 rented billboards, 16 million posters and pamphlets, 1,200 radio spots, and 3,000 ads in the press. It is very likely that the party's expenditure of money and effort was greater than these figures suggest. Nevertheless, they faithfully reflected one tendency apparent in the campaigns of all the parties: the growing role of radio compared with other means of communication, even television.

In any case, the electoral program was probably not what made up the voters' minds. As Garrigues pointed out, the parties' programs did not differ substantially, and the electorate's understanding of the special character of each group was intuitive, based partly on which adversaries it chose to attack. In the first phase of the campaign, the UCD concentrated its fire on the groups that could compete most directly for its vote, especially the right. A vote for the Popular Alliance—now the Democratic Coalition (CD), often referred to as the AP/CD—it argued, would be wasted, even counterproductive, since its effect would be to strengthen the left; the PSOE, meanwhile, was excessively radical and "infantile." The "coherent, efficient, and logical" choice for the conservative elector was a vote for the UCD.[33]

Luis Apóstua, a candidate in Madrid, was quoted as saying that the "true rivals" in this election were the UCD and the PSOE, insofar as they were the only parties that could realistically hope for victory.[34] Arias Salgado went even further: to vote for the AP/CD was to be "an objective ally of the Marxist left" and "to cast a vote for socialism." The need to use one's vote in the way most likely to promote the conservative cause—to cast a "useful vote"—became a major theme of the UCD campaign. Centrist candidates, meanwhile, stressed the conservative aspects of the UCD ideology in their statements to the press. The minister of justice declared, "While the UCD governs, abortion will be a crime," and the minister of the interior, in a daily column in *Ya*, the principal Catholic daily, expressed concern about the radicalization of the nation's youth.

The AP/CD, of course, fought back. In an article published in *El Imparcial* on 1 February, Manuel Fraga rejected "the three UCD arguments." In his opinion, the UCD could not claim to be responsible for the transition since it had not succeeded in having its draft constitution adopted; the statement that a vote for the UCD was "a useful vote" made no sense since the Centrists had repeatedly and overtly joined forces with the leftist adversary; and the touted "new style" was nothing more than a promise. And Osorio told the conservative newspaper *ABC* the difference between the AP/CD and the UCD was that the former had "definite ideas": what the UCD had to do to hold its own against the right was clarify its ideas and demonstrate its firmness to the electorate during the campaign. But on the whole, the arguments of the right were weak and easily refuted.

The UCD's attacks on the right virtually disappeared as the campaign developed, and sallies against the PSOE multiplied. Beginning on 15 February, the principal Centrist candidates and spokesmen (though not Suárez himself) harshly criticized the Socialist party, specifically its proposal for negotiations with the Basque terrorist organization, Basque Land and Liberty (ETA), its incoherence on the matter of public order, and the demagogy of its social and economic promises. The more conservative sectors of the UCD expressed this sentiment most emphatically, but Fernando Abril, deputy prime minister and an intimate associate of Suárez, was a vigorous critic as well. Various ministers called the PSOE's program a new version of Disneyland; the Socialists' accession to power, they said, would "double unemployment in six months." Pérez Llorca affirmed that a Socialist victory would strengthen the radical wing of the PSOE. Even Abril said that the PSOE would only stop being Marxist if it were punished at the polls.[35] This kind of argument, particularly in the final phase of the campaign, probably made up more conservative voters' minds than the earlier plea for a "useful vote." In any case, what is clear is that the electorate voted UCD for lack of a better option. *Ya* (which had briefly advocated a coalition of all groups to the right of the Communists) endorsed the UCD on February 28, arguing that this choice was dictated by the electoral system.

An unexpected development in the middle of February may have had an important effect on the outcome. Early on it had been announced that Prime Minister Suárez would play the key role in the UCD campaign, traveling to twenty provinces. At first, his tour proceeded smoothly. In León and Galicia, Suárez's audiences were relatively small, his tone moderate, his criticisms of the PSOE cautious; this Giscardian approach, as some called it, seemed successful. But in Estremadura and above all Andalusia, in the strongholds of the left, the prime minister encountered heckling and other forms of protest. Suárez's trip south concluded with a very tense visit to Atarfe, a small town in Granada, where he barely escaped physical abuse. Thereafter he suspended his personal campaign appearances until the last phase of the campaign.

It is very likely that this final phase was decisive. As we shall argue, the electorate was largely undecided in mid-February 1979. It is very probable that the UCD's early electoral propaganda stressing the transition to democracy was inappropriate and even counterproductive at a time when a large part of the electorate had seen no improvement in its socioeconomic situation. By and large, the centrist campaign was overconfident and self-satisfied. It has been argued that in the final phase, specifically in his last speech on national television, Suárez really took control of the campaign, which up to then had been led by Federico Isart, a close collaborator of Fernando Abril. Up to that point Suárez had appeared confident of victory and proud of his government's record, but in his last speech he made a dramatic attack on the Socialists. The country was voting not just for a government, Suárez affirmed, but for a model of society. The UCD's model was well known; the PSOE favored a collectivist society in which, among other things, abortion would be permitted. The UCD, he went on, did not seek a vote of fear but a clear endorsement, and clarity required knowledge of the alternatives.

The Electoral Results

Before we discuss the electoral results in detail, we should look briefly at the forecasts published shortly before the election. Naturally enough, these had considerable impact on public opinion.

The UCD's position just before the election was not completely satisfactory. The Centrist electorate was lethargic (few attended meetings, and according to an unpublished survey taken in 1978, a mere 2 percent were party activists), and the party could only hope that some of the undecided would vote UCD. This is in fact what happened. Yet on 6 February *El País* spoke of "a slight Socialist advantage": 21 percent, according to the paper's survey, to the UCD's 18.4 percent, but it is quite possible that fewer voters were undecided than the polls suggested. More important than either party's share of the popular vote was which would control the Parliament. Analysts close to the UCD noted the possibility that an increase of the UCD vote in a very few districts would give the Centrists an absolute majority of seats (176). More careful surveys taken nearly eight months before the election had suggested a decline in the Centrist vote in several regions where the UCD enjoyed a clear majority, such as the Balearic Islands, Estremadura, and Galicia; these predictions were borne out by the results. By contrast, the suggestion that the UCD would maintain its vote in Andalusia and grow significantly in Catalonia proved mistaken. The forecasts published in late February, however, gave the UCD between 153 and 156 seats to the PSOE's 132 to 140.

The elections saw the victory of the UCD, with 6,268,593 votes, representing 35.0 percent of the total, and 168 seats in the Chamber of Deputies. The government party finished comfortably ahead of the Socialists, who enjoyed a slight increase to 5,469,813 votes (30.5 percent) and 121 seats in the Chamber of Deputies.[36] Clearly, the UCD managed to resist the growing leftward trend of the electorate. On the other hand, the UCD actually saw its vote decline; the greater fragmentation of the electorate was the key to its increase in seats. Since this fragmentation benefited the nationalist/regionalist parties, the UCD felt its impact less than the PSOE: both in the Basque country and above all in Andalusia, the voter who shifted to the nationalist parties had previously voted for the left.

Some surveys suggest that the Centrists' emphasis on the threat represented by the Socialist "model of society" may have been decisive in preventing centrist votes from leaking to the Socialists. Meanwhile, given the heterogeneous character of the AP/CD's support and its bleak outlook, this campaign theme probably reinforced the UCD's earlier calls for a "useful vote" and allowed the UCD to obtain a good number of votes from the right.

There was little change in the voter turnout between 1977 and 1979. As for the regional and provincial characteristics of the vote, the UCD did well in agricultural regions with dispersed populations, high rates of literacy and religious observance, and conservative or centrist political traditions. Regions with high unemployment, leftist political traditions, and high proportions of immigrants or young people saw the defeat of the UCD. For the UCD as well as, to a lesser extent, for the Socialists and the Communists, the 1979 elections brought greater homogenization and nationalization. The vote was most stable in Castile-León and New Castile. In three of the five electoral districts in New Castile the UCD vote rose; in two it declined but very modestly. In Castile-León the situation was similar: in only one of the six provinces was the UCD's gain more than five points. In five provinces the UCD suffered losses of less than five points. In Logroño, where there was a sharp increase in the centrist vote, the UCD picked up votes that had formerly gone to independents; something similar happened in Castellón, Zaragoza, and Ceuta, while in Melilla, an independent candidate took votes away from the UCD. The increase in the centrist vote was most striking in those areas where the AP/CD lost, as in Burgos; the AP's vote held in 1979 in Salamanca, and so did the UCD's. The two Castiles remained loyal to the UCD; the Balearic Islands and Galicia, while easily won by the Center in both elections, gave it fewer votes in 1979. In Galicia the drop was due not only to a rise in the nationalist vote but also to a rise in the AP/CD vote.

In Orense the five percentage points gained by the AP/CD coincided with a similar decline in the centrist vote. Estremadura is another region where the influence of the Center declined, though the UCD retained control of the parliamentary delegation. In all of the Basque country, the UCD suffered losses, compensated in part by the presentation of a Centrist list in Guipúzcoa where none had stood in 1977. Evidently the vote loss in the Basque country benefited the PNV, especially in Alava. By contrast, in Catalonia the Centrists, rather than losing votes to the regionalist parties, actually gained, though by less than the party had expected and surveys had predicted. Perhaps relevant in the case of Gerona was the presence of an independent centrist list. The relatively small growth in the Centrist vote (in Catalonia compared with what had been predicted) was due to the failure to attract the Christian democratic vote. In Barcelona the Centrist vote could hypothetically have reached 20 percent, but the UCD attained only 17 percent. In fact, surveys had suggested it would be difficult for moderate Catalan nationalists to vote UCD. Lérida may have been an exception: the rise in the vote for the Centrist candidates may have been due to the composition of the UCD list. In any case, it hurt nationalists, who lost their seats to the centrists. (Later, however, in the municipal and then the regional elections, the UCD did not continue to grow.) The results in Asturias and Aragon were satisfactory for the UCD: in both regions, there was modest growth—and in Teruel, a major setback for the AP/CD. In Murcia the UCD vote declined slightly, while in Albacete it grew slightly. Finally, in Andalusia the electoral results clearly reflected the homogenization of the electoral map: the decline in the UCD vote was evident in those provinces where the UCD had received the most votes in 1977, that is to say, Huelva, Granada, and Almería. By contrast, in provinces controlled by the left (Cádiz and Jaén) the UCD vote grew most. In the case of Andalusia, it is evident that the Center increased at the expense of the AP/CD, which dropped to fifth place in the region, behind the Socialist party of Andalusia.

Survey data and an analysis of the 1977 and 1979 results suggest certain conclusions. It appears that neither the lowering of the voting age nor the decline in turnout affected the outcome decisively. Nearly six of ten UCD voters were women, according to a 1978 survey;[37] their level of education was relatively high; and there is a positive correlation between the Centrist vote and areas where family enterprises and agriculture predominated. Whereas the UCD took about 40 percent of the vote in cities with more than 100,000 voters, it received more than 50 percent in the smallest towns (in 1977 in Galicia, the UCD won in 302 municipalities and was beaten in only nine). The Centrist electorate tended to be mature, though generally younger than the AP/CD electorate. Finally, the Centrist vote was not a nationalist/regionalist vote—particularly in Catalonia. In working-class districts in Catalonia's industrial belt, the UCD did better than the nationalists.[38]

In sum, the 1979 general election consolidated the UCD electorate. Surveys had shown that the Centrist electorate, despite a certain diversity, had a very specific profile.[39] But in 1979 the UCD was able to attract centrist votes that had been dispersed in the previous election; a good part of its gains in Madrid, for example, came from the Christian Democratic Team. At the same time, the UCD's strong campaign against the Socialists forestalled any significant loss of votes toward the left (and foiled the PSOE's plan to expand toward the center).

If the UCD was more sure of its electorate after 1979, it was also stronger in Parliament, with three seats more than in 1977. Given the fragmentation of the electorate, the electoral system worked to the Center's advantage. The UCD lost seats in nine provinces, including where it had been the predominant force. This was the case in the three Galician provinces, in Granada, and in Cáceres. The UCD was also affected by the rise in the nationalist/regionalist vote and by its own losses in two of the Andalusian provinces. Meanwhile, the UCD won twelve new seats, three in Catalonia and others in Castellón and Zaragoza, provinces where the Centrist vote became consolidated, in Guipúzcoa, in Madrid and Valencia where the middle class may have feared a Socialist government, and in Zamora, where the AP/CD lost votes.

The UCD did even better in the Senate, where it went from 106 to 116 seats and gained a majority. Actually, the elections to the upper chamber were doubly beneficial to the UCD. Not only did the UCD gain from adding to its lists candidates who had run as Senators for Democracy in 1977, but since Senate elections were contested exclusively between parties under a plurality system, the parliamentary impact of the party's showing was much more significant. In nine provinces the UCD gained a senator, in two provinces it gained two, and in Zaragoza three. These gains more than made up for the loss of a senator in each of three provinces and of two senators in one. Meanwhile, the PSOE also improved its position in the Senate, moving from 35 to 59 seats. The UCD won its senatorial victory at the expense not of the Socialist party but of the various independents, who dropped from 56 to 29 seats.

Conclusions

The story of the birth of the UCD and the demise of Christian Democracy as a viable alternative in Spanish politics illustrates the difficulty of bringing a party system into being in a democracy newly emerged from a long dictatorship. It also raises the question why one party triumphed and the other failed. Clearly the errors and sound judgments of each are an important part of the answer. The Christian Democrats were overconfident, not realizing that their potential electorate might move toward other political options. Although the UCD made mistakes (more in 1977 than in 1979), it was able to capitalize on its role as leader of the transition that culminated in the constitution.

It would be excessive, however, to conclude that these facts alone explain the early party organization of the center and center-right in Spain. In postwar Italy the party identified with the center and center-right was Christian Democracy. It drew on a higher level of Catholic participation in Church-affiliated organizations than was found in post-Franco Spain and above all on the less secular character of Italian society. Spanish society had already begun to undergo a process of secularization by the time political mobilization occurred. It is quite probable that a Spanish Christian Democratic party would have emerged in 1945 or even in the late 1960s, but no later. By 1970 its potential electorate was gone.

The leading role of the UCD in the transition was important. One could even say that democracy could not have taken the form it did in Spain without the contribution of this centrist party. But the conditions under which it developed were unique to Spain. Unlike its Portuguese counterpart, the Democratic Alliance, the UCD was born in power; it did not first learn the role of opposition. Nor was the UCD's experience that of the Greek governing party, New Democracy, which enjoyed a large majority for the first seven years after the reinstitution of democracy. In Greece the memory of the political clienteles dating from the predictatorial period, the fact that Karamanlis had been in exile, and the advantage the electoral system gave his party all helped New Democracy secure its majority. In Portugal, although some share of political power has always remained in the hands of the army, the Democratic Alliance was able to secure a clear victory at the polls in the wake of government by the left. In Spain the proportional electoral system and, above all, the fragmentation of Spanish society not only by political, social, and religious cleavages but also by the religious ones meant that the parliamentary majority of the governing party was always precarious. This precariousness, together with the endemic factionalism of the party and the challenges Spain has faced since 1977, explains why tensions persisted within the UCD and ultimately destroyed it.

The Socialist Alternative: The Policies and Electorate of the PSOE

JOSÉ MARÍA MARAVALL

———The Spanish Socialist Workers' party (PSOE) was created in 1879. In the general election of February 1936, the last before the fascist dictatorship, the party obtained 21.4 percent of the seats: it was the largest minority in the Cortes and the most important political organization of the Popular Front.[1] Forty-one years later, in the first election after the dictatorship in July 1977, the PSOE obtained 29.3 percent of the vote and 33.7 percent of the seats. The second largest party in the country, the PSOE almost matched the Union of the Democratic Center (UCD), the new center-right party created a few months before. These results were confirmed by the elections of March 1979, when the PSOE reached 30.5 percent of the vote and 34.6 percent of the seats.

Aside from the political importance of the PSOE in the context of Spanish and southern European politics, these electoral results raise several important questions for political analysis. Some come under the general heading of political continuity and refer to the political experiences of the party between 1939 and 1979: the degree of organizational persistence and change; the extent to which the geographical distribution of Socialist allegiance varied or remained stable over time; the maintenance of partisan loyalties between generations. The answers to these questions should explain to a large extent why the PSOE retained (or, rather, increased) its political relevance in spite of nearly forty years of dictatorship. Other questions have to do with the impact of deep social and economic changes on party ideology. The problem of the political orientations of the PSOE will be analyzed through an examination of the ideological characteristics both of the party organization and leaders and of its supporters.

To what extent was the Socialist party of 1977 the direct successor of the party of 1931-39? How did the party organization survive? To answer these questions, I shall briefly examine the politics of the PSOE under the Republic and during the Civil War, about which there is an extensive literature, and under Francoism, about which there is very little information. I shall then discuss the Socialist party during the transition to democracy and in the new party system, which started to crystallize in 1977.

Throughout its history the PSOE has partaken of the traditional "two souls" of social democracy: a revolutionary soul that defended revolutionary objectives and a reformist soul that pursued moderate practices. The attempt to reconcile them, by combining parliamentary and institutional politics with extraparliamentary and mass-mobilization strategies, was fraught with tension, manifested in internecine disputes, during the Second Republic (April 1931 to April 1939). These disputes opposed the three main leaders of the PSOE and the socialist trade union UGT (General Workers Union). Thus Julián Besteiro represented an amalgam of Fabian doctrine and Bernsteinian influence; he conceived socialism as a slow process of maturation, based on education and trade union strength. Indalecio Prieto saw the consolidation of democracy and Republican institutions as the first priority for the PSOE; whether freedoms were more or less "bourgeois" was secondary. Prieto's way to socialism required alliance with center-left Republican parties and a process of cumulative reform under Republican legality. For Francisco Largo Caballero and the socialist tendencies represented by the magazines *Claridad* and *Leviatán* after 1933, socialism could only be revolutionary, following a strategy of mass mobilization and leading to the collapse of the bourgeois order.

This dilemma, as well as an ambiguous political strategy, affected the PSOE very deeply under the Second Republic; indeed, the Spanish Socialists' situation was very representative of the drama of the European left in the 1930s.[2] The Civil War turned into a tragedy, and fascism put an end to the problem of reconciling democracy with radical egalitarian change.

The threat of fascism increased the radicalism of the party after January 1934; the impact of events in Germany and Austria on the political orientation of the party was to be very great. The challenge from the right (a right-wing government ruled from December 1933 to December 1935) and the challenge from the left (the Anarchist National Confederation of Labor [CNT] was influential and the power of the Communist party grew after the outbreak of the war in 1936 because of the Republican government's dependence on Soviet help) also contributed to the Socialists' difficulties in finding an adequate strategy. The experience of the Republic and the Civil War was indeed terrible for the Socialist party: torn by factionalism, it was unable to achieve revolution or protect democracy, and its alliance with the left ended in disaster. Besides the war that the Communists launched in 1937 against the Anarchists and Trotskyists, the Communist party played the Socialist factions against one another, thus bringing down the Largo Caballero government in May 1937 and forcing Prieto out as minister of defense in April 1938; it infiltrated the UGT; and it captured half of the Socialist Youth and the Catalan Socialists by incorporating them into the Communist-controlled Unified Socialist Youth (JSU) and the Unified Socialist party of Catalonia (PSUC). Eventually the Republican surrender of April 1939 took place after a street battle between Socialists and Communists in Madrid. But the drama of the Spanish Socialist party in the 1930s was also a reflection of the fratricidal struggles throughout the European left in the same period, of its conflicts and strains over the issues of reform and revolution, radical change and representative democracy, hostility, and alliance between working-class parties. The PSOE enjoyed a high degree of working-class support, partly through the UGT, whose membership reached 1.4 million in 1939. Socialist politics in the Second Republic included genuine reform measures, particularly in labor relations, education, trade union protection of the agricultural work force, and social security. Finally, Socialist governments at the local level and the political presence of the Socialist party within local communities through the Casas del Pueblo (Houses of the People) were an important influence in the political socialization of many Spaniards during the Second Republic. There is a sense in which the brevity of Spain's democratic experience before fascism was offset by its particular intensity for the people who lived through it.

The Republican defeat in 1939, followed by massive exile and internal repression under the new regime, caused the collapse of the PSOE. It was only in 1944 that the first post–Civil War party congress was held,[3] and it was little more than a regrouping of exiled militants, with poor representation of the few thousand underground Socialists inside Spain. The party in exile fell into the hands of its right wing (first under Prieto, later Rodolfo Llopis) and turned toward strong anticommunism in reaction to the experiences of the Republic and the Civil War. This anticommunism was reinforced by the Soviet-German pact of 1939–1941 and later by the setting up of dictatorships in eastern Europe and the cold war. The Socialists' rejection of the old policy of alliance with the Communists took different forms. In Catalonia the Catalan Socialist Movement (MSC) was the answer to the socialist-communist unification in the PSUC. The PSOE set up the Junta for Spanish Liberation (JLE) in 1943, as a democratic alliance without the PCE (although the Communists entered a National Alliance of Democratic Forces—ANDE in 1947), but successive party congresses after 1944 declared the unwillingness of the Socialists to enter into joint ventures with the Communists. More important, the Socialist leadership in exile imposed its anticommunism on the party inside Spain.

The Socialists within the country reorganized inside the jails. In 1940 the UGT set up a national committee for the coordination of prisoners, which soon had a nucleus of some 500 militants, and the liberation of France in 1944 and a political amnesty in the same year improved the condition for restructuring the PSOE. The socialist party was active in the first strikes under Franco in 1947, 1951, 1953, and 1956; it must also be noted the socialist guerrilla movement survived until 1948, when the last guerrilla group led by José Mata escaped from Asturias. In 1944–1945 the UGT had between 7,000 and 8,000 members organized within Spain. Nevertheless, the Socialists were badly fragmented, and one main reason was repression. In 1949 there were still some 3,000 Socialist prisoners in the jail at Puerto de Santamaría and over 1,200 in Burgos; in addition, socialists were the largest group of prisoners in San Miguel de los Reyes, Santona, Alcalá de Henares, Carabanchel, and Yeserias. Between 1941 and 1969 more than 1,000 party militants were arrested: the losses were particularly great in 1941, 1946, 1947 (over 300 arrested), 1949 (150), 1953, 1965 (again over 300), and 1969 (some 250). In 1968 the members of three consecutive executive committees were in prison simultaneously; in 1953 the leader of the PSOE and general secretary of the UGT, Tomás Centeno, died from torture in the General Directorate of Security; in 1958 the leader of the Socialists inside Spain, Antonio Amat, and more than 100 militants were arrested.

The Socialists inside Spain also suffered from poor leadership. From 1945 to 1951 the main strategy of the organization in exile had been to rely on the Allied governments to liberate Spain from the dictatorship. The closing of the French border and the withdrawal of the ambassadors of democratic governments isolated Spain only temporarily, and in 1951 the Socialist strategy collapsed. Prieto resigned as first secretary of the PSOE in great bitterness against the western democratic governments, although his successor, Llopis, was still placing hope in social democratic and liberal governments as late as 1956. Meanwhile, organizational work had been poor, there was a growing lack of coordination of socialist activities, and the exiled leaders increasingly lost touch with what was happening inside the country. The Socialist leadership exerted very strict control of the Socialist groups in Spain, but these groups were denied a vote at PSOE congresses until 1972, on the grounds that clandestine struggle made it impossible to verify the members claimed by representatives from the interior. The 1960s were thus a period of crisis for the Socialists, largely because of the misguided politics of the PSOE leadership. The crisis of the PSOE created a space for other Socialist groups inside Spain, such as the left-wing Popular Liberation Front (called Catalan Workers Front [FOC] in Catalonia and Basque Socialist Front [ESB] in the Basque country), the Galician Socialist Movement (MSG) in Galicia, the Valencian Socialist party (PSV) in Valencia, and the Union of the Canary People (UPC) in the Canary Islands; the Workers' Syndical Union (USO) also emerged in the early 1960s as a trade union alternative to the UGT. It is important to note, however, that the PSOE groups inside Spain did not disappear: though very often isolated from the party organization and from one another, they were frequently very active.[4] This activity was perhaps most visible in Asturias and in Vizcaya, among miners and steelworkers, but the PSOE retained strong influence in Valencia and in Andalusia.

There were several attempts within the party to overturn a strategy and an organization that were weakening the party inside Spain. One of the earliest attempts was carried out by the Socialist University Group (ASU), a Socialist organization set up in 1956, which later joined the Socialist Youth (JJSS) and which has provided several of the present party leaders (Luis Gómez-Llorente, Francisco Bustelo, Miguel Boyer, Miguel Angel Martínez). At the congress of 1961 there was a confrontation between Gómez-Llorente and Prieto; at the congress of 1964 the Paris delegation opposed the other delegations, defending a greater autonomy for the groups of the interior. Another attempt took place in the 1967 congress, when delegates from Paris and members of Socialist Youth tried again to wrest some of the powers of the bureaucratic leadership in exile.[5] The most important attempt to renovate the party started in Andalusia in 1965. In 1969 a group of young professionals (mainly university teachers, labor lawyers, and doctors) were very active in rebuilding the party in the region.[6] Their efforts took two directions: on the one hand, visiting old militants and reestablishing political contacts that had been lost; on the other hand, promoting the UGT as the Socialist trade union by providing legal services to workers and by acting as a sort of rallying point for groups of organized, potentially Socialist workers. The UGT and the PSOE gathered new impetus after several industrial conflicts in Andalusia,[7] and these activities were extended to other areas of the country.[8] In July 1969 Felipe González represented this Andalusian group at a meeting of the PSOE National Committee in Toulouse, and after that meeting strong links were established with the two most powerful Socialist strongholds inside the country: Asturias and the Basque country.[9] The triangle Andalusia-Asturias-Basque country then became the basis for the reorganization of the PSOE. González wrote:

> We knew that it would not be possible to revive the organization without the support of the Basques and the Asturians, so we worked very hard with their organizations.... In 1970 I traveled all over the Basque country raising money for the strike at Siderúrgica Sevillana and establishing contact with comrades. I met with all our comrades in Eilbar, in San Sebastián, in Bilbao; I went from factory to factory.... I had connections with the entire organization, with Asturias and the Basque country, and I knew all the people involved personally.... I visited Spain from end to end.[10]

On this basis the many scattered Socialist groups were reconnected, above all those in Madrid, where the Socialists' fragmentation was particularly serious: "We went to Asturias, to the Basque country, and again and again to Madrid. We spent more of our time in Madrid than anywhere else, trying to restore the party organization and put it to work. It was badly fragmented.

There was X's group over here and Y's group over there and then all the rest of ASU, all frequently at odds with one another."[11]

The reconstruction of the party required a change of leadership, which was accomplished in three stages in 1970, 1972, and 1974. In August 1970 the Eleventh Congress in exile took place in Toulouse. Six zones of the interior were not represented, although their delegates still had no votes.[12] The issue of the political autonomy of the Socialists within Spain was again a cause of internal disputes: Felipe González defended this autonomy against Rodolfo Llopis, then first secretary of the party, and won the support of 80 percent of the vote for a new document on party organization. This change opened up the possibility of reorganizing the PSOE inside the country—a possibility that was strengthened after the UGT congress in 1971, when a new Executive Committee, composed mainly of leaders in the interior, was elected.[13] But the party's change of direction was not just a matter of organization: in fact, the organizational changes were only the expression of a political and strategic reorientation within the PSOE. The party's political strategy was no longer defined almost exclusively by anti-Communism; there was a positive attempt to produce a specifically socialist program and to identify the political space of socialism in Spain.

The next congress was called by ten of the fifteen members of the Executive Committee[14] and took place, again in Toulouse, in August 1972. The old leadership tried to boycott this congress in a final effort to retain some control of the new party, and subsequently they organized a splinter group. The new congress decided to transfer the leadership of the party and control of its economic resources to the interior. It also lifted the ban on joint actions with the PCE. It was decided that the Executive Committee would have a collegiate leadership and that the post of first secretary remain temporarily vacant.[15] In 1974 the Socialist International voted to recognize the renovated PSOE as the genuine one, disallowing the claims of Llopis and his old guard, the only abstention was that of the Italian PSDI. In October 1974 the PSOE held its last congress in exile, at Suresnes, a suburb of Paris. Eleven zones of the interior were now represented,[16] and the party claimed 4,000 members, half of them in exile. In addition, it had many supporters within Spain who did not pay dues regularly. Felipe González was elected first secretary, and the party adopted the strategy formulated in what was known as the Declaración de Septiembre.[17] The PSOE defended a struggle of positions against the dictatorship, which it called "conquest of parcels of freedom," through mass mobilization, pressure, and negotiation, with the aim of achieving a *ruptura democrática*—a break in the nation's political history that would open the way for democracy.

The timing of this last congress in exile was important: it took place after Franco had suffered a very serious illness in the summer of 1974; after the death of the Spanish prime minister, Admiral Luis Carrero Blanco, at the hands of terrorists in December 1973; and after Portugal's turn to democracy in April 1974. The end of the dictatorship was no longer a remote dream for which, however unsuccessfully, one had to fight. Furthermore, the working-class movement was gathering strength after a long crisis produced by extensive repression between 1968 and 1973. Illegal strikes increased by 84 percent between 1972 and 1973 and by another 62 percent between 1973 and 1974, and the number of work hours lost through these illegal strikes reached a record of some 14 million. The Spanish Communist party (PCE), together with the small Popular Socialist party (PSP) led by Enrique Tierno Galván and an odd assortment of liberal groups, small Marxist-Leninist parties, and independent individuals had set up the Democratic Junta in 1974. The PSOE refused to join the junta *after* it was set up, expressing disagreement over the participation of individuals on the same basis as parties, the support the junta offered Juan de Borbón (the father of the present King Juan Carlos), the manipulation of the PCE, and several other points of strategy. The Socialists then joined with other Marxist-Leninist groups and Christian Democrats in the Platform of Democratic Convergence. Eventually the junta and the Democratic Convergence group would reach an agreement and fuse, adopting the name Democratic Coordination in the spring of 1976.

It is now established that the transition from dictatorship to democracy was brought about in part by an autonomous policy of democratic reforms *from above*. It is also clear that this policy was stimulated by powerful demands for democracy *from below*. Indeed, the government's reform policy might well have failed in the face of Francoist resistance had this pressure from below not existed. The whole process of movement toward democracy was the outcome of the joint dynamics of reform *and* rupture. The first part of the transition from dictatorship was marked by a very militant working-class movement. Thus the number of hours lost through strikes reached 149 million in 1976 and 109 million in 1977, the first two years of the monarchy. This pressure brought the first post-Franco government, that of Prime Minister Carlos Arias Navarro, to a political impasse: the goal of this first government was to introduce a modality of restricted pluralism, semicontested elections, and a limited reform of the Francoist Fundamental Laws without a new constitution. This goal proved impossible, and the strategy threatened to bring the future of the monarchy into question. Arias Navarro's replacement by Adolfo Suárez changed the situation rapidly. Suárez adopted a strategy of full democratization through cumulative legal reforms. These included a very broad political amnesty, the legalization of parties, the acceptance of limited national self-government in Catalonia and the Basque country (together with regional decentralization in Valencia, Galicia, Andalusia, and other regions), and, finally, general elections to a constituent assembly.

The first PSOE congress held in Spain after the forty years of Francoism took place in Madrid in December 1976, five months after Suárez's appointment as prime minister but before many of his reforms had been implemented. The PSOE, though tolerated, was illegal, and the transition to democracy was at its very beginning. The party had over 8,000 members inside Spain and was expanding fast. The Twenty-seventh Congress approved an ideological declaration that defined the PSOE as "a class party, and therefore a mass party, Marxist and democratic," which rejected "any accommodation with capitalism" and sought "the suppression of the capitalist mode of production through the conquest of political and economic power and the socialization of the means of production, distribution, and exchange by the working class."[18] In a first stage the ten largest banks and 50 of the two hundred largest corporations would be nationalized. The party's political objectives also included the extension of "participatory" grass-roots democracy beyond its limits of the "capitalist state." In order to achieve its goals, the PSOE defended the necessity of combining parliamentary action with "popular mobilization."[19] The Twenty-seventh Congress also passed a declaration on strategy, which insisted on the twin ideas of a break with the past and the "cumulative conquest of freedom"; it also called for a "constitutional compromise"—general elections to a constituent assembly and, as a prerequisite to the elections, the establishment of fundamental rights and freedoms, the legalization of all parties, a general amnesty, the suppression of all autocratic institutions (especially the Francoist trade unions), and equality of access to the mass media and the neutrality of the state during the campaign.

At this stage the PSOE was already moving toward the leading role within the Spanish left. Early in 1977 the party absorbed a small but highly influential socialist organization in Madrid, the Madrid Socialist Convergence, and reached an agreement with the Catalan Socialist party (PSC) to carry out a joint political strategy, which eventually led to the integration of the PSC in a federal association with the PSOE. Affiliation in the PSOE was taking place at a very high rate, and this was simultaneous with the growth of the UGT. The Socialist party tried to maintain pressure on Suárez with street demonstrations and strong propaganda; the week from January 31 to 6 February 1977, for example, was used for public mobilization and a massive recruitment drive. The PSOE also took a leading part in the great demonstration on 1 May 1977, which again revolved around the themes of amnesty, freedom, and a break with the past.

Like all the relevant groups of the left—including the PCE and the Leninist Revolutionary Workers' Organization (ORT) and Labor Party of Spain (PTE)— the PSOE essentially cooperated with the transition course charted by Suárez. Indeed, the chief threat to the transition toward democracy was not left-wing militance but right-wing violence, including the murder of five PCE members in

January 1977. Gradually the break with the past became a strategy of "negotiated break." In December 1976, the Law for Political Reform was approved by 94.2 percent of those casting votes in a national referendum. The legalization of the parties began in February 1977, the Francoist party and unions were dismantled in March and April, and a new amnesty was granted in March. These measures met the most important demands of the anti-Francoist opposition and of the PSOE in particular.[20] The Suárez government and a representative committee of the opposition parties (which included Christian Democrats, Liberals, and Social Democrats, Socialists, Communists, and representatives of regional parties) agreed on an electoral law establishing proportional representation with the d'Hondt system. The law also regulated different aspects of the electoral campaign, providing for equality of access to television and public financing of the parties' campaigns in proportion to their share of the seats and votes.

The campaign leading up to the elections of 15 June 1977 lasted three weeks. The PSOE fought a very dynamic campaign, largely centered on Felipe González, who covered some 200,000 kilometers throughout the country. The party's main slogans were "Freedom is in your hand," "Socialism is freedom," and "A vote for socialism is a vote for liberty." It used thirty minutes of government-authorized television time and forty-five minutes of radio. The electoral program of the PSOE insisted on the "conquest" of freedoms, the need for the new Parliament to produce a democratic constitution, the struggle against corruption, and the general goal of dissolving all remnants of Francoism; the more specific policy proposals referred to tax reforms, the extension of free education, social security, changes in rural properties, and employment measures. The elections were a great success for the socialist party, which became the second largest party in the country with 29.4 percent of the vote against the UCD's 34.4 percent, while the minor roles fell to the Popular Alliance (AP) on the right and the communists on the left. The PSOE became one of the two poles of a party system that has been characterized as "polarized pluralism."[21]

Once the elections were over, the Socialist party turned to the business of establishing itself as the major opposition party—the *alternativa de poder*. It concentrated on the task of offering alternatives to the government's programs. Thus the PSOE presented to Parliament twenty-one legal proposals between August 1977 and January 1979. At the same time, the PSOE tried to increase its strength: the party claimed 75,000 militants before the elections, and in the following months membership went up to nearly 200,000. But the party needed to secure two additional pillars of its power: it had to consolidate the UGT as a powerful socialist trade union and to gain local bases of power. Thus the PSOE pressed the government to return to the UGT the property that had been confiscated by the Franco regime, which would mean considerable additional resources; and it called for municipal elections to replace mayors and councilors appointed by the dictatorship.

But the conciliation was still called for, especially while the delicate process of drafting the new constitution was going on. After all, the PSOE itself had demanded a "constitutional compromise." In addition, the economy was in a vulnerable state. Thus the Socialists came to view the period between the elections of June 1977 and March 1979 as one of "provisional democracy."[22]

The committee drafting the constitution was composed of centrists, socialists, communists, regionalists, and conservatives. Both houses of Parliament approved the final draft on 31 October 1978 and by national referendum on 6 December. The PSOE had a very positive view of the constitution, particularly the articles regulating fundamental rights and liberties of individuals and collectivities, regional autonomy, the abolition of the death penalty, the lowering of the voting age to eighteen, and state education. The party considered that the constitution left enough room for a Socialist government to implement a program of substantive reforms; for example, article 9 stated in general terms that all obstacles to freedom and equality among individuals and groups should be removed.

In order to consolidate democracy the economy had to be cared for. Thus in October 1977 the PSOE reluctantly signed the Moncloa Agreements, which introduced a program of austerity, along with additional democratic reforms in the state structures. The austerity measures included a 20 percent ceiling on wage increases, restrictions on credit, and an increase in public expenditure, and the reforms covered a new and more progressive tax system and modifications in the educational system, social security, the national health service, a new Public Enterprise Statute, a rather ambitious employment program, and an expansion of public land and housing. The reforms also extended parliamentary control to several areas of governmental activity that had remained largely autocratic, such as the social security system. The PSOE viewed these agreements as inevitable and as making it possible to distribute the costs of the economic crisis more fairly, with compensation for wage earners, the unemployed, pensioners, and small enterprises. Indeed, the agreements incorporated large parts of the economic program of the Socialist party. The problem was how to ensure the implementation of those aspects of the agreements that were progressive. The PCE demanded a supraparliamentary supervisory commission, but the PSOE rejected this as a communist attempt against what should be orthodox parliamentary control of the executive, in order to compensate for the Communists' weak position in Parliament. Large portions of the Moncloa Agreements were never implemented—including the employment policies, the Public Enterprise Statute, the policies on land and housing, the reforms of the health system, the devolution of trade union property, and the new system of industrial relations. As a result the PSOE did not want to participate in further interparty socioeconomic pacts, which might weaken the role of parliament and the party system. Unlike the PCE, the Socialists agreed that negotiations ought to take place between the trade unions and the employers' federations, not between the parties.[23] In fact, the UGT never supported or signed the Moncloa Agreements, but the Workers' Commissions did. The pacts were effective, however, in bringing down the annual rate of inflation from 26.4 to 16 percent, stimulating exports, increasing the inflow of tourism, cutting dramatically the deficit in foreign trade, and increasing the reserves; on the negative side, unemployment was nearly 8 percent of the active population, investment was stagnating, and the credit squeeze damaged many firms.

Conciliatory politics could hardly satisfy expectations created by the elections of 1977. A mood of disenchantment characterized the next stage of transition. The PSOE argued that this disenchantment was largely the result of the policies of the government: the slowness with which democracy was being extended to vast areas of social life and, particularly, the delay in calling municipal elections and the delay in returning confiscated property. The PSOE thought that political apathy might well end as soon as individuals began to see that democracy meant more than the existence of a parliament and the occasional election. It must be possible to avoid a repetition of the disenchantment and skepticism that had followed the adoption of the liberal constitution of 1812 and that Marx and Engels had commented upon: political enthusiasm unleashing expectations of a dramatic reversal of everyday miseries had created widespread disillusion and resentment.[24]

Two problems for which no immediate solution was at hand increased frustration: economic difficulties and violence. There had been thirty-six civilian deaths from political violence between 1964 and 1975 (twenty-two of them in the Basque country); from January to November 1978 the number of deaths reached fifty-three. The increase of violence was fundamentally associated with Basque terrorism—both directly and indirectly. Between the summer of 1978 and the summer of 1979, ten high-ranking military officers were killed by ETA, and from January to July 1979 there were eighty-four victims of political violence. The decline of public order encouraged the increasingly aggressive parafascist groups, which began again to take the initiative in 1978 and 1979, causing disturbances within the army and in the streets that left several people dead. The Basque problem was the main destabilizing force for the new democracy, however, and the polarization of the Basque population between right-wing centralism and regional nationalism did much damage to the PSOE, which had presided over a largely ineffective Basque General Council. Indeed, the UCD had been very reluctant to increase the powers of the organs designated to preside over devolution, in which the PSOE had the majority. (Besides the Basque General Council, these included the Consell in Valencia and the

Junta de Andalucía; the Socialists were also the largest political force in the Catalan Generalitat.)

The PSOE began to press for both local general elections immediately after the constitution was approved in the referendum of December 1978. There was no alternative to elections: the dramatic situation in the Basque country, the decline of public order, the unions' refusal to reach an economic pact with the government, and the PSOE's refusal to extend the Moncloa Agreements had brought the government to an impasse. The PSOE demanded that local elections take place first so that all the local authorities appointed under the Franco regime would be removed before the campaign for the general election began. The government rejected this demand, and Suárez called the general election for 1 March 1979, the local elections for 3 April. The PSOE centered its campaign for the March election on the themes of employment, public order, a new system of industrial relations, greater public investment, and democratization of the state. The issues were much more specific than in 1977. The PSOE concentrated its campaign resources in the areas where the UCD was strong: the most rural parts of Spain—Galicia, Estremadura, New and Old Castile, and the Canaries.

The second general election of the new democracy largely confirmed the results of the first, and this in itself was a major success for the UCD. The PSOE increased its share of the vote to 30.5 percent from 29.3 percent, but the UCD and the PCE also increased theirs (from 34.4 to 35.0 and from 9.4 to 10.8 percent, respectively) at the expense of a collapsed CD (the Democratic Coalition, which had absorbed the authoritarian right-wing AP) and of the PSP, which joined the PSOE in April 1978.

Perhaps the two most important results of the 1979 election were the increases in abstention (which went up from 21.6 percent of the electorate to 33.6 percent) and in the strength of the nationalist/regional parties, which captured 9.9 percent of the vote (up from 5.4 in 1977). Both results harmed the PSOE in particular. Abstention was especially high in working-class areas that had a long tradition of Socialist loyalty and had voted PSOE in 1977. This was particularly so in the industrial areas of Vizcaya (where abstention reached over 40 percent of the electorate) but was also significant in all the places where the PSOE was strong (Madrid, Valencia, Barcelona, and Andalusia). This abstention was seen by the socialist leaders as a "vote of punishment" on the part of a loyal electorate that had not turned to any other party (neither to the PCE nor to the nationalist PNV in the Basque country) but felt strongly about the politics of conciliation that the PSOE had had to follow from the autumn of 1977 onward. The growth of regional nationalism also harmed the PSOE, particularly in Andalusia where the Socialist party of Andalusia (PSA) took an important share of the potential Socialist vote. Abstention and nationalism were above all a threat to the stability of the new democratic order,

Table 6.1 Vote Switching, 1977–79: Where the Votes Came From (percent of party's total 1979 vote)

	Party supported in 1979		
Recalled Vote, 1977	UCD	PSOE	PCE
UCD	75.8	8.6	4.3
PSOE	2.5	65.6	9.9
PCE	0.3	1.8	61.9
Other	21.4	24.0	23.9
Total	100.0	100.0	100.0
N	(1,150)	(1,117)	(307)

Source: EMOPUBLICA survey for the PSOE, May 1979 (N=4,175).

Table 6.2 Vote Switching, 1977–79: Where the Votes Went (percent of party's total 1977 vote)

	Recalled Vote, 1977		
Party Supported in 1979	UCD	PSOE	PCE
UCD	71.2	10.0	5.3
PSOE	3.0	76.3	12.2
PCE	1.4	8.0	75.7
Other	24.4	5.7	6.8
Total	100.0	100.0	100.0
N	(1,225)	(960)	(251)

Source: EMOPUBLICA survey for the PSOE, May 1979 (N=4,175).

which could hardly survive left-wing terrorism, right-wing conspiracies, and a severe economic crisis unless it could count on the deeply rooted political allegiance of the population. The terrorist blackmail of ETA appeared to be supported by a sizable part of the Basque population, and "antisystem" parties now had parliamentary representation (from the parafascist National Union [UN] to Herri Batasuna, the political arm of the left-wing terrorist "military ETA").

The distribution of electoral forces seemed to have crystallized, and the UCD and PSOE electorates appeared to be firmer than expected.[25] Indeed, the UCD became stronger where it had been weaker (it won votes in Catalonia, the Basque country, Asturias, and the large cities), just as the PSOE did (gaining in Estremadura, Galicia, and La Mancha). Tables 6.1 and 6.2 indicate the transfers of votes to and from the three major parties between the elections of 1977 and 1979. The first table shows where the parties' support in 1979 came from, the second where their 1977 support went. The stability of the UCD electorate is confirmed by both: most of the UCD's support in 1979 came from loyal UCD voters (75.8 percent), and most of the 1977 UCD voters remained loyal (71.2 percent).

Whatever loyalties of the electorate, the parties were caught up in the dynamics of polarized pluralism: each of the major parties faced competition from both the left and the right.[26] The PSOE, however, faced more competition on its left than the UCD did on its right: in 1979 nearly twice as many votes went to parties to the left of the Socialists (15.2 percent of the vote) as went to the parties of the right of the government (7.5 percent). The left/right divide appeared then to be rather stable. Although the percentage of the total leftist vote had gone from 42 to 46 percent, it seemed unlikely to increase further given the strength of the UCD in the cities and the stability of its electorate. (There was a correlation coefficient of .88 between the vote of the UCD in 1977 and in 1979.) Moreover, the d'Hondt system of proportional representation with a three-seat minimum meant that a victory of the left would require a switch in the rural vote of massive proportions. Thus, although the PSOE improved its position in rural areas, the impact in terms of seats was minimal.[27] This raises a question about the strategy of the PSOE in 1979, which focused on the peasantry and rural areas. Party militants criticized the Socialist leaders for trying to win over "those sectors of the population that, with a lower average income than socialist voters, voted UCD"—that is, sectors with an allegedly "objective" interest in the Socialist program. The leaders claimed that they could recover these "natural" supporters without watering down the Socialist program.[28] It would take time, however, and a serious organizational effort to break the peasantry's traditional, perhaps deferential, allegiance to a conservative party and to overcome the biases of the electoral system.

Figure 6.1 indicates the geographical distribution of the PSOE vote in the general elections of 1977 and 1979 and in the local elections of 3 April 1979.[29] It must be noted that, to reflect the postelectoral pact between the PSOE, the PCE, and the PSA (the Andalusian Socialist party), the shaded areas of the map indicate victory for the left as a *whole*; however, except in Córdoba and Granada (where the PCE and the PSA obtained more votes), the PSOE was the largest party of the left, and PSOE mayors were elected in the twenty-one other provincial capitals—including Madrid, Barcelona, and Valencia. Overall, 11,019 Socialist councilors were elected in the local elections of 1979.

Yet it seems to me that beyond the euphoria raised by the results of the left-wing pact, Felipe González was right in urging caution.[30] True, the PSOE vote reached 35.4 percent while the UCD dropped to 31.7 percent and the PCE rose to 16.7 percent, but the socialists' expectations for the local elections, only a few months before, had been very high. These elections had been seen as the great opportunity to rid the country of Francoist-appointed mayors and councilors; yet many of these were reelected on UCD lists. On the whole, there does

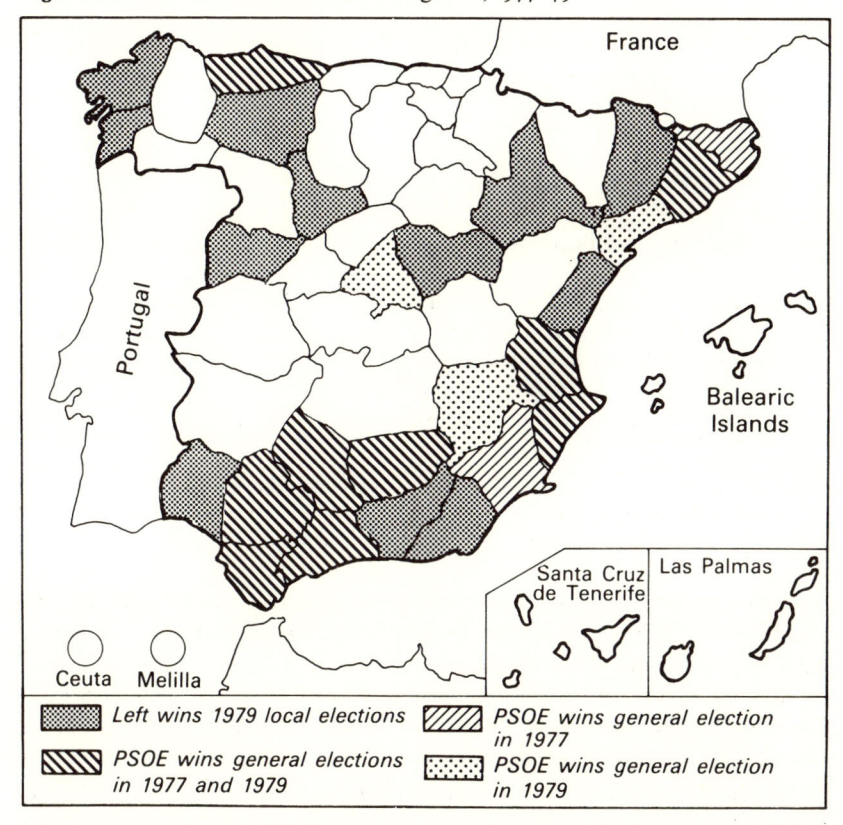

Figure 6.1 The Socialists' Electoral Strongholds, 1977-79

not seem to have been a very large departure from the pattern of the general elections.[31] Indeed, two trends apparent in the 1979 general election results were present again in the local elections, and both were very negative for the Socialist party. On the one hand, the PSOE lost still more support in Andalusia, where it had obtained a very high proportion of the votes in 1977. The independent Socialist party in Andalusia drained 188,125 votes away from the PSOE, 17.3 percent of the regional total. Thus the only Andalusian province and capital won by the PSOE were those of Málaga. The PSOE's losses were the PSA's gains—both parties together won a large majority over any other party. Simultaneously, except in Cádiz, the UCD lost votes in Andalusia. On the other hand, the municipal elections confirmed the weakness of the PSOE in the Basque country, where, except in Vizcaya, its share of the vote was still lower than in the general election one month before. The difficult and complex situation of the Basque country was further illustrated by the near absence of the other parties of the Spanish left, including the PCE. The PSOE could take little comfort

Table 6.3 Ecological Correlations of the PSOE, UCD, and PCE

		Correlation
1.	PSOE vote (1977) and proletarian areas[a]	.57
	PSOE vote (1977) and urban areas[b]	.46
2.	PSOE vote (1977) and UCD vote (1977)	−.50
	PSOE vote (1977) and PCE vote (1977)	.57
	PCE vote (1977) and UCD vote (1977)	−.59
3.	PSOE vote (1977) and PSOE vote (1979)	.79
	UCD vote (1977) and UCD vote (1979)	.88
	PSOE vote (1977) and PSOE municipal vote (1979)	.48
	UCD vote (1977) and UCD municipal vote (1979)	.69
	PCE vote (1977) and PCE municipal vote (1979)	.84

Source: Author.

[a] Measured by percentage of wage earners in the active provincial population.

[b] Measured by percentage of provincial population living in centers with more than 10,000 inhabitants where agriculture was not the predominant activity.

from the fact that it retained important support in some Basque working-class communities (such as Portugalete, Sestao, Baracaldo, and Basauri in Vizcaya; Irún, Rentería, and Eibar in Gupúzcoa).

The PSOE's most important electoral gains in the local elections came in Catalonia (all four provinces), Valencia (Valencia, Castellón, Murcia), Galicia (La Coruña, Orense, and Pontevedra, though here the PSOE remained well below the UCD), Asturias, and a large number of provinces in the northern half of the country that were right-wing strongholds (Teruel, Soria, Logroño, Zaragoza, Guadalajara, Valladolid, Segovia, Salamanca, León, and Palencia). The PSOE also won the province of Madrid. The eastern coast (Catalonia and Valencia), together with Asturias, now appeared to be the Socialists' strongholds, along with a few large cities in rural areas (Zaragoza, Valladolid, Málaga) and the province of Madrid. It was a very powerful position, but little more than a consolidation of the support already evident in 1977. Regional nationalism and abstention continued to harm the PSOE, impressive as its showing was for a party legalized only three years before.

Table 6.3 provides a series of ecological correlations of the Socialist vote. These correlations seem to indicate (1) an important association between proletarian/urban areas and the Socialist vote, (2) a considerable territorial overlapping between areas of Socialist strength and areas of Communist strength, and (3) a high degree of crystallization of the vote. It must be borne in mind that calculations of partisan municipal vote have been made through the aggregation of the municipalities of each province for which data are available; the correlations show, however, that the PSOE was the party whose progress was least associated with former areas of strength. This could be the starting point of a process of "colonization" of areas of weakness—if the PSOE also manages to maintain more stable support in some of its areas of strength than seems to have occurred.[32]

The Socialist share of the vote went from 29.3 percent in June 1977, to 30.5 percent in March 1979, to 35.4 percent in April 1979. Although the organizational, strategic, and ideological difficulties that the party faced were quite formidable, the "Italian scenario" did not seem likely to recur in Spanish politics in the foreseeable future. While the first general election had shown the important of "political memory" in the Socialist vote, the subsequent elections had suggested an important stability *and* extension of partisan support (with losses in Andalusia and the Basque country and successes in eastern, central, and northern Spain). It must be remembered that in only seven years, from 1946 to 1953, the Italian Socialists' vote collapsed from 20.9 to 12.7 percent, with the result that the DC and the PCI increased their share of the electorate from 54 percent in 1946 to 73 percent in 1976. It is of course difficult to pinpoint the political differences between Spain and Italy and between the competing parties;[33] that such differences exist, however, explains why the expectations of Spain's communist leaders since 1965 have been unfulfilled.

How can the largely unexpected Socialist electoral strength be accounted for? In search of the answer I shall examine, first, the interpretation that focuses on "political memory"—the persistence of political loyalty in particular sections of society. I shall also discuss the social foundations of partisan support to determine whether the PSOE represents the interests of a homogeneous or a heterogeneous population. Finally, I shall analyze the political-ideological views of Socialist supporters in order to see whether their ideological position fits that attributed to the PSOE.

"Political memory" and ideological continuities have characterized other societies that had experienced long disruptions of their party systems. Italy is one, where the degree of continuity was hardly less than in countries with stable party systems. But Italy was different from Spain in important respects: the source of its political continuity after Mussolini was essentially cultural; it had more to do with the persistence of a Catholic and a leftist subculture than with the specific organizations that would give these subcultures political expression. In Spain the PSOE was able to preserve a connection between the leftist subculture and the "traditional" political organization of the left, but the situation of the Spanish center and right was quite different. The UCD was heir to the CEDA tradition, but it also embraced a large part of the former Republican electorate.[34]

The continuity in the geographical distribution of leftist loyalties before and after the Francoist dictatorship was indeed remarkable. The major change was the Socialist party's success in former anarchist strongholds in Catalonia, Valencia, and southern Andalusia. At the same time, the left's influence persisted in its old areas of strength. The main difference thus was that the major component of this subculture after the dictatorship was socialism, in an otherwise surprisingly similar territorial distribution of ideological cleavages.

Thus the Spanish case did fit the argument that "the party alternatives, and in remarkably many cases the party organizations, are older than the majority of the national electorates."[35] This argument is obviously easier to defend for societies whose national party systems have been fundamentally stable: in such societies the institutionalization of political traditions leads to a highly crystallized party support, to what Butler and Stokes call "the tenacity of generalized partisan identification."[36] The argument, however, becomes much more perplexing when it applies to societies that have experienced a long disruption in their party systems, such as Italy or Spain, where what has been euphemistically termed "the forgetting process,"[37] associated with periods of nondemocratic rule, should replace the cultural transmission of partisanship.

Postwar Italian democracy has often been described as presenting strong continuities with the period before Mussolini. Samuel Barnes has stressed that "amazing political continuity between cohorts despite massive social change and political discontinuities," and several authors have shown the geographical persistence of political ideological loyalties.[38] As I have argued, however, political continuity in Italy refers more to broad tendencies than to support for specific parties; the PCI has replaced the PSI as the hegemonic political organization within what could be loosely called the Italian leftist political subculture, although this subculture has remained highly stable.[39] Broad ideological continuities between prefascist and postfascist Italy have been interpreted as a result of the political traditions of communities, the organizational strength of the parties, and, to use Converse's term, the "transmission process" (that is, the patterns of socialization that ensure the intergenerational transmission of political and parapolitical values). Communities, parties, and families would have acted as the "social carriers" of ideologies, beyond the restrictions and repressions of a nondemocratic regime.[40]

There is still very little empirical evidence on political continuities and discontinuities in Spain. That political continuity seems to be, again, a major question to be investigated by sociopolitical research is evident from the correlations between the pre-Francoist and the post-Francoist left-wing vote shown in table 6.4.[41] The data indicate a long-term stability of the electoral map of the left, despite dramatic changes in the Spanish economy and occupational structure and nearly four decades of dictatorship.

Table 6.4 Correlations between Pre- and Post-Francoist Left Wing Vote

	Correlation
PSOE vote (1931) and PSOE vote (1977)	.70
PSOE vote (1936) and PSOE vote (1977)	.61
Popular Front vote (1936) and PSOE vote (1977)	.50
PCE vote (1933) and PCE vote (1977)	.25
Popular Front vote (1936) and PCE vote (1977)	.69

Source: Author's calculations from official electoral returns.

Table 6.5 PSOE or UGT Background of Delegates to the Twenty-Eighth PSOE Congress, 1979

	Parents affiliated	Parents not affiliated	No answer
Male delegates	117	147	9
Female delegates	14	7	1
Total	131	154	10

Source: Survey carried out by the Secretariat of Organization of the PSOE, May–June 1979 ($N = 295$, or about 27 percent of delegates).

To interpret this stability we must explore the survival of left-wing loyalties in communities and families. Elsewhere I have studied this survival in enclaves of working-class militancy (miners in Asturias, metal and steel workers in the Basque country, Barcelona, and Madrid), as well as in the family backgrounds of working-class and student activists under Franco,[42] but the analyst must go beyond these atypical communities and political groups to explain voting patterns. That the intergenerational transmission of ideological orientations seems to be important for interpreting political continuities before and after forty years of dictatorship is suggested by the fact that as many as 37.3 percent of the delegates to the Twenty-eighth Congress of the PSOE were the children of parents who had been affiliated either to the PSOE or to the socialist trade union, the UGT (see table 6.5).[43] This finding suggests that the case of Spain would support the theory of intergenerational ideological transmission through processes of socialization within the family. It is true that other studies of party militants have shown higher percentages of ideological continuity,[44] but these refer to rather broad political orientations and not to intergenerational affiliation to the same organization. Moreover, the very low number of individuals in the Spanish sample who could not recall whether their parents had been affiliated must be contrasted with the roughly 73 percent of French and Italian voters who could not remember their fathers' political leanings; the difference

Table 6.6 Delegates with Socialist-Affiliated Parents, Twenty-Eighth PSOE Congress, 1979, by Region and Occupation

	Number of delegates from region or in occupational group	Percentage with socialist-affiliated parents
Region		
Andalusia	53	37.7
Asturias	30	63.3
New Castile (including Madrid)	48	45.8
Catalonia	37	21.6
Basque country	40	42.5
(Vizcaya only)	(20)	(75)
Valencia	35	40.0
Occupation		
Manual workers	49	61.4
Nonmanual workers	44	38.6
Civil servants and employees	44	20.5
Liberal professions	70	35.7

Source: Same as table 6.5.

could stem from the much higher political involvement of the sample of PSOE delegates.[45] Sani has noted: "In political systems characterized by basic discontinuities in the nature of the political regime ... there might be reasons to wonder whether the family plays an important role, simply because the transmission of orientations appropriate to a given political regime makes little sense in a drastically changed context."[46] Nevertheless, in Spain as in Italy, political socialization in the family encouraged "political memory."

The role of the family seems to have been reinforced by community and class traditions. Thus intergenerational partisan continuity is much stronger than elsewhere in those enclaves where the PSOE and UGT survived the dictatorship—the close-knit communities of Asturian miners and of metal and steel workers in Vizcaya. Continuity characterized 63.3 percent of the delegates from Asturias and 75 percent of the delegates from Vizcaya. Table 6.6 shows the regional and occupational background of delegates with socialist parents. It suggests that industrialized areas, homogeneous communities, and working-class collectivities reinforced the inheritance of socialism.

No empirical evidence is yet available on continuity in partisan support among socialist voters in general, but it would seem that the strength of socialism after Francoism must at least partially be examined from the point of view of the *cultural* and *organizational* survival of the PSOE—that is, *both* its underground politics *and* the persistence of political symbols, images, and perceptions (and hence loyalties) in particular sectors of Spanish society.

Which sectors were these? In other words, who came to support the PSOE once the dictatorship was over? I shall analyze this question from two points of view: first, by focusing on the social and ideological profile of Socialist supporters, both voters and militants; second, by looking at potential sources on interparty competition stemming from the ideological characteristics of partisan support.

Who voted Socialist in Spain? It had often been predicted that in post-Francoist Spain the PSOE would find its support not among the working class but in the "moderate" middle strata.[47] The strength of the PSOE would depend on its capacity to attract not a homogeneous section of the population but a heterogeneous electorate reflecting the national population as a whole. The argument that socialist parties increase their interclass appeal as they increase their voting support has been powerfully presented by Otto Kirchheimer.[48] Analyses of the PCI in Italy and of the PS in France have drawn on Kirchheimer's concept of the "catchall 'people's' party": thus Cayrol has shown the increasing similarity between the composition of the PS electorate and the composition of the French adult population since 1973. While the attraction of the PCF has remained limited to the working class and that of the *majority* prior to 1981 to the middle class, the PS has attracted support from all sectors —as much from the working class as the PCF and one-quarter of the liberal professions, the higher cadres, and the peasantry.[49] There is, of course, an apparent contradiction between a "class" party and a party that absorbs multiple sectors of society and fairly represents the overall occupational structure of the nation.[50] The Socialist reply to that apparent contradiction usually is that of socialization of production and the extension of large bureaucracies have produced a huge category of wage and salary earners, which, though profoundly different from the "traditional proletariat," has an "objective" interest in a modern Socialist project—as well as an increasingly "subjective" one.

Table 6.7 gives several background characteristics of socialist voters and militants in Spain, and it is possible to compare them with the traits of voters of the other main parties (UCD and PCE) as well as with those of the sample as a whole. Socialist voters and militants were rather more often in the lower income category and in the lower educational levels. Socialist voters were also more often male, thirty-five or under, and not practicing Catholics. Communist voters tended to be more educated, younger, more often male, and less often Catholic, and UCD voters showed just the opposite traits.

The occupational structure of the Socialist vote, however, is the crucial point

Table 6.7 Socioeconomic Background of Party Supporters (percent)

	PSOE Voters	PSOE Militants	PCE Voters	UCD Voters	Sample
Income					
35,000 pesetas or less	64	39	64	63	65
Over 35,000	36	61	36	37	35
Education					
Less than secondary	74	80	62	76	72
Secondary or more	26	20	38	24	28
Sex					
Male	51	91	65	41	48
Female	49	9	35	59	52
Age					
35 or under	45	28	53	37	37
Over 35	55	72	47	63	63
Religion					
Practicing Catholics	32	23	15	73	54

Source: EMOPUBLICA survey for the PSOE, May 1979 (with don't know and no answer excluded, $N = 3,077$).

regarding the arguments about catchall parties. Table 6.8 gives the 1979 distribution of the party vote within each broad occupational category. The internal distribution of the PSOE vote did differ much from that of the electorate as a whole. It was the overrepresentation of the working class (particularly of skilled workers) that was most atypical. The results were markedly similar to those of other surveys, both of national samples and of industrial workers only.[51] The data examined in tables 6.7 and 6.8 suggest that the underprivileged, working-class component was still important in the electoral support of the PSOE and that none of the other main parties, on either its left or its right, could attract a similar proportion of the working class. The PSOE, then, retained its class appeal in 1979 while at the same time winning an important share of the middle-class, white-collar, and peasant vote—a higher share, apparently, than that achieved by the PS in France.

All left-wing parties face the difficulty of making compatible what Cayrol has called their "class preferential linkage" and their "social linkage"; they strive to be the political embodiment of a class, to follow a "class mandate," and to carry out an egalitarian (or "class preferential") program while at the same time attracting majoritarian electoral support and a national mandate and defending a program that takes into account all interests. It may well be that the historical development of capitalist society makes this possible—if not by reducing all sectors of society to a massive homogeneous class, then perhaps by creating enough common interests between different social groups that a socialist program can defend them all. Certainly this is the view held by the PCI or the PS, whatever the differences of nuance, and it is also the view of the PSOE.[52] The theory of the catchall party offers a very different interpretation, however: a catchall party would pay little attention to ideology, and the commitments and loyalties of its supporters would not be intense. This is why Parisi and Pasquino are opposed to analyzing the development of the PCI in terms of the evolution of a catchall party: to the extent that ideology is not abandoned, that winning elections is not the only goal, that internal democracy matters, a party of the left (and the PCI in particular) cannot be seen to conform to Kirchheimer's type.[53]

I shall examine now the political universes of PSOE supporters and compare them with those of supporters of the UCD and the PCE, the Socialists' main rivals on the right and the left in the first years of democracy. Finally, I shall discuss briefly the ideological dilemmas of Spanish socialism. This last part of the chapter will allow us to see whether the case of the Spanish Socialist party confirms the familiar theory that it is in the least-advanced industrialized countries that communism has proved to be stronger than socialism and the related argument that leftist ideologies become diluted with economic development.[54]

The voters' self-placement and their placement of parties on a left-right

Table 6.8 Party Vote of Occupational Groups, May 1979 (percent)

Occupation	PSOE	PCE	UCD	N
Inactive	34.6	7.7	41.6	1,623
Workers				
Skilled	45.0	16.5	24.3	455
Unskilled	41.6	13.1	29.1	161
Agricultural laborers	41.9	19.0	28.9	105
Employees, civil servants, liberal professionals	34.9	8.6	34.7	392
Small landowners	30.3	3.1	57.6	76
Independent workers	32.7	12.2	38.9	217
Managers, businessmen, employers	19.1	5.4	47.4	47
N	(1,117)	(307)	(1,150)	(3,077)

Source: EMOPUBLICA survey for the PSOE, May 1979.
Note: The entries are percentages of the stated occupational group who voted for the stated party. "no answer" excluded.

152 The Socialist Alternative

Figure 6.2 Left-Right Self-Placement of Party Voter

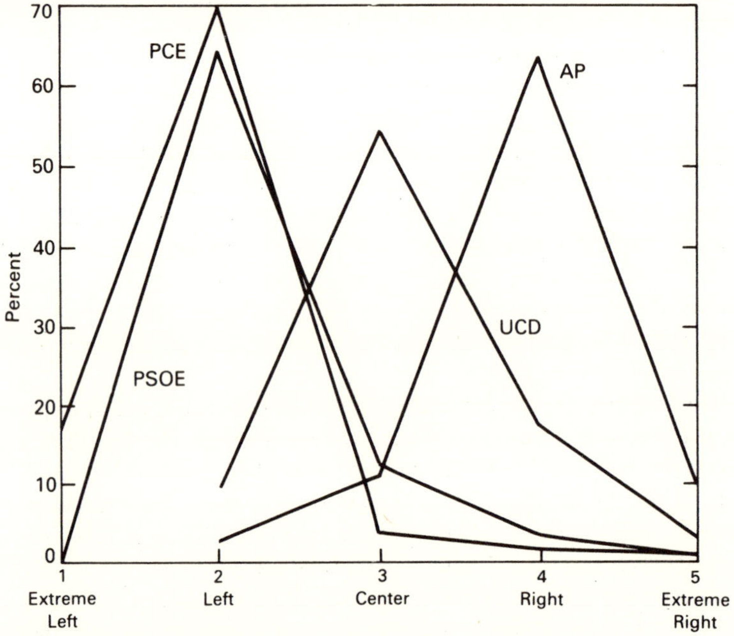

[Figure: Line graph showing percent (0-70) on y-axis versus left-right position (1 Extreme Left, 2 Left, 3 Center, 4 Right, 5 Extreme Right) on x-axis, with curves for PCE, PSOE, UCD, and AP.]

Source: CIS survey, July–August 1978.

continuum have been the subject of endless academic discussion. It has been argued, on the one hand, that the subjective political space of the electors is highly structured, that there is a great deal of general agreement on the position of the parties and the electors, and that this left-right identification can predict party preference.[55] On the other hand, it has been argued that "partisanship" does not follow "ideological position," that the left-right identification has only peripheral importance in the subjective political universe of the individual and no bearing on his party commitment—indeed, that ideological position is only a way of labeling partisanship.[56] It is important to note, however, that the importance of the individual's identification of himself and parties on the left-right dimension appears to vary cross-culturally: thus, while only one-quarter of British voters cared to identify their position in the left-right continuum, 76 percent of Italian voters and 85 to 90 percent of French voters were prepared to do so.[57] If we turn to Spain, 69 percent of the voters indicated their left-right position (90 percent of Communist voters, 81 percent of Socialist voters, 81 percent of UCD supporters). Thus I would agree with Sartori that the variable *left-right subjective identification* has possibilities and limitations rooted in national cultures. It is clear, however, that as an independent predictor of the vote it explains only a small part of the variance: the assumption of "spatial rationality" is only one factor in determining choice.

Figures 6.2 to 6.5 show the 1979 distribution of the supporters (voters and militants) of the main Spanish parties on a five-point, left-right continuum. The average self-ranking of the PSOE voter on this five-point, left-right scale 2.23, that of the Communist voter was 1.71, and that of the UCD voter was 3.14. The figures show an extensive overlapping between the Socialist and Communist pyramids: 68 percent of PCE voters situated themselves at point two of the continuum, as did 65 percent of Socialist voters. The overlap in the ideological space of socialists and communists is again remarkable if we consider PSOE and PCE militants (figure 6.3). Some differences emerged, however, if we limit ourselves to voters and divide the second point, "left," into two alternatives, "left" and "center-left." In this case, 20 percent of PSOE voters

Figure 6.3 Left-Right Self-Placement of Party Militants

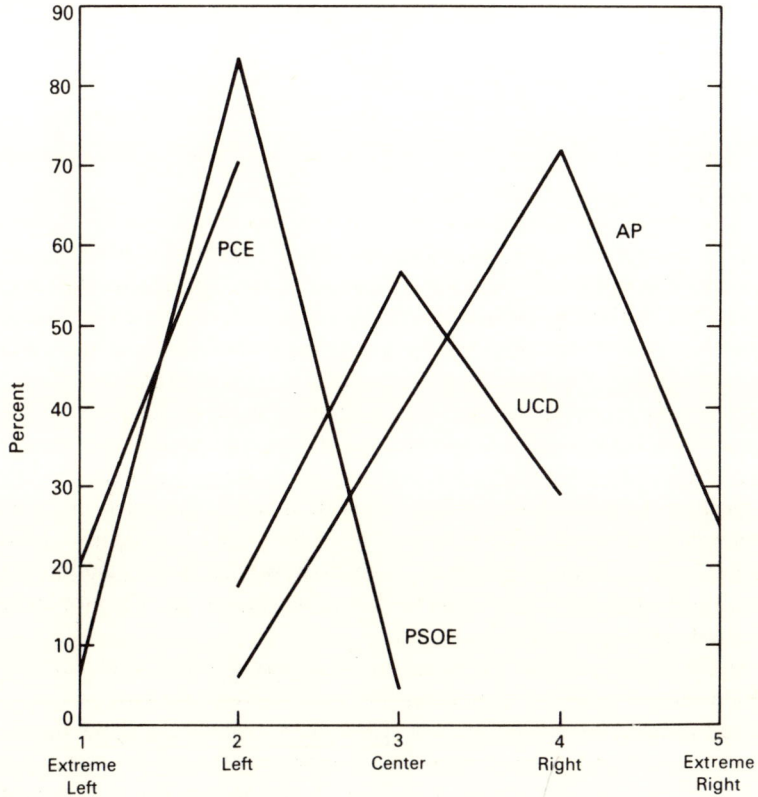

Source: CIS Survey, July–August 1978.

154 The Socialist Alternative

Figure 6.4 Voters' Left-Right Placement of Parties

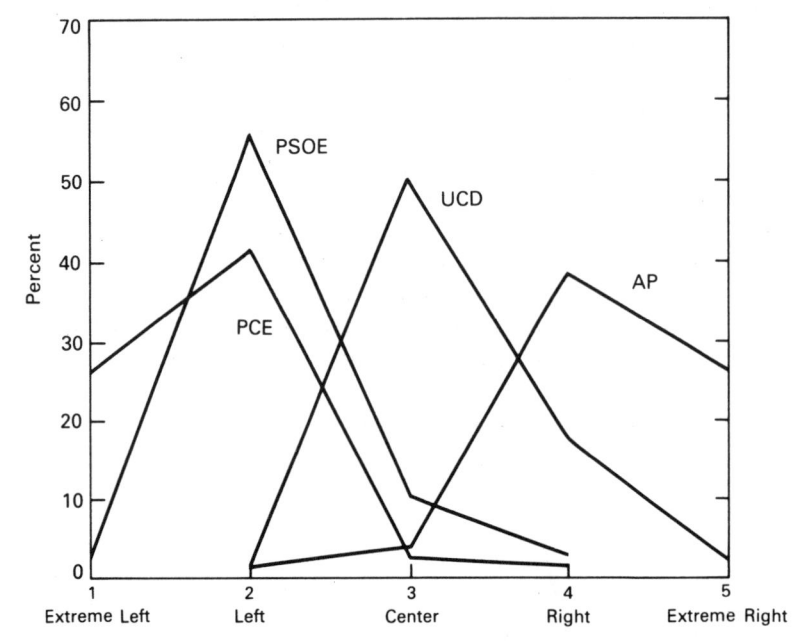

Source: CIS survey, July–August 1978.

located themselves in the first and 45 percent in the second, while the corresponding figures for PCE voters are 46 and 22 percent. The internal distribution of the "left" within the two parties was thus diametrically opposed. It must be remembered, however, that, because the Socialist electorate was much larger, the PSOE's share of the pure left vote was still much greater than that of the PCE (45.2 versus 27.0 percent), as was a fortiori its share of the center-left vote (55.9 versus 7.1 percent). Thus the PSOE attracted a much larger section of both areas of the left in 1979, but the more moderate part contained a higher proportion of socialist voters. (The center-left area was also much larger in the electorate as a whole.) The proximity of Socialist and Communist voters is revealed again in figures 6.4 and 6.5, which show where voters and militants, respectively, placed the parties on the five-point continuum. The PSOE and PCE pyramids again considerably overlapped.

Aside from numerical rankings and scores, there are three issues that should should shed some light on the image the voters have of the PSOE as a party of the left differentiated from the PCE. These three issues refer to the degree to which the party was seen as the political representative of the working class and to the extent of its radicalism (including whether the PSOE is a Marxist or a social democratic party). Answers are given in table 6.9 for PSOE and PCE voters, for skilled and unskilled manual workers (what Cayrol called the "preferential link" of both parties), and for the electorate as a whole.

These data would suggest that the PSOE was widely seen as the main working-class party in the Spanish party system, and as one which stood in a moderate left-wing position. It is worth mentioning that a higher percentage of workers than of the general electorate saw the PSOE as a working-class party and that the largest share of workers and Socialist voters saw it as a social democratic party.

Inferences from this information, however, must be drawn with caution. Thus, when PSOE voters and militants were asked to indicate to which tendency of the party they felt ideologically closer, almost nine times as many of the voters aligned themselves with the left as with the right; the percentage of

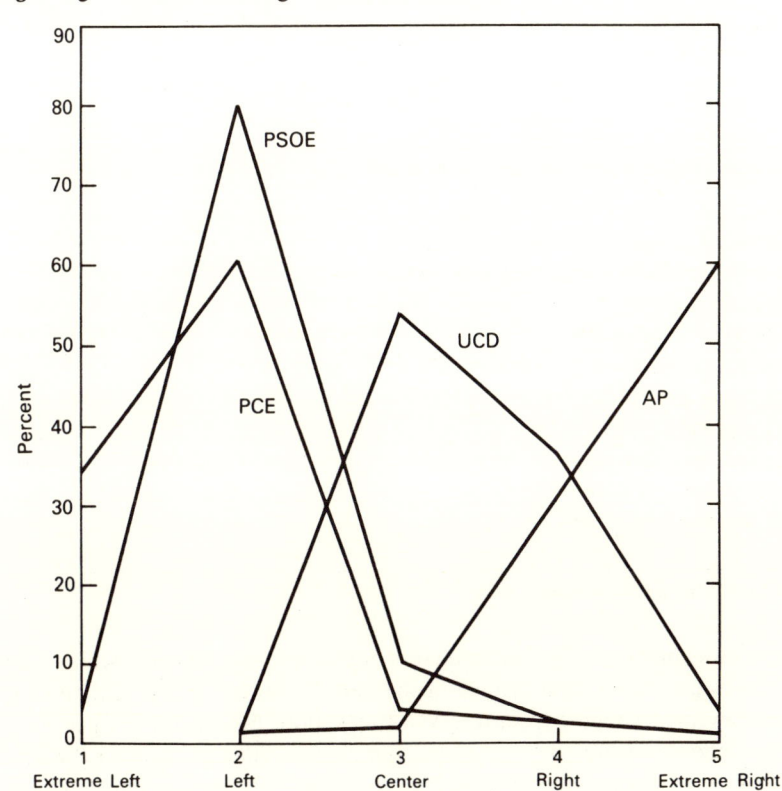

Figure 6.5 Militants' Left-Right Placement of Parties

Source: CIS survey, July–August 1978.

156   The Socialist Alternative

Table 6.9 How "Left" Is the PSOE? (percent)

Survey question	PSOE voters	PCE voters	Skilled workers	Unskilled workers	Total electorate
Which party is more working class?					
PSOE	47.7	7.0	37.6	38.2	34.4
PCE	21.2	73.7	29.9	22.1	24.3
Which party is more to the left?					
PSOE	8.6	2.4	6.5	8.1	5.6
PCE	63.0	83.7	67.4	57.3	60.0
Is the PSOE					
a Marxist party?	19.6	11.7	19.3	16.6	18.0
a social democratic party?	41.5	56.5	46.3	33.2	33.4
N	(1,117)	(307)	(573)	(217)	(4,175)

Source: EMOPUBLICA survey for the PSOE, May 1979

Table 6.10 Support for Ideological and Strategic Tendencies within the PSOE (percent)

Tendency	PSOE Militants	PSOE Voters
Left wing	43	26
Right wing	1	3
Against a turn to left	8	15
Against a turn to right	55	43
For an alliance with the PCE	57	37
For an alliance with the UCD	36	37
N	(86)	(1,229)

Source: CIS Survey, July–August 1978.

leftists was higher still for the militants (see table 6.10). When Socialist supporters were asked what change in the party's strategy might lead them to withdraw their support from it, seven times more militants and three times more voters answered a "turn to the right" rather than a "turn to the left." Left-wing alliances were preferred to center-left alliances among militants, although PSOE voters gave equal support to both (which suggests that many did not see alliance with the UCD as a turn to the right).

A majority of Socialist voters and Socialist militants, then, appeared to have a perception of the party characterized by the following traits: (1) they placed both the party and themselves at left or center of the left-right continuum, (2) they ranked the PSOE high on a sympathy scale, far above the other parties, but of these they ranked the PCE higher than the UCD; (3) they saw the party as more working class than any other; (4) they tended to support a strategy of moderate leftism, conceiving the PCE as clearly to their left and viewing the PSOE as social democratic; (5) they seemed to oppose any move by the party toward the right of its present position; (6) they saw themselves as part of the left wing of the party; (7) they had no clear preferences as between left and center alliances. Most of these views about the PSOE were strongly held by one central element of the Socialist electorate: manual workers, especially skilled workers.

There was thus a desire for radical change and at the same time a desire for moderation, not unconditional change and pure leftism among Socialist voters in 1979. To analyze in detail the content of such expectations lies beyond the scope of this chapter. But it is worth asking what sort of impact Socialist voters—and Spanish voters at large—thought that the PSOE would have on Spanish society if it came to power (see table 6.11). If "no answers" are excluded, two-thirds of the Socialist voters and half of the electorate expected important changes in Spanish society if the PSOE were to come to power. As I have said, the content and direction of the change expected may vary: the PSOE has attracted an electorate that is quite heterogeneous. To what extent can the PSOE reconcile these different interests and aggregate them in a Socialist strategy and program? To what extent would such a program produce significant changes in the structure of Spanish society?

To the first question, one answer that has found an important echo within the PSOE is the strategy of "class front," or "class bloc," put forward by the PS and the PCI, which has its roots in Gramscian thought. The leadership of the PSOE has repeatedly stressed the need for a Socialist program to represent all "dependent" sectors of society; economic and social exploitation on the one

Table 6.11 Change Expected under a Socialist Government (percent)

If a socialist government were elected, Spanish society would undergo:	PSOE Voters	All Voters
Important changes	66	49
Small changes	28	35
No changes at all	6	16
Total	100.0	100.0
N	(1,117)	(4,921)

Source: EMOPUBLICA survey for the PSOE, May 1979.

hand and political and ideological domination on the other are seen as the common denominator of such a front or bloc.[58] A second answer, also of Gramscian origin is the strategy of "penetration of civil society by the party": by establishing its "presence" in all areas of society, the party would increase both its grass-roots support and its ideological penetration. These parallel strategic directions, the "class bloc" and "presence in civil society," would produce, according to this view, an open political organization, receptive to the demands of different sectors of society and capable of overcoming the political apathy widespread in the new Spanish democracy. In addition, the Socialists distinguished between "institutional politics" (*política institucional*) and "mobilization politics" (*política reivindicativa*), which together would reconcile reforms from above with exigencies from below and which would complement parliamentary with extraparliamentary action.

What has been the PSOE's program for social transformation? I think it has three main objectives: (1) an egalitarian reform of society affecting, for example, income distribution, education, health, social security, and housing policies, (2) a democratic transformation of the state including both devolution of power to regional and national communities within Spain and full political openness and accountability of the state apparatus, especially the state-controlled media, the police, and areas of civil service, and (3) a more dynamic role for the public sector. In this third area a PSOE government would seek three goals: to prune down "public waste," which had grown under Francoism with the absorption of unprofitable firms, and cut back nonredistributive components of public expenditure; to encourage growth and employment through a more efficient, profitable, and larger public sector; and to redistribute wealth, both geographically and between social groups.

Clearly this program has important similarities to those of the PS and the PCI; no wonder PSOE leaders have sometimes acknowledged common ground with these parties.[59] Particularly since the summer of 1977, the PSOE has faced the same dilemmas and difficulties as other Western European parties in finding a distinctively socialist program of social transformation that is credible, attractive, and politically feasible.

Obviously, such difficulties have been increased by the permanent threats to the new democratic order in Spain; the basic question, however, remains: how is it possible to implement a program of social egalitarianism and political participation within a pluralist system that is also immune to subversive challenges, either military or economic? This question is obviously much more serious when it is faced by a party that may accede to power.[60] The problem of finding an answer was one cause of the organizational crisis within the PSOE following the party's Twenty-eighth Congress in May 1979,[61] as well as of the debate precipitated by Felipe González in Barcelona in May 1978 when he spoke out against the PSOE's self-definition as a Marxist party—a debate that, though largely symbolic, tore the party apart.

The history of the PSOE has been one of deep internal conflicts and strains. Often dramatic, sometimes tragic, these have reflected the basic difficulties that beset the European left. Historical events, unfortunately, do not always repeat themselves as farce. It is true that the PSOE's electorate has remained stable, for three reasons discussed in this chapter: the persistence of "political memory," the party's ability to attract the largest share of the working-class vote and significant support from other social sectors, and the ideological proximity of the party and its voters.

People and parties help make their own history. If the PSOE can keep the traditional strains under control, it will go on disproving the thesis of communist preponderance in countries where industrial capitalism is less advanced. If the PSOE can overcome the historical tension between revolution and reform and move beyond the dilemmas that produce strategic paralysis—most likely in the direction of what has been called "revolutionary reformism" or "constitutional radicalism"[62]—it will also disprove the thesis of the irrelevance of left-wing politics in industrialized societies. At the same time, it will strengthen democracy in Spain.

The Spanish Communists and the Search for Electoral Space

EUSEBIO M. MUJAL-LEÓN

———The first elections of the post-Franco era not only signaled the return of democracy to Spain, they also marked the formal entry of the Spanish Communist party (PCE) into the political arena. Operating illegally after the end of the Civil War in 1939, the PCE had functioned for most of the Franco years as the most effective opposition force in the country. That background and the moderate domestic policies and independent international line pursued by the Spanish Communists suggested that the PCE might assume a dominant position on the left and play a decisive role in the politics of a democratic Spain. But the June 1977 and March 1979 parliamentary elections showed otherwise.

The Spanish Communists captured 9.4 percent of the national vote in June 1977 and received just over 1.7 million votes. This was enough to make them the third largest electoral force in the country, but they trailed well behind the Union of the Democratic Center (UCD), led by incumbent Prime Minister Adolfo Suárez and a resurgent Spanish Socialist Workers Party (PSOE), which took 34.4 and 29.3 percent, respectively. As it was, despite the claims PCE leaders had made in the early 1970s about the future role and influence of their party, the Spanish Communists' performance in June 1977 did not compare favorably with either that of the French and Italian Communists in the post–World War II period or with the 15 percent the Portuguese party polled in April 1976. The PCE did well only in the four Catalan provinces (where it secured eight deputies and over 550,000 votes, 18 percent of the national total) and in parts of Andalusia (five deputies and nearly 250,000 votes in Cádiz, Córdoba, Málaga, and Seville). In the conflict-ridden Basque country and in Galicia, the party did not capture a single chamber seat, and even in Madrid and Asturias, where the PCE had been thought to have much influence, it barely topped 10 percent of the vote. PCE leaders could take solace only from the fact that the various extreme left groups—still illegal in June 1977 and forced to run in electoral fronts under assumed names—did considerably worse. Nevertheless, even if they received less than 3 percent of the national vote, this was more than a third of the PCE vote (without counting left nationalist groups) in 1979.

There was no dramatic increase in the Communist vote in the second parliamentary elections, held in March 1979. Once again, the PCE emerged as the third largest force in the country, increasing its percentage 10.8 and its votes to over 1.9 million. These gains, well below what many Communist leaders and militants had expected, left little room for optimism. Particularly worrisome for the party was its continued inability to do well in two major Spanish regions, the Basque country and Galicia. Yet there were favorable signs too, suggesting that the party might eventually be able to narrow the gap separating it from the PSOE. For one thing, the Communist party was the only national organization to increase its vote in March 1979 in absolute terms, which it did in all but ten of the fifty-one constituencies where it presented candidates. The gains were especially notable in Madrid, Seville, and Valencia, where the PCE picked up an additional 130,000 votes. Significantly, the Communists took more than 10 percent of the vote in fifteen provinces, up from nine in 1977.

This chapter analyzes the Spanish Communists' performance in the first two elections in the post-Franco era. The first section assesses the reasons for the Communists' failure in June 1977. The second section focuses on the degree to which the efforts the Communists made to reverse the verdict of 1977 were successful two years later, with closer looks at several important regions and provinces. The concluding section sizes up the prospects for Spanish communism.

The 1977 Elections

In the months and weeks preceding the June 1977 elections, the Spanish Communist party ran an electoral campaign aimed at overcoming the bitter memories many Spaniards had of the PCE's conduct during the Civil War and the virulent anti-Communist propaganda the Franco regime had promoted for four decades. They tried to put across the image of a moderate, profoundly democratic party that had abandoned all reliance on Leninist methods of seizing power as well as any subservience to the Soviet Union. Basking in the limelight of Eurocommunism, one of whose principal exponents the PCE had become, Communist leaders ceaselessly reminded their audiences of their commitment to political and civil rights and the rules of parliamentary democracy. It was in keeping with the general spirit of the campaign that at one rally in the province of Teruel the Communist candidates for the Chamber spent two hours addressing the crowd and did not mention the word "communism" once.[1]

The political and economic program the PCE presented to the nation placed special emphasis on the need for measures to ensure the consolidation of the democratic system. Unable to carry through on plans for a provisional government to be set up to oversee the elections and rule the country during the transition to the post-Franco era,[2] the Communists called in early 1977 for the creation of an "arc of constitutional parties" ranging from the UCD to the socialists and the Communists to agree on a new national charter.[3]

The economic component of the Spanish Communist program was similarly unprovocative.[4] It gave no hint of socialist transformations, and, although the PCE rejected any suggestion that it might agree to anything resembling a *social pact*, the party showed a willingness to enter negotiations with other groups with a view to setting up a four-or five-year plan for economic recuperation. Their only condition, PCE leader Santiago Carrillo declared, was that "the sacrifices and advantages be adequately distributed."[5] Specifically, the PCE called for extensive fiscal reform, an end to urban speculation, and that priority be given to restoring confidence among small and medium entrepreneurs. All in all, the Communists' economic program could be judged less radical than that of the socialists. Whereas the PCE generally avoided the subject of nationalization (declaring that expropriation with compensation would be indispensable in the longer run, but that the issue should not be raised until democracy had been consolidated), the PSOE talked as if the nationalization of banking and credit institutions and energy-related industries were realizable in the not too distant future.

The Campaign The Communists ran one of the best-organized campaigns. The size and orderliness of their rallies were impressive. One rally at Torrelodones outside Madrid and another at Gavá on the outskirts of Barcelona attracted over 500,000 people. (Such displays, on the other hand, helped mislead Communist leaders: after the June elections, it was evident that in places like Vizcaya, Seville, and Santander, to name only a few, Communist rallies had attracted more people than had voted for the party.) The PCE also organized work sessions where lawyers instructed militants and sympathizers on how to function as poll watchers (*interventores*). In Barcelona, Madrid, and some other large cities, the party mobilized thousands of these poll watchers in an effort to minimize vote fraud. The strategy was particularly effective in Madrid, where the Communists were able to successfully challenge a sufficient number of votes to retrieve an apparently lost Chamber seat. Because the poll watchers also participated in the vote-counting procedure, the PCE was able to tabulate the results coming in from urban centers long before the government itself. Indeed, in some localities officials verified their numbers against those of the Communists in the hours after the polls closed.

The PCE directed most of its campaign fire at the Popular Alliance (AP) and its leader, Manuel Fraga Iribarne. "*Fraga, el pueblo no te traga*" (Fraga, the people won't swallow you) became a favorite slogan at rallies, and Carrillo declared on more than one occasion that the former minister of the interior belonged in an insane asylum. Suárez, on the other hand, received little or no criticism. The strategy had its logic, but, as we shall see when we discuss the Communists' performance in specific regions, it may well have hurt the PCE. Only once in a while did Carrillo lash out at the prime minister. For the most part, attacks on Suárez were left to second-ranking figures in the party like Simón Sánchez Montero or Ramón Tamames. This may have been because after a secret meeting between the two men in early January 1977 at which Carrillo had rejected a Suárez proposal that the PCE run in the elections under a different name and wait for legalization until after 15 June, they had developed a respect for each other's political abilities.

Next to the AP, the favorite Communist targets were Felipe González and the PSOE. True, Communist leaders could be heard to insist that the PSOE was a natural ally in the struggle for socialism, with more in common with the PCE than divided them; but they also strongly attacked the PSOE for its "social democratic" orientation. The PCE held several things against González and his party. In the first place there was the fact that for the Senate races the PSOE had allied itself with Joaquín Ruiz Giménez and José María Gil Robles's Christian Democratic Federation rather than with the Communists. Second, and perhaps more important, the PSOE, through a combination of skill and luck, seemed first in line to reap the fruits of what the PCE considered were its unique contributions to the anti-Franco struggle and the democratization process. All the more since Carrillo and other PCE leaders had been important members of the PSOE left wing before the Civil War and had abandoned it after becoming convinced that only the Communist party could lead the Spanish working class to socialism, it was difficult for many Communists to accept the notion that the PSOE was far ahead of them in the opinion polls.[6]

The Results The PCE's performance was not altogether unexpected, but it disappointed the Communists deeply. For one thing, garnering only 9.4 percent of the total vote constituted a political defeat of the first order: only a year before, the PCE had been telling its militants that reform of the Francoist system was bound to fail and exhorting them to press forward and lay claim to "the hegemonic role in the process of change."[7] By late 1976, of course, the PCE had changed its public stance on this score and indicated a willingness to accept the reality of Adolfo Suárez's reforms once the party had been legalized.

During the early stages of the campaign, PCE leaders had tried not to raise the expectations of their militants unduly. Instead of dwelling on the party's prospects, they emphasized the importance of minimizing the AP vote and bringing about a working center-left majority in the new Cortes. As election day approached, however, some Communist leaders, buoyed by the impressive turnout at rallies, began to talk of a surprising showing by "the party that had struggled most vigorously against the dictatorship and for democracy."[8]

After 15 June the militants who had listened to them had to be reassured. Carrillo did his best to comfort them, describing the Communist vote as "honorable" and emphasizing that the "most dynamic sectors of the population" had supported his party.[9] The Communist vote, he said, had "an enormous expansive capacity," and the vote certainly did not match the "outpouring of heroism and sacrifice" the PCE had made during the Franco years.[10]

The Central Committee met in late June to analyze the party's performance. In rationalizing their defeat, Communist leaders underscored the fact that their party, illegal until less than two months before the elections, could not in the space of a few weeks have overcome the effects of forty years of anti-Communist propaganda, especially when radio and television still remained under the influence and control of the government. Moreover, they said, there was the electoral system under which the balloting took place. The Suárez government had fashioned a law that quite clearly discriminated against the left. Although it purported to set up a system of proportional representation, its provisions worked against the smaller parties and overrepresented the more conservative, agricultural parts of the country. The electoral law discriminated in other ways as well. It set the voting age at twenty-one, keeping out some 2 million young people among whom the left generally and the PCE in particular had gained an audience, and it placed numerous obstacles in the way of the more than half a million Spaniards working abroad.

The extent of the Communist defeat in 1977 was magnified by the PSOE's remarkable performance. The Spanish Socialist Workers' party received three times as many votes as the PCE and captured 118 seats in the Chamber, 47 in the Senate. Calling the Socialist vote "disposable," "transitory," and "nonmilitant," Carrillo explained to the Central Committee in late June that the PSOE had done so well because it had been legalized earlier than the Communists and had been shown greater toleration by the regime. He threw down the gauntlet with the charge that the Socialists had found support among the "bourgeoisie," who believed the PSOE more able to attract foreign investment, and among workers, who thought it "in a better position to enter the government." The PCE, he went on, had been victimized by fear. It had been unable to overcome the atmosphere created at the time of the legalization of the party by statements like that of the army officers who expressed "revulsion" at the government's decision.[11]

The Aftermath As we can see, the PCE leadership left few stones unturned in their efforts to explain away the Communist showing in the June 1977 elections. Many of the arguments made sense, but they were hardly a sufficient explanation. Indeed, after 15 June Communist leaders worked hard at blaming extrinsic factors instead of taking a careful look at their own analyses and strategy.

The Spanish Communists had assumed that the influence they exerted as the best-organized opposition force in the country could easily be translated into electoral strength. They were wrong about this, as they were wrong in thinking that the virulence of their public disagreements with Moscow after the Czech invasion would overcome the visceral distrust many Spaniards felt for the PCE. In my book *Communism and Political Change in Spain*, I outline in some detail the policies the Spanish Communist party followed during this period with respect to such important sectors of society as the labor movement and the Catholic church and subculture as well as its ideological and organizational evolution and the development of its foreign policy. I argue there that the Communist leaders not only misjudged and overestimated the efficacy of their efforts within Spain but also failed to go far enough in shedding the undemocratic attitudes and habits that had been part of the PCE for so long. These failures might not have mattered quite as much had the Communists managed to wrest the political initiative from King Juan Carlos and Prime Minister Suárez in the year after Franco's death. But the fact is they did not. Unable to galvanize the forces necessary to impose a clean break between the Francoist past and the democratic future, the PCE could not capitalize on its organizational superiority. The success of the *reforma* over the *ruptura* option thus worked to the advantage not only of the UCD but of the PSOE.

Communist discussions of the June 1977 election invariably emphasized the negative impact forty years of antiCommunist propaganda had had on the Spanish electorate. They were right, of course, but there was more to it than that. Did not the propaganda have some factual basis, and did not the PCE's analysis of the changes needed in Spanish society bear the imprint of the Civil War and of the hatred Communist leaders and militants had developed toward the regime? Certainly the success PCE had had with a Popular Front strategy during the Civil War encouraged the party leadership to pursue its broad alliance strategies and the prescient call for "National Reconciliation" in 1956.[12] But the PCE did not emerge from the war with particularly clean hands, and there was no self-criticism, no public apology, for the Spanish communists' role in the assassination of Andreu Nín by the Soviet secret police and of Leon Trotsky by a Catalan Communist in Mexico, for the slavish adherence to Stalinist directives, or for the deaths of Anarchists at the hands of party members in Catalonia in 1937 and 1938. The enmities engendered by the Civil War isolated the Communists on both their right and their left. The Communist insistence that the Franco regime could not be reformed but had to be brought down (a view the PCE did not abandon formally until 1976) also led many people to wonder about the Communists' commitment to moderation. Other groups in the opposition (including the PSOE) subscribed to the thesis that there had to be a clear break with Francoism, but it is likely that Spaniards took the Communist position a bit more seriously, saw the PCE as more radical and likely to carry through on its intentions than the other parties. Indeed, one survey showed 40 percent of the Spanish electorate as believing the PCE did not have the skill to prevent a confrontation between Spaniards.[13] To an electorate whose dominant desire was to forget the Civil War and the quarrels that had engendered it and move quickly toward psychopolitical integration with Europe, the Communists resurrected unwelcome memories. Their still fresh statements about the unviability of the Suárez reform program suggested a desire to reverse, not simply to forget, the verdict of the Civil War. Indeed, all who watched Santiago Carrillo on his one nationally televised campaign appearance in June 1977 saw a man whose repeated references to the war indicated he had failed to lay down the burdens of the past.

The moderation of the Communist campaign may well have backfired. Had the PCE acted less "responsibly" during the transition, Suárez could easily have delayed its legalization until after the elections. Indeed, Communist leaders justified the moderate policies they pursued by alluding to that possibility and to the danger of an involution toward authoritarian government. This approach may have convinced some restive rank and filers of the virtues of restraint — but posing the alternatives as democracy and dictatorship and raising the specter of *pinochetismo* probably scared away some voters.

The PSOE undoubtedly benefited from this state of affairs. Led by a vigorous and photogenic thirty-four-year-old first secretary named Felipe González, the PSOE was successful in its effort to project a reformist image along with a commitment to thorough-going change. The PSOE retained its allegiance to Marxism, but the Marxism of the early twentieth century, not that of Lenin and Stalin. Unlike the Communist party, it had never been subservient to Moscow. The PSOE had always been unabashedly pro-European. Continental socialists like Willy Brandt, François Mitterrand, Pietro Nenni, and Olaf Palme lent their prestige to a campaign that offered the PSOE as the best vehicle for European integration. This was important at a time when Spaniards badly wanted their country accepted at last as a full and equal partner in Europe. The PSOE, as José María Maravall notes in his chapter, was also helped by the phenomenon of historical memory and the return to the Socialist family of many Spaniards who, though never themselves members of the party or its trade union, remembered some relative who had been.

The Socialists' success in preempting what might have been the political space of Eurocommunism in Spain was partly due to the ambiguities of the Communists' evolution and campaign. There was, for example, the openly pro-Soviet attitude adopted by the eighty-three-year-old president of the PCE, Dolores Ibárruri, upon her return from exile in Moscow in early May 1977.

The Spanish Communists had gone to great lengths in the years after 1968 to demonstrate their independence vis-à-vis the Soviet Union. Relations had deteriorated sharply, and in early 1977 in a book entitled *"Eurocommunismo" y Estado* Santiago Carrillo had questioned the socialist nature of the Soviet system (an unprecedented step for the secretary general of a Communist party in Western Europe), implying that deep structural changes would be necessary before it could claim that status.[14] The presence of Ibárruri on the Communist list in Asturias and her statements during the campaign did little to shore up what credibility Carrillo had developed on this score. Although her appearances were short (Ibárruri suffered from a heart ailment and was growing senile), she wasted no opportunity to tell her audiences about the accomplishments of the Soviet bloc.[15] Indeed, her defense of the Soviet Union was so strong at times that on more than one occasion Carrillo felt compelled to explain away her remarks, reminding people that she had, after all, lived nearly forty years in Moscow and had lost her only son fighting in the Russian army at Stalingrad in World War II. Ibárruri was, of course, essentially a symbolic figure within the PCE. She wielded little effective power, but her statements lauding "those countries where socialism is being built," when coupled with the unwillingness of others in the leadership to address the issues forthrightly, undoubtedly raised questions about how deep Eurocommunist doctrine ran in the PCE.

Communist organizational practice raised similar doubts. The leadership openly admitted that during the Franco era their party (like all the others) had emphasized centralism over democracy. That was the only way, they argued, the PCE could have survived the rigors of clandestinity. They promised that once democracy were restored and the party legalized, they would put the combat-party model aside and begin the full democratization of PCE internal structures.[16] There was progress in this regard in the year and a half after Franco's death, but the Communist record up to and during the campaign did not help the party recast its image among liberal intellectuals and others. The candidates were selected behind closed doors, with the decision as to which individuals would run and in what slot left largely in the hands of the Central Electoral Commission, especially those of its members who also sat on the Secretariat. The Central Committee, ostensibly the highest policy-making body in the party between congresses, was there to rubber-stamp the results. That would not have been so bad had the party leadership permitted at least a semblance of debate on these matters at the various provincial conferences that met during the spring. Instead, when individual members of the party or units like the lawyers' group in Madrid sought to spark a debate on organizational questions or specific party policies, they were quickly cut off.[17] The most glaring confirmation that old methods still had quite an influence in the PCE came in mid-April 1977 when the Central Committee dropped the traditional

Communist opposition to the monarchy and its flag. The members of the Central Committee took what was for the PCE a decision fraught with symbolism after a largely pro forma debate, before which there had been no discussion within the party. As if this were not enough, the Communist leadership apparently ordered its security forces to remove all who during rallies shouted slogans in favor of the Republic or raised its flag. There were quite a few scuffles, and the press carried articles and letters condemning the overzealous behavior of the *servicio*.

The Struggle for Political Space

There was keen disappointment in Spanish communist ranks after the June 1977 election. Although most polls had indicated the PCE would garner no more than 10 percent of the national vote, many in the party had held on to the hope that the predictions would be proved wrong. In the end, of course, they were not, and, despite the preeminent role the PCE had played in the opposition to Franco, the Communists found themselves outstripped by a resurgent PSOE by better than three-to-one. Most galling the Communists was their inability to translate their trade union influence into votes. Not only did the overwhelming majority of people who eventually supported the General Workers' Union (UGT) in the 1978 syndical elections vote for the PSOE in 1977 (72 percent, versus a mere 2 percent for the Communists), but even among those who later voted for the Communist Workers' Commissions (CC.OO.) the PCE did poorly. Thus, while 44 percent of the eventual *Comisiones* voters supported the PSOE in 1977, only 39 percent voted for the PCE.[18]

In the months after June 1977 the Communists tried to reverse the balance of forces on the left and in the country. They had several points in their favor. One was the presence they had developed in the labor movement. The Communists had begun to work within the official Francoist vertical unions as early as 1948. Although this policy did not bring them immediate results, by the late 1950s the structural conditions for worker unrest and dissent had developed, and spontaneous workers' commissions began to appear. When they did, the Communists were in place, ready to seize the opportunity. Communist labor activities created provincial and national structures to coordinate plant-level commissions. Eventually they developed a dominant presence in the organization that came to be known as the *Comisiones Obreras*. PCE leaders had ceaselessly predicted that after the break with Francoism the CC.OO. would emerge as the dominant trade union organization in Spain. Their hopes had been dashed by the political dexterity of King Juan Carlos and Prime Minister Adolfo Suárez, but even so the PCE entered the post-Franco era with a decided advantage in organization and trained cadres over their closest rival, the socialist UGT. The Socialists made a determined effort in the months after June

1977 to overcome the Communist advantage among organized labor, but they did not have much success. With their presence in labor and the power to call strikes and demonstrations that went along with it, the Communists had an ace in the hole to play against any effort to render them marginal spectators in the political arena.

Another circumstance that worked in favor of the PCE was the organizational discipline of the party and the influence it could expect through the network of organizations, such as housewife and neighborhood associations, it had developed since the 1960s. Surveys taken in 1976 and 1977 indicate that the average Communist militant inclined more to the left in his personal preferences than official party policy; even so, there could be no doubt about the party's ability to deliver support for the "responsible" policies advocated by Carrillo and his closest associates. This discipline increased the PCE's political weight—and contrasted with the PSOE's lack of cohesion.

A final element that worked in favor of the Communists was the electoral weakness of the UCD. That party had been able to parlay 34 percent of the vote into a nearly absolute majority in the Chamber (165 of 350 seats) thanks to the d'Hondt system of representation used to distribute the seats, but this was an artificial abundance. If push came to shove, Suárez could probably count on the support of the Popular Alliance and its sixteen deputies, but he did not relish this option. Suárez and Fraga Iribarne, the secretary general of the AP, disliked each other intensely, and, what was worse, the prime minister desperately wanted to avoid being tarred with the brush of Francoism. The presence of an aggressive Socialist party complicated matters for Suárez. The PSOE called for elections immediately upon completion of the constitution, denounced Suárez as the heir of an illegitimate regime, and saw itself as likely to succeed him.

That Suárez succeeded in maintaining a degree of normalcy during the transition from Francoism should not obscure the fact that a delicate transformation was taking place, breaking one bond of political legitimacy and creating another. With the drafting of a new national charter, all the issues that had traditionally divided the Spanish polity were raised again—the role and power of the monarch, the devolution of power to the regions, the place of the Catholic church in Spanish society and in the educational process, and so on. Communist support for the document and for other measures adopted by the government would go far toward taking the bite out of the anticipated Socialist opposition and would ensure the new constitution a national consensus.

The Communists, of course, were more than happy to oblige Suárez. Preventing the PSOE's accession to the government or, alternatively, making sure that if the Socialists entered, the Communists too would join became the paramount Communist objective. The PCE's proposal for a "government of national concentration" to include all parties from the UCD to the PCE along with the Basque and Catalan nationalists had as its stated objective preventing polarization and saving democracy in Spain, but behind it lay an obvious effort to frustrate the Socialists' desire to rule and the conviction that Communist entry into the government would dramatically speed up the legitimization of the PCE.

During this period, the Communists moved on a broad front to strengthen their organizational/political capabilities and diminish the virulence of anticommunist feeling in Spain. Some of their initiatives were designed to reinforce the influence of Communists in labor and of Communist labor activists within the party as a whole, but their best-publicized efforts came in the fields of ideology and foreign relations.[19] The PCE and Santiago Carrillo, we noted earlier, had developed quite a reputation for their outspoken criticism of the Soviet Union and other so-called socialist states in the years after 1968. There had been ambiguities in this development, and it was clear that many militants did not share the bitingly critical opinions Carrillo and his chief foreign policy adviser, Manuel Azcárate, voiced about the Soviet bloc. Nevertheless, when Carrillo's *"Eurocomunismo" y Estado* appeared in the spring of 1977, it posed a serious ideological challenge to the Soviet Union. Carrillo had hoped the publication of the book would have a direct effect on the June 1977 election; and indeed, if the Soviet blast had come several weeks earlier, it might have brought the party some additional votes. But the Soviets did not respond until after the election, when they charged that Carrillo's views "accorded only with the interests of imperialism." Their bitter attack brought relations between the PCE and the Soviet party to the brink of rupture, but both sides pulled back in the ensuing weeks and months. Then in early November 1977 the Soviets refused to allow Carrillo to speak at celebrations commemorating the sixtieth anniversary of the October 1917 revolution. There is evidence to support the proposition that Carrillo provoked the Soviets into taking this unprecedented step in the hope of assuring himself a good reception during his first visit to the United States a few weeks later and perhaps even access to the Carter administration. Carrillo perceived the United States as perhaps the principal obstacle to the PCE's entering the government and achieving full legitimization. If he were judged sufficiently anti-Soviet, Carrillo thought, the United States might not pressure Suárez to keep the Communists out, and Suárez could not use supposed American displeasure as an excuse to keep the PCE out of the cabinet. The gambit failed: although during his visit to the United States Carrillo addressed gatherings at prestigious universities and institutions like the Council on Foreign Relations, he did not have official contacts with the Carter administration and did not come away from his trip with the expected waiver of the American veto to Communist participation in government. It is difficult to know whether his expectations were ever realistic, but unless Carrillo had been willing to break with Moscow completely (which would have meant a fundamental critique of the Soviet system and would probably have led to a break with the Italian Communists as well), there was little he could have offered the United States government in return.

During his visit to the United States, Carrillo announced what was to be the final thrust in the ideological campaign the party had embarked upon several months before: he would propose to the PCE Central Committee that in the draft theses to be presented to the Ninth Congress in the spring of 1978 the description of the PCE as a Leninist organization be dropped. After one of the most open debates to be held inside a communist party anywhere since Stalinization in the late 1920s, delegates to the Ninth Congress approved the change. But those who thought the move would accelerate change within were mistaken; in fact, quite the opposite occurred. Many "liberal" party members subsequently left the party and Carrillo, in order to have the proposal approved, struck a tacit deal with more traditional elements within the party to slow the process down.

A straightforward up-or-down assessment of Communist policies in the months after June 1977 is difficult, if not impossible, to make. In the weeks after the signing of the Moncloa Agreements, the PCE came close to forcing the PSOE into a government of national unity, but it ultimately failed—not only because of the Socialists' opposition but also because of Suárez's reluctance. He did not relish the idea of sharing power and preferred to use the Communists to keep the PSOE off balance. Yet, despite this failure, any objective analysis of the PCE's strategy and its relations with Suárez and the UCD would have to emphasize that the Communists received as much from that relationship as they gave. The PCE captured only 9.4 percent of the vote in June 1977, but in the months after the election Carrillo and his party became key figures on the Spanish political scene, playing important roles in the drafting of the constitution and legislative proposals. Suárez had to take their views into account, and occasionally he had to backtrack from his original intentions when faced with Communist opposition.

One example of this was the municipal elections law debated in the Cortes in February and March 1978. Putting their heads together in an effort to extract maximum partisan gain, the UCD and PSOE had drafted a proposal stipulating that after municipal elections the head of the list with the most votes would automatically become mayor. There can be little doubt as to the intention of the document: it aimed to freeze out the other parties and distribute the mayoralties between the UCD and the PSOE. Well aware of the likely impact of such a law, the Communists attacked the proposal and mounted a vigorous campaign against it. Needing the PCE to support him on various controversial provisions of the constitution, Suárez backed down and agreed (as did the Socialists, but they had little choice in the matter) to a compromise. Only a candidate whose list had won an absolute majority automatically became mayor. Otherwise, the councilors elected the mayor. On the first round, an individual had to receive an absolute majority of the votes cast by his fellow municipal councilors. Only if no victor emerged at that point did the second round become necessary, at which time a plurality sufficed. The change was vitally important for a smaller party like the Communists, as the municipal elections in April 1979 amply demonstrated. Unable to win an absolute majority in most cities, the Socialists had to turn to the PCE for support on the mayoralties. The PSOE-PCE municipal pact put Socialist mayors in over one thousand Spanish cities, but in return the PSOE had to share authority and patronage with the Communist councilors.

Whatever advantages the PCE may have derived from its privileged relationship with Suárez, it was nonetheless clear that the political initiative remained in the hands of the prime minister. He was very much the dominant partner, and when in December 1978 he decided to call new elections, there was not much the Communists could do about it, even though they did not want a return to the polls. Indeed, it was reported that shortly before dissolving the Cortes Suárez asked the PCE to join his party in creating a stable parliamentary majority.[20] We do not know how serious he was in this offer or what its exact terms were, but Carrillo declined the overture, insisting that for the Communists to enter the government or sign any sort of agreement with the UCD, the Socialists also had to take part. The reasons for this stance should be evident. The Communists might not have wanted an election, but they could reasonably expect to hold their own in one. There was not all that much to be gained from entering into the relationship proposed by Suárez. It might keep the PSOE out of the government, but by making the PCE appear too blatantly anti-Socialist, it would also stoke the Socialists' fire and perhaps indirectly help them do well in the coming municipal campaign. The Communists preferred to chance new national elections. They clearly did not want the Socialists to win and would to their best to take votes away from them. If a close election materialized, the UCD-PSOE or PSOE-UCD coalition government might ensue, and the Communists could then be asked to join the government or support it formally in some way. If the Socialists were to veto such an arrangement, however, the PCE could assume the role of principal (albeit moderate and responsible) opposition party and thus benefit from the disenchantment that would set in once the inevitable austerity measures were instituted. On the other hand, if, as Carrillo believed, Suárez were to win again, little would change for his party, but the socialists would lose much of their momentum.

The 1979 Elections The Communists' chief objectives in the March 1979 electoral campaign were to prevent a PSOE victory and to prepare for the municipal elections by extending their organizational network and influence. To this end they mounted an aggressively anti-Socialist campaign. Although there was some debate within the PCE as to how much criticism should be directed at the Socialists, the general tenor of the campaign was harsh. Communist speakers roundly denounced the influence of the West German Social Democratic party was having on the PSOE and ridiculed the Socialists for thinking that they could constitute a left-wing government in 1979 Spain. In a clear pitch to the left-wing PSOE voter, Communist candidates argued that a vote for the PCE was the only way to keep the PSOE on a "progressive" course. Communist attacks on the Socialists were also aimed at discouraging PCE voters from going over to the PSOE. This possibility posed a real threat. Surveys taken over the previous two years indicated that half the Communist voters would opt for the Socialists as their second choice, and polls commissioned in January and February 1979 indicated some 8 percent of those who had voted Communist in 1977 intended to vote for the PSOE.[21] Some may have felt that Carrillo overdid his attacks on the PSOE—one highly respected independent on the left described him after the election as having an "anti-Socialist phobia"[22]—but his sarcasm sprang from a resentment deeply felt by the PCE rank and file over the PSOE's ability to outmaneuver the Communists and maintain a position of strength on the left. The standing joke in many Communist groups was that the PSOE had a record of "one hundred years of honesty and firmness" (the official Socialist slogan for 1979, the party's centenary) but had spent forty of them on vacation, a not too flattering reference to the atrophy of the PSOE organization during the Franco years.

Aside from the jabs at the Socialists, there was little electricity to the Communist campaign this time around. Once again, the PCE had the most impressive and largest rallies and mounted the best-organized campaign. But, perhaps because the novelty had worn off and the previous two years had been so exhausting, not to mention the fact that another campaign was looming in just a few weeks, there was little visible excitement. The program the PCE presented to the nation was like that of 1977 but if anything more moderate. There was no mention of nationalization in short or medium term, just calls for greater efficiency. Who could quarrel with demands that the administrative apparatus, the municipal structures, and the social security system be reformed, that the fight against terrorism be carried forward, and that autonomy measures for the various regions be enacted? Perhaps the only controversial measures put forward by the PCE related to the *Estatuto de los Trabajadores*, a sort of labor charter, and the proposal for breaking government control and censorship over radio and television.

As slogans like "Put your vote to work" and "Employ your vote against unemployment" suggested, the Communists directed their campaign propaganda at the working class. At one level, of course, this was not surprising. The PCE claimed to be the party of the working class, found its raison d'etre in representing proletarian interests, and had preferential relations with the largest trade union, the Workers Commissions. But, in fact, the Communists had received fewer working-class votes than the PSOE in 1977: an estimated 60 percent of the CC.OO. membership had voted for the PSOE ticket in that election. Communist leaders were determined to reverse this trend. Already at the Ninth PCE Congress, a definite effort was made to promote working-class activists and move those with working-class backgrounds into the highest policy-making bodies of the party: over one-quarter of the new Central Committee were from the CC.OO., as were seven of the thirty-four members of the new Executive Committee. Many CC.OO. leaders—notably Marcelino Camacho, Nicolás Sartorius, Julián Ariza, Tomás Tueros, and Fernando Soto, all members of the CC.OO. National Secretariat and of the PCE Executive Committee—made their way onto PCE lists in March 1979. Although a detailed statistical breakdown is not possible given the paucity of biographical information about the Cortes candidates, it is worth noting that, according to a report published in *Mundo Obrero*, of 30,000 national and municipal candidates put forward in 1979 by the Communists, approximately 10,000 were members of the CC.OO.[23]

Assessment of the Outcome

In an interview published the day after the March 1979 elections, Santiago Carrillo described the PCE's results as "what we had hoped for and somewhat more."[24] Carrillo was trying to put the best face on an election about which he must have had mixed feelings. Suárez had won, and the Socialists were not going to enter the government, and this was, of course, reason for rejoicing in the PCE camp. The UCD had lost some 50,000 votes, even as it had once again outdistanced the PSOE by nearly five percentage points. This was a serious setback for the PSOE, whose leaders had virtually predicted that they would defeat Suárez, at least in the popular vote, and form the government. In his chapter on the Socialists, José María Maravall presents a detailed analysis of the electoral results as they relate to the PSOE and, more broadly, to the socialist family in Spain. There is no need to repeat it here. What is important to remember, for it bears heavily on why the PCE's assessment of the election was generally favorable, is that, even though the PSOE had incorporated various regional socialist groups and Enrique Tierno Galván's Popular Socialist party (PSP) and had made efforts to strengthen the UGT, the PSOE increased its total vote by only 100,000. The mergers did not bring an automatic gain for the PSOE, much less the "multiplier" effect predicted by Socialists leaders. Only in Catalonia, where the Reagrupment organization formerly headed by Joseph Pallach fused with it, did the PSOE improve perceptibly. Elsewhere, and particularly in Andalusia, there was a hemorrhage of the PSOE vote, with losses of 56,000 in western Andalusia. In Madrid, where the PSP had garnered 212,000 votes, the PSOE advanced by only 38,000; the admittedly heterogeneous PSP vote appears to have split several ways, part going to the UCD, part to the PSOE, part to the Communists. The Basque country had always been an area of PSOE strength, but when the returns were in this time around, PSOE candidates had lost 70,000 votes and three deputies relative to 1977.

Besides drawing favorable conclusions from the Socialists' failures, the Communists pointed to positive aspects in their own showing. The PCE increased its vote in forty-one of the fifty-one districts where it presented candidates and, as we indicated earlier in this chapter, was the only national organization to register both a relative and an absolute increase in its vote over 1977. The PCE gained the bulk of those 300,000 votes in a few provinces. Nearly 65,000 came from Andalusia, more than half from the provinces of Córdoba, Granada, and Jaén. The party also picked up 63,000 votes in Madrid province (going from 10.6 to 13.5 percent of the vote there) and 12,000 in Oviedo. Perhaps the most spectacular rise in the Communist vote came in the province of Valencia, where the PCE total increased by nearly 45,000 votes, from 9.2 to 13.3 percent.

There was a less positive side to the Communist performance, however. The party had gained some 300,000 votes—but the lowering of the voting age to eighteen had brought in 3.2 million new voters, as few as 10 percent of whom may have voted Communist. In addition, as Communist leaders were well aware, their party had quite a distance to go before it could pretend to have a nationwide base: approximately 65 percent of its vote had been concentrated in just eight provinces, and five-sixths of that total came from only five. The party had gained votes in parts of Andalusia, but in some provinces where it had expected to do much better than in 1977—like Cádiz, Málaga, and Seville—its increases had not been very significant. There had also been a loss (admittedly small) in the four Catalan provinces, a region where the Communists had done very well in the previous elections, and this was a source of concern for PCE leaders. Even more alarming were the results in the Basque country and Galicia: in none of the eight provinces there did the PCE win a single Chamber seat or attain more than 5.1 percent of the vote. The party gained marginally in La Coruña, Orense, and Pontevedra but lost votes in all the Basque provinces.

Several general characteristics were exhibited by the Communist voters in 1979. By a margin of 65 to 36 percent, more men than women voted for the PCE. The ratios were 51 to 49 for the socialists and 41 to 59 for the UCD.[25] Along with this failure, and despite an ostentatious effort to make itself attractive to Catholics, the PCE attracted only 18 percent of those who described themselves as practicing Catholics.[26] The educational profile of the Communist voter showed him to be slightly better educated than his Socialist or Centrist counterparts. Thus, although the Communists trailed the UCD and the PSOE among voters in all educational categories, the proportion of the PCE vote coming from those with high school degrees or higher educations was higher than for the UCD or the PSOE.[27] This may relate to the influence the PCE exerted over the university and student movements during the 1960s and into the 1970s. Most predictably, the Communists did relatively well among the working class, with skilled and unskilled workers making up nearly 32 percent of the Communist vote.[28] But even so, it was the Socialists who gained the support of a majority of the working class (48 percent, and only 19.5 for the PCE) and could more accurately claim to be the principal worker's party in Spain.[29]

Much of what I have said in this chapter about the reasons for the PCE's failure in June 1977 applies to its performance in March 1979, but some additional factors may have intervened. One of these has to do with the polarization of the electorate around the UCD and the PSOE. Neither party came out of the 1979 election unscathed, but between them they managed to collect nearly three-quarters of the votes cast. The PSOE did not do as well as many Socialist leaders had expected, but it was still successful in convincing those who voted left that the only truly useful vote, the only vote that could have a real impact on policy, was one for the Socialist party. A second factor that probably affected the PCE's performance was the dimming of its Eurocommunist image. We noted earlier the ambiguities in the Spanish Communists' evolution away from Stalinism but insisted on the depth of the ideological challenge posed to the Soviet Union by Carrillo in *"Eurocommunismo" y Estado*. In the aftermath of the incident in Moscow and of his failure to have the Carter administration waive its opposition to Communist entry into the Spanish government, Carrillo backed off from confrontation with the Soviet Union and consciously withdrew from the limelight of controversy in the international Communist movement. The Spanish Communists by no means abandoned the positions they had developed, but they began to sound more restrained. They were now more ready to incline toward the Soviet Union and its allies—to take an anti-Chinese stance, for example, during the Sino-Vietnamese conflict in late 1978 and early 1979. A third factor that might be adduced to explain the PCE's failure to expand its electoral base significantly has to do with the political-organizational choices the party made after June 1977. Although the Communist vote in the first election of the post-Franco era had been remarkably broad-based (in the sense that a significant proportion had come from outside the working class), in the months thereafter the party had opted to strengthen its ties with the labor movement. This was logical enough given the PCE's base in the Workers' Commissions, but it meant that within the party itself preference was to be given to labor activists over younger professionals. This choice made it much more difficult for the PCE to broaden its electoral appeal and led to strong polemics within provincial and regional organizations, eventually contributing to the disintegration of the party. In the final analysis, the campaign the party directed at the working class was a failure: aside from picking up support among agricultural laborers in parts of Andalusia and from workers in the industrial belt in Madrid and in Valencia, the PCE did not reap a more bountiful harvest of CC.OO. votes this time. Indeed, one postelectoral analysis suggested there was no significant correlation between increases in the PCE vote and strong CC.OO. showings in the 1978 syndical elections.[30]

The factors we have just discussed are those that strongly affected the Communists' national performance, but our sense of the strengths and weaknesses of the PCE would be incomplete without a more detailed analysis of its performance in several important provinces and regions. It is to this that we now turn.

Asturias The Communists had high hopes for their ticket in Asturias in 1979. Heading the party list were Horacio Fernández Inguanzo, a miner who had played a leading role in organizing the PCE and the CC.OO. in Asturias during the Franco years, and Gerardo Iglesias, the thirty-three-year-old secretary general of the Asturias PCE and a member of the National Secretariat of the CC.OO. Dolores Ibárruri, the legendary La Pasionaria of Civil War fame, had been first on the ticket in 1977, but she, like fellow octogenarian Wenceslao Roces, the only Communist senator elected in 1977, was not presented by the party again.

Asturias—more precisely the province of Oviedo—had long been considered an area where Communist influence was strong. The PCE had played an important role in the mine workers' strikes that had paralyzed the region in 1958, in 1962, and again in 1970. The party had received only slightly more than 10 percent of the vote in 1977, however, and had won only a single Chamber seat. What must have been particularly disconcerting to Communist leaders was that their party came in fourth in the voting (behind the Popular Alliance) and in the capital city of Oviedo ranked fifth. The PSOE, meanwhile, had captured seats in the Chamber and nearly 32 percent of the vote.

In 1979 the Communists hoped to improve on their 1977 performance by running a ticket heavy with CC.OO. activists and gearing their campaign to take advantage of discontent among former PSP supporters who were unhappy about the merger with the PSOE. Dissatisfaction on this score had been rather evident in May 1978 when the Communist candidate picked up 26,000 votes in the senatorial by-election, but it seemed to have less effect in March 1979. The PCE did better this time than before, but its total—74,000 votes, or 13.5 percent of the tally—was lower than in the by-election.

The PCE had been hurt in Asturias by abstentions in the mining region, a phenomenon that reflected not only general worker discontent but disillusion with the bitter squabbles that had shaken the Asturias PCE in 1977 and 1978.[31] The first signs of tension had appeared before the June 1977 election when some party members, mostly young and including many professionals, objected to La Pasionaria's heading the list in the region. They saw her as too old and too controversial a figure, a person who could not help the PCE expand its audience and put the quarrels of the past behind it. This conflict boiled over in the fall when, despite the objections of the Central Committee, the Asturias Regional Committee formally asked Ibárruri to resign from the Cortes. But the deeper issue was the political orientation of the party in the region, and it came to a head during the debates over whether the party should drop Leninism from its program. The Young Turks in the organization objected to the proposal not because they opposed dropping Leninism but because they felt a four- or five-week debate was insufficient to eliminate the residues of forty years of Stalinism from the PCE. Finally, in April 1978, a few weeks before the Ninth PCE Congress, one-third of the delegates to the provincial conference walked out of the proceedings when it became apparent they could not defeat the motion on Leninism. Many either quit or were expelled from the PCE in subsequent weeks, and the loss undoubtedly hurt the party in the March elections.

The Basque Provinces and Navarre Shortly after the returns were in in June 1977, the secretary general of the Basque Communist party (PCE-EPK), Ramón Ormazábal, declared: "We consider the PCE results to be unsatisfactory. We have done poorly."[32] His successor, Roberto Lertxundi, could have said the same in March 1979. The formally autonomous Basque Communist party won only 4.2 percent of the vote in the three Basque provinces and Navarre in 1977, and in 1979 it lost some 4,700 of the 56,000 votes it had collected two years before. Although the PCE could take some solace from the dismal Socialist showing in this region (the PSOE lost 60,000 votes and three deputies and fell more than 120,000 voters behind the front-running Basque Nationalist party, PNV), it could neither overlook its own horrendous performance or ignore the eruption of extreme left nationalist sentiment that had produced groups like the Euzkadi Left (EE) and Herri Batasuna (HB). Both those groups had ties to rival factions of the Basque terrorist movement known as ETA, and each outpolled the Communists handily in Guipúzcoa, Navarre, and Vizcaya.

The Communists' disappointment was all the greater because the Basque country, or Euzkadi, is the most highly industrialized region in Spain. Over 50 percent of the 1969 active population were part of the industrial working class, and this figure went up to nearly 70 percent if the service sector were included.[33] Moreover, its reputation for combativeness against the Franco regime was second to none. During the years 1967–72, when strikes were illegal and more severely punished in Euzkadi than anywhere else in Spain, they averaged over one thousand yearly in the region.[34] From this point of view, the region appeared to be ideal for a recently clandestine opponent of Francoism whose program included a call for Basque autonomy. What happened?

For one thing, the moderate strategy pursued by the PCE ran into the virulent nationalism of the region. In so politicized an area, the Communists could not gain by arguing, as they so often did, for restraint and against popular mobilization. Less than a month before the June 1977 election, in fact, the PCE had opted not to participate in a general strike called by other organizations to protest the shooting of five workers during a demonstration demanding amnesty for all political prisoners—and this despite the fact some of the dead had been members of the Workers Commissions. Or again, in the fall of 1979 the new secretary general of the PCE-EPK led two hundred Communist militants and sympathizers on a march to dramatize their opposition to ETA and terrorism. This was an act of political and physical courage on the part of the demonstrators, and the national PCE said it proved how stalwart the Communists were on the issue. But it cannot have won much favor on the nationalist left, and it cast the PCE-EPK as just one more organization supporting the central government that had stationed over 13,000 police and security forces in Euzkadi.

The Basque Communists invariably supported demands for the autonomy of the region, but they were never able to shed the image of an organization that took orders from Madrid. Not only that, but the PCE-EPK never seemed really to appreciate why radical nationalist ideas exercised such an influence on younger Basques. Whatever the reasons for this insensitivity on the nationalities' questions—and some would cite the preponderance of non-Basque immigrant workers in party ranks—the point that needs to be made here is that moderate groups like the PNV and the PSOE used the issue to isolate the Communists during the Franco era and thereafter. The PCE never managed to reenter the Basque government in exile from which it had been excluded in at the 1947 onset of the cold war, and the coalition known as the Euzkadi Democratic Alliance that it sponsored in the early 1970s as a rival to the government-in-exile never got off the ground. Even the partial renovation that took place at its first legal congress in late 1977, when Ormazábal was replaced as secretary general by ex-ETA member Lertxundi, appeared to be too little too late. Supporters of greater autonomy from the national party for the PCE-EPK ironically found their influence lessened by the move.

But the last word may be that the PCE just did not have as strong an organization in the provinces of Euzkadi as it liked to let on. Indeed, as one official document noted after June 1977, that organization was "more a magma than a cohesive whole."[35] Even in Vizcaya, where the party was strongest, its influence did not extend much beyond the metallurgical industry in Bilbao.

Catalonia This region was the one Communist success story in June 1977. Running as the Unified Socialist party of Catalonia (PSUC), the Communists elected eight deputies (seven in the province of Barcelona and the other in

Tarragona) and played an important role in the overwhelming victory obtained by the senatorial coalition known as the Agreement of the Catalans. In the region as a whole the PSUC received over 550,000 votes, 18.2 percent of the total cast.

The results were more disappointing in March 1979. The party lost votes in all four provinces and attained only 17.1 percent of the votes in the region. The voters also handed the PSUC a serious setback in the senatorial race when they overwhelmingly supported the candidates proposed by the PSOE in the New Agreement for Catalonia and Socialism. Of the candidates supported by the PSUC, only Josep Benet made his way against the tide. Elected with more votes than any other senator in Catalonia in June 1977, he now trailed Socialist Josep Andreu Abelló by over 170,000 votes.

The PSUC was hurt in the 1979 election by abstentions in the industrial belt around Barcelona and specifically in the Vallès Occidental (where Sabadell and Terrassa are located) and in the Baix Llobregat, areas where it had done very well two years earlier. Part of the explanation for this drop is the damage internal tension did to the effectiveness of the Communist campaign.

The breadth of the Communist vote in 1977 had been due in large measure to the PSUC's success in projecting the image of an open and socially heterogeneous organization. Thus a survey conducted in 1978 showed the PSUC vote to present some interesting contrasts with that of the PCE in the rest of Spain. Of PSUC voters asked to place themselves on a ten-point left-right scale, only 17 percent (as opposed to 43 percent of PCE voters) chose the two leftmost positions). Only 46 percent of the PSUC voter sample accepted the label "Marxist," in contrast to 64 percent of PCE voters. Whereas only 17 percent of PCE voters described themselves as "socialist" (and 75 percent as "communist"), approximately 39 percent of the PSUC voters did so. On another question— asking voters how close they felt to the Socialist party—20 percent of the sample from the PSUC electorate said "very," and only 8 percent of the PCE voters polled gave that answer.[36]

Although not legalized as a separate party until May 1977—that is, a little over a month before the election, and on the fortieth anniversary of a bloody Anarchist-Communist confrontation in Barcelona—the PSUC had stopped functioning as a clandestine organization many months before and had begun to break the style and habits of underground activity. One of the most important decisions taken by the PSUC as it resumed public activities in early 1976 was the modification of its organizational structures. The Catalan branch of the PCE abandoned the traditional cell structure—some six months before the Spanish Communist Central Committee (in which it is represented) approved that reorganization for the party as a whole—and set up sixty- to eighty-member workplace and neighborhood *agrupaciones*. This transformation, which in other regions of Spain had not been completed by early 1978, had been virtually wrapped up in the PSUC by the time of the June 1977 election, and the Catalan Communists were able to influence the electorate more effectively through their penetration of neighborhood and housewives' associations. The PSUC also benefited from many years of patient work in the vertical syndical structures set up by Franco. The Workers' Commissions were stronger in Catalonia than anywhere else in Spain. Also relevant in this respect was the absence of an organized socialist movement in Catalonia—the PSUC having been the result of a fusion between various socialist parties in 1936—and the virtual disappearance of the anarchist CNT.

Any explanation of the success of the Catalan Communists must also take into account the ability to come across as at once an authentically regional and a national force. In this regard the Catalan Communists presented quite a contrast with other regional parties (those in the Basque country and Galicia particularly), which had a difficult time shedding the charge of *sucursalismo* aimed at them by nationalist groups. The PSUC had been in the forefront of efforts to restore autonomous government to the region, and even its well-publicized struggles with Josep Tarradellas (president-in-exile of the Catalan Generalitat until October 1977 and appointed head of that body when it was reconstituted in Catalonia by King Juan Carlos) did not lessen the image it had gained while forging such regional opposition coalitions as the Coordinadora de Forces Politiques (1969), the Catalan Assembly (1971), and the Council of Political Forces (1975). But the PSUC had never been extreme in its regionalism—many Catalanistas even doubt its sincerity—and this too also helped the party, particularly in the district of Barcelona, where an estimated 42 percent of the voters were of non-Catalan origin.[37]

Galicia There was deep disappointment in Spanish Communist ranks both in 1977 and in 1979 about the PCE's results in the four Galician provinces. Preelection hopes had been high in 1977 that the secretary general of the Galician Communist party, Santiago Alvarez, would win a seat in Pontevedra and that fellow Executive Committee member Rafael Pillado would likewise in La Coruña. These expectations went up in smoke on 15 June. Pillado proved unable to capitalize sufficiently on his leadership of the Workers' Commissions in La Coruña, and the PCE as a whole came up with only 3.7 percent of the vote in the province. Not only did the Communists trail the UCD, the PSOE, and the AP by sizable margins there, but they received fewer votes than Tierno Galván's PSP and managed to surpass a small nationalist group, the Galician Socialist party, by only some 117 votes out of approximately 448,000 cast. Alvarez, for his part, led the PCE to fifth place in Pontevedra with 3.2 percent of the vote. In both Lugo and Orense provinces, the PCE came in sixth with less than 3,000 votes to its credit.

The March 1979 election was in many ways a repeat performance. Alvarez and Pillado once again headed the Communist lists in Pontevedra and La Coruña, and the party increased its votes in these provinces by 5,300 and 3,284 respectively. The increase was nowhere near enough to bring the Communists deputies in either province. In both districts the party came in sixth, trailing two small, rather recently formed nationalist groups, Galician Unity and the Galician National Popular Bloc.

It is difficult to understand why the Communists ever expected to do better than this in Galicia. From a sociostructural point of view, despite significant industrial growth of some cities over the last two decades,[38] the region is still primarily agrarian and dominated by a *minifundio* system of land exploitation; politically it is a rather conservative part of Spain. It closely resembles, politically and sociologically, the northern Portuguese provinces where the left as a whole (and the Portuguese Communists in particular) fared so poorly in the months after the military coup in April 1974. Apparently the PCE hoped to capitalize on the resentment spawned by the massive outward migration the region had endured since the 1960s and on the growing labor unrest in larger cities like Vigo, La Coruña, and El Ferrol. If so, they misjudged the region and its people: emigration may well have removed potential labor activists from the region, and the older population cohorts were probably more amenable to influence under the still existent *cacique* system in the rural areas.[39] Moreover, despite much propaganda to the contrary, the Communists presented an unimaginative agrarian program.[40] Their call for the redistribution of land to "those who till it" sparked little excitement in an area full of small landowners who were under the influence of *caciques* and who feared that the Communists' real objective was the collectivization of all land.

A final element in an explanation of why the Communists did not do so well in Galicia is the reputation and structure of the Galician party organization. The ideas of Eurocommunism, so much in the air in the Catalan provinces, had found unfertile ground in Galicia. The party in this region retained the sectarian, *ouvriériste* orientation typical of heavily repressed clandestine parties and had the reputation of being intolerant of dissent. In this context, we might note that at the height of the Portuguese revolution, which was also the nadir in relations between the Portuguese and Spanish Communist parties, the Galician party kept contacts with the Portuguese Communists open.

Madrid Like all other national parties, the PCE attached great importance to doing well in the Spanish capital. Despite having one of the largest organizations in the country and running an efficient campaign, the PCE had been disappointed by its showing in Madrid in 1977: one-tenth of the approximately 2,340,000 votes cast in the province (the UCD captured 32 percent, the PSOE 31.9, the AP 10.5, and the PSP 9.2) and four seats in the Chamber of Deputies.

The fourth seat came at the expense of the UCD after Communist lawyers challenged the balloting in various parts of the city.

Determined to improve their position, the Communists redoubled their efforts in Madrid. They streamlined their list by dropping controversial candidates like Victor Díaz Cardiel or those with little connection to the organization in the city like Federico Melchor, editor of *Mundo Obrero*, and replacing them with younger people, many of whom, like Adolfo Piñedo and Begoña San José, were prominent in the Workers' Commissions. The PCE had won no Senate seats in 1977; now it tried to attract voters linked to the CC.OO. and the PSP by running a slate headed by a former member of the PSP, José Alonso, who sat on the National Secretariat of the Workers' Commissions. He received the endorsement of five ex-members of the PSP Executive Committee who had opposed the fusion with the PSOE.

The results of the March 1979 election represented an improvement for the Communists over their performance in 1977. The party increased its vote by 63,000 and its share went up from 10.6 to 13.4 percent. The Communists placed second in one district of the city (Mediodía), third in six (Vallecas, Villaverde, San Blás, Hortaleza, Moratalaz, and Carabanchel), and fourth in the rest. The PCE did most poorly in the seven central districts of the capital, with a high of 10.3 percent in Tetuán (where it was strong in the neighborhood association) and a low of 5.3 percent in the upper-class residential district of Salamanca. It did better in the eleven peripheral districts (with highs of 24.7 percent in Mediodía, 20.1 percent in Vallecas, and 20.0 percent in Villaverde) but saved its best performance for the towns and small cities outside Madrid that form part of the industrial belt around the city, where the CC.OO. was very strong. Significantly, in the fourteen towns of that belt—where nearly 75 percent of the city population lives—the combined vote of the left in 1979 generally went over 55 percent, in some places over 70 percent. The PCE attained its high mark there in San Fernando de Henáres with 37 percent of the vote.

As elsewhere, however, the PCE did not really challenge the PSOE for hegemony on the left and had to content itself with picking up a sizable share of the old PSP vote in some districts. Even if it slipped, the PSOE picked up some 30,000 votes (increasing its share from 31.3 to 33.1 percent), and even in the district of Vallecas, whose popular nickname was Little Russia and where the PCE captured 20.1 percent of the vote, the PSOE easily outdistanced the Communists, collecting over 42 percent of the tally. The most telling point about their performance was that a fifth congressional seat, which the Communists felt sure would go to CC.OO. leader Nicolás Sartorius, did not materialize.

Generally, the factors that worked against the PCE nationally were evident in Madrid as well. The only significant factor relating specifically to the province has to do with the party organization there. Historically, the PCE in Madrid had relied heavily for support and the bulk of its membership on the industrial working class. Under the leadership of Díaz Cardiel, the Executive Committee member responsible for the organization in the Spanish capital, the PCE had not made much of an effort in the years after Franco's death to expand its influence in non-working-class districts and among the middle class or the service sector. The party paid lip service to do so, but in effect the organization was too *ouvriériste* and sectarian to have much success at that enterprise. Even after Díaz Cardiel was defeated for reelection at a provincial conference in March 1978, the organization's character did not really change. Moreover, as a result of the internal turmoil that shook the PCE in Madrid, a plan for organizational consolidation in the party as a whole was slowed by acrimonious debates over how to reconcile sectoral, workplace, and neighborhood *agrupaciones*.

Andalusia The Communist party needed and expected to do well in this region. Not only was it a relatively underdeveloped part of the country with latifundist characteristics and many agricultural laborers, but its bloc of ninety-one deputies and senators was the second largest in the country and would account for 16.3 percent of the new Cortes. Saddled with high unemployment —the regional average was one and a half times the national rate, and the situation was particularly acute in Granada, Málaga, and Seville—the region could be expected to vote rather heavily for the left. Accordingly, the PCE brought out its big guns, and Executive Committee members headed the lists in four of the eight provinces.

The Communists' showing in 1979 represented a notable improvement over 1977, but it was still under what party leaders had hoped to achieve. By comparison with regions like Galicia or the Basque country, the PCE did very well: it came in third in Andalusia as a whole, with a high of 18.9 percent in Córdoba and a low of 6.9 percent in Huelva. It captured 392,000 votes and seven seats in the Chamber of Deputies, a gain of five seats over 1977. But the Communists still trailed the Socialists by a significant margin and, more important, barely beat the Socialist party of Andalusia (PSA) in the race for third place. The PSA ran a strong campaign with a nationalist thrust that bordered on the demagogic: "*Andaluz, vota por tu tierra.*" It also capitalized on the PSOE's errors in the region. The PSOE had done very well in 1977 but lost heavily this time around, leading in four instead of five provinces and losing 55,000 votes into the bargain.

The Communists had anticipated that the influence the Workers Commissions had developed among metal workers and in the transport sector in the region would improve the party's electoral performance. They had also hoped to profit from sharp competition between the PSOE and the PSA for the socialist space on the political spectrum. A bitter struggle between those two parties did indeed develop, but the Communists were not the principal beneficiaries. The PSA emerged as the real victor of the March 1979 elections in Andalusia. It gained 190,000 votes with respect to 1977, an impressive 84 percent of which came in the four most populous provinces. The PSA beat the Communists in Cádiz and Huelva and trailed the PCE by only 2,000 votes in Málaga, 10,000 in Seville. In this last province the PCE ticket was headed by two members of the Executive Committee who had been active in the Workers' Commissions in the region. Although both won election to the Cortes, the PSA made an impressive showing with just over 14 percent and 100,000 votes.

Córdoba was the bright star in the 1979 Communist electoral galaxy. A list headed by former Organizational Secretary Ignacio Gallego and backed up by Manuel Rubia, the secretary general of the CC.OO. in the province, received 18.9 percent of the vote, the highest Communist total in the country. The Spanish Communists did particularly well in the capital city of the same name and in the La Campiña area south of the Guadalquivir, where the margin separating them from the PSOE (which received 29.7 percent of the vote) was less than anywhere else in Andalusia. Perhaps to prove that their performance was no fluke, the Cordoban Communists staged an impressive municipal campaign a few weeks later and elected the only Communist mayor of a provincial capital.

Conclusion

The first two elections of the post-Franco era did not leave the Communists in a very favorable position. Some consolidation and broadening of the PCE vote took place in March 1979, but that expansion brought the party nowhere near the takeoff point anticipated by most party members. Indeed, it was eruption of nationalist sentiment in various regions and the misjudgments of the PSOE, not the successes of the Communists, that made the situation in mid-1979 still fluid and unpredictable.

Having failed to defeat Suárez and the UCD in the legislative contest, the PSOE had to settle for an agreement with the Communists after the April 1979 municipal elections. Whereas without PCE votes the Socialists could not govern many cities, a united left was capable of electing mayors in more cities with more than 50,000 people. This fact impelled the Socialist-Communist pact, produced Communist mayors in 150 of the nearly 1,200 cities where the left had won a majority, and gave the PCE a parcel of power from which it might expand its organizational and support network.

Another consequence of the Socialist defeat in March 1979 was the crisis loosed within the PSOE at its May 1979 Congress when Felipe González moved to drop the reference to Marxism from the party program. The defeat of the proposal whose objective was to give the party a more center-left cast, and

González's subsequent refusal to run for reelection as first secretary led to heated intraparty polemics during the summer and forced the convocation of an extraordinary congress in September.

The dynamic of the municipal pacts and the convulsions shaking the PSOE suggested that the PCE was not irremediably locked into a margin position on the left. But the satisfaction with which the Communists viewed the situation faded in a few months. Not only did González reimpose his authority at the extraordinary congress and decisively defeat the more left-wing *sector crítico*, but the PSOE also expanded its influence in the trade union movement, making important inroads (as the syndical elections in late 1980 demonstrated) into the strength of the *Comisiones Obreras*. Even where the Socialists showed signs of weakening—as in the Catalan and Basque regional elections of March 1980—the PSOE, headed by the most popular politician in Spain, maintained its image as the only viable national alternative to the UCD. The Communists, in the meantime, did not improve their electoral performance perceptibly.

The Communists' inability to make headway against the PSOE also showed in the municipal sphere, where, despite their previous efforts in the neighborhood associations and the labor movement, the Communists remained very much a junior partner. Any expectations they may have had of outmaneuvering the PSOE evaporated in the face of Socialist political skill and of budgetary constraints; given the highly centralized character of governmental administration in Spain, left-wing city councils could hardly embark on ambitious social projects or significantly expand services. Moreover, as popular participation in civic associations declined, so did the influence the Communists exerted through the neighborhood associations.

The Communists' failure to expand their audience significantly after 1979 aggravated latent tensions within the party. In the wake of its July 1981 Tenth Congress, the PCE confronted two crises: one, a crisis of identity, related to its abandonment of many traditional Leninist precepts and its search for a new political image; the other, an organizational crisis, related to its still unconsolidated structures and to its inability to renew its leadership while maintaining a certain amount of continuity in policies and perspectives. How to resolve these crises was the principal issue on the Communist agenda. Were the party to fail to make significant headway on them, its chances for reversing or shifting the correlation of forces on the left would evaporate. But the problem the Communists faced among the electorate was an extraordinarily difficult one. One survey showed the PCE outpacing the Socialists (by a 34 to 16 percent margin) among only one group of voters, those describing themselves as "extreme left."[41] The group comprised only 3 percent of the Spanish electorate, however. By contrast those who considered themselves to be center and center-left (a group encompassing 35 percent of voters) went handily to the PSOE, by margins of 38 to 7 and 35 to 27 percent, respectively. Thus, in its struggle for electoral space, the PCE not only had to overcome the advantage the Socialists derived from a public perception that they were the only viable left-wing alternative but also to project an image capable of attracting the more "moderate" voter. A final obstacle stood in the way of implementing such a strategy. The principal source of Communist organizational strength was among working-class activists, but excessive reliance on them and an explicitly *ouvriériste* orientation would only inhibit the expansion of Communist influence to other sectors of Spanish society, further compounding the PCE's identity crisis.

Francoist Reformers in Democratic Spain: The Popular Alliance and the Democratic Coalition

RAFAEL LÓPEZ-PINTOR

This chapter deals with the electoral performance of two groups that can be considered representative of the reformist sector that grew up inside the Franco regime in its final years. Both were electoral coalitions composed of minor parties and significant personalities from the right.

The Popular Alliance (AP) emerged before the general election of June 1977 and was replaced by the Democratic Coalition (CD) before the general election of March 1979. Both were led by Manuel Fraga Iribarne. Within the party system, both occupied the space between the Union of the Democratic Center (UCD) and the parties of the extreme right. Their electoral programs had much in common, including an emphasis on law and order.

A great deal of public attention focused on these groups, both before and during the electoral campaigns of June 1977 and March 1979. Many observers were surprised when the Popular Alliance took only 8.3 percent of the popular vote and less than 5 percent of the seats in the Chamber of Deputies, and in 1979 the Democratic Coalition's performance was even poorer: 6 percent of the vote; it won fewer than 3 percent of the seats in the Chamber. For all their campaigning, each finished fourth, right behind the Communist party. Nevertheless, the significance of the Popular Alliance and the Democratic Coalition in Spanish politics should not be underestimated, for among their leaders were politicians who represented clusters of interests that had the utmost importance within Spanish society.

This chapter outlines the origins of the Popular Alliance and the Democratic Coalition and describes their leaders, their programs, and their campaigns. The last part of the chapter is an analysis of the electoral returns.

Origins

As a political formation, the Popular Alliance (known at the time as the Conservative Electoral Alliance) was born in October 1976, a few months after the inauguration of the second government under the monarchy of King Juan Carlos. This was the period when Prime Minister Adolfo Suárez and his cabinet were preparing reform legislation that would make possible the transition to a democratic regime. It is important to note that the Law for Political Reform would be supported, with minor objections, by the leaders of the Popular Alliance, who were members of the Francoist legislative chamber that provided for its own demise by approving the reform bill. Thus the Popular Alliance was part of the new Spain from its very beginning.

Formally, both the AP and the CD were electoral coalitions rather than political parties. They were made up of minor parties with conservative leanings.[1] Like most Spanish parties, these had neither solid organizations nor large memberships. Their leaders were well-known representatives of the Franco regime of the 1960s and early 1970s, when it was broadly associated with economic development, planning, public works, and some moderate attempts at political reform.

All the leading personalities in the Popular Alliance and then the Democratic Coalition had civilian backgrounds and were men in their early fifties or even younger. They had outstanding university records and usually held the top post in the bureaucratic careers in which they were engaged. Many had pursued two or more bureaucratic careers at the same time. Most had held cabinet or other prominent positions under Franco and maintained important connections in the business and financial world. Most were outspoken people with intellectual leanings—professors or writers—who cultivated an image of authority and efficiency.

In their manifesto to the Spanish public, the seven organizers of the Popular Alliance defined themselves as "a group of citizens who represent various political tendencies and who, setting aside personal preferences, think it their duty to establish a political and electoral alliance."[2] In fact, they represented most of the ideological "families" of the Franco regime short of the most explicitly authoritarian. Together, they might be said to embody the "limited pluralism" that existed under Franco.[3] Yet while they were serving the Franco regime, they did not always cooperate with one another and sometimes were bitter enemies.

As we shall see, some of these politicians came out of the Falange, the fascist organization from which the Franco regime drew its ideological basis at its earliest stage; some came from Catholic organizations representing either the most conservative Catholicism (for example, Opus Dei) or the wing of the church associated with Christian Democracy; others had various and shifting identifications. Yet they were united not only by generational ties but also by professional and political experiences under the late Franco regime. They seemed also to share a basic view of politics, which has been labeled "liberal-authoritarian": within the Francoist elite, they had tended to play liberalizing roles; yet when the path to democracy was open, they displayed authoritarian leanings and some major objections to reform. Moreover, all had helped bring about important achievements under the Franco regime in the 1960s, once the repressive period that followed the Civil War was over.

Broadly speaking, they occupied positions somewhere between the most recalcitrant authoritarian right and the progressive modern right of Suárez's Union of the Democratic Center. Insofar as such comparisons are meaningful, they tended to see themselves as close to parties like the Republican party in the United States and the Conservatives in Britain.

The Popular Alliance had a collegial executive of seven members and a secretary general. From the very beginning of the coalition, this latter position was held by Manuel Fraga Iribarne, the strongest personality within the group and almost its only spokesman. At the first National Congress in March 1977 in Madrid, the seven constituent parties formally became a federation under the name Popular Alliance, and the earlier name was dropped.[4] Previous to this congress, each of the seven parties had held its own general assembly where the possibility of joining a federation had been discussed and approved. As we have seen, none of the seven had either a strong organizational apparatus or a large membership, and in at least three cases, it seems clear that the party (like many parties in the early days of Spanish democracy) was actually created to give its leader a power base from which to negotiate with his colleagues over the formation of the coalition.

Why did the Popular Alliance emerge when other political forces on the right and in the center already existed or were in the making? The answer has much to do with the proliferation of political groups and the feuds between personalities with similar ideologies that are so characteristic of contemporary Spanish politics. In the case of the Popular Alliance, the emergence of the coalition was definitely related to the rift that split the elite of the Franco regime once it became clear that King Juan Carlos would democratize the country and the opposition groups would accept his initiative.

In July 1976 the king dismissed Prime Minister Carlos Arias Navarro and chose as his successor a relative unknown, Adolfo Suárez, who turned out to be a decided reformer. Suárez's appointment ruled out several important figures of the Franco regime who might have aspired to leading the transition to democracy. These included Manuel Fraga, Federico Silva, and Laureano López Rodó, who became leaders of the Popular Alliance.

Even before Franco's death, it had been Manuel Fraga's objective to organize a large political party of the center-right, but once Suárez started to build up his own center-right coalition from so privileged a position as the prime ministership, Fraga moved toward the right. Theoretically, Fraga could have joined the Suárez coalition, and there may even have been some discussion of the possibility, but in practical terms, this would have proved very difficult. There might have been conflicts over leadership since both Suárez and Fraga were strong personalities, and to many groups inside the Suárez coalition Fraga was ideologically unacceptable.[5]

The Democratic Coalition emerged on the eve of the general election of 1979. Several factors led to its birth. First, and most important, there was the process of constitution building, which lasted from the opening of the first democratic legislature in 1977 to December 1978, when the new general election was announced. By the end of this period, the Popular Alliance was split. Some of its representatives in parliament—above all Fraga—held the view that the Union of the Democratic Center was shifting to the left, leaving a vacuum on the center-right into which the Popular Alliance should move. Others—particularly those who had voted against the draft constitution—advocated a shift to the right. Outside the Popular Alliance, meanwhile, several politicians who had been close to the UCD, shared Fraga's views. These included José María de Areilza and Alfonso Osorio. Areilza, like Fraga, had been a member of the first cabinet under King Juan Carlos, and Osorio had been a member of the first Suárez cabinet before the general election of 1977.

Under these circumstances, the more rightist politicians of the Popular Alliance left the coalition, and Areilza and Osorio joined Fraga in building up a new electoral force. The Democratic Coalition finally crystallized in January 1979, once the new general election had been announced. What its leaders hoped and claimed was that their coalition would collect the center-right vote, attracting people who had supported the Union of the Democratic Center in 1977 but had been disappointed by the Suárez government.

Leaders

Manuel Fraga (Democratic Reform)

The main spokesman and secretary general of the Popular Alliance, Manuel Fraga Iribarne, was one of the most controversial politicians in Spain in the 1970s. He might also have been the leader most scorned by the print media during the 1977 campaign. Some observers saw Fraga as a "liberal-authoritarian," which may be a clue to his position and importance in Spanish politics.[6]

Interestingly enough, Fraga tended to see himself in very much the same terms as some of his critics: a career man above all, an active leader, an outspoken personality and prolific writer, and an advocate of controlled reform and strong government.[7]

More than any other leader of the Popular Alliance, Fraga took risks by pushing for liberalization under the Franco regime and speaking up for conservatism in the transition to democracy. In both endeavors he partly failed and partly succeeded. Perhaps for this reason, the Spanish historian Ricardo de la Cierva has referred to Fraga as "the unburnable."

Fraga joined the Falange in his youth. Taking a rather standard path to social mobility for middle-class Spaniards of his time, he pursued several bureaucratic careers through the *oposiciones* system—a public examination system for recruitment into the different branches of public service, including the universities. Like most of the other leaders of the Popular Alliance, he was very successful in these careers, serving as a legal expert in the Cortes, a diplomat, and a tenured professor of political science. From the time he was in his thirties, Fraga occupied important government positions: secretary general at the Ministry of Education, seats on no fewer than five national councils (top public advisory boards concerned with political, economic, and educational matters), and membership in the Cortes by appointment. He kept his seat in the Cortes until 1971, when Franco dismissed him. From 1962 to 1969, Fraga was minister of information and tourism. From this position, he managed to obtain the passage of a bill reforming the laws on the press, which had been in force since the end of the Civil War. In 1969 Fraga was ousted from his cabinet position after a feud within the cabinet relating to the MATESA scandal (a financial scandal in which several members of the cabinet were indicted) and the declaration of a state of emergency, which was followed by severe repression of the labor movement and opposition groups.

Between 1969 and 1977 Fraga taught at the University of Madrid and occupied important positions in the private and public sectors. He was president of a large beer company and an oil company and sat on the executive boards of several business firms. Then he served as Spanish ambassador to Britain for two years. By the time he returned to Spain in 1975, he was trying to organize a large party of the center. Although this was not a complete success, Fraga was a key figure in the transition to democracy. In the first cabinet of King Juan Carlos, Fraga served as deputy prime minister. This experience lasted only six months. Fraga resigned when Adolfo Suárez was appointed prime minister in June 1976 and started organizing the Popular Alliance.[8] From his background, his extensive writings, and his public declarations, it is appropriate to conclude that Fraga was a conservative as much as a reformer from the right. It seemed likely that he would remain a controversial figure in Spanish politics.

Laureano López Rodó (Regional Action)

López Rodó was one of the most powerful politicians in the last decade of the Franco regime. His power was mostly a function of his close friendship with Carrero Blanco—the regime's strongman, who was assassinated in 1973—as well as of the fact that he was the creator and director of the National Planning Agency, which functioned during the period of most spectacular economic growth, 1962-73.

The oil crisis of 1973 posed a threat to the planners' blueprints in Spain as in other countries. By this time, López Rodó had already left the Ministry of Planning, which was finally abolished in 1975. Yet López Rodó continued to speak proudly of the three development plans that were devised and implemented under his authority, claiming that planning was chiefly responsible for the economic and social modernization of Spain. His critics maintained, on the contrary, that even without planning the country's economy would have developed under the impact of foreign investment, tourism, and the exporting of Spanish labor to other European countries.[9] Whatever the truth, López Rodó seems entitled to associate himself politically with the economic development of Spain.

By the time development planning was on its way out and Prime Minister Carrero Blanco was assassinated, López Rodó headed the Ministry of Foreign Affairs. He had to leave the ministry when a new wave of politicians were appointed to the strategic positions that had been held by Carrero and his friends in Opus Dei, the Catholic organization of which López Rodó was a member. He went to Vienna as Spanish ambassador but soon returned to Spain to participate directly in the new stage of Spanish politics.

Unlike Fraga, López Rodó had never been widely known to the general public. Like many other well-established politicians of Franco's Spain, he became better known just at the time when he was losing power, during the electoral campaign.[10] Yet it should not be forgotten that López Rodó was the most active and effective economic and administrative reformer in Franco's Spain.

López Rodó, too, had been a member of the Falange since his youth. He early attained tenure as a university professor of public administration. Then, from his position within the prime minister's entourage, he tried to modernize the state apparatus and the structure of government. It was under his influence that basic legislation on administrative procedures and personnel was enacted. He was also responsible for legislation about the structure of public administration that is still applicable. After the new Spanish constitution was approved by the Chamber of Deputies in November 1978, López Rodó left the Popular Alliance. By this time Fraga was attempting to build up the Democratic Coalition, and López Rodó did not stand in the elections of 1979.

Federico Silva (Spanish Democratic Action)

Silva, like López Rodó, had strong ties to Catholic organizations. One of the three candidates for the prime ministership in July 1976, he had a reputation for efficiency, mostly in the area of public works. He too was an outspoken person and had had a successful career in both the higher civil service and the business sector.

Silva was given a seat in the Franco legislature in 1961. By 1965 he joined the cabinet as minister of public works and devised and started implementing a plan for the construction of a national network of highways.[11] Four years later, when Silva resigned, some claimed it was the first time one of Franco's ministers had resigned instead of being dismissed.

Taking advantage of the law passed in 1974 that permitted some forms of political association, Silva organized a party under the name Spanish Democratic Union (UDE) in 1975. This party split in less than a year; Silva remained the head of the more conservative wing, while the more reformist members decided to cooperate with Prime Minister Suárez, first in his predemocratic cabinet and then in the Union of the Democratic Center. Silva was one of the few members of the Cortes elected in 1977 who voted against the draft constitution. Shortly thereafter, he left the Popular Alliance in order to build up an electoral coalition of the extreme right that never got off the ground. He did not run in the elections of 1979.

Licinio de la Fuente (Social Democracy)

Like other leading members of the Popular Alliance, Licinio de la Fuente rose from rather humble origins and made a very successful career, both bureaucratic and political. At twenty-five he held the prestigious title of *abogado del estado*; subsequently he was appointed to a provincial governorship and to other important political offices. In 1969 he became minister of labor, which remained he until 1975; like Silva, he resigned rather than being dismissed by Franco. Licinio de la Fuente was best known for his programs for the elderly and the retired. He also promoted technical and vocational schools. Yet basic legislation on industrial relations—even regulation of the right to strike along widely accepted Western standards—was not enacted during the time when he was minister of labor. Soon after gaining a seat in Parliament as a Popular Alliance deputy he left the coalition. He did not run in the 1979 elections.

Cruz Martínez Esteruelas (Spanish People's Union)

In his mid-forties, the president of the Spanish People's Union was the youngest of the Popular Alliance leaders. He had been a successful higher civil servant and a member of the Falange since his youth and sat in the last two Franco cabinets, presiding over the Ministry of Planning in 1974 and the

Ministry of Education in 1975. Before becoming a minister, he had occupied important positions in both the public and private sectors. The author of several books, he wrote a doctoral thesis about planning in the United States, which he submitted to the University of Madrid while he was minister of planning. Besides Manuel Fraga, Martínez Esteruelas was the only Popular Alliance leader who joined the Democratic Coalition in 1979 as a candidate, but he failed to win a seat.

Gonzalo Fernández de la Mora (Spanish National Union)

Like Licinio de la Fuente, Fernández de la Mora chose not to dissolve his party when it joined the Popular Alliance. De la Mora had been a diplomat and director of the Spanish School of Diplomacy and for a few years a member of the Private Council of Don Juan de Borbón, King Juan Carlos's father. Like Federico Silva, he had been engaged in public works planning, serving as minister of public works during the early 1970s, just after Silva's resignation.

Fernández de la Mora was a prolific writer, claiming to have written over 4,000 pages.[12] His best-known book, *El crepúsculo de las ideologías*, is a study of the decay of political ideologies in industrial societies along the lines of Daniel Bell's *The End of Ideology*, published a few years earlier. He has consistently advocated strong government oriented toward efficient, practical action—what he came to define as an *estado de obras*, or public works government. He classified the Franco regime as a government of this type, comparing it to Athens under Pericles, Rome under Caesar, Victorian England, and France under Napoleon.[13] Like Federico Silva, Fernández de la Mora voted against the draft constitution in parliament and left the Popular Alliance soon after. He was not a candidate in 1979.

Enrique Thomás de Carranza (Popular Social Union)

Thomás de Carranza was the least known and perhaps the most conservative of the leaders of the Popular Alliance. Never a minister, he held a law degree and occupied important second-level positions under Franco. He did not fit the pattern, so common among his colleagues in the Popular Alliance, of a successful career civil servant, nor was he known as a writer, lecturer, or intellectual. His ideological bent, however, can be deduced from the fact that he was a founding member of New Force, the most right-wing group in Spain and one frequently associated with violent action. He was not elected in 1977 and made no public appearances thereafter.

José María de Areilza (Liberal Action)

Manuel Fraga Iribarne's chief new collaborators in building up the Democratic Coalition were two politicians from the center-right, José María de Areilza and Alfonso Osorio. A member of the Spanish nobility, Areilza joined the

Falange and played an important role in the early years of the Franco regime. He was appointed mayor of Bilbao, the most important northern Spanish city, in the 1940s and Spanish ambassador to the United States in the 1950s. In the 1960s he was a member of the Private Council of Don Juan de Borbón. By this time he had shifted to a liberal ideological position which put him in trouble with the Franco regime; there was even a time when he was denied a passport. But after Franco's death, Areilza was, for six months, minister of foreign affairs in the first government named by Juan Carlos.

Areilza was not a candidate in the 1977 election, although he had been a founder of one of the parties making up the Union of the Democratic Center. Instead, he publicly endorsed the Senators for Democracy lists, which included Christian Democrats, Liberals, and Socialists and had the support of the Communist party and other forces of the left.

Alfonso Osorio (Progressive Democratic party)

The youngest of the three Democratic coalition leaders, Osorio was a conservative Christian democrat who had always been affiliated with Catholic organizations. He held prominent administrative positions in the late Franco regime and became deputy prime minister under Suárez in the first cabinet of the transition. A member of the Union of the Democratic Center, he was appointed to the Senate by the king in 1977. After the first general election, Osorio left the cabinet, and later he publicly stated his disagreements with Prime Minister Suárez's policies. Shortly before the general election of 1979, Osorio founded his own party and then joined the Democratic Coalition with Fraga and Areilza.

Programs and Campaigns

The Popular Alliance

At least three main points about the Popular Alliance campaign in 1977 must be stressed. First, it was both intensive and extensive. Second, a rather ambiguous image of the party emerged from its campaign activities: moderation was cultivated in the program and written statements, while an aggressive conservatism was conveyed at meetings and in spoken statements. Finally, like many other parties, the Popular Alliance began by stressing party but ended by calling support for its leading personality, Manuel Fraga.

The Popular Alliance campaign actually started long before the official date. Fraga traveled the country for several months, giving lectures and meeting people. In all, he probably traveled about 150,000 miles—more than any other politician.[14] Once the campaign was officially under way, the Popular Alliance increased its activities. Fraga's lectures as well as meetings and printed and broadcast propaganda proliferated throughout the country. At least during the first half of the campaign, the Popular Alliance's propaganda was probably more conspicuous than any other party's. Besides posters and pamphlets, the party published several books and a campaign journal.

Both the amount and the sources of the party's financial support are hard to assess, but one thing should be clear to anybody familiar with the administration of Spanish electoral campaigns: the figures quoted by newspapers and party spokesmen fell far short of reality. In the case of the Popular Alliance, six months before the election one leader declared that the party would need about $21 million in order to get 9 million votes.[15] By the end of the campaign, some newspapers suggested that it had spent about $7 million.[16] A few days after the elections, in which the Popular Alliance did rather poorly, official coalition sources publicly requested from members and sympathizers financial support to the tune of about $3 million to make up the deficit between campaign expenses and the reimbursement the coalition would receive from the government on the basis of its vote.[17] Nevertheless, according to some experts in campaign activities, the Popular Alliance may have spent more than $30 million on its campaign, as much as a major party. As for the sources of the Popular Alliance's campaign funds, sixty-one business firms and banks, where important members of the Popular Alliance had some standing or connections, publicly reported making contributions,[18] but the amounts were difficult to guess.

The program and written declarations The AP's program and written publicity—interviews, posters, pamphlets, books and articles—clearly reflected an ideology of the center-right within the Spanish context. From the founding manifesto of October 1976 to Manuel Fraga's last article before election day, its written campaign material consistently defined a moderate center-right position.[19] The main principles can be summarized as follows.

First, the Popular Alliance advocated the free-market economy, where private property and initiative were respected and fostered. Within such a system, social policies should promote a more just distribution of income. A free, independent, and democratic trade unionism was considered necessary to the development of a modern industrial order. Second, with regard to the structure of government, the Popular Alliance favored constitutional reform but not a complete break with the past. As for the functioning of government, much emphasis was placed on law and order. Greater autonomy for the different regions of the country was endorsed, although the Popular Alliance seemed deliberately unspecific on this sensitive point. The constitutional role of the armed forces should include both the defense of the territorial integrity of the country and the defense of the constitutional order. Third, in the realm of foreign policy, the Popular Alliance advocated Spain's integration into the European Economic Community and NATO, maintaining a close relationship with the United States, and pursuing diplomatic relations with all the countries of the world. Finally, the Popular Alliance was in favor of women's rights and equality as well as divorce reform, although the legalization of divorce would be possible only after changes had been made in the legal relationship between church and state.

All Popular Alliance campaign advertising bore the slogan "Popular Alliance. Spain is the only important thing." A variety of posters and press notices mentioned parts of the Popular Alliance program, sometimes in colloquial terms. There were references to youth, the elderly, the industrial and agricultural sectors, the family, education, the problems of those on the fringes of society, the economic crisis, and so on. Much emphasis was also placed on security, peace, and law and order. Thus Popular Alliance advertisements read:

> Today Spain is in need of better communications and transportation [education, jobs, etc.]. If you think so too, vote for the Popular Alliance. Spain is the only important thing. Worker, if you want social cooperation instead of class struggle, vote for the Popular Alliance: Spain is the only important thing.
> We need the support of our youth [we seek conciliation, foster education, science and culture, etc.]. Popular Alliance: Spain is the only important thing.
> Because we need justice and honesty [progress and imagination, democracy and freedom, etc.], vote Fraga. Fraga will be useful.[20]

This last advertisement was typical of those that appeared at the end of the campaign even outside Madrid, where Fraga was running. In districts outside Madrid a sentence was added at the bottom of the advertisement: "Give your vote to the candidates of the Popular Alliance."

At least from their printed materials, it is hard to see major differences between the Popular Alliance's program and those of other center parties, particularly the Union of the Democratic Center, beyond the special emphasis the Popular Alliance placed on law and order and on gradual constitutional reform. Yet two facts should be underscored: First, almost every party in Spain presented its program as moderate and expressed a commitment to democracy. Second, and more important, written propaganda is but one key to understanding political behavior. One must look to the leaders' backgrounds as well as their actions to assess the real position—ideological, strategic, and tactical —of any given group within the polity.

Meetings and speeches It was apparent during the campaign that the moderate tone of the printed materials of the Popular Alliance was inconsistent with the aggressive right-wing stands and nostalgia for the Franco regime that the Popular Alliance leaders displayed in their statements to the press, public speeches, and television appearances. When Prime Minister Suárez legalized the Communist party, for example, Manuel Fraga publicly accused him of having staged a coup d'état. Later the leader of the Popular Alliance was very critical of legislation forbidding military personnel to engage in electoral activities. Above all, at mass meetings and on television the leaders of the Popular Alliance appeared at their most conservative.

Throughout the campaign, the mood at Popular Alliance meetings was very much the same. The party opened its campaign with a rally at the Escorial, where Philip II is buried; the speakers recalled the Spanish Civil War, from which Franco had emerged victorious, and claimed that the country was crumbling politically, economically, and morally.[21] A month later, at the party's last meeting in the main bullring of Madrid, former prime minister Arias Navarro exalted the memory of Franco and warned that Spain was going through a prerevolutionary phase, while Manuel Fraga attacked every political party except his own.[22] In their two main television appearances, Arias and Fraga struck a similar note. It should also be pointed out that the Popular Alliance was the only party that tried to associate its campaign with the king, using pictures of him from the time when Arias was prime minister as backgrounds for its television broadcasts. The contrast between this kind of maneuver and the moderation of the party's printed publicity left room for real doubt about the fundamental political identity of the Popular Alliance as an electoral coalition and as a group of politicians.

Some scholars publicly speculated that a major reason for the poor showing of the Popular Alliance at the polls was the aggressive right-wing outlook its leaders were forced to adopt by the audiences at meetings and public gatherings.[23] This line of reasoning might lead to the conclusion that the Popular Alliance leaders were less conservative than they appeared. Observers from the center and the left, on the other hand, claimed that the Popular Alliance leaders were much more conservative than they wanted to appear.[24] Five days before the election, *El País* ran an editorial to this effect headed: "Popular Alliance: The Ashes of Francoism." Another analyst concluded after the elections that the more intensive the Popular Alliance campaign became, the lower the party's standing fell among the electorate.[25]

The Democratic Coalition

The electoral program that the Democratic Coalition presented to the electorate in early 1979 was a general political declaration rather than a platform in the strict sense. Its content was similar to that of the Popular Alliance program two years earlier, although more emphasis was placed on security, especially the fight against terrorism, the defense of the right to life, and the liberalization of the economic system through a reduction of state intervention and a progressive but not vindictive system of taxation. Although the political orientation of the CD program did not differ too much from that of the Union of the Democratic Center, the CD criticized the government party for its failure to protect law and order and provide strong government as it had promised to do in 1977. The CD campaign itself was at least as ambitious as the one AP had run in 1977. Most observers estimated that the Democratic Coalition spent no less than $15 million on its campaign, although CD sources claimed they had spent a maximum of $10 million.

With the winter not quite over, the 1979 campaign took place mainly indoors. Public meetings tended to be held in theaters, restaurants, and convention halls, and audiences tended to be modest. These were not the massive rallies of 1977. Once again Fraga played the most important role, making some sixty appearances in the twenty-one days of the campaign, while Areilza and Osorio were more concerned with other campaign activities such as relations with the mass media and elite groups.

The Democratic Coalition's campaign passed through two clearly distinguishable phases, each lasting about ten days. With so little time between the coalition's creation and the election, its strategists made mistakes that they tried to remedy halfway through the campaign. In the first phase, the party's printed material stressed themes—prices, unemployment, security, the family, and so on—and criticized the government. The underlying message was the government's inability to cope with existing problems because of its lack of definition and its weakness. Thus one CD message was: "The family: One of the things that is being destroyed. To put things in order, the Democratic Coalition defends the family." In the second phase CD advertisements asked the voter to support the "center-right solution." The Democratic Coalition's television broadcasts followed the same pattern: the first two broadcasts stressed the government's "mistakes," the last asked for support. In the television campaign the three leaders of the Democratic Coalition shared the spotlight in proportion to the assumed importance of their respective groups: Fraga was on longer than Areilza, Areilza longer than Osorio.

The two different phases of the CD campaign seem to have reflected two different assessments of the party's electoral possibilities. The first phase seemed devised under the assumption that the Democratic Coalition would be able to attract an important share of the vote that had gone to the Union of the Democratic Center in 1977, while the second, disregarding that possibility, merely aimed at maintaining the support of the people who had voted for the Popular Alliance in 1977.

The Electoral Returns

Eight months before the 1977 elections, some leaders of the newly created Popular Alliance declared that they hoped to take more than 50 percent of the popular vote—Martínez Esteruelas even spoke of something between 60 and 70 percent.[26] This was long before some of the nonleftist parties had taken shape, notably the Union of the Democratic Center under the leadership of Prime Minister Suárez. In fact, the Popular Alliance fell far short of its leaders' original expectations, the support of 1.5 million voters giving it only sixteen seats in the Chamber of Deputies, two seats in the Senate.

Only a few opinion polls accurately predicted this outcome—and some placed the Popular Alliance as low as 2 percent. In all the surveys taken during the campaign, however, the number of undecided respondents was unusually large—generally more than 50 percent.[27] This made projecting the outcome a hazardous venture, although the margin of error was likely to be smallest for parties at the extremes of the political spectrum. It was a safe bet that the Popular Alliance would be one of these once Prime Minister Suárez decided to head a coalition of the center-right and the Popular Alliance to stress its conservative features. The Popular Alliance came to be identified with what was left of Francoism and therefore had little public appeal. In this connection it is worth noting that in several opinion surveys conducted during the last few years of the Franco regime (some of them by this writer) only 10 to 15 percent of the adult population identified themselves as sympathetic to the Falange or the Movement, the Francoist organizations from which the Popular Alliance leaders came.[28]

Nevertheless, in 1979 again, the Democratic Coalition leaders publicly predicted that they would take an important share of the vote, although they would not say how much. The opinion polls, meanwhile, predicted a small CD vote. And, as in 1977, the coalition came in fourth, right after the Communists, with a million votes. This was six percent of the tally—2.3 percent and almost half a million votes less than the Popular Alliance had taken in 1977. For representation in Parliament, this meant ten seats—down from sixteen for the Popular Alliance in 1977.

Apparently, the Democratic Coalition failed to make a dent in the UCD constituency on the one hand and lost part of the former Popular Alliance vote to the extreme right on the other. The latter more than doubled the far right's share of the vote, from less than 0.5 percent in 1977 to 2 percent in 1979. Clearly, the Democratic Coalition had little appeal for either the moderate voter or the voter of the far right in either 1977 or 1979.[29]

The geographic distribution of the vote for the Popular Alliance and the Democratic Coalition was similar and uneven (see table 8.1). It is important to note that several historic voting patterns reemerged. First, support for these

Table 8.1 Popular Alliance and Democratic Coalition Election Returns by Region and Province, 1977 and 1979

		Chamber				Senate	
Region and Province	Total Seats in Province	Percent of AP 1977	CD 1979	AP 1977	CD 1979	AP Seats, 1977	CD Seats, 1979
Andalusia							
Almería	5	8.1	4.4	—	—	—	—
Cádiz	8	4.9	3.3	1	—	—	—
Córdoba	7	9.3	5.7	—	—	—	—
Granada	7	7.1	4.7	—	—	—	—
Huelva	5	5.0	3.3	—	—	—	—
Jaén	7	8.6	3.6	—	—	—	—
Málaga	8	8.4	3.9	—	—	—	—
Seville	12	6.3	4.7	—	—	—	—
Aragón							
Huesca	3	5.9	4.5	—	—	—	—
Teruel	3	16.1	8.3	—	—	—	—
Zaragoza	8	8.0	5.4	—	—	—	—
Asturias							
Oviedo	10	13.5	8.6	1	1	—	—
Balearic Islands	6	8.8	9.2	—	—	—	—
Basque Country							
Alava	4	6.4	6.2	—	—	—	—
Guipúzcoa	7	8.2	1.0	—	—	—	—
Vizcaya	10	6.5	4.3	—	—	—	—
Navarre*	5	8.4	—	—	1	—	—
Canary Islands							
Las Palmas	6	5.6	3.0	—	—	—	—
Tenerife	7	9.2	4.6	—	—	—	—
Castile-Leon							
Avila	3	6.8	6.9	—	—	—	—
Burgos	4	14.6	8.2	—	—	—	—
Leon	6	12.4	11.4	—	—	—	—
Palencia	3	14.5	9.5	—	—	—	—
Salamanca	4	7.8	7.7	—	—	—	—
Segovia	3	8.7	6.6	—	—	—	—

Table 8.1 continued.

		Chamber				Senate	
Region and Province	Total Seats in Province	Percent of AP 1977	CD 1979	AP 1977	CD 1979	AP Seats, 1977	CD Seats, 1979
Soria	3	6.3	10.1	—	—	—	—
Valladolid	5	8.4	8.4	—	—	—	—
Zamora	4	24.1	16.4	1	—	—	—
Castile-La Mancha							
Ciudad Real	5	12.5	4.8	—	—	—	—
Cuenca	4	8.2	6.0	—	—	—	—
Guadalajara	3	15.7	10.8	—	—	—	—
Toledo	5	16.6	5.6	1	—	—	—
Albacete	4	9.5	4.9	—	—	—	—
Madrid	32	10.5	8.6	3	3	—	—
Cantabria							
Santander	5	14.4	—	1	—	—	—
Catalonia							
Barcelona	33	3.2	3.7	1	1	—	—
Gerona	5	3.2	3.4	—	—	—	—
Lérida	4	5.4	3.2	—	—	—	—
Tarragona	5	6.0	4.0	—	—	—	—
Estremadura							
Badajoz	7	6.8	3.4	—	—	—	—
Cáceres	5	9.3	4.1	—	—	—	—
Galicia							
La Coruña	9	11.0	11.8	—	—	—	—
Lugo Orense	5	13.3	18.8	1	1	—	—
Pontevedra	8	11.4	11.7	1	1	—	—
Murcia	8	6.8	5.7	—	—	—	—
Rioja							
Logroño	5	21.8	19.3	1	1	1	1
Valencia							
Alicante	9	6.5	5.2	—	—	—	—
Castellón	5	6.0	3.5	—	—	—	—
Valencia	15	5.4	4.4	1	—	—	—

Table 8.1 continued.

		Chamber				Senate	
Region and Province	Total Seats in Province	Percent of AP 1977	CD 1979	AP 1977	CD 1979	AP Seats, 1977	CD Seats, 1979
Spanish Cities in North Africa							
Ceuta	1	—	7.9	—	—	—	—
Melilla	1	10.9	4.9	—	—	—	—

Source: Institute for Political Studies, *Partidos políticos y elecciones* [Political parties and elections] (Madrid: Instituto de Estudios Políticos, 1977), pp. 305–40; *El País* (Madrid), 2 May 1979, pp. 13–18, and 3 May 1979, pp. 17–22; Ministry of the Interior, "Advances del Ministerio del Interior"; and data supplied by José Ignacio Wert Ortega, # Centro de Investigaciones Sociológicas, Madrid.
* Navarre is sometimes referred to as both a region and province, however, natives of Navarre do not refer to themselves as Basques.

coalitions was highest in those areas of Spain where the right had done relatively well in the elections of the Second Spanish Republic (1931–36).[30] Second, it was particularly low in the industrial areas of the country—with the partial exception of Madrid—as well as in those areas with a latifundia pattern of land tenure and a tradition of peasant radicalism (southern and western Spain). It was higher in the provinces in central and northwestern Spain, which did not have an industrial past, are not densely populated, and have an agricultural pattern of small and middle-sized farms.

Although the coalition leaders were disappointed, the importance of the AP and CD vote could not be underestimated in either 1977 or 1979. More than 1 million voters supported a conservative-reformist alternative in preference either to the most conservative groups of the right or to Suárez. As Juan Linz has stressed on several occasions, however, the support of Spanish voters for groups at both extremes of the political spectrum has a double importance. First, such voters tend to be people of strong ideological commitment; this was true of Popular Alliance and Democratic Coalition voters as much as of Communists. Second, the parties they support are rather special, precisely because they operate at the fringes of the democratic system. Despite their minor electoral support, they can play a crucial role in stabilization or destabilization of the political system.[31]

Even after two general elections, it was not wise to conclude that the relatively small share of the vote attracted by the Popular Alliance and the Democratic Coalition necessarily spelled final defeat for either the interests or the ideology these parties represent. Out of the various parties and coalitions of the Spanish right, which have been preoccupied with personal feuds and minor ideological disputes until now, there still could emerge a solid political party. And quite apart from any party's electoral performance, some of the leaders of the Popular Alliance and the Democratic Coalition remained significant figures on the Spanish political scene.

Catalan Nationalism and the Spanish Elections
JUAN F. MARSAL AND JAVIER ROIZ

──────Any serious student of Spanish politics and society is struck by most foreigners' ignorance of the role played by the so-called historic minorities: Galacia, Euzkadi, and the subject of this chapter, Catalonia. By contrast, no one inside Spain is unaware of Catalonia's importance. On the contrary, the "Catalan question" arouses so much passion that one nineteenth-century Iberian historical compared it to the "Jewish question" in Germany, even though the political class in Madrid has traditionally exploited prejudice against the cultural minorities to prevent them from offering a political and cultural alternative to the prevailing *españolismo*.

It is difficult to account for the ignorance manifested by foreigners interested in Spanish affairs, including some who come from Spanish-speaking countries that have already freed themselves from the same centralist yoke the Catalans are trying to throw off. The universal acceptance of Spanish hegemony, with all the prejudices involved, can be considered one of the few real successes of Madrid diplomacy in the twentieth century. As José Goytisolo—a poet who writes in the Castilian language—has lamented: "Catalan culture is still seen as a kind of nebula made up of the glow from a thousand wrecks and a language not taught in Madrid schools."[1]

According to Oriol Pi-Sunyer, a Catalan anthropologist working in the United States, there are historic reasons for the Western world's ignorance of Catalonia's fight to preserve its independent identity. "From the Renaissance to the present," he writes, "the history of Europe suggests that the national directing elites distrust pluralism and view the monoethnic state as the ideal goal. With only a little exaggeration, post-medieval political philosophy could well be paraphrased as *one state, one language, one culture*."[2] Pi-Sunyer quite properly reminds us that it was not always so, for during the Middle Ages "pluralism was the rule rather than the exception." But the problem is not only historical. In recent times an anticolonialist mood in the United States and the other Western powers has diverted attention from the element of internal colonialism in these nations' dealings with their own cultural minorities and directed it toward colonies still dependent on foreign powers.[3]

Modern European regionalism, such as that found in Catalonia, is anything but an atavism. Indeed, it is a product of substantially industrial or postindustrial societies. The present-day reawakening of national or regional consciousness (Flemish, Slovakian, Cypriot, Croatian, Breton, Scottish, and so on) is emerging just when central European nationalism is on the decline. Catalonia could be, for Pi-Sunyer, a crucial illustration of this paradoxical reawakening, for Catalonia is the opposite of underdeveloped. Bearing in mind the numerous studies that posit the Mediterranean as a paradigm of traditionalist underdevelopment, Pi-Sunyer adds: "A social and cultural entity that is both *Mediterranean* and *developed* is apparently difficult to conceptualize; almost, in fact, a contradiction in terms."[4]

Jaume Vicens Vives, the respected Catalan historian who died at the height of his creative life when he was the head of one of the most prestigious schools of economic and social history in Catalonia, referred to the Catalans as a "transient people" with a "mestizo culture."[5] It was founded by what he called *homines undecumque venientes*, men from everywhere. The Catalan coast was the site of Iberian, Greek, and Roman cities visited by travelers from all the great Mediterranean empires, while the inland sections were populated by waves of soldiers and settlers from the Gothic monarchies Christianized between the fifth and eighth centuries. Catalonia emerged as a country with its own individual identity and territory between the seventh and the ninth centuries, when Christianity and Islam were the major political forces in the Mediterranean. Catalonia was a buffer state; at first a feudal territory with its own culture and political institutions, and then, from the ninth century, a principality comparable to Florence, Milan, and Venice. But ultimately its neighbors, France and Spain, turned into Renaissance states, whose languages have spread across the world, while Catalonia, with its minority language and culture, remained in their shadow, seldom noticed by foreigners save during the turbulent periods of its history.

Given this general ignorance of the Catalan question, it is difficult to discuss Catalonia in analytical terms without touching on the historical background of Catalan nationalism. To consider the Catalan case, as many have, under the heading of sociology and politics of the Mediterranean area is, in our opinion, a tremendous mistake, a distortion of history that impairs any subsequent analysis.

Nationalism in Spain

Let us begin with an excursus into the concept of nation. Essentially three different conceptions of the nation have enjoyed some currency in Europe since the mid-nineteenth century. There is the romantic conception created by the "doctrinaires" of German idealism and historicism, for whom the nation is a spiritual entity, the mystical embodiment of the spirit of the people (*Volkgeist*) and a whole greater than its parts. Their view is summed up in the claim: "Peoples are spiritual principles."[6] This doctrine was espoused by the great nineteenth-century movements for national unification of Germany and Italy —and by the Catalan nationalist bourgeoisie during the same period, when its hegemony was threatened by class struggles and workers' organizations. Luis Durán i Ventosa, a prominent right-wing Catalan nationalist, expressed it clearly:

> Catalan regionalists should never be so naive as to think that the majority of the citizens' votes represent the nation—particularly when they base the legitimacy of their decisions upon representation, assuming that only what their representatives agree upon is legitimate. No, the national will does not consist merely of the sum of individual wills, which is deceptive most of the time: if the nation, as regionalism contends, is not a mere aggregate of individuals but a superior living entity, its will, instead of being the sum of individuals' wills, must be the independent will of a distinct entity, with its own personality, of which those individuals are just constituent parts.[7]

The opposition between this right-wing nationalism and democracy could hardly be stated more starkly.

Second, contrasted to this spiritual and ultimately totalitarian concept of the nation stands the Marxist theory, summed up by the formula "the market is the primary school where the bourgeoisie learns its nationalism." This interpretation is followed by Pierre Vilar, the great French historian of Catalonia[8] To Vilar, who rejected the static conception held by the political right, "the nation is a historic category produced by a specific age: that of rising capitalism." Therefore, national problems become intimately linked with those of a specific class. National identity and a sense of community are merely instruments used by the different social classes in their attempts to establish their political predominance. To Vilar the economic structure is, of course, the independent variable on which group feelings depend; Catalan nationalism is explained by the ties between Catalonia's leading elites and the political personnel in Madrid, the backbone of the Spanish state.

Max Weber formulated subtler ideas about the nation and nationalism. For Weber (and it is surprising for such a notorious nationalist) the nation was an ambiguous concept, permeated by many others—class interests, prestige, the intelligentsia, religion, culture, and, above all, native language—none of which by itself is necessary or sufficient. In this as in everything, Weber emphasizes the multiplicity of causes. But Weber's view coincides with that of the Marxists in that only collective political action can empirically prove the existence of a nation in the international political arena. Once national feeling has crystallized, it tends to produce an autonomous state: "A nation," in Weber's words, "is a community of sentiment which would adequately manifest itself in a state of its own; hence, a nation is a community which normally tends to produce a state of its own."[9]

But the problem is that in Spain "community feeling" and "group national consciousness" do not have a single clear focus precisely because the struggle between Castilian centralism and the federalism of the peripheral peoples has never been resolved. "The Castilian attempt at the formation of a Spanish national consciousness failed," wrote Vicens Vives about the sixteenth century. But the federalists from the periphery also failed to impose their pluralist concept of the state, both in the sixteenth century and in the nineteenth century. No one has described better than Juan Linz the aftermath of these failures: "Spain might have succeeded in state-building, but it has had somewhat less success in nation-building . . . [it] went far but not far enough." It is not surprising that a long historical process should produce an "ambivalent outcome." Linz believes that "Spain today is a state for all Spaniards, a nation-state for a large part of the population, and only a state but not a nation for important minorities."[10] This is a fact no student of the social and political reality of Spain can ignore. At the present time, the different conceptions of the national community, objectively and subjectively, exist in equilibrium; and it seems that all of them have missed opportunities to determine the shape of the Spanish nation. Castile and Catalonia, or rather Madrid and Barcelona, are doomed to live together on a political seesaw, to travel a common road along which each will sometimes lead and sometimes follow. Not even forty years of Francoist dictatorship, we now see, was able to erode, much less destroy, Spanish pluralism.

Historical Background

Spain and, within it, the Kingdom of Aragon and Catalonia emerged as political entities in the Middle Ages.[11] This was a prenational era, and Vicens Vives was entirely correct when he denied the validity of the ideological constructions created by later Castilian and Catalan historians and projected, out of nationalist zeal, a posteriori onto quite different realities. National histories cannot apply to a time when there were no nations. What existed in the Middle Ages was a pluralist conception of political life, general to the whole Iberian peninsula, which evolved gradually into the Hispanic monarchy of the Hapsburgs in the sixteenth century, a sort of personal monarchic confederation in which the Kingdom of Castile always played a central role.

Castile's predominance was inevitable, for many reasons of which population was one of the most important.[12] In addition, Castile was embarked upon an imperialist adventure in America. The crown of Aragon had no international endeavors under way, and neither did the Principality of Catalonia, which, on the basis of its wealth and its prosperous Mediterranean trade, intended to become an independent "signoria" on the Italian model.

The greater dynamism of Castile rapidly brought its logical consequence: an attempt to unify the whole of Spain under Castilian domination. Led by the Generalitat,[13] the Catalan people struggled to defend their *fueros*[14] and resist absolutist pretensions of the Crown. Repeatedly from the fifteenth to the eighteenth century, conflict developed into open war, each time ending in a Catalan defeat and a subsequent erosion of Catalan independence. After 1707 Catalonia lost its autonomy and a distinctive political arrangements, becoming just one more Spanish province, administered more or less as the others were administered and like them subject to Madrid's executive power.[15] In addition, there was social unrest in Catalonia, including in the seventeenth century an egalitarian peasant revolt with all the characteristics of a *Jacquerie*.

Each time its independence was threatened, Catalonia tried desperately to find European allies to help in the defense of its territory and its laws from the pretensions of the Spanish Crown. But here is a constant feature of Catalonia's turbulent history: France, instead of being a potential ally against Castile, itself posed a serious danger to Catalan autonomy. Had Catalonia had a different neighbor on its northern border—for example, a pluralist federal state —the history of the principality would have been very different. It is no coincidence that the height of Spanish patriotic fervor in Catalonia, during the war against Napoleon, coincided with the strongest hostility toward the French state.

Spain entered the nineteenth century ruined by its fight against Napoleon's army and by the insurrection of its American colonies. Unable to regain the American colonies by force of arms or to find an administrative and legal solution to its problems, Spain returned to absolute monarchy in 1815. Thus the task commended to successive ministers of the treasury was impossible: "to accommodate the old absolutist regime to the necessities of the new times, without adopting any measure that could alter the existing social structure or touch the privileges of the ruling social sectors."[16]

Spanish liberals realized that this could not be done. Like other European countries, Spain had to get rid of its *ancien régime*. But in Spain change was pursued very cautiously. As Fontana says, Spain had "a bourgeois revolution that was hardly a revolution and that changed very little: it secured a momentary respite, but not enough to stave off a future of economic underdevelopment and social conflict."[17]

Amid the institutional collapse and economic default of the old regime and the growth of a tepid new liberalism, the industrial takeoff of the Catalan economy occurred between 1830 and 1850. It had been preceded by demographic growth due to improvements in agricultural techniques and crop production in the eighteenth century. At the beginning of the nineteenth century, Catalonia contained approximately 10 percent of the total population of Spain. Peasants no longer needed in the agricultural sector provided the initial labor force for economic development. Later, by the end of the century, as those human resources became depleted, they were replaced by waves of immigrants coming from the rest of Spain, particularly the Levant.

During the nineteenth century, Catalonia controlled 40 percent of Spanish industry, and its businessmen, after the loss of their American markets, needed to find new ones to replace them. A division between the bourgeoisie and the people of Catalonia dates to the nineteenth century, this social cleavage intertwined with a cultural one. Catalan particularism inside the Spanish framework began to turn into Catalan nationalism in bourgeois circles but into indifference to politics among the proletariat. Both stemmed from the same frustration. "This apoliticism, which was not always a synonym of Bakuninism," the historian Albert Bacells has written, "clearly reflected scorn and mistrust toward the centralist state, cut off from the real life of Catalonia; it was in fact a working-class variant of Catalan particularism."[18]

Pierre Vilar defined Catalan bourgeois nationalism in terms of an everlasting "frustrated bourgeoisie." Similarly, Solé-Tura describes the history of Catalan nationalism as the "history of a frustrated bourgeois revolution." A speech delivered by the movement's leader, Francesc Cambó, in 1916 in the Spanish parliament illustrates this frustration:

> We Catalan regionalists are unique among Spanish political flora, perhaps among European ones; we spend our lives fighting and opposing the government; but I must add, gentlemen, and let me not speak hypocritically, that we are a group of governing men, men born to govern, and who have prepared ourselves to govern; that we have shown our aptitude for governing in all the spheres we have worked in; and that, nonetheless, we are forever condemned to be men of opposition.[19]

In 1898, after the obvious disaster of the monarchy and the loss of Spain's remaining colonial empire (Cuba and the Philippines), the Catalan bourgeoisie was utterly disillusioned with the Spanish state, which could control nothing and orient no one. Now it advocated a Catalan nationalist solution, an independent state. Once the American colonies, which had been the major market for its products, were lost, the Catalan bourgeoisie became bolder. In 1901 it provoked and led a widespread movement of Catalan solidarity, but the attempt fell short.

As the twentieth century advanced, the nationalist bourgeoisie lost its hegemony in Catalonia to the nationalist left. On the coming of the Second Republic in 1931, this was an accomplished fact. When the Francoist rebellion erupted in 1936, the choice for the Catalan bourgeoisie was between fidelity to the Catalan nation in its struggle for self-government and fidelity to class. Beginning with Cambó himself, it chose the latter, joining forces with Franco. Luis Valls i Taberner, one of the leaders of bourgeois Catalan nationalism, wrote this dramatic mea culpa in 1939, at the end of the Civil War:

> Catalonia has followed an erroneous path, becoming to great extent the victim of its own failures. This wrong path has been nationalist Catalanism. . . . Catalanism, including its generous hope for renovation in the midst of general decadence, turned against Catalonia in the end. On the other hand, what it contained of fidelity, doubtless imperfect but full of candid hope, the longing it represented for reform and perfection—even if it was sometimes too proud and passionate—all has been ignominiously prostituted and sacrificed in the course of these last years. . . . Given that God's providence saved us from irredeemable ruin at the most dangerous and grievous moment through the overwhelming excellence of our Generalissimo Franco and our glorious national army, it is necessary that our rectification, contrition, and amendment mark a new orientation in the life of Catalonia, definitively incorporated into Spain.[20]

In the hard times that followed, the pluralist ideals of the Catalan bourgeoisie vanished, and law and order became the supreme value as it had been elsewhere in such situations.

The left wing of Catalan nationalism followed a completely different course, though also with bourgeois leadership, in the 1930s. This movement originated in nineteenth-century federalism and reached its peak in the 1868 revolution, a delayed manifestation of the revolutionary tide that swept Europe in 1848. Catalan participation in the 1868 revolution was notable.[21] Spanish federalism reached its climax under the First Republic (1873), which perished quickly, undermined by its own failure and eventually swept away by a military coup d'état that brought the monarchy back.

Most historians of leftist Catalanism agree that this nineteenth-century peripheral federalism was the only modernizing and democratic movement in modern Spain. In Catalonia, after the failure of bourgeois nationalism, the party of the industrial and urban lower-middle classes, the Catalan Left, imposed its will through its electoral superiority during the Second Republic (1931–36), with the support of an organized proletariat. A clear majority within the proletariat were non-Catalan-speaking and were heavily influenced by anarchism. This left-wing Catalanism, free of any bourgeois check or tie, carried Catalan autonomy to its furthest point in the middle of the Civil War.[22]

With the republican defeat in the Civil War in 1939 and the military occupation of Catalonia by the Francoist army, the left's experiment with self-rule ended. A long, dark forty years of economic, cultural, and political persecution then began. As we can verify today, this endeavor was as malignant as it was fruitless. In any case, the paranoid repression of the Catalan language and culture under the Francoist regime, as well as the unchecked enrichment of the local oligarchy—the bourgeois minority who had deserted from the Catalan right to cooperate with Madrid—have been documented in every detail.[23]

It is not our task to recount the vicissitudes of the Catalan resistance to the Franco government's efforts to annihilate it after the collapse of the Second Republic in 1939 or to relate all the obstacles the Catalan collective consciousness stumbled against in its long journey through the Francoist night. Let us say, however, that a tremendous growth in self-awareness has characterized the intelligentsia in the last three decades.[24]

What had been barely perceptible in the late 1950s and early 1960s became evident to even the clumsiest observers in Spanish society and politics in the 1970s amid the physical decline of the dictator and his regime. Entire sectors of Spanish society such as the universities and the working class slipped outside the control of a regime whose only recourse was the crudest police repression. The problems of the post-Franco era were already present: an evolution of attitudes was under way. It is, of course, absurd to imagine that the Spanish people went to bed Francoists on 19 November 1975 (the day of General Francisco Franco's death) and woke up democrats the next morning. But what no sociologist dared predict was that one of the most durable authoritarian regimes of our time would cave in, to the astonishment of its followers and supporters.

The Elections of June 1977 in Catalonia

The complicated political process that carried Spain to its first general election after the longest period of dictatorship in its modern history is described in other chapters of this book. Here it is enough to repeat that the electoral law governing the selection of members of the Cortes established a proportional representation system clearly biased in favor of the large parties and the less populous agrarian provinces, which were presumably conservative. This was especially evident in the case of the Senate.

More important for our purposes are the features of the elections that were peculiar to Catalonia. Throughout the electoral campaign the old claims of Catalan nationalism and all the grievances of Catalan particularism were reasserted a common goal was announced: to regain the autonomy lost in Civil

War. The parties affiliated with nationwide parties were denounced as *sucursalistas*—mere subsidiaries or appendages of Madrid politics—even though they repeatedly stated their concern for Catalan autonomy. Only the Popular Alliance (AP), a nationwide right-wing party, which also acknowledged Catalan particularism in its campaign in Catalonia, dared to praise the unity of Spain, one of the leitmotifs of the Franco era. In fact, Franco's repressive use of Spanish unitary nationalism made it easy to identify the worst of Francoism with Spanish nationalism. As we will see, the electoral outcome in Catalonia demonstrated a shift to the left of the entire political spectrum, making the Catalan electorate distinctive. More completely than anywhere else in Spain, the groups, parties, and political movements that were the staunchest supporters of Spanish nationalism, such as the New Force and the Falange, simply dropped out of sight. In Barcelona this was not a surprise: in Franco's last days, when tens of thousands of people gathered in Madrid to demonstrate in favor of the unity of Spain, only a few thousand turned up in Barcelona.

Three types of groups ran in the 15 June Chamber elections:

1. One the right stood the Popular Alliance, a branch of the neo-Francoist party in Spain, whose lists were headed by Franco's ex-minister Laureano López Rodó, a native Catalan. There were also candidates put up by what pretended to be a revitalized version of the traditional party of the Catalan bourgeoisie, the League of Catalonia.

2. There was much more competition in the center. First, there was a Christian Democratic coalition in Catalonia called the Union of the Center and Christian Democracy of Catalonia (UCDCC). But a much stronger force was the Democratic Pact for Catalonia (PDC) led by Jordi Pujol. This important coalition embraced a range of groups from center-right elements to social-democratic offshoots of Catalan socialism. Its expectations were high and its propaganda modern and efficient. Its political coloration was center-left with a strong Catalan nationalist base chiefly among professionals, though it aimed to attract support from immigrant workers and to develop into an interclass party. Prime Minister Adolfo Suárez's government, believing it could make some kind of arrangement with several other centrist groups, also made up its mind to enter the political arena in Catalonia, and submitted a Union of the Democratic Center (UCD) list just before the legal deadline.

3. The classic left was represented by two lists: the Unified Socialist party of Catalonia (PSUC) and the Socialists of Catalonia, the latter embracing both the Catalan Socialist party (PSC) and the Catalan branch of the Spanish Socialist Workers' party (PSOE). This coalition, which would win a plurality of the votes in the region, emerged only two months before election day. Remarkably, it was built up without any serious resistance from either of the two component parties, both of which retained their independent existence. Some sectors of the PSC accused the PSOE of *sucursalismo* and lack of real interest in Catalan

Table 9.1 Results of the 1977 Chamber Election in the Catalan Provinces, by Party

	Barcelona		Tarragona		Lérida		Gerona	
Party	Seats	% of vote	Seats	% of vote	Seats	% of vote	Seats	% of vote
Popular Alliance	1	3.2	0	6.0	0	5.4	0	3.2
Catalan Left	2	4.7	0	4.3	0	7.3	0	[a]
Democratic Pact for Catalonia (CDC, EDC, PSC-R, and FNC)	6	15.2	1	18.0	1	23.4	2	26.8
PSUC (Communist)	7	19.4	1	20.5	1	12.2	0	10.0
Socialists of Catalonia (PSC-PSOE)	11	30.5	1	28.3	1	15.0	2	24.0
Union of the Center and Christian Democracy	2	5.3	0	5.7	0	9.1	0	5.0
UCD	5	15.2	2	27.8	1	24.3	1	18.2
League of Catalonia-Catalan Liberal party of Gerona	0	[a]	—	—	—	—	0	4.0
Independents of Gerona	—	—	—	—	—	—	—	[a]

Source: *El Correo Catalán*, 17 June 1977, p. 4.
Dash: (–): Party did not run.
[a] Under 3 percent.

problems, while the Catalan federation of the PSOE blamed the PSC in turn for its lack of working-class rank and file. Also on the left, the Catalan Popular Socialist party, connected with Enrique Tierno Galván's Popular Socialist party (PSP) ran a few candidates, as did two coalitions of assorted groups (most of them not yet legal) including republicans, Trotskyists, feminists, minor communist splinter groups, and so on—in a word, what the French call *gauchistes*.

In the Senate elections—where candidates ran as individuals, not part of lists—the situation was much simpler. Socialists and Communists joined forces in a sort of popular front; the PDC ran its own list, as did the right-wing League

216 Catalan Nationalism and the Spanish Elections

Figure 9.1 Distribution of Chamber Seats in Catalonia and the Four Catalan Provinces, by Party, 1977

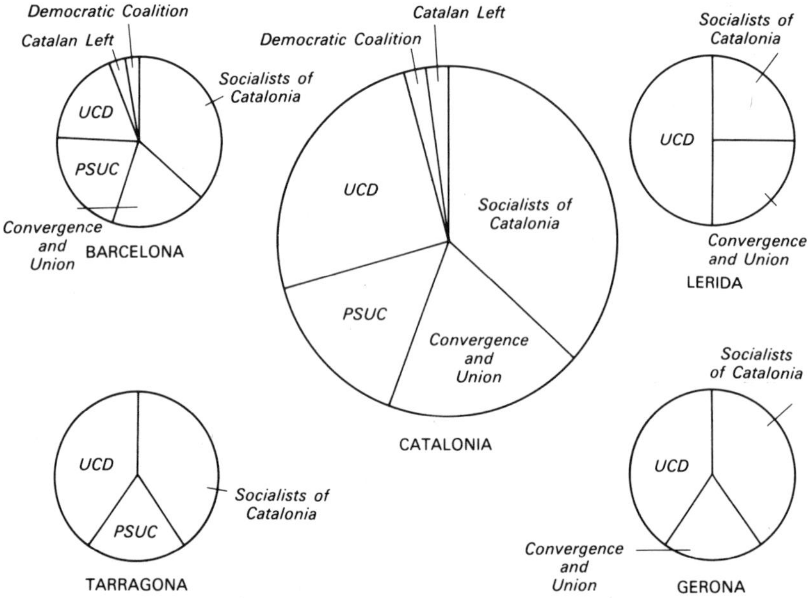

of Catalonia and the UCD. At the same time, many well-known individuals entered the race. One of these was Luis M. Xirinács, a Catholic priest popular for his stubborn fight to secure a general amnesty for political prisoners.

The 1977 election results in Catalonia are shown in table 9.1 and figure 9.1. A glance at the figures confirms the success of the classic left in Catalonia, especially in the province of Barcelona—which, by the way, was the largest in Spain in number of electors. The electoral system favored front-runners and worked to the advantage of the Socialists, who won fifteen seats in the Chamber. In the Senate, the Socialists, Communists, and independents running under the label Agreement of the Catalans scored a landslide victory, taking twelve of the sixteen seats for Catalonia. Of the remaining four seats, Jordi Pujol's centrist alliance took two, independent leftist Xirinacs one, and the UCD the fourth.

One study of Barcelona carried out by a team of electoral analysts from the Autonomous University of Barcelona, shows that there is a bourgeois nucleus in the city of Barcelona, surrounded by a "red belt" with a high density of Socialist and Communist votes (see figures 9.2 and 9.3). Commenting on this study, a political scientist from Barcelona, González Casanova, wrote: "The voting distribution in the different districts of Barcelona induces us to believe that an approximate but significant correlation exists between Barcelonians' voting behavior and their social extraction.... The logic of the vote seems to correspond to the social logic of Barcelona." There is a certain percentage of interclass votes, but, even though Barcelona as a whole is further left than the rest of Catalonia, in González Casanova's opinion, class is still "the great fundamental division."[25]

The sociologist Esteban Pinilla de las Heras (himself a defeated PSP candidate) made his own analysis two days after the elections. Pinilla tried to explain the winners' success in terms of "their ability to make a sum (rather than a synthesis) of the electorate's tendencies and orientations." The PSOE, in Pinilla's view, was well on its way to becoming a catchall party. Its votes, and to a lesser degree those of the Communists, he saw as coming from a working class that opposed private economic power, as well as from intellectuals and professionals.[26] This mixture corresponded quite accurately to the structure of the coalition Socialists of Catalonia: the PSC was basically a party of intellectuals with an efficient rank and file, while the Catalan PSOE was a mass party, supported for the most part by the immigrant working class, which in Catalonia included about 40 percent of the total population from the very bottom of the social ladder. Evidently the Catalan electorate, and especially that of Barcelona, sought a leftist and autonomist solution to its problems. Arguably, the election

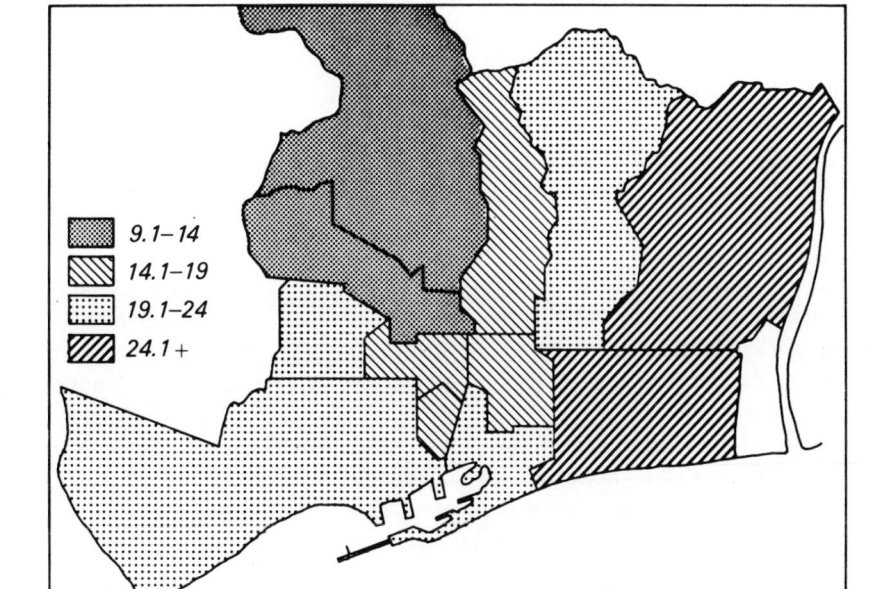

Figure 9.2   Socialist Votes in the City of Barcelona, 1977 Chamber Elections

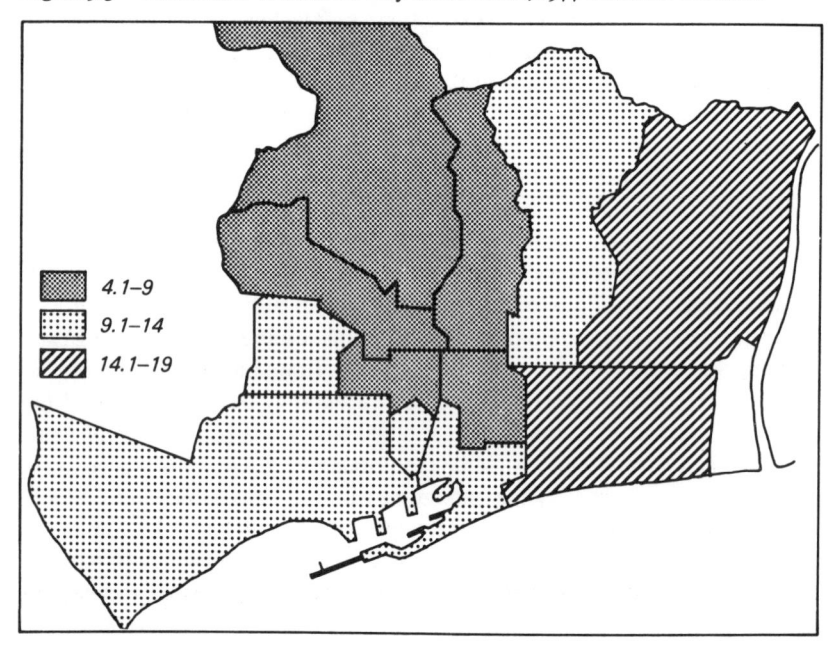

Figure 9.3 Communist Votes in the City of Barcelona, 1977 Chamber Elections

showed blue-collar and white-collar strata seeking protection for their class interests of a sort they could not get from the Spanish state. The Socialists, though Catalonia had not previously been one of their strongholds, had secured new life through the PSC-PSOE coalition—and a huge Castilian-speaking base among immigrants and blue-collar workers.

Pinilla adds—in our opinion, correctly—that the PDC (the Catalan center-left) was the most conspicuous loser, in spite of its considerable percentage of the votes, since it had been expected to be the overwhelming winner and the keystone of the party system in a future democratic Catalonia. But in the end, the PDC was unable to win over a suspicious working class, by and large not Catalan and obviously mistrustful of Catalan pressure groups supported by the managerial class.

On the other hand, Prime Minister Suárez's party, the UCD, came out quite well, particularly considering how late it was constituted and how completely dependent the Catalan branch was on the staff in Madrid. All in all, the UCD chose attractive candidates in Catalonia, and attained approximately the same number of votes and seats in the Chamber as the Pujol-led PDC.

By contrast, the neo-Francoist Popular Alliance was badly defeated in Catalonia, as in all of industrial Spain; it elected only one deputy, for the province of Barcelona. No doubt the idea of political continuity, which Suárez as the incumbent prime minister represented, was a magnetic pole that attracted the well-to-do sectors of Catalan society; the study of voting in Barcelona suggests as much. Moreover, historically these classes had always turned to the rightist governments in Madrid in search of adequate protection for their interests against the increasing radicalization of the Catalan electorate.

The rightist League of Catalonia also lost, despite the considerable financial resources invested in its electoral campaign by one of its main backers, the millionaire José María Figueras. Indeed, the League and the Christian democrats (who had never been strong in Catalonia) were the biggest losers in all of Spain. Another big loser was Esquerra de Catalunya, the great Catalanist party of the left under the Second Republic, which barely won its one seat in Barcelona, and did so only thanks to the support of an assortment of *gauchiste* groups. It must be added that these *gauchiste* groups had been remarkably successful in organizing street demonstrations, which supports the suspicion that there is a vast difference between people's behavior in demonstrations and their electoral choices. Within the Catalan left, it is clear that the "useful vote" prevailed on voting day, decisively favoring the PSC-PSOE coalition.

The Elections of March 1979

Almost twenty-one months after the first legislative elections, Catalonia again went to the polls. Those results permit a study of the evolution of the electorate (see table 9.2 and figure 9.4).

The Role of the Suárez Government Once the constitution had been approved in the referendum of 6 December 1978, Prime Minister Suárez con-

Table 9.2 Results of the 1979 Chamber Elections in the Catalan Provinces, by Party

Party	Barcelona Seats	Barcelona % of vote	Tarragona Seats	Tarragona % of vote	Lérida Seats	Lérida % of vote	Gerona Seats	Gerona % of vote
Democratic Coalition	1	3.7	0	4.0	0	3.2	0	3.4
Catalan Left	1	3.8	0	4.6	0	7.6	0	4.1
Convergence and Union	6	15.5	0	14.1	1	15.7	1	24.4
PSUC	7	19.1	1	14.3	0	10.8	0	9.4
Socialists of Catalonia	12	29.8	2	28.9	1	24.6	2	27.6
UCD	6	17.0	2	28.3	2	31.8	2	25.0

Source: *El País*, 26 March 1979, pp. 15–16.
Note: Percentages are percentages of votes cast.

Figure 9.4 Distribution of Chamber Seats in Catalonia and the Four Catalan Provinces, by Party, 1979

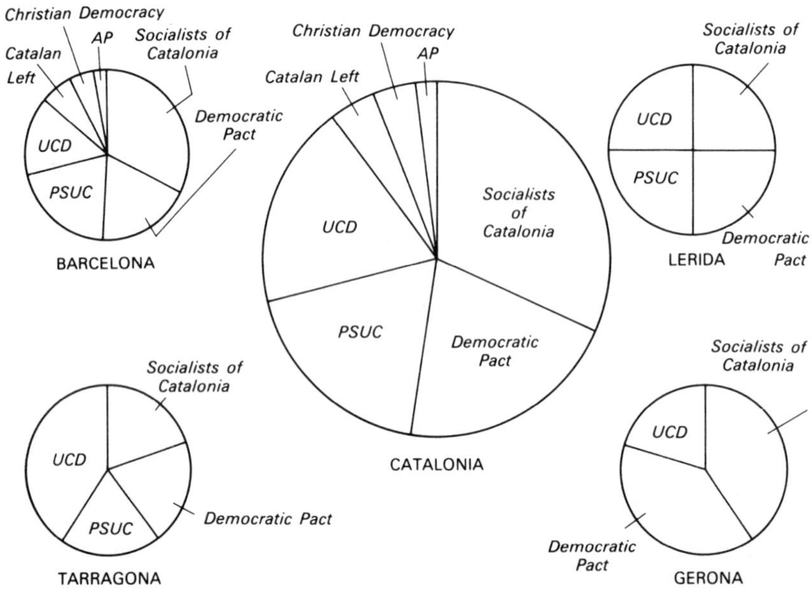

sidered his government's task done. His two options were to obtain a new vote of confidence from the Chamber [27] or to dissolve the Parliament and call new legislative elections.[28] Suárez opted for the second course. The party in power, the UCD sought a clear majority in the Chamber, while the opposition considered it indispensable to measure the exact strength of each party, once the transition period was over and the agreed moderation during the constitution-making process was no longer needed.

For Catalonia new elections meant a delay in the Autonomy Statute, which had been submitted to the ad hoc commission in the Chamber some minutes before the Basque one and just before the deadline. The statute had been supported by all political forces in Catalonia and was gathering momentum in the Chamber, but the parties shelved it once elections were called.

Election day, 1 March 1979, brought no major changes in the balance of forces. Nonetheless, several new factors—such as growing unemployment, the policy of consensus, economic crises, and the deterioration of public order that had set in while the parliament had been working on the constitution—affected the outcome. Moreover, the constitution-making process had taken priority over ideological debate and tighter control over the executive by the opposition.

One of the most remarkable characteristics in the 1979 election was the increased abstention rate. In Catalonia it ranged from 36.8 percent in the province of Barcelona to 30.3 percent in Gerona, averaging 35.8 percent for the region as a whole. The progressive increase in abstention since the referendum in 1976 might suggest alienation from the new democratic regime—or simply fatigue induced by four trips to the polls in less than twenty-seven months.[29] In any case, people's expectations about the new political class were too high. Coming out of a dictatorship where clandestine opposition was the parties' and labor unions' main role, the new politicians had to adjust their attitudes as together they sought to stabilize and defend the Spanish democracy.

One of the hindrances they faced was lack of cooperation by the state-run media, especially television, the most powerful opinion-making force in Spain. Mostly in the hands of old Franco supporters, the media constantly promoted the idea that politicians were inefficient, forever struggling for office, and disconnected from their constituencies. The top positions in both television channels were occupied by well-trained professionals who maintained close contact with Prime Minister Suárez's personal staff; and Suárez himself, director general of Spanish television for seven years under Franco, had a keen appreciation of the medium's power. Viewing politics as a dirty game might be said to have been the attitude passed on to the new democracy by the right, which was always eager to prove the evils of politics no matter what the regime. It is not clear whether Suárez favored this outlook or was unable to prevent the Francoist elements in the media from promoting it.

The Two Centers The UCD improved its position in Catalonia considerably in March 1979. It had already done well in 1977, considering the strong Catalanist mood of the electorate, and in 1979 it did even better. Its advance was twofold: a gain of three seats (in Barcelona, Gerona, and Lérida) and consolidation in the region as a whole. In principle, Catalonia offered scant opportunity for centralist—or Castilian—parties, but the UCD staff in Catalonia was successful in persuading Madrid to work toward the restoration of the Catalan Generalitat. Suárez's government took the initiative of working with Josep Tarradellas, president-in-exile of the Generalitat, in restoring a measure of Catalan autonomy. At the same time, the Catalan UCD attracted to its lists some prestigious democrats, which helped to balance the ideological composition of the party. It might be said that the UCD's greatest success was its ability to attract a wide range of Catalan centrists; in effect, the party became Catalanized as it defined its ideological boundaries and political appeal. In 1979 the UCD attained a position that had seemed out of reach not long before: the leadership of Catalan centrism. In particular, it took more votes than Jordi Pujol's party, which, lacking the UCD's operating facilities, remained in its previous position.

In 1979 Catalonia was the only part of Spain where the center was clearly split in two. Pujol had in the meantime formed the Convergence and Union (CIU), an electoral alliance that now included the Catalan Democratic Union (UDC). CIU was a bourgeois Catalanist group drawing on a long tradition of nationalist demands, while the Catalan UCD was a branch of the Spanish UCD. Each took six seats in the Chamber elections. Each also had a well-defined identity, and their programs differed as much as their constituencies. Sooner or later, however, they would be forced to come to terms with each other.

The CIU's distinction was its Catalanism and its impeccable democratic record. It reaffirmed Catalan values in the face of Madrid's overwhelming influence, and its electorate was extremely sensitive to nationalist issues, and regarding Madrid as a colonialist power and an impediment to any political solution for Catalonia. Indeed, Madrid remained the symbol of all Catalan misfortunes: the Catalan holidays commemorate defeats in battle against Madrid and signify the Catalans' frustration in determining their political future. By contrast, the UCD was identified with Madrid, a fact its opponents continually stressed. On the other hand, the UCD controlled the power of the state, and thus had an immense role in the formation of public opinion. In any case, CIU proved to be a growing force and a well-qualified representative of the democratic tradition within bourgeois Catalanism.

The Socialist party   The most remarkable feature of the 1979 election results was no doubt the great success of the left and, in particular, the Socialist party. In 1977 the PSC-PSOE coalition had taken fifteen of the forty-five Chamber seats for Catalonia, and in 1979 it took two more. While the Socialists' performance elsewhere in Spain was somewhat less favorable than expected (particularly in the Basque country and Andalusia), in Catalonia they improved their position considerably. The Catalan branch of the PSOE saw its policy of autonomy (which sometimes led it far afield from the positions adopted by the Madrid-based leadership) rewarded with a gain in seats that was greater than that recorded by the PSOE in any other region. On the other hand, the PSOE's incorporation of Tierno Galván's PSP in 1978 (it had taken seven seats and almost 5 percent of the votes in 1977) did not produce any appreciable gain for the PSOE in 1979.

The reason for the Socialists' remarkable success could be found in their blend of Catalanism and socialism. The Catalan Socialists had sought the support of Castilian-speaking immigrants; at the same time, they had committed themselves to a socialist Catalonia for all. Their success was even more complete in the Senate elections. In 1977 the Socialists and Communists had run joint lists, and the Agreement of the Catalans took twelve of the sixteen seats; but in 1979 the Socialists ran on their own, winning ten seats.

As result of these strategic successes, the Catalan Socialists saw their position in the national PSOE strengthened. Through the intervention of General Secretary Felipe González himself. Their leader, Joan Reventós, secured from the Madrid party staff a commitment to set a deadline for Catalonia's Statute of Autonomy. The date chosen was 11 September 1979, Catalonia's National Day, in commemoration of the final surrender of Barcelona to Philip V in 1714 after more than a year's siege. As Pinilla de las Heras wrote shortly after the elections, "Were it not for the strength of the PSC-PSOE in Catalonia, the conservative European media would be clamorously cheering what they have already labeled the PSOE's defeat."[30]

The Communist party   The PSUC vote was stable in 1979 despite the great efforts of the party's militants to improve its position. Less independent of Madrid than their socialist counterparts, the Catalan Communist leaders suffered a serious setback. While in the rest of Spain the PCE moved forward, winning three new seats for a total of twenty-three, the Catalan Communists fell back from eight seats to seven. It is difficult to explain why the Communists were not able to increase their votes despite the efforts of well-trained cadres and highly motivated rank and file, but tentative explanations include the possibility that, for the time being, communism reached its peak in Catalonia and the theory that the electorate, increasingly moderate and interested mainly in the Catalan statute, felt more attracted to the federal structure of the Socialist party. The Senate elections lend support to the second hypothesis, for the Socialists were clearly right to end their joint candidacies with the Communists: in 1979 only one Communist obtained a seat, while the Socialists took ten.

The Coalition of the Right   A final word should be said about the conservative right. The Popular Alliance did not survive intact its defeat of 1977, but a spruced-up version, the Democratic Coalition (CD) fared no better in 1979, only retaining the AP's single seat for Barcelona. The CD spurned the ultraright, offering a much more moderate image than the AP had in 1977 in the hope of appealing to a wide range of conservatives from Franco supporters to moderate bourgeois sectors. The failure of this strategy was doubtless due in part to the growing strength of the UCD and the CIU in Catalonia.

The Difficulties Ahead

The landslide victory of Catalan nationalism in the 1977 election, supported by at least some of the Castilian-speaking population (which is almost half the total), had encouraged the central government to quicken the devolution of Catalan autonomy. Without waiting for the new constitution to be approved, the Suárez government provisionally had restored the autonomy Catalonia had lost as a result of its loyalty to the Second Spanish Republic. By so doing, Madrid capitalized on the prestige of Josep Tarradellas, president-in-exile of the Catalan Generalitat,[31] and seized the initiative from the left. As time passed, however, it became plain that Madrid would not rush to fulfill Catalan expectations as long as the eighty-year-old Tarradellas remained cooperative and willing to adapt to Madrid's official policy for Catalonia.

The 1978 constitution (formally approved by the Cortes on 31 October, then by the referendum on 6 December 1978) was reasonably hospitable to Catalan hopes for autonomy, though not for independence.[32] Theoretically it opened the way for the creation of a great many self-governing communities, although the framers' immediate purpose was to find a solution to the Basque and Catalan problems.

The long-awaited statute was finally promulgated on 18 December 1979. In it, the Spanish state recognized the Catalans as a nation with a capacity for self-government and recognized the Generalitat—made up of a parliament, a president, and an executive council or government—as the chief institution of their government. The statute specified a long list of powers that within a two-year span were to be transferred from the Spanish state to the Generalitat, and a mixed commission including members from both sides was appointed to oversee the process.[33]

By the early 1980s the transfer had advanced quite reasonably in administrative areas such as control of agriculture, industry, tourism, environmental protection, welfare, labor regulation, urbanization, youth, libraries, housing, education, consumer protection, mining, energy, and culture. Comparable progress had not been made, however, in more political matters such as control of the mass media, the creation of a local police force, and the institution of a Catalan supreme court.[34]

There were bound to be problems ahead. Juan Linz has described some of them in detail.[35] Thus far the Spanish state has done no more than return to Catalonia its language, national anthem, and flag, banned for many decades, along with an increasing administrative burden. The political importance of these symbolic transfers should not be underestimated, but they will not be enough unless they pave the way for real political autonomy and not a mere delegation of bureaucratic tasks. Their failure to do so might produce a radicalization of Catalan nationalism and incalculable frustration among the population.

Plainly, no Catalan government would have the slightest chance of succeeding without drawing on the fiscal and economic resources—and the mass media—controlled by the Spanish state. Negotiations with a view to sharing these powers were delicate inasmuch as they imply the possibility of reducing the omnipotence of the elite in Madrid. The other Spanish regions, poorer than Catalonia, have opposed any arrangement that makes their situation inside

Spain more difficult. To these difficulties was added the shadow of the attempted coup d'état of February 1981. The attempt carried out by a small group of discontented officers in the name of the unity of Spain, served to test the resonance of this issue on the armed forces generally.

The threat was not lost on the parties, which by now appreciated the importance of the autonomy question for the future of the state. That is why the government and the PSOE agreed to regulate the timing and scope of the whole process by means of Organic Law for the Harmonization of the Autonomy Process (LOAPA). On 31 July 1981, the UCD and PSOE agreed on a draft law, ending negotiations in which the Communist party and Democratic Coalition also participated but to which the Basque and Catalan nationalist parties were not even invited. Several months later the parliament approved the law with only slight modifications.

The obstacles that now faced a Catalan government were enormous and, while failure was possible, the benefits of success made it an effort well worth the risk. What was at stake was a political model not only for a decentralized and pluricultural Spain but also for other European countries struggling to free themselves from obsolete centralist structures.

Regional Nationalism and the Elections in the Basque Country

JOHN F. COVERDALE

———The Basque country includes four Spanish provinces: Alava, Guipúzcoa, Navarre, and Vizcaya. Their combined population of 1.2 million occupies an area of 18,000 square kilometers (see table 10.1). The largest city in the region is Bilbao, the capital of Vizcaya, with 472,000 inhabitants. Guipúzcoa and Vizcaya constitute the core of the Basque country. Alava is less enthusiastic about the Basque cause, and Navarre, as we shall see, is the scene of bitter conflict between pro-Basque and anti-Basque forces.

The more extreme Basque nationalist groups include in their plan for a future Basque state the three historic French regions of Labourd, Basse-Navarre, and Soule. A few Basque activists come from the French side of the Pyrenees, the Spanish Basques have often found temporary refuge there. Basque nationalism is not, however, a powerful factor in the three French provinces. Their population does not enter significantly into the dynamics of Spanish Basque politics and will not be considered here.

In most areas of Europe, regional nationalism is accompanied by, and to a large extent is a result of, relative economic deprivation. Clearly this is not the

Table 10.1 Estimated Population and Population Density of the Basque Country, 1975

Province	Population	Area (Km^2)	Population (Km^2)
Alava	240,513	3,047	79
Guipúzcoa	707,308	1,997	354
Navarre	491,076	10,421	47
Vizcaya	1,194,612	2,217	539
Total	2,633,509	17,682	149[a]

Source: Instituto Nacional de Estadística, *Espana 1976 Anuario Estadístico* (Madrid, 1976).
[a] Average population per sqaure kilometer.

Table 10.2 Per Capita Income in the Basque Country, 1971

Province	Per Capita Income (Pesetas)	Index (Spanish average = 100)	Rank among the 50 Spanish provinces
Alava	101,718	143.75	3
Guipúzcoa	104,111	147.13	2
Navarre	84,160	118.93	8
Vizcaya	105,947	149.72	1

Source: Ramon Tamames, *Introduction a la economia espanoloa*, pp. 422–23.

case of the Basques. Not only has the Basque country been historically the wealthiest area of Spain, it has also benefited from the recent Spanish economic boom. In the period 1964–71, per capita income in Vizcaya, Guipúzcoa, and Navarre grew at the same rate as in the country as a whole. Alava's growth rate was one and a half times the national average. Consequently, the region as a whole registered a slight increase in its percentage share of gross national product (GNP).[1] In 1971 Vizcaya enjoyed the highest per capita income of any Spanish province, and the next two positions were occupied by Guipúzcoa and Alava (see table 10.2). The poorest of the Basque provinces, Navarre, ranked in the top sixth of the nation and was almost 20 percent above the national average. Taken together the four provinces accounted for 10 percent of Spain's GNP in 1971.

Because of its high degree of industrialization, the Basque country carries on a lively commerce with the rest of Spain, with which its economy is closely linked. Other Spanish regions constitute the best market for Basque manufactured products—steel, fabricated metal goods, appliances, and so on. In addition, Bilbao's great banks carry on operations at a national level and have major investments in all parts of Spain. The leaders of the business community recognize that they benefit economically from the availability of Spanish markets and of Spanish labor.

Basques complain, however, that they pay dearly for the advantages they derive from being part of Spain. In 1968 the Basques paid 14 percent of all taxes collected in Spain, whereas only 6 percent of governmental expenditures took place in the region.[2] The central government argues that the larger sum the Basques pay is justified by the region's prosperity and contributes to a socially beneficial transfer of resources from wealthy to poorer regions. Most Basques are willing to concede that they ought to pay more in taxes than other regions, but nationalist sentiment is fostered by the belief that current disparities are excessive and constitute discrimination against them.

Demands for autonomy also feed on a sense of superior economic skill in comparison with Castile, which exercises administrative and political power but lags behind economically.[3] A disproportion between political and economic

Table 10.3 Spanish Immigrants in the Basque Provinces, 1970

Province	Number of Persons	Percent
Alava	25,873	16
Guipúzcoa	68,075	14
Navarre	34,765	9
Vizcaya	124,325	15
Basque provinces	253,038	13

Source: Calculated from *Estudios sociológicos sobre la situación social de España* 1975 (Madrid, 1976), table VII.5, pp. 74–79.

Note: Immigrants are persons over ten years of age registered in the stated province in the 1970 census but in a non-Basque province in the 1960 census. The base for the percentages is the provincial population over ten years of age.

power caused by the relative economic weakness of the political center contributes to discontent. The periphery feels, with considerable justification, that its interests would be better served by a more decentralized system under which decisions affecting the region could be made at the regional level.

The demand for labor has also produced a strong current of immigration from poorer regions of Spain into the Basque region during most of this century. As early as 1950, slightly over one-fourth of the population of the province of Vizcaya was made up of people born in other provinces.[4] The economic growth of the 1960s increased the influx of immigrants from other regions of Spain (see table 10.3), and the percentage of ethnic Basques and of Basque speakers has declined steadily.

Basque Nationalism

The outstanding political question in the Basque country has been the region's future status and its relations with the rest of Spain. A desire for autonomy, even independence, has found expression in frequent acts of political violence. Only a minority of Basques favor severing all ties with Spain or approve of terrorism, but the majority of the population has supported amnesty for political crimes, and many vote for declared nationalist parties.

Affective identification with the region has been strong though not as widespread as in Catalonia. In 1975 32.4 percent of those interviewed said they considered themselves primarily Basques, whereas 41.1 percent reported that their primary identification was with Spain and a surprising 19.6 percent considered themselves "citizens of the world."[5] Basque nationalism has traditionally been much stronger in rural areas than in the cities. In 1969 a survey in three of the four Basque provinces found that twice as many respondents in rural areas as in urban areas identified themselves as Basques.[6] In recent years the development of left and far-left Basque nationalist movements in industrial centers has somewhat changed the situation, but the countryside remains the stronghold of traditional Basque nationalism.

The linguistic base of Basque regional nationalism is weak: nineteen percent of people surveyed in the four Basque provinces in 1975 reported that they were able to speak Basque easily. Only 10 percent used it most of the time at home, and a mere 4 percent used it most of the time in other situations.[7] Few people in the larger cities speak Basque with any regularity. A survey published in 1969 showed that Basque was used only one-third as much in large urban centers as in the countryside.[8] Recently Basque academies have grown in number and popularity, and Basque has been introduced in the state schools; but Castilian is likely to remain the language of instruction in most schools. Few teachers know Basque well enough to be able to teach in it, and even in the areas with the highest percentage of Basque speakers many children do not know the language. Attachment to the Basque language is and will probably continue to be for some time cultural, sentimental, and symbolic rather than practical or economically advantageous. Ability or inability to speak Basque does not help or hinder career opportunities. Even many political leaders of Basque nationalist parties cannot speak Basque.[9]

Historical Roots Basque regional nationalism has roots deep in the history of Spain. At the time of the formation of the Spanish state in the sixteenth century, the provinces of Alava, Guipúzcoa, and Vizcaya had belonged to the crown of Castile for several centuries. The sub-Pyrenean section of Navarre was annexed by Ferdinand II in 1512. Each of the four regions retained its local customs, institutions, and language. Though linked by geographic proximity and the Basque language, they had no common institutions and little sense of common identity.[10]

The four Basque provinces retained their special status throughout the sixteenth, seventeenth, and eighteenth centuries. Philip V's centralizing measures, which incorporated Catalonia more fully into Spain in the early eighteenth century, did not affect them. Local questions continued to be decided locally. Taxes were negotiated with the central government and apportioned and collected by provincial assemblies. Since the early Middle Ages, Basque had been limited to domestic use; Castilian was the language of both government and culture. Basques participated actively in the life of Spain and in all its major enterprises. There was no significant Basque revolt against the Spanish Crown during this period.

Serious Basque opposition to the central Spanish government began in the 1830s. A dynastic dispute between Carlos de Borbón and his infant niece Isabel gave rise in 1833 to a civil war, which lasted until 1839. Liberal politicians, who controlled the government in Madrid and were trying to centralize Spanish administration along the lines established earlier in France, supported

Isabel. Basque peasant defenders of the region's traditional local liberties supported Carlos and were consequently called Carlists. At the end of the war a negotiated settlement left the Basque provinces with considerable autonomy in matters of administration and taxation.

During the 1870s a second civil war between liberals and Carlists again saw massive Basque peasant resistance to liberalism, in large part because the liberals intended to deprive the Basques of their autonomy in the name of uniform central administration. The defeat of this new generation of Carlists brought with it the loss of administrative autonomy, but the Basques retained the right to negotiate their taxes with the central government and apportion and collect them locally. The amount of taxes collected in the Basque country remained fixed between 1841 and 1893.

Until late in the nineteenth century, rural Carlism was the most significant expression of Basque regional nationalism. Urban groups were willing to give verbal support to local liberties and to lament their loss in 1876, but the Basque urban elite had no real quarrel with the Spanish state and no sense of being oppressed by it. Throughout the nineteenth century the use of Basque even as a domestic language declined, especially in the cities. Two of the greatest literary figures of the early twentieth century, Miguel de Unamuno and Pío Baroja, were Basques, but they wrote exclusively in Castilian.

Basque economic growth in the second half of the nineteenth century was based on nearby iron ore and coal deposits. By the 1890s the Basque country, especially Vizcaya, had become the center of Spanish heavy industry and mining. Spanish tariffs worked to the advantage of industries that could not compete with foreign producers because of their small scale and inadequate natural resource base. Iron and steel production, shipbuilding, and other heavy industries made the region the most dynamic in Spain. Basque entrepreneurs proved the most daring and modern in the country, and they participated actively in the economic and political life of the nation as a whole.

The foundations for Basque regional nationalism were laid in the 1880s and 1890s by Sabino de Arana y Goiri, a conservative, devoutly Catholic son of a Basque entrepreneur. Arana's Basque nationalism was based on close identification with the church and on a desire to maintain the ethnic purity of the Basque people. The movement gave rise to the Basque Nationalist party (PNV), which elected its first candidates in 1898 and remained the chief expression of Basque regional-nationalist politics for over half a century.

Until the proclamation of the Republic in 1931, the political significance of Basque regional nationalism and of the PNV was minor compared with that of the Spanish political parties. The relatively small size of the region, the weakness of the linguistic base, the integration of Basque elites into Spanish economic and political life, and the continuing strength of Carlism as an alternative way of defending autonomy prevented the PNV from recruiting mass support before the proclamation of the Republic.

Under the Republic, Basque regional nationalism grew rapidly, and the PNV became a major political force. Regional nationalism remained conservative and Catholic in its orientation. In fact, the electoral success of the PNV in the early 1930s was due to its position as a defender of the church against the anticlericalism of the Republic. In Navarre interest in a Basque autonomy statute survived only so long as it appeared that an autonomous Basque region might be able to follow a religious policy more favorable to the church than that of the rest of the Republic. As soon as it became clear that religious policy would be excluded from the competence of any autonomous region, the Navarrese lost interest in the project. Navarre would be the stronghold of the Carlist party and would provide Franco his most important civilian support in the Civil War. Alava also lacked enthusiasm for Basque regional nationalism, partly because the linguistic base there was weaker than in the two remaining Basque provinces, partly because its mostly rural population distrusted a movement that seemed to be dominated by more industrialized areas.

During the five years between the proclamation of the Republic and the outbreak of the Civil War, Basque politicians in Vizcaya and Guipúzcoa became more intransigent and more radical in their demands for autonomy, although they continued to be socially and politically conservative. The PNV won the majority of the two provinces' seats in the 1936 election, not so much because of its own strength as because of the division of its opponents.

The outbreak of the Civil War posed a serious dilemma to Basque politicians. Their aspirations for regional autonomy dictated that they support the Republic, but their Catholicism and their political and social conservatism made them natural allies of the insurgents. In the end, regionalist sentiment prevailed in Guipúzcoa and Vizcaya, which supported the Republic. Navarre and Alava were Franco's strongholds. The fighting in the north during the summer of 1937 saw many Carlist units from Navarre opposing Basque Republican units from Vizcaya.

Basque Nationalism under Franco   The Franco regime made every effort to uproot the remnants of regional nationalism in the Basque country. In 1937 it deprived the Basque provinces (expect Navarre, which had supported the Nationalists during the Civil War) of their last vestiges of economic and administrative autonomy. As in Catalonia, the local language was suppressed, but with less traumatic effects since Basque had been losing ground steadily and by this time was confined almost exclusively to isolated farming communities. The prohibition of Basque songs and symbols, however, provoked frequent clashes between the Civil Guard and inhabitants of the area.

Despite repression, members of the Basque elite continued to play important roles in Spanish life during the Franco regime. In the economic sphere this was a natural result of the scope of Basque industrial and financial activities, but Basques were also active in politics. Of the eighty-nine ministers who served in Franco's cabinets between 1938 and 1969, six were from Navarre and six more from other Basque provinces. The percentage of ministers from the Basque country was almost two and a half times as great as the percentage of Basques among the population. Needless to say, the men who served in Franco's cabinet had no ties to Basque regional nationalism. Over half of them were Carlists, and the others were closely identified with Franco and his policies.[11]

During the first two decades of the Franco regime, Basque regional nationalism found political expression mostly in the very limited activities of the PNV, which staffed the Basque government-in-exile and tried to keep alive a sense of Basque identity within the region. Its most valuable ally proved to be the clergy, from whom it had traditionally received support. During the Republic and the Civil War many priests and member of religious orders overcame their natural aversion to collaborating with the anticlerical Republican left in order to foster Basque regional aspirations. After the war, priests were in large measure responsible for keeping alive a sense of Basque identity. The Basque country continues to be one of the most Catholic regions in Spain,[12] and the support of the older members of the clergy in rural districts is even today a source of strength for the PNV.

The best-known of the radical Basque nationalist groups, ETA, took shape in the 1950s when younger members of the PNV began to form their own groups under the name *Euzkadi ta Askatasuna* (Basque Land and Liberty).[13] These groups soon detached themselves from the main body of the PNV and by the end of the decade had attracted to their ranks most of the younger Basque activists.

The formation of ETA coincided with the campaigns in which the Algerian provisional government finally won autonomy from the French. The Algerian example contributed to the genesis of ETA's combination of radical socialism and radical nationalism. The party's First Congress formulated its program in 1962, and by 1967, when the Fifth Congress was held, the tension between nationalism and socialism had split ETA. The more nationalist elements stressed the precedence of the fight against Spain, primarily through terrorist violence, in the fashion of Ireland's provisional IRA. Socialist elements, like the official IRA, stressed the fight against capitalism, for which the solidarity of the working class was of fundamental importance.

Until 1968, ETA violence was limited to blowing up monuments, setting off bombs in front of Civil Guard stations, and other acts that stopped short of bloodshed. Gun battles between ETA members and the Guardia Civil in June

Table 10.4 Results of the Referendum on Political Reform in the Basque Country, December 1976 (percent)

Province	Abstention	Votes cast		
		Yes	No	Invalid
Alava	13.7	91.9	5.4	2.7
Guipúzcoa	55.1	91.5	5.8	2.7
Navarre	26.4	92.8	2.9	4.3
Vizcaya	46.8	90.7	3.9	2.5
Spain, national average	22.3	94.2	2.6	3.2

Source: La Actualidad Española, 20–26 December 1976, p. 13.

1968 were followed in August by ETA's "execution" of a police inspector, whom they accused of having tortured ETA members. The government responded with a state of emergency, numerous arrests, and torture. This was the beginning of a spiral of violence that led to arrests, trials, shootings, kidnappings, and bomb attacks, including the assassination of Prime Minister Luis Carrero Blanco in downtown Madrid on 20 December 1973. At first the demands of ETA extremists found little support from the population of the Basque provinces, but the violence and brutality of police efforts to stamp out ETA greatly increased antagonism toward Madrid.

The General Election of June 1977

As in the rest of Spain, political parties and groups proliferated during the year and a half between Franco's death and the elections. Until early 1977 the parties that classified themselves as *abertzales*, that is, purely Basque parties unsubordinated to any larger Spanish group, seemed to dominate the scene. Their power first became apparent in the results of the December 1976 referendum on Adolfo Suárez's proposals for political reform. The *abertzales* joined the parties of the left in criticizing the proposals for the autocratic way in which they had been formulated by Suárez and urged their followers not to take part in the referendum. As can be seen in table 10.4, their campaign was strikingly successful in Guipúzcoa and Vizcaya but failed in Navarre and Alava.

The most important *abertzale* party was the PNV, which occupied in the Basque provinces the political ground held by Christian Democrats in other parts of Spain but combined centrist economic and social policies with a vigorous defense of Basque autonomy. It called for the immediate restitution of the statute of autonomy granted to the Basques by the Republic in 1936. To the left of the PNV there appeared a plethora of other *abertzale* parties ranging from social democrats through socialists to Marxist-Leninists, which combined their various social and economic polemics with a call for Basque autonomy and in some cases independence.

The *abertzale* parties seemed at first to be encountering considerable success in their efforts to present themselves as the sole legitimate representatives of Basque interests, even though virtually every party defended Basque autonomy in one form or another. The campaign for the general election of June 1977 centered on local issues, chiefly political ones; throughout Spain social and economic issues remained in the background. In the Basque country the range of issues was further narrowed, to the related questions of autonomy and amnesty for Basque political prisoners.

Some smaller *abertzale* groups, including representatives of ETA, spoke in favor of total independence for the Basque country, although even they represented it as a long-range goal and called for autonomy within Spain as an immediate solution. The larger *abertzale* groups, including the PNV, the Basque Left Socialist party (ESB), and the Basque Nationalist Action party (ANV), focused their attention on demanding more autonomy, starting with the restitution of the rights granted by the 1936 autonomy statute. They did not go so far as to demand independence, but their critics in the rest of Spain felt they should speak out more firmly than they did in favor of Basque participation in Spanish national life and condemn more vigorously the terrorism of ETA.

Almost all the non-*abertzale* parties in the Basque country also demanded autonomy for the region. The Spanish Socialist Workers' party (PSOE) stressed its commitment to a federal structure for Spain within which the Basque country could easily find its proper place. The Union of the Democratic Center (UCD) rejected federalism but proclaimed its commitment to regional autonomy for all regions whose history, geography, and economic situation might lead them to desire it. The orthodox Communist party of Euzkadi (PCE-EPK) also proposed a federal constitution for Spain and as a short-term solution suggested the reinstatement of the 1936 statute.

Since most parties defended some form of Basque autonomy, their differences lay in the extent of the autonomy they advocated and the perceived sincerity of their commitment. The UCD was vague and cautious in its declarations and seemed to be moved more by the requirements of electoral politics than by any principled commitment to decentralization. The PSOE hammered away at its proposals for a federal constitutional structure but deliberately avoided hard questions about how to reconcile regional fiscal autonomy with demands for a more equitable income distribution between rich and poor regions. The *abertzale* parties were all clearly pledged to Basque autonomy, but the PNV was markedly more moderate in its demands than the far-left groups of recent formation.

Even more important than the question of autonomy were demands for full amnesty for political prisoners. They dominated the electoral campaign in the

Table 10.5 Basque Seats in the Chamber, by Party and Province, June 1977

Party	Alava	Guipúzcoa	Navarre	Vizcaya	Total Basque provinces
PSOE	1	3	2	3	9
PNV	1	3	0	4	8
UCD	2	—	3	2	7
EE	0	1	—	0	1
AP	0	0	0	1	1
Totals	4	7	5	10	26

Source: Diario 16, 22 July 1977.
Dash (–): Not applicable.

Basque country and were supported by all important parties. Frequent, often violent, demonstrations shook the region as police and demonstrators clashed. The issue of amnesty united the majority of the Basque population against the government of Madrid and for a time threatened to lead to massive Basque abstention in the general election similar to that in the December 1976 referendum. The Suárez government's decision to allow the few remaining Basque political prisoners to go into exile succeeded in calming public anger temporarily and persuaded most Basque parties to urge their members to vote. The scale of the demonstrations in favor of amnesty, however, had clearly shown the extent of Basque awareness of and antipathy toward the central Spanish government.

Despite fears that ETA might unleash a new campaign of violence to disrupt the polling, the elections took place in an atmosphere of calm, marred only by a few minor incidents. Voter participation in the region as a whole was only slightly below the national average in 1977: 76.6 percent of eligible voters cast ballots, compared with 79.2 percent in the nation; 83 percent participation in Navarre and Alava contrasts with 75.5 percent in Vizcaya, and 71.8 percent in Guipúzcoa. In Guipúzcoa it seems that 5 to 10 percent of the eligible voters chose not to cast ballots in order to protest the conditions of the election and particularly the government's refusal to legalize certain far-left Basque political parties. On balance, however, the salient fact was a high index of participation, which appeared at the time to point toward at least momentary willingness of the public and of the parties to try to achieve Basque goals within the established political framework.

The electoral results gave the *abertzale* parties a much less prominent role in the Cortes than they had played in the Basque provinces during the campaign. The eight seats won by the PNV and the single seat won by the Euzkadi Left (EE) accounted for just more than a third of the total (see table 10.5).

The PSOE had the largest number of Basque deputies in the Chamber and

Table 10.6 Results of the Chamber Elections in the Basque Country, June 1977

Party	Popular vote (percent)	Seats	Index of over representation
PSOE	25.1	9	+0.38
PNV	22.8	8	+0.35
UCD	16.1	7	+0.67
EE	4.7	1	−0.18
AP[a]	7.3	1	−0.47
Other center parties[b]	4.8	0	−1.00
Other far-left parties[c]	6.1	0	−1.00
PCE	4.4	0	−1.00
Basque Socialists and Social Democrats[d]	3.7	0	−1.00
PSP	1.9	0	−1.00
Other	0.2	0	−1.00
Invalid	3.1	—	—

Source: *Diario 16*, 22 July 1977.
Note: Index = (% seats − % votes)/% votes.
[a] Includes Alianza Foral in Navarre although this group laid heavy stress on local issues and differed on some other points from AP.
[b] DCV, DIV, FDI, FNI.
[c] FUT, FDI, AET, AETE, UNAI, Montejurra, FDI, AETNA, APN.
[d] ESB, ANV.
Dash (−): Not applicable

was the only party to win at least one seat from each of the four provinces. "Spanish" parties took seventeen of the twenty-six seats. The UCD was not on the ticket in Guipúzcoa and ran a poor third to the PNV and the PSOE in Vizcaya, but it elected more deputies than any other party in both Alava and Navarre. The Francoist party Popular Alliance (AP) picked up one seat in Vizcaya.

The PNV took over 30 percent of the region's seats, clearly establishing itself as the chief representative of Basque aspirations in the Spanish Cortes. The only other *abertzale* group to win a seat was EE, a list backed by ETA, although the Workers' Revolutionary Organization (ORT), and a number of other radical left Basque parties ran in the election. Regional nationalist sentiment was by no means confined to these parties, but their deputies would prove to be the chief exponents of the Basque positions in the Cortes.

If the results in seats are examined in left/center/right terms, rather than in *abertzale*/Spanish terms, the election represented a clear victory for the center-right parties. The PNV and the UCD elected fifteen of the region's twenty-six deputies and accounted for more than half the seats in every province except

Guipúzcoa. The left (PSOE and EE) accounted for ten of the remaining eleven seats, leaving only one for the far right represented by the Popular Alliance.

The choices and preferences expressed by the voters were, of course, more complex than the results in seats would indicate. The popular vote of the four provinces treated as a single unit reveals a significant degree of fragmentation of voter opinion (see table 10.6). The division of their opponents and the workings of the electoral law benefited the three largest parties (PSOE, PNV, and UCD). They won more than 90 percent of the seats with only two-thirds of the popular vote. Conversely, the smaller groups received less that 10 percent of the seats although they won a third of the popular vote. *Abertzale* groups accounted for almost 40 percent of the popular vote. Thanks to the eight deputies of the PNV, *abertzale* opinion was only slightly underrepresented in the Cortes, but the PNV deputies stood well to the right of many Basques who voted for *abertzale* candidates of other parties. The far left accounted for more than one-tenth of the total popular vote but received only one seat. Splintering into ten separate groups deprived these parties of due representation in the Cortes, but they were obviously a force to be contended with locally, especially since they had a high proportion of militants and activists.

Many Spanish commentators stressed the unexpected strength of the PSOE in the Basque region, where it ran almost as well as in the country as a whole,

Table 10.7 Distribution of the Vote for the Chamber in the Basque Provinces, June 1977 (percent)

Party	Alava	Guipúzcoa	Navarre	Vizcaya
PSOE	27.6	28.2	21.3	24.5
PNV	17.4	30.8	—[a]	29.9
UCD	30.9	—	29.0	16.3
AP	6.4	8.2[b]	8.1[c]	6.5
EE	—	9.4	—	5.2
Other far-left parties	2.7	1.1	23.2	0.1
Other center parties	2.7	9.6	6.9	—
PCE	3.3	3.7	2.4	6.0
Basque Socialists and Social Democrats	2.1	6.0	—	3.4
PSP	1.3	1.4	2.4	2.1
Other	3.1	1.3	—	—
Invalid	2.6	2.0	1.9	4.8

Source: *Diario 16*, 22 July 1977.
Dash (–): = Party did not run.
[a] In Navarre, *Alianza Foral*.
[b] In Guipuzcoa, *Guipúzcoa Unida*.
[c] In Navarre the AP ran in coalition with the ANV and the ESEI.

despite the stigma of being a "Spanish" party. Equally striking though less often noticed was the strength of centrist opinion in the Basque provinces. The PNV, UCD, and other center and center-right parties accounted for 44 percent of the popular vote. This contrasted sharply with Catalonia and other highly industrialized parts of Spain, where the left was stronger and the center considerably weaker.

Table 10.7 reveals striking differences in the electoral behavior of voters in the four Basque provinces. Navarre stands out for the extremely low percentage of votes won by the PNV, which was less than one-fourth as strong there as in Vizcaya and Guipúzcoa. Even in coalition with two other Basque regionalist parties, it failed to win as much as ten percent of the vote in Navarre. The weakness of the PNV and other Basque parties was not due to a lack of sense of local identity. In fact, a strong sense of provincial identity found expression in votes for *Alianza Foral* (a conservative group pledged to the restoration of the historic local rights and privileges of Navarre), for local centrist candidates (who won more votes than the PNV), and for certain far-left parties. Even among UCD supporters there were voters with strong provincial attachments. The leading UCD senatorial candidate, Jaime Ignacio del Burgo, vigorously defended Navarre's right to achieve autonomy in its own right but opposed all plans for including the province in a future Basque region. Many Navarrese from various parts of the political spectrum shared del Burgo's rejection of plans for including Navarre in a unified Euzkadi but proposed to win greater local autonomy for themselves.

A second striking feature of Navarre was the strength of the far left. Until the mid-1960s, Navarre was the most conservative province in Spain. As a result of rapid industrialization and the radicalization of the clergy, who were extremely influential, it became the most radical. Almost one-half the electorate cast ballots for parties to the left of the Social Democrats, and nearly one-fourth voted for parties to the left of the Basque branch of the Spanish Communist party (PCE-EPK). The moderate left (from the social democrats to the PCE) took 39 percent of the vote in Guipúzcoa, 36 percent in Vizcaya, 33 percent in Alava, but only 25 percent in Navarre. In contrast, groups like the Workers' Revolutionary Organization, which ran under the name Workers' Electoral Group (AET), showed their greatest strength in Navarre. Maoist, Marxist-Leninist, and Trotskyist groups took many votes away from the less radical left.

In Alava what sense of provincial identity existed related directly to the wider Basque cause, but Basque regional nationalism was weak, as shown by the modest success of the PNV and of Basque Socialist and Social Democratic candidates. The provincial capital, Vitoria, witnessed a particularly bloody clash between police and demonstrators in 1976, but tension in the province arose primarily from social and economic conflicts and was not successfully harnessed by Basque regional nationalists. About 38 percent of the votes in Alava supported left and center-left parties, but the specifically Basque parties within this group received only about 5 percent of the vote. The PSOE alone accounted for over 70 percent of the left and left-center vote in Alava. The strength of the UCD, which took almost twice as many votes as the PNV, shows that center and center-right voters also preferred national parties over regional ones from the same part of the political spectrum.

Alava was the least radical of the four Basque provinces. The far left took a smaller percentage of the votes there than in the other three provinces. The far right also registered its lowest percentage in Alava. Moderate parties, those to the left of the AP and to the right of the PCE, made their best showing in Alava, where they took 79.1 percent of the vote.

In Vizcaya, the birthplace of Basque regional nationalism, regionalist candidates won 40 percent of the vote. The PNV was the strongest party in the province, where it captured nearly twice as many votes as the UCD. Moderate opinion in Vizcaya identified closely with Basque regional nationalism, which drew most of its strength from the center. The left in Vizcaya was less inclined to support regional nationalism, because a high percentage of the working class was composed of immigrants from other regions who did not identify closely enough with Basque claims to vote for Basque parties. The strong tradition of the PSOE in Vizcaya and its fervid defense of federalism also made it an attractive alternative even for native Basque workers.

As in Alava, voters in Vizcaya largely resisted the lure of both the far left and the right. Parties to the left of the AP and to the right of the PCE accounted for more than three-fourths of the vote. The UCD ran a poor third, but the PNV and the UCD together totaled almost half the vote.

Specifically Basque parties took over half the vote in Guipúzcoa, the province in which Basque regional nationalism won its greatest electoral success. The PNV won a slightly higher percentage of the vote there than in any other province, but it was above all the strength of left-wing Basque groups that made Guipúzcoa the stronghold of *abertzale* politics. In Guipúzcoa, more than in any other province, working-class discontent was harnessed to Basque causes.

After Navarre, Guipúzcoa was the most polarized of the four provinces. The AP, running under the name United Guipúzcoa, won 8 percent of the vote, and far-left parties took slightly more than 10 percent. This combination of very strong Basque regionalism with considerable political radicalization helps explain the frequency and violence of confrontations in Guipúzcoa between demonstrators and police. The province has been the most conflict torn of Spain and is likely to continue to be so.

From the June 1977 Elections to the Constitutional Referendum

The holding of free elections in June 1977 did little to restore peace to the Basque country.[14] In the weeks and months following the elections, terrorism and political violence continued to dominate events there. Basque nationalist leaders condemned ETA violence when it occurred, but they refused to support governmental action against its authors. The government's attempts to obtain extradition of Basque terrorists from France and security measures in the Basque provinces provoked widespread popular demonstrations usually backed by the leaders of all Basque parties including the PNV.

The PNV and the PSOE had demonstrated their strength in the 1977 elections, but they soon allowed the initiative to pass to more extremist groups, which set the tone in the Basque country. In October 1977 a sweeping new amnesty, which was designed to benefit principally Basque nationalists, temporarily eased tensions, but its effects did not prove lasting.

Negotiations between the government and the Assembly of Basque Representatives (a group made up of recently elected Cortes members from Alava, Guipúzcoa, and Vizcaya) over the draft of a "preautonomy" statute encountered serious difficulties during the fall. The two most hotly discussed issues were fiscal autonomy for the Basque region and the inclusion or exclusion of Navarre from such a region. At the end of the year an agreement was reached. It granted the Basques no significant fiscal autonomy and provided that Navarre would be excluded from the Basque region until after the municipal elections. On 31 December 1977 the government announced a preautonomy status for a Basque region comprising Vizcaya, Guipúzcoa, and Alava.

The most obvious result of the statute was the formation of a Basque General Council with five members each from the PSOE and the –7, three from the UCD, one from the EE, and one independent. The Basque General Council was of almost exclusively symbolic importance. It had no real authority and virtually no funds to spend. Unlike the Catalans, who seemed willing to accept symbolic concessions as a pledge of future real ones, the Basques were not pacified by the formation of the Basque Council. Marches, demonstrations, and violence continued to be the order of the day throughout the Basque region.

While demonstrators marched through the streets of San Sebastian, Bilbao, Vitoria, and Pamplona and bombs continued to explode in the Basque country, Basque representatives engaged in a long and arduous series of negotiations with the leaders of the UCD over the new constitutions's provision for regional autonomy. Article 2 states: "The constitution is based on the indissoluble unity of the Spanish nation, the common and indivisible country of all Spaniards, and recognizes and guarantees the right to self-government of the

Table 10.8 Results of the Constitutional Referendum in the Basque Primaries, December 1978 (percent)

Province	Turnout[a]	Votes Cast Yes	No	Invalid
Alava	59.2	71.4	19.2	9.4
Guipúzcoa	43.4	63.9	19.8	16.3
Navarre	66.6	75.7	20.0	4.4
Vizcaya	43.9	70.9	21.6	7.5
Spain, national average	67.7	87.8	7.9	4.3

Source: Coverdale, *Political Transformation of Spain*, p. 124.
[a] Votes cast as a percentage of eligible votes.

nationalities and regions of which it is composed and solidarity amongst them all."

Article 3 establishes Castilian as the official language of the state and affirms the right of all Spaniards to use it and their duty to know it. It also provides, however, that the other languages of Spain will be co-official with Castilian in their own regions and promises that the government will respect and protect linguistic diversity as part of the country's cultural heritage.

The constitution provides a framework in which future regions may exercise significant authority over various areas of regional life. It authorizes them to collect surtaxes or other taxes ceded to them by the state as well as to impose taxes of their own and take out loans. The central government, however, retains the right to regulate their activity.

As a concession to Basque nationalists, the Committee on Constitutional Affairs of the Chamber of Deputies added an additional clause, which declared, "The constitution protects and respects the historic rights of the territories with *fueros* [special statutes and liberties dating from the Middle Ages]. The exercise of the *fuero* system shall take place within the framework of the constitution and of the Statutes of Self-Government." The clause obviously had little specific juridical content and was added primarily to please the Basques. Basque representatives, however, angrily rejected it. They argued that their historic rights, their *fueros*, were part of their patrimony, and not dependent for their legitimacy on the constitution.

Most leftist Basque groups and parties urged their voters to reject the constitution as wholly inadequate because of its failure to provide sufficient autonomy or, in the view of some groups, the right of self-determination. The attitude of the PNV toward the constitution remained in doubt for a long time. In the end, however, the PNV decided not to call for a "no" vote, since the

Table 10.9 "Positive Abstention" in the Basque Provinces, December 1978, Referendum

Province	"Positive Abstention"[a]	PNV Vote, June 1977 (percent of eligible voters)
Alava	11.2	14.1
Guipúzcoa	28.4	24.9
Navarre	1.1	6.7
Vizcaya	24.2	24.0

[a]Positive abstention = (percentage of Basque voters abstaining − national average abstaining) + (percentage of Basque voters casting invalid ballots − national average casting invalid ballots).
Source: Coverdale, *Political Transformation of Spain*, p. 125.

constitution did provide for significant democratic liberties. Instead it urged its followers to abstain as a way of demonstrating their dissatisfaction with the provisions on regional autonomy.

The results of the constitutional referendum held in December 1978 are summarized in table 10.8. They confirm what the general election of June 1977 had already demonstrated: the strength of Basque nationalism in Guipúzcoa and Vizcaya, its intermediate position in Alava, and its weakness in Navarre. In both Guipúzcoa and Vizcaya, over half the voters stayed away from the polls. It is impossible to say how many did so out of inertia, how many out of political conviction, and how many out of fear either of violence from ETA terrorists or of pressure from friends and neighbors. Although fear certainly played a significant role, particularly in the small towns in which most people's political opinions would be well known to their neighbors and to the poll watchers, the very high rate of abstention indicates the strength of Basque nationalism in these areas.

Table 10.9 shows quite clearly the correlation between the strength of the PNV, which was the only major group to urge its supporters to abstain or cast blank ballots rather than vote yes or no, and "positive abstention," a level of nonvoting and invalid voting higher than the national average. Vizcaya and Guipúzcoa had very high rates of positive abstention, with significantly lower ones in Alava and almost none at all in Navarre.

In all four Basque provinces, approximately one-fifth of the voters cast "no" votes—about two and one-half times the Spanish national average. "No" votes came from very different sources: from right-wing extremists, leftist Basque nationalists, other fringe groups on the far left, and Navarrese nationalists disgruntled by the constitution's attempt to force them into becoming part of the Basque region. The proportion of "no" votes coming from each of these groups varied widely from province to province. It is surprising that the "no" vote in Navarre was not considerably higher than 20 percent in view of the strength of the far left, the far right, and Navarrese nationalists there. Some far-left voters who would otherwise have rejected the constitution must have voted "yes" in Navarre because of the provisions for including Navarre in the Basque region.

In the Basque country it is important to consider not only the percentage of votes cast for and against the constitution but also the *percentage of eligible voters* who voted "yes" and "no." Thus we see in table 10.10 that in Guipúzcoa only 27.8 percent of eligible voters actually voted "yes." This certainly does not mean that three-fourths of the voters opposed the constitution, but it does mean that support for it was much weaker than the "yes" share of the votes cast—63.9 percent—suggests.

During the months immediately preceding the constitutional referendum, the members of the Basque General Council prepared a draft autonomy statute for the region. The draft claimed exclusive jurisdiction for the autonomous institutions of the Basque country in thirty-seven areas, including local government, local law, agriculture, prisons, and economic planning in the Basque country. It also claimed exclusive jurisdiction over education in the Basque country at all levels and in all forms "with no other restriction than respect for the principles contained in Article 27 of the Constitution." It further established that Basque institutions would exercise full control over an autonomous police force and that the national police would be allowed to exercise public order functions in the Basque country only if requested to do so by the Basque government or in cases in which the national government has declared a state of alarm, exception, or siege.

The draft stipulated that fiscal relations between the Basque country and the national state would be regulated, as they traditionally had been, by an economic agreement under which each province would pay a certain sum to the national government but would retain discretion over how that sum was to

Table 10.10 Results of the Referendum on the Constitution in the Basque Country, December 1978 (percent)

Province	Distribution of Eligible Votes			
	Abstained	Voted	Voted	Cast invalid ballot
Alava	40.8	42.3	11.3	5.6
Guipúzcoa	56.5	27.8	8.6	7.1
Navarre	33.4	50.4	13.3	2.9
Vizcaya	56.1	31.1	9.5	3.3
Spain, national average	32.3	59.4	5.4	2.9

Source: Coverdale, *Political Transformation of Spain*, p. 23.

be collected. It established that all taxes would be collected within each province by the provincial authorities, in sharp contrast to the existing system, which was highly centralized.

The General Election of March 1979

Shortly after the approval of the constitution in the referendum of December 1978, the electoral campaign for the general election of March 1979 began. The distinctive aspects of the campaign in the Basque country centered on four issues, all of them relating to Basque nationalism: (1) acceptance or rejection of the draft autonomy statute, (2) inclusion of Navarre in the future Basque region or its separate autonomous status, (3) amnesty for Basque political prisoners and the extradition of Basques from France, and (4) condemnation or approval of the terrorist tactics of ETA in the Basque country.

Most parties supported the draft autonomy statute, with greater or lesser enthusiasm. The PNV made it a central piece of its campaign, presenting it as the only possible framework for peace and progress in the Basque region, and the far-left group EE showed scarcely less enthusiasm. Not surprisingly, the PSOE and the UCD also announced their acceptance of the draft, although the UCD expressed reservations about the constitutionality of certain provisions. Opposition to the draft came principally from two groups, the Communist Movement of Euzkadi-Organization of the Communist Left of Euzkadi (EMK-OIC) and Herri Batasuna. The latter was the political arm of the most radical ETA faction and had not competed in the 1977 election. Herri Batasuna rejected not only the specific provisions of the draft but the whole concept of the inclusion of Euzkadi within a unitary Spanish state.

The various amnesties and pardons granted by King Juan Carlos in the course of the transition had set free all Basques imprisoned for political crimes. A small group of them had been exiled, but most of the exiles quickly returned to Spain and succeeded in establishing themselves there. Ongoing ETA violence, however, led to new arrests of Basque activists. The fact that these terrorists were arrested and imprisoned for crimes committed not during the Franco regime but under a democratically elected government did not lessen the sympathy of Basque nationalists for their countrymen. Throughout the period of the electoral campaign, numerous demonstrations were held in the Basque country, demanding the liberation of Basque political prisoners and the transfer to the Basque country of Basque prisoners held in prisons in other parts of Spain. There were also numerous protests against Spanish attempts to obtain the extradition from France of suspected Basque terrorists as well as against the internment by the French of other ETA activists in towns far from the Spanish border. In the course of these demonstrations, a well-known leader of Herri Batasuna was arrested and subsequently imprisoned for apology of violence. He immediately became a martyr of the Basque cause, and numerous marches demanded his immediate liberation. Most of the demonstrations were organized by parties on the far left of the Basque spectrum, but the PNV, out of conviction or necessity, lent its support to some of them.

The frequency and size of the demonstrations and marches, together with the continued violence of ETA terrorists, led the government vastly to increase police patrols in the Basque provinces. The presence of numerous heavily armed police units, frequent roadblocks, checks of people along highways and on city streets, and other preventive measures contributed to the climate of tension and hostility between the police and population through most of the electoral campaign.

In sharp contrast to all other parties, Herri Batasuna refused to join the chorus of condemnation of ETA's terrorist activities. On the contrary, it defended ETA's actions as necessary in the struggle for Basque liberation from the repression of Madrid. In its view, ETA terrorists were soldiers fighting for their country's freedom, and their victims were either fascists or representatives of a repressive foreign power.

This made Herri Batasuna the most radical of the three major Basque nationalist groups. The PNV advocated broad autonomy within the Spanish state and a market economy, although its leaders seldom explicitly rejected full independence as a long-term possibility. The EE openly spoke of independence as a possible long-term goal and based its social and economic policies on Marxian socialism. It accepted the constitution and the autonomy statute as immediate answers to Basque aspirations. Both parties advocated the use of peaceful political means for achieving their goals. Herri Batasuna proposed independence as the necessary framework for the fulfillment of Basque aspirations. It rejected both the draft of the autonomy statute and the constitution and announced that any of its candidates who were elected would refuse to take their seats. In addition, as we have just seen, it endorsed the violence of ETA as the proper means of achieving Basque goals.

The elections were held in the Basque country without disorder. The percentage of voters who stayed away from the polls (34 percent) was slightly higher than the national average (33 percent), but the difference was not significant. If some voters refrained from voting for fear of ETA violence or subsequent reprisals, the intensity of political emotion in the region brought out other voters to take their place.

The elections signaled a sharp increase in the importance of the purely Basque parties (see table 10.11). From the nine seats they had held in the previous Parliament, they increased their representation to eleven, although the fact that the Herri Batasuna representatives had pledged themselves not to participate in the activities of the Cortes meant that the number of deputies actually sent to the Cortes by purely Basque parties would decline to eight.

Table 10.11 Basque Sects in the Chamber, March 1979

Party	Alava	Guipúzcoa	Navarre	Vizcaya	Total
PSOE	1	2	1	2	6
PNV	1	2	0	4	7
UCD	2	1	3	2	8
EE	0	1	0	0	1
UPN	—	—	1	—	1
HB	0	1	0	2	3
Total	4	7	5	10	26

Source: El Diario Vasco, 3 March 1979; and *El País*, 2 May 1979.
Dash (—): Party did not run.

The greater loser in this election was the PSOE, which lost one seat in Guipúzcoa, one in Navarre, and one in Vizcaya so that its total representation declined from nine to six. From being the party with the largest number of Basque deputies in the Cortes, it became the third party of the region in numbers of representatives. The UCD managed to retain all the seats it had won in June 1977 and picked up one seat in Guipúzcoa, where it had not presented candidates in the previous elections. This success made it the party with the largest number of seats in the region. The PNV lost one seat in Guipúzcoa but remained far and away the largest of the purely Basque parties. Its relative success was eclipsed, however, by the striking and almost totally unexpected victories of Herri Batasuna, which won one seat in Guipúzcoa and two in Vizcaya to become suddenly a major force on the Basque political scene.

In terms of left-center-right positions on socioeconomic issues, the electoral results expressed in seats presented a significant shift to the left. The center and center-right parties (the PNV and the UCD) retained their fifteen seats, and the left as a whole failed to increase its representation, but the victory of three revolutionary Marxist candidates of Herri Batasuna clearly indicated a sharp shift to the left in electoral sentiment. The right, running this time under the name of Union of the People of Navarre (UPN), retained the single seat it had won in Vizcaya in 1977.

The distribution of the popular vote showed less dispersion than in the previous election (see table 10.12). In 1977, 20.7 percent of the voters had cast their ballots for parties, groups, or coalitions that had failed to win a single seat in the Cortes; in the 1979 election that percentage declined to 13.2. Consequently the difference between the distribution of the popular vote and the distribution of seats in the Chamber was less than in 1977. The UCD continued to benefit most from the workings of the electoral mechanism, but even it was less overrepresented than previously. The two other major parties (the PNV and the PSOE) both benefited slightly from the d'Hondt proportional voting system, but their share of the seats was only slightly greater than their share of the popular vote.

The PSOE was the greatest loser in the Basque country in popular votes as well as in seats. Its share of the popular vote declined by 5.6 percentage points, or almost one-quarter. The PNV retained almost exactly the same percentage of the popular vote it had had in 1977. The UCD, largely because it presented a full slate of candidates in Guipúzcoa, where it had not run in 1977, increased its share of the popular vote by four percentage points. As a result of these changes, the PNV became the party with the largest number of votes in the Basque country, and the UCD edged out the PSOE for second place.

The impressive performance of Herri Batasuna, which managed to garner 13.5 percent of the vote, brought the total share of the far left to slightly more than one-fourth of the vote. Nowhere else in Spain did parties of the far left show anywhere near such strength. It is impossible on the basis of current evidence to differentiate between nationalist and other components in the vote for the far left. It seems probable, however, that conflict in the Basque region has contributed to a general radicalization of the population on all issues, rather than merely on the issues of Basque autonomy or independence.

Table 10.13 once again reveals sharp differences between the four Basque provinces. Navarre continued to stand out for the low percentage of the vote given to the PNV, which even in a coalition achieved only about one-third as many votes in Navarre as it did alone in the other Basque provinces. Even

Table 10.12 Results of the Chamber Elections in the Basque Country, March 1979

Party	Popular vote (percent)	Seats	Index of over representation
PNV	22.0	7	0.22
UCD	20.2	8	0.52
PSOE	19.7	6	0.17
HB	13.8	3	−0.16
EE	6.4	1	−0.93
UPN	2.2	1	0.73
Other far left[a]	4.9	0	−1.0
PCE	4.1	0	−1.0
Far right[b]	3.6	0	−1.0
Other	0.7	0	−1.0
Invalid	2.4	—	—

Source: Author's calculation from data in *El País*, 2 May 1979.
Dash (—): Not applicable
[a] EMK-OIC, ORT, EKA, LKI, IR, UNAI.
[b] UF, UN, UFV, UNE.

248 The Elections in the Basque Country

Table 10.13 Distribution of the Vote for the Chamber in the Basque Provinces, March 1979 (percent)

Party	Alava	Guipúzcoa	Navarre	Vizcaya
PNV	23.0	26.5	—[a]	29.3
UCD	25.5	15.4	33.0	16.0
PSOE	21.4	18.2	22.0	14.1
HB	10.0	17.6	8.9	14.5
EE	4.7	12.9	—	5.9
Union Foral Vasco	6.0	1.0	—	4.2
UPN	—	—	11.0	—
Other far left	2.9	4.1	14.0[b]	2.2
PCE	3.3	3.1	2.2	5.8
Other far right	0.9	0.8	—	1.5
Other	1.9	0.1	—	0.5
Invalid	3.2	2.1	1.9	2.4

Source: *El País*, 2 May 1979
Dash: (–): Party did not run.
[a] In a coalition called Nacionalistas Vascos.
[b] Includes 7.6 percent from the Partido Carlista.

more striking is the fact that Herri Batasuna won more voter support in Navarre than did the PNV. Incorporation into the Basque country is such a hotly disputed issue there that voters who support Basque nationalism are more inclined toward the extreme parties. Despite the striking success of Herri Batasuna, the parties of the far left did not improve their positions with respect to 1977. They remained, however, a formidable political force in Navarre, accounting for close to one-quarter of all votes cast.

At the opposite end of the political spectrum stood the UPN, which vigorously rejected the union of Navarre with the other Basque provinces and proposed a conservative social and economic program. The UPN captured the votes that in the previous election had gone to Alianza Foral and in addition won some of the voters away from other parties. The UCD remained the strongest party in Navarre and in fact slightly improved its position with respect to 1977. Navarre was the only one of the four Basque provinces in which the UCD held a commanding lead over its closest rival. In Alava it was also the largest party, but the PNV was less than two percentage points behind. In Navarre the UCD received half again as many votes as the second largest party, the PSOE. Despite its relative weakness compared with the UCD, the PSOE did better in Navarre than in any of the other Basque provinces. Navarre was also the only province in which the PSOE improved its position with respect to 1977.

Alava remained less enthusiastic about Basque nationalism than Vizcaya or Guipúzcoa, but Basque nationalists made striking gains there between 1977 and 1979. Their share of the vote increased from one-fifth in 1977 to more than a third in 1979. The extreme Basque nationalism of Herri Batasuna received the support of almost one in every ten voters. EE more than doubled its vote, although it still accounted for less than 5 percent of the vote in Alava. The more moderate PNV grew from 17.0 percent to 22.3 percent. Basque nationalists from all parts of the political spectrum had clearly been very successful in building their positions in Alava.

In sharp contrast, the two major national political parties, the UCD and the PSOE, each lost about six percentage points in Alava. If in 1977 the PSOE had counted for more than 70 percent of the total vote of left and center-left parties there, in 1979 it constituted barely 50 percent. In 1977 the UCD had accounted for close to two-thirds of the total vote of the center and center-right in Alava. In 1979 it accounted for little more than half.

In Vizcaya the PNV continued to dominate the political center, winning almost twice as many votes as the UCD. Leftist voters apparently shifted away from the PSOE toward Basque nationalist parties. Herri Batasuna won the support of one voter in every seven, and the other parties of the Basque left maintained their positions. The PSOE in contrast lost one-fourth of the votes it had received in 1977. The two principal national parties together accounted for only one-third of the vote in Vizcaya, a clear sign of the strength of Basque nationalism in the province.

Guipúzcoa presents a picture very similar to Vizcaya, except in heightened colors. The strength of the Basque nationalist movement was even greater there than in Vizcaya. The extreme Basque nationalists Herri Batasuna and EE together accounted for almost 30 percent of the vote, and the PNV took more than one-fourth of it. The radicalization of Basque nationalism in Guipúzcoa was evident in the decline of votes for the PNV and the sharp increase in votes for more extreme nationalists. It seems probable that many voters who had cast their ballots for the Popular Alliance in 1977, in the absence of its successor, the Democratic Coalition (CD), voted UCD in 1979.

Our analysis thus far has failed to mention two important matters pertinent to the 1979 election: the vote of the newly enfranchised eighteen- to twenty-one-year-olds and the vote of the large immigrant working-class population. On the basis of impressionistic evidence, it would appear that young voters gave their support disproportionately to Basque nationalist parties and to parties of the far left. Most observers agree that Herri Batasuna recruited its support especially among the younger voters. It would also appear, although the evidence is even less reliable, that the success of the Basque nationalist parties in the March 1979 elections reflected in part their having made some inroads into the immigrant working-class population. A number of working-class neighborhoods in and around Bilbao with a largely immigrant population, voted heavily for Basque nationalist parties in the 1979 election. It seems that some immigrant workers, disgruntled with the difficult economic situation, chose to express their rejection of the government's policies by voting for radical Basque parties, even though they themselves were not Basques and would ordinarily not be expected to support Basque nationalism.

The Municipal and Provincial Elections

In three of the four Basque provinces (Guipúzcoa, Navarre, and Vizcaya), elections for provincial assemblies were held simultaneously with the municipal elections conducted throughout Spain little more than a month after the March 1979 general election. In Alava there was a single election; the voters there elected only members of municipal councils, who in turn would choose the representatives to the provincial assembly. The nationalist parties centered their campaign on the issues of Basque autonomy. Personalities were, naturally, of great importance in the municipal elections, but a disproportionate percentage of the propaganda of the Basque parties dealt with regional and national rather than local issues.

In Alava, Guipúzcoa, and Vizcaya, the elections of 3 April confirmed the patterns established in the national elections a month earlier. As most observers expected, the PNV showed great strength, increasing its vote in many places and taking the majority of seats on many municipal councils. Local institutions in all three provinces would be dominated by the PNV members. The extreme Basque nationalists of Herri Batasuna also strengthened and consolidated the positions they had gained in the 1 March elections. In many municipalities their candidates ran second only to those of the PNV.

In contrast to the marked success of the nationalist parties, the PSOE continued to lose ground in the Basque country. Even in many areas of traditional Socialist strength and of heavy immigration from other parts of Spain, the PSOE lost votes to the nationalists. The PNV established itself as the leading political force in such traditional Socialist strongholds as Eibar, Baracaldo, and Santurce. The UCD, like the PSOE, did less well in the municipal elections than it had a month earlier. The UCD's strength in the Basque country is clearly a function of its national position. The party lacks solid structures and implantation at the local level, and this was evident in its relatively weak showing in these elections.

Unlike the other three Basque provinces, Navarre showed a sharp shift in opinion between the two elections. At the municipal level, independent candidates, many of them backed by left-wing nationalists, ran very strongly. Seventy percent of the members of town councils elected in Navarre were independents. In the elections for the provincial parliament (*parlamento foral*) voters opposed to the incorporation of Navarre into the Basque country shifted away from the UCD to the more radically anti-Basque UPN. The UCD received

83,000 votes on 1 March but only 68,000 on 3 April. In contrast, the UPN increased its vote from 28,000 to almost 41,000. Voters who favored the incorporation of Navarre into the Basque country also tended to shift their support to the most radical Basque country, Herri Batasuna. A complex pattern of coalitions in the various districts that make up the province prevents any direct comparison of the vote for Herri Batasuna in the two recent elections. In the capital city of Pamplona and its surrounding district, however, where Herri Batasuna presented its own candidates in both elections, it increased its vote from 16,000 to 28,000.

Conclusion

The results of the elections analyzed in this chapter clearly point to the diversity of the Basque region. Basque regional nationalism is not a uniform phenomenon. It is far stronger in Guipúzcoa and in Vizcaya than in Alava. In Navarre it enters into open conflict with a Navarrese identity that is both more "Spanish" and more conservative in its orientation. In all four provinces Basque nationalism has played a large and growing role in the elections. This is evident in the growth of the regional parties and the decline of the national ones in the Basque region. The decline of the Socialists was particularly striking since the Socialist party had a long and solid tradition of presence in the Basque country.

Both the electoral results and the content of the electoral campaigns make it clear that there is no real consensus in the Basque country, even among Basque nationalists, about the shape of a future Basque region. The PNV and its supporters would probably be at least temporarily satisfied by a grant of broad autonomy compatible with the provisions of the current Spanish constitution. Other more extreme Basque nationalists, both those of Herri Batasuna and those of the EE, may not be satisfied with even the most far-reaching concessions that any Spanish state is likely to make. Their demands could probably not be met even within a federal structure, and they certainly exceed the possibilities of the unitary constitution approved in December 1978.

The most extreme Basque nationalists are usually also socioeconomic radicals. Many are Marxist-Leninists, who accuse the Communist party of Spain of having sold out to the establishment. As we noted earlier, this brand of leftwing Basque nationalism is a recent development. Until twenty years ago, Basque nationalism was almost exclusively conservative. The PNV, with its conservative social and economic program, is still the strongest single force in the Basque regionalist movement. The development of Herri Batasuna, of EE, and of smaller radical groups, however, has deprived it of its monopoly on Basque nationalism.

The addition of a Marxist social program to the traditional demands of Basque nationalism helps to explain, at least in part, the growing radicalism of

Basque nationalism. It also explains the growing appeal of Basque nationalism among the industrial working class of the region. Twenty years ago the typical representative of Basque nationalism was a small farmer in an out-of-the-way village. Such people continue to provide much support for the PNV. The left-wing Basque nationalist parties, however, have found strong support among the metalworkers of Vizcaya and other industrial workers who were previously socialist in their orientation. Some immigrants from other parts of Spain have been won over by the radical social protest of these groups. Their definition of Basque as anyone who sells his labor in the Basque provinces provides a basis for attempts to extend their appeal further among populations who know no Basque and who trace their ancestry to other parts of Spain.

These patterns all seem to point in the direction of increasing conflict in the Basque region. Approval of the autonomy statute has not brought peace to the region. The situation in the Basque country poses a serious threat to Spanish democracy. The electoral results analyzed in other parts of this volume by and large seem to indicate a relatively optimistic prognosis for the new Spain, but the facts discussed in this chapter are less encouraging. The Basque question demands generous and creative solutions if it is not to jeopardize Spain's future.

Portions of this chapter were previously published in *The State of Europe* (The Chicago Council on Foreign Relations) and *The Political Transformation of Spain and Portugal* (Praeger) and appear here with the permission of the publishers.

The Media and the Elections
JUAN ROLDÁN ROS

───── The electoral process and political institutions of any Western democracy often take different paths but sometimes intersect in the field of mass and social communications. During the two months of political campaigning that preceded the elections of 15 June 1977, the daily newspapers and weekly magazines of Spain performed the information-participation-influence functions, commonplace in the other Western democracies. Radio and television, both government-controlled, performed similar functions but in the manner of those European countries where television is generally a patrimony of the party in power.

But the true significance of the role of the Spanish press during the campaign and the election lies in the contribution it made to the first democratic elections in forty years. During the period between the death of Franco and the 1977 elections, the press played a major role by informing the citizens and thereby strengthening the processes of democracy. Again in 1979, the press contributed to a relatively informed public for the national and local elections. To understand recent legislative elections in Spain, it is necessary to take a retrospective look at the role played during this period by a few magazines and newspapers and a handful of journalists throughout the country.

Development of Free Expression

In 1977 Spain was a country just beginning to restructure itself as a modern democracy after forty-one years of Franco's rule that had isolated it from the Western democratic world of liberties and human rights. During its long history, the Spanish people, especially those of the lower classes, had enjoyed few liberties. Until the middle of the nineteenth century, however, the Spanish situation was more or less comparable to that of the rest of Europe. The absence of an industrial revolution in the 1800s and of a religious reformation a few centuries earlier, however, left Spain unprepared to enter the modern age with its new inventions and especially its advances in communications and technology. Not until the late 1950s did the forces of development in the world surrounding Spain encourage the transformation of Spanish society.

The change from absolute to constitutional monarchy in the late nineteenth century did little to improve fundamental popular liberties and rights; neither did the continuing flirtation between the political leaders and the military establishment improve the nation's situation. The stratified Spanish society that existed well into the twentieth century left power in the hands of the nobility, the clergy, and the military, while the poor, the craftsmen, and the peasants had few rights and virtually no representation. Hardly a fertile soil for democracy to take root. Not until 1931 did Spain reach a republican period when the first faint stirrings of a democracy developed.

The population of Spain during the Second Republic (1931-36) was less than half that of the late 1970s and only one-third of the current population of the metropolitan areas of Madrid and Barcelona. In 1936 some 500,000 papers were sold daily in Madrid, although many of its 1 million people were illiterate. In 1977 the sale of papers remained at 500,000 for a population that had risen to 4.3 million. Essentially the same situation prevailed in Barcelona. In the rest of the country no paper had a circulation of more than 50,000. Today, television—with one national channel and another channel that reaches only half of the fifty provinces—is practically the only source of information for half of the Spanish people.

Radio Nacional de Espana (RNE) until 1977 was another virtual state monopoly in the field of information. Local stations were not permitted to broadcast their own news bulletins, and they were instructed to rely on official news transmitted twice a day by RNE. The importance of radio and especially of television was underscored by the results of a poll taken by the National Institute of Public Opinion (I.N.O.P.), which revealed that only 9 percent of the adult population read a newspaper on a daily basis. Some 50 percent of the population read nothing at all, while 23 percent read a newspaper or magazine only "from time to time."[1]

Even in the mid-1970s the largest national newspapers, printed in Madrid and Barcelona, sold no more than 120,000 copies on weekdays and a maximum of 180,000 on Sundays. *La Vanguardia* of Barcelona, *El País*, *Ya*, and *ABC* of Madrid are the only papers that reached these circulation figures. Evening papers such as *Pueblo*, *Informaciones*, and *Diario 16* of Madrid rarely reached an individual daily circulation of 50,000. Spain is one of the few industrialized countries where the system of home subscriptions is practically nonexistent. Spain, according to the economic daily *5 Dias* in 1979, placed last in European newspaper circulation.[2]

The weekly general newsmagazines that outnumber the daily newspapers also have small circulations. Only *Cambio 16* (whose role in the reform process will be analyzed later) and *Interviú* (with its suggestive nude pictures on the cover) have maintained an average circulation between 150,000 and 300,000.

Television had an average maximum audience of 13 million viewers daily, and the evening news broadcasts were seen by between 3 and 5 million people. According to a 1979 poll by the Institut Oficial de Radiofusion y Television, 90 percent of the people in rural Spain watched television every day, 75 percent listened to the radio, and 40 percent said they had never read a newspaper. The survey suggested that news and cultural information that reach perhaps one-third of the 47 million Spaniards was presented by the one national television network. These figures not only showed that many more Spaniards turned to the electronic media rather than the press, but they also indicated that it would be easier and more effective to change the television news programming than to change the reading habits of the public.[3]

Censorship: Ministry of Information

After the Civil War the Franco regime established a system of censorship of the mass media, the theater, and so on. The regime established the Department of Press and Propaganda in the mid-1940s and later the Ministry of Information, the purpose of which was to reinforce censorship. The ministry not only sought to keep the press in line, but also radio, television, popular cultural programs, the theater, and the cinema.

The control and repression exercised over journalists and the media between 1939 and 1975 is difficult to summarize in a few lines. The main political means for controlling the press took two forms: on one hand, strict control over the news material published by the private press; on the other hand, the creation of competing official publications to disseminate information directly to the people.

When Franco gained control of Spanish territory, he expropriated private and political party publications. These were then incorporated into the Prensa y Radio del Movimiento (Press and Radio of the Movement),[4] an organization under the control of the National Movement, the only legal party. In all, nearly one hundred publications, thirty-nine newspapers, and several radio stations were taken over. All journalistic establishments in two-thirds of the Spanish provinces belonged to this official chain. From Madrid, where the official organ *Arriba* was published, the provincial press and radio received from Pyresa, a domestic news agency, not only the news but also editorials and daily political guidelines imposed by the government.

Symbolically, many of the new official papers were printed in buildings and with machinery that had formerly belonged to the papers that during the Second Republic had been the organs of anti-Falangist parties. In quarters that had housed *El Socialista* (The Socialist), the official newspaper of the Spanish Workers Socialist party (PSOE) and its union, the General Workers' Union (UGT), the government established the evening daily *Pueblo*, the organ of the only legal union, the Syndicate of the Organization of Management and Workers. Most of the papers have been reclaimed by their original owners. During the constitution-writing process, a decision concerning the ownership and control of the papers confiscated by the Franco regime was postponed because other matters were considered more important and because the party in power benefited from the existing situation. The same was true of official radio and television. Curiously, the opposition political parties did not strongly press the issue with the Suárez government, and at the beginning of 1979 administrative control of these "official" newspapers was shifted from the Ministry of Culture to the prime minister's office.

The Franco regime also had at its disposal the main news agency in the country, CIFRA-EFE, with an annual budget (in 1979) of $15 million. This agency was considered a private corporation (*sociedad anónima*) even though 75 percent of the stock was owned by the government. Through CIFRA (EFE's national wire service) and Pyresa domestic news was controlled and censured. EFE, which controlled the distribution of foreign news services, sharply curtailed the purchase of foreign information from large international news agencies such as UPI, AP, Reuters, and AFP.

Aside from direct government intervention through its own news media, the Franco government maintained a complex and primitive form of censorship. From 1940 and 1966 newspapers could not be sold without prior approval of the government in each municipality. News stories, photographs, and advertisements had to pass a prepublication check by a team of censors in the Ministry of Information. Over a thousand persons were assigned this duty in Madrid and in the provinces. These bureaucrats, generally with limited education, interpreted the arbitrary guidelines printed in monthly or daily bulletins by their superiors. The print and electronic media were only two of the casualties of censorship; Spain's great literary and artistic tradition was cut off at the roots.

The newspapers that remained in private hands—about a dozen—included *ABC* of Madrid and *La Vanguardia* of Barcelona, both family enterprises. During these years, they were the most powerful papers in the country. They and *Ya*—official organ of the Catholic church hierarchy and the Conference of Catholic Laity—survived because they collaborated with the government. Since all papers depended on the government's distribution of ink and paper, they did not criticize it and were therefore able to make tremendous profits. Only the privately owned newspapers that started up in the 1970s were more willing to openly attack those in power. The older newspapers, in exchange for their collaboration, occasionally pressured the government into granting or denying publishing licenses to those who sought to form new publications.

Change Begins

The state-controlled Official School of Journalism and the Catholic journalism schools in Madrid, Barcelona, and Navarra (the latter was controlled by Opus Dei) were the only educational institutions entrusted by the Franco regime to teach journalism. Persons who had not studied journalism in a state- or church-run school could not join a newspaper staff. In addition to the requirement of a professional degree, the Franco regime erected another quasi-political barrier requiring a journalist to have a membership card issued by the Federation of Press Associations, a professional organization controlled by the regime. These credentials were sometimes issued to persons who had not graduated from a journalism school, but who had a long list of services to the regime in the early days of the dictatorship.

In June 1966 then-Minister of Information Manuel Fraga Iribarne (later the leader of the conservative Alianza Popular) presented a new press law that eased the 1939 rules by substituting postpublication censorship for prepublication censorship.[5] Under the new law, publications could go on sale without prior approval but could be confiscated later by the Ministry of Information if the censors objected to their articles. Fraga's law outlined an "administrative decision-making" process that made the bureaucracy, not the courts, the final arbiter.

Article 2 of the new law soon became infamous for its threat of punishment for any text that the administration deemed offensive. The article provided:

> Liberty of expression and circulation as contained in the first article, will have no limitations except those imposed by the law. These limitations are: respect for truth and morals; adherence to the law of the principles of the National Movement and other fundamental laws; the demands of national defense, the security of the state and the maintenance of domestic law and order, and foreign peace; due respect to the institutions and persons entrusted with political and administrative duties; independence of the Courts and the respect of privacy, personal and family honor.[6]

Broadly interpreted, this article left little room for critical writing on public affairs. And yet there were changes in the last years of Franco's rule. He did not prevent the new generation of journalists from acquiring liberal ideas. Working trips to and exile in Europe and the United States helped these new journalists develop a different outlook. The more they became acquainted with the foreign press, the more they worried about their own system. Savings policies, development, and "moonlighting" encouraged economic change in the 1960s and brought about the growth of an authentic apolitical and consumerist middle class. The influx of tourists into Spain, lured by prices lower than those found in most Western countries, and the prospects of change once Franco left the scene, slowly turned Spain away from its former isolation.

Some newspapers reflected the new mood. After a change of ownership, the evening paper *Madrid* sought to return to the great tradition of the capital by blending intellectual writing with popular journalism. In the 1960s, under the editorial leadership of Rafael Calvo Serer and Antonio Fontán, it became the first paper to publish the facts clearly and courageously, thus constituting a direct threat to the regime. An article in 1968 entitled "Retiring on Time" that discussed the fall of de Gaulle in France, was interpreted by the government as an assault on Franco's person under the 1966 press law. The paper was suspended for four months. The minister of information finally closed *Madrid* on 25 November 1971, alleging that there had been administrative irregularities when the paper was originally licensed. At the time of its death, *Madrid* had a circulation of 80,000 to 90,000 copies. It took seven years and the death of Franco before Calvo Serer, who lived in exile in France during Franco's last years, won a Supreme Court decision that awarded him an indemnity of 300 million pesetas (approximately $400,000).

Cambio 16 A new weekly magazine with a nationwide circulation, *Cambio 16*, began publication in the capital shortly after *Madrid* had been closed. Although the magazine was originally allowed to publish only economic news, by 1974 it had become the first weekly magazine covering national political events, with a style and format akin to *Time*, *Newsweek*, or *Le Point*. By 1976, without the aid of home subscriptions, it became the largest mass circulation, Spanish-language newsmagazine in the world, selling a million copies at home and producing an international edition.

The founders of *Cambio 16* were sixteen almost unknown individuals of the moderate opposition who had meager economic means and were trained in different professions. They used the magazine to denounce the policies of Franco and his successors. Juan Tomás de Salas aided by Ricardo Utrilla, Luis Gonzalez Seara, and others set the line and style of the magazine. The firm (IMPULSA, S.A.) grew rapidly. It published a magazine dealing with historical themes, *Historia 16*; founded a paperback publishing house; and in October 1976 it launched an evening paper, *Diario 16*. Journalists with these and other publications wrote of political and administrative abuses, repression, and the use of torture. On the positive side, they called for new leadership to move the country toward a pluralistic democracy, vigorous measures to revitalize the economy, and an end to terrorism by extremists of both the left and right. Journalists deserve credit for speeding an end to the dictatorship. Although their articles were still published under difficult circumstances, censorship had become more lenient in the later Franco years. The administration did not silence critical publications as it had done earlier in the case of *Madrid*.

The last years of the dictatorship saw a relaxation of censorship of magazines, but not of the daily papers. This encouraged the weeklies to hire professional journalists who eventually joined the daily papers that appeared after Franco's death. Various reforming weeklies including *Posible*, *Cuadernos para el Diálogo*, *Triunfo*, and *Guadiana*, although smaller than *Cambio 16*, contributed to the struggle for democracy and a free press.

The traditional Spanish press, perhaps because of censorship policies or its own incapacity or lack of desire to change the status quo, did not emerge quickly from the lethargy of forty years. National papers like *La Vanguardia*, *Ya*, *Arriba*, and *ABC* did not alter their reporting style even after the death of Franco. In 1977 these, like the press of the National Movement, were put under the Ministry of Information. Without subsidies some of the papers collapsed.

The provincial press was insensitive to the changing nature of Spanish society. None of the five state or private newspapers in the Basque region reported on the problems of the area. These papers continued to favor a strong central government in Madrid, even as Basque opinion preferred regional autonomy or even independence. *Cambio 16* stepped into this void by devoting many cover stories to the Basque news. This policy also provided financial reward because half of its issues were sold in the region.

A change in the information process did not really reach the Spanish public until the appearance in 1976 of two new national newspapers in Madrid—*El País* and *Diario 16*. Their style and professionalism took advantage of the new mood of the country, and they became the largest-selling morning and evening papers, respectively. *El País* was founded by José Ortega Spottorno, son of the philosopher José Ortega y Gasset, who owned *Alianza Editorial*, a paperback publishing house. The magazine had a style similar to that of the French *Le Monde*. Because it presented a sober and independent outlook and adopted an editorial policy that forcefully favored democracy, its impact on national opinion was very strong. For its part, *Diario 16* broke away from the traditional style that had dominated the Spanish press for forty years and featured heavy photographic coverage and often sensational, though bold and informative, headlines. Within a years its total sales and influence surpassed those of the other evening papers—*Informaciones*, *Pueblo*, and *El Alcázar*. Economic and labor problems as well as poor administration beset *Diario 16* during its first two years, and it lost much of its initial influence. By the end of 1978, many members of the original editorial staff had left the newspaper. Even with credit that was widely thought to be given by the UCD, the party in power, its circulation dropped by 50 percent.

Two separatist newspapers appeared in the Basque country before the 1977 elections: *Egin* and *Deia* filled the information vacuum on regional political, economic, and social problems that were left unreported by the Catholic newspapers published in the Basque provinces.

Egin, with a circulation of 15,000 copies, later became more radical and moved closer to the separatist and revolutionary ideas of the Herri Batasuna party. It usually printed national news in the "foreign" or "international" sections. The more conservative *Deia* was closer to the Partido Nacionalista Vasco (PNV) and had a daily circulation of 60,000 copies. In spite of their defense of the Basque language and culture, neither paper devoted more than 10 percent of its news in the Basque language.

The Press and the 1977 Election

In December 1976 the Spanish people approved the Law for Political Reform in a referendum. An election for deputies and legislators to write a new constitution was announced 15 April 1977. The campaign, officially limited to twenty-one days, was set to begin 24 May. Both the press and the candidates sought to inform the public of the issues in the elections.

While all traditional political parties had been legalized in 1976, the Communist party (PCE) was not legitimized until 9 April 1977. The press, other than the most conservative journals, had argued that the public would benefit from PCE participation in the elections because the readers could then learn the true strength of the Communists and would not have to depend on the exaggerated claims made by the PCE from its clandestine quarters.

When the government of President Adolfo Suárez legalized the Spanish Communist party, the PCE's paper *Mundo Obrero* was sold on the streets after years as an underground publication. A few months before this occurred, *El Socialista*, the PSOE weekly newspaper that changed to a magazine, once again became the official organ of the Socialist party and was openly sold.

Of the major publications, only *ABC* and *El Alcázar* termed the legalization of the Communist party an "error" and accused the government of authorizing the presence of the Communists in the mainstream of Spanish life. *El Alcazar*, a staunch supporter of Franco, attacked the Communist party as being "totalitarian." On the other hand, *Arriba*, the former organ of the Falange or National Movement, congratulated the government for making this "realistic" decision.

El País and *Diario 16* and magazines such as *Cambio 16, Cuadernos para el Diálogo, Triunfo,* and *Posible* viewed with satisfaction the consternation felt by some conservatives in the armed forces over the legalization of the PCE and President Suárez's dismissal of the minister of the navy, Admiral Pita da Veiga, who had publicly criticized the decision. In 1977 political opinions and debates flowered in the national Spanish press in Madrid and Barcelona where years earlier Franco's policies had centralized control of the media. Outside of Catalonia, the regional press devoted more than two-thirds of its political coverage to national news from Madrid, while largely ignoring local candidates and issues.

Only in Madrid, Barcelona, and in the northern provinces were there any privately owned, independent papers. In most of the fifty provinces, each of which was an electoral district, the major papers had belonged to the National Movement and in 1977 were still largely controlled by the government. Many of the editors still seemed to live in the age of Franco.

Another reason for the excessive centralization of campaign coverage lay in the expectation that major changes in the politics of the whole society would develop out of the June elections. Even the candidates made scant mention of local themes or their personal programs. Television and National Radio of Spain, as previously mentioned, had a national monopoly over virtually all television and radio reporting, so that the news generally reflected the views of the government.

The common goal of the parties and coalitions from the center to the left was to return the country to a democratic form of government, to a pluralistic political life, and to recover lost individual liberties. Themes common in election rhetoric of any Western democracy, such as education, economics, and foreign policy problems, were rarely debated. Nor did the press write about them. Once a candidate had distributed his party's platforms, neither the candidate nor the press analyzed their content in any detail.

Reform of the "Law of the Press"

The Suárez transition government attempted in early 1977 to soften the impact of the press law of 1966.[7] Liberal, private, and independent publications had already begun to ignore its provisions, and on 1 April 1977 the information and propaganda sectors of the old Movement were transferred by government decree directly to the Ministry of Information and Tourism. Article 2 and part of article 69 of the 1966 law, which referred to sanctions that the ministry could impose on the press and journalists, were abolished by the government. Nevertheless, article 2 was replaced by a third article that continued to give the government broad administrative powers to influence or control the press. The new article stated that the administration could seize "any audio or visual materials that contain news, commentaries or information considered contrary to the unity of Spain, that constitute an attack on the monarchy or royal family, and that in any manner attempt to decrease the institutional prestige or the public regard of the armed forces." In commenting on this new press law in its 13 April 1977 edition, *Diario 16* stated:

> They have rescinded Article 2, but in return, they have given us a third article by which they can seize anyone who writes about regionalism in a manner not liked by the censor of the moment, anyone who brings his literary or graphical eroticism beyond the bounds tolerated by the righteous bureaucrat, or anyone who loyally expresses his point of view on the form of government or of the military organization. Why this obsession with maintaining taboos and silent zones where only the official dogma can tread? Do they want to impose on us new fundamental principles, permanent and unalterable by their very nature?[8]

The new law also emphasized the "direct and sole" coresponsibility of the author and the chief editor, where previously, under the penal and civil codes, editors had had only secondary responsibility. Under the new, more liberal norm, a private citizen's claim was nevertheless cause enough for a public official to begin legal proceedings against the press for damages alleged to have been incurred by the citizen. The new law was intended to make editors more fearful and cautious of what was printed in their publications.

The government advised the editors when these new regulations were issued that a "gentlemen's agreement" was needed to ensure the peaceful transition from a dictatorship to a democracy. The press was urged to refrain from criticizing three institutions: the monarchy and the royal family, the armed forces, and the geopolitical unity of Spain. Although the country was still officially a Catholic state, the Catholic church was not included in the list of taboos because the church hierarchy and the clergy were no longer considered as necessary allies. This change may be attributed to the ideological and generational differences that had weakened the church after the Second Vatican Council.

Among members of the press, respect for the Crown and King Juan Carlos was universal. The young Borbón king was considered the moving force responsible for the peaceful transition to the democracy so ardently desired by the politicians and the Spanish people. On the other hand, the sacred cow status accorded to the armed forces, including the paramilitary units and the policy, was supported by very few newspapers and magazines and, then, only with reluctance. Significantly, during the 1977 campaign, several journalists were jailed for what the military considered an infringement on its honor, and they were brought to trial before a military tribunal.

During the preelectoral period the Spanish press often took a united stand favoring amnesty for political prisoners. The substantial press coverage accorded to street demonstrations, political party statements, and editorials defending amnesty helped bring about the release of all political prisoners not charged with murder. Eventually the government deported most imprisoned terrorists, generally members of the Basque separatist group ETA.

The press denunciation of terrorist acts by groups described by the government as "extreme leftists" were less effective. Some politicians and other press sources voiced the suspicion that the terrorist groups were ultra-rightists, or at least had been heavily infiltrated by the right. These elements certainly shared the goals of the Revolutionary Antifascist Patriotic Front (FRAP) and the Groups of Antifascist Resistance (GRAPO) whose avowed objectives included the destabilization of Spanish society, impeding the elections, and provoking a military coup. The liberal press published allegations about these groups, but it was unable to force the government to take strong measures against terrorist groups that had kidnapped well-known persons, set bombs, and killed law enforcement officers. The reasons for the lack of effective measures by the government were difficult to ascertain. Perhaps the government was reluctant to move against them because this might require dismantling the intelligence and police apparatus that had grown up during Franco's forty years in power. Perhaps there were other reasons.

The government, for its part, alleged that GRAPO, FRAP, and similar groups had been infiltrated by international fascists newly arrived from Latin America, Germany, and Italy. Their activities continued even after the elections. In August 1977 an attempt was made on the life of King Juan Carlos and the prime minister as they traveled in Palma de Mallorca. A bomb placed in the road over which their car would pass was discovered minutes before the king and prime minister arrived. On 25 June, ten days after the election, two bombs were allegedly placed by GRAPO, damaging the printing presses of *Diario 16*, which had denounced their activities and had charged that GRAPO was controlled by the extreme right.

A Sense of Mission

One press, the political parties, and indeed most Spaniards displayed a sense of mission in the period before democracy became a reality. The press helped to fill the political-ideological vacuum that existed because heretofore the illegal political parties lacked communication facilities and the legislative power had been in the hands of the Francoist reformers. The press sought to educate the public on the role that elections could play in promoting a free, representative, and democratic society.

Except for the conservative *ABC* (which editorially supported Popular Alliance) and *El Alcázar* (which opposed holding elections), no other information media overtly tried to influence its readers. However, Suárez's UCD and the PSOE were the parties that seemed to be most preferred by the media. For its part, the state-controlled press in the provinces favored the UCD. Aside from simple bias, there were occasional abuses by the press. *Diario 16* and *El*

Alcázar—the former initially supporting the left and the latter the right—sometimes abused their power by the manner in which they discussed opposition candidates and their political beliefs. *Posible*, a weekly political magazine that disappeared within a year, was sometimes guilty of similar abuses.

Less than ten days before the elections, *Diario 16* published a series highly critical of Manuel Fraga Iribarne, the secretary-general of Alianza Popular. *Posible* also published several stories recalling past activities of war prosecutor Arias Navarro, a former prime minister under Franco and now a senatorial candidate on the Popular Alliance ballot. In two successive editions it listed the names of 1,880 persons executed in the province of Malaga in 1936 and linked Arias to the event. The government responded by ordering the seizure of the 201st edition of *Diario 16* because of the article published on Fraga. Arias Navarro and Fraga sued the papers.

The extreme right press—particularly its most visible spokesman, *El Alcázar*—continued a campaign against Santiago Carrillo, secretary-general of the Communist party. It blamed Carrillo for war crimes and called him "the assassin of Paracuellos." As noted earlier, *El Alcázar* editorially opposed holding the elections.

El País offered the most moderate editorial coverage of any Madrid newspaper during the 1977 campaign and tried to inform its readers about the parties and coalitions and their platforms. Articles by the most important and representative leaders of the political parties were published in this paper. Other newspapers and magazines tried to give broad coverage of the campaign, but none succeeded as well as *El País*. The treatment by *El País* of the recurring themes prior to the elections was full and dispassionate. Its attitude in favor of formal liberties was clear.

Polls

The weekly *Cambio 16* and the daily *El País* were the only papers to commission opinion surveys. The research firm Consulta worked for *Cambio 16* for the two months prior to the elections. Their surveys showed that a high percentage of Spaniards did not know or would not say for whom they planned to vote. One private poll fifteen days before the election found that more than half of the population (57 percent) did not know or refused to name the candidates of their choice. Two days before the elections, *El País* published a Sofemasa poll of 18,000 citizens that produced the most accurate, privately published election forecast. Under the title of "A Strong Move Toward the Left," Sofemasa predicted that the UCD and PSOE would place 141 and 121 deputies, respectively, in the lower chamber of parliament.[9] The final results were 165 and 118, respectively.

National Radio and Television of Spain

The wire services of CIFRA and Pyresa (the latter formerly of the Movement), National Radio (RNE), and Spanish Television (TVE) made up the so-called state- or government-controlled media. Television was used during the campaign in a manner faintly reminiscent of the Francoist era—only now it was Suárez and his followers who used this control to their advantage. Since television had a daily national audience of 13 million viewers and reached 50 percent of the population, it was the major source of news. Because its directors were appointed by the government and because it had no direct competitors, TVE by and large acted as a government spokesman during the transition period from the death of Franco to the 15 June elections. Directives were transmitted through Rafael Ansón, the director general of RTVE and a personal friend of Suárez. Because Ansón was a publicity expert who now in effect managed the media campaign for the UCD, *Cambio 16* and *Diario 16* baptized the TVE as TELEVIANSON. Radio Nacional had a monopoly over all the information transmitted by radio and had the same director general as RTVE. Because it was less important than RTVE, the government did not bother to subject it to the same control as television.

Television was certainly important in promoting the candidacy of Suárez. The official TVE budget for the year was over 7,000 million pesetas (approximately $100 million), and probably a significant share of these funds were spent during the campaign. Even so, it is difficult to estimate the exact amount spent by RTVE on the campaign. Some say it far exceeded the budgeted sum.

Analysts generally say that RNE and TVE propaganda was most effective in the news broadcasts. Paid political announcements were banned by these two media. The news broadcasts of radio and television during the dictatorship were forced to stress positive political events while concealing negative developments among the people. After Franco's death, the general information transmitted by radio or television remained under strict government supervision. The television and radio news programs read only press statements sent by the parties but declined to comment on their contents. If, for example, Felipe González as leader of PSOE or Gil Robles, the leader of the Christian Democrats, delivered an important speech anywhere in the country, the television cameras were not there to record this event for its viewers. But if President Suárez or any UCD candidate or a minister made even an appearance, critics said that the television and radio broadcasts covered the event.

The nine parties or coalitions registered in at least half of the nation's fifty districts were each granted one half-hour of free time on television and radio, an allotment that was divided into three ten-minute periods spread over the duration of the campaign. The nine parties were the Popular Alliance, Spanish

Falange, PCE, PSOE, Social Spanish Reform, Popular Socialist party, UCD, Federation of Christian Democrats, and Democratic Federation of the Left. A peculiar practice of Radio Nacional, which was also followed by the private radio stations, allowed no candidate's voice to be heard during the official time given a party on radio. Instead, the texts of the statements were read by a professional broadcaster.

The print media and the parties (except UCD) complained about the manner in which information was manipulated during the campaign, but their complaints came to naught. The bureaucracy remained unreformed, and no institution outside the government attempted to end these abuses.

Prompted by widespread dissatisfaction with the government's handling of the media, *El País* published an article on 22 June 1977 entitled "Changing the Official Information," which said:

> These days, after a change in headquarters, the official news agency EFE is also trying to change its image. The state-controlled radio and television is suffering from a barrage of criticism for the delays and errors in the electoral facts and figures.
>
> One thing appears clear: The profound changes which the country is experiencing make unacceptable a continuation of the uses and habits of Francoism in the field of information.
>
> The reporting of the old regime was based on [these] guidelines: Information and criticism should be doled out by the state, open debate is harmful for the country's interests and should therefore be kept to a minimum.
>
> The government has legalized during the last twenty months almost all the political tendencies, it has called and carried out legislative elections, it has opened a dialogue between Madrid and the other regions, it has broken the last existing diplomatic blockade, it has broadened the margins of liberty, and has freed almost all the political prisoners. But, in spite of this, the information apparatus of state remains intact with its vices, inertia, and corruption.
>
> The old Press of the Movement, RTVE, and EFE should be radically remodeled in order to place them at the service of the community, divorced from political tendencies and bias. But the same face and servility of the past should not be part of the image of a government ministry.
>
> A few days ago eight political parties published an *initiative* to intervene in a reasonable manner to change television. We believe that, the project aside, it is pertinent to point out the need for change a public debate on a subject that affects and sometimes intoxicates the conscience of millions of Spaniards. The information media of the government cannot be left at the mercy of the government, any government, in any

democracy. A juridical statute to guarantee the impartiality and independence of this media is necessary as soon as possible.[10]

Constitutional Period and Elections of 1979

Evidence of fatigue in the press developed in the years following the democratic elections in 1977. The fatigue translated into a loss of professional interest in keeping abreast of the details of political events. There was a corresponding shift to writing about subjects or views that appealed to the general public, even while protecting or criticizing public policies and activities. In some cases *El Alcázar*, *El Imparcial*, and, less directly, *ABC* openly opposed democracy, blaming it for all major weaknesses in the system such as the increase in violence; on several occasions *El Alcázar* and *El Imparcial* even supported the return of the previous military regime.

The most representative case of a nondemocratic new press was the daily established in Madrid, *El Imparcial*, a curious mix of the Falangist syndicalism in the style of the daily *Pueblo* under Franco, extreme rightists such as the Fuerza Neuva (New Force), and some retired military officers. *El Imparcial* began publishing in January 1978 and immediately became the standard-bearer of *golpismo* (military interventionism), while criticizing Suárez and the UCD. The paper considered them and their military colleagues, and especially Deputy Minister of Defense Lieutenant General Gutiérrez Mellado, as "traitors" to the country. The daily presentation of *crónica negra* (black events) was its trademark during its first year. Rarely did it fail to emphasize violence by terrorists, by the police, or by criminals in order to show how poorly the country functioned under democracy. When the second general elections were called, *El Imparcial* asked in an editorial: "Doesn't Mr. Suárez realize that in Spain these elections can still divide, as they are in fact doing, the Church, the military, and the families?"[11]

By contrast, nationally circulated publications by left-wing parties were never as radical or did they blame democracy or advocate an armed revolution against it. *La Calle*, a general newsweekly financed by the Communist party, which began publication in March 1978, and two other weeklies, *El Socialista*, the official organ of the PSOE, and *Mundo Obrero*, published by the PCE, were generally cautious and moderate in tone.

During 1978 the government subsidies to newspapers totaled 5,500 million pesetas (approximately $75 million), and in March two lines of credit with very favorable terms, based on copies sold, were approved for modernization of equipment. These lines of credit were approved by the government during the electoral period and were distributed by the ministry of culture and the prime minister's office. The feature magazine *Sabado Gráfico* criticized making grants without parliamentary approval and compared them to the awards given to the "faithful" newspapers during the Franco years. The editorial went on to say: "Regarding the aid from the state to the press, we insist aid must come from the state and not the government, and only clear, objective public legislation can protect reporting from the pressures of authority. . . . It is necessary that the next parliament approach this matter for the first time."[12]

El País also criticized the "aid to the press" and suggested that rather than distributing the aid arbitrarily, the government should

> remove measures protecting the country's low-quality print and reduce import duties, create a national system of distribution in the rather difficult Spanish geography, reduce communications tariffs and eliminate the national television's monopoly, recipient of one-third of all the publicity revenues, and above all, eliminate expenditures of approximately 30,000 million pesetas [approximately $248 million] in publications of the so-called "state press."[13]

Within the press sector, weeklies and monthlies suffered the most during the economic crisis. In a twenty-month period magazines known for their opposition to the Franco tradition, such as *Cuadernos para el Diálogo*, *Posible*, *Ilustracion Regional*, *Berriak*, *Austurias Semanal*, and *Actualidad Española*, or the more recent *Qué* and *Opinión*, among others, closed down. The only national newspaper whose reputation kept growing, albeit not its circulation, was *El País*. *Cambio 16*, though still ranked as the top-level national political newsmagazine despite declining influence, went through an identity crisis in the late 1970s that affected its editorial line, modified its contents, and decreased its circulation.

The 1979 Electoral Campaign

The popular approval by national referendum of the Spanish Democratic Constitution on 6 December 1978 marked the beginning of the electoral campaign for the next parliamentary elections. These were followed by the first municipal elections since 1931. The general elections took place on 1 March 1979, and the local elections were held 3 April 1979.

The excessively centralized distribution of information to newspapers published both in Madrid and the provinces meant that all of them, whether under private or government control, devoted so much space to reporting national developments that they did not foresee the political changes developing in the Basque country, Andalusia, Aragon, and the Canary Islands. *El País* sponsored two polls by Sofemasa Institute that did not predict the reappearance of the separatist parties and only partially succeeded in forecasting the results in the Basque country on 27 February, just two days before the elections. Even the oldest private daily in the Basque country *El Correo Español*, established in 1910 and with the largest circulation in the area through five subregional editions (Vizcaya, Alava, Guipúzcoa, Rioja, and Miranda del Ebro), failed to report any increasing support for leftist separatist parties that in some instances were backed by the terrorist organization ETA. The first regional poll, conducted by the specialized regional institute Abaco, was published on 9 February and showed 45.2 percent of the electorate still undecided; PSOE and PNV were tied with 10 percent of the electorate supporting them in the three Basque provinces. Behind these national parties in the poll were Herri Batasuna (pro-ETA) with 6 percent and Euskadiko Eskerra with 2.6 percent.[14] The second poll, published on 26 February, showed that 37.5 percent of the electorate was still undecided and came closer to the actual results by giving 14.2 percent to PNV and 5.4 percent to Herri Batasuna. The results of the 1979 general elections in the Basque country showed the PNV winning seven seats in the National Congress; Herri Batasuna won three; Euskadiko Eskerra, one; PSOE, five; and UCD, five.[15] In the 1977 elections neither Herri Batasuna nor the Euskadiko Eskerra had won any seats.

The failure to report these developments in the Basque country was repeated in Andalucia, Aragon, Canarias, Navarre, and other regions. In Andalucia virtually all papers failed to predict the reappearance of the Partico Socialista Andaluz (PSA). Only in Catalonia, where results including those of the separatist parties were similar to those in the previous election, did the regional press accurately forecast the results.

Terrorism

ETA led the outbreak of violence during the two years following the 1977 democratic elections, but other extreme left and right groups played an important part in the violence. All newspapers and magazines stressed terrorism as an issue in the 1979 campaign. Several papers seized on the problem of terrorism as a reason to criticize the government, parliamentary democracy, the political parties, and even as a basis for defending the need for a military coup and the return to a dictatorship. In February *Ya* published a statement by the undersecretary of the interior, Julio Famuñas, reporting that during the period from October 1977 to February 1979, 460 terrorists had been arrested in Spain, 154 of whom were members of ETA. From October 1977 to June 1978, the statement continued, 115 terrorist acts occurred that were attributed as follows: ETA, 29; GRAPO, 38; MPAIAC (Movimiento para la Independencia del Archipielago Canario), 29; anarchists, 14; and others, 5. During 1978 there was even a high level of violence against ordinary citizens.[16]

Coverage of organized and unorganized violence has long been used by the media in free countries to draw readers. Reports in Spain, especially of organized violence in 1978 and 1979, may sometimes have had the additional political motive of weakening the new and still fragile democracy and encouraging a return to authoritarian government. Space for stories on the campaign and policy issues were sacrificed to make way for violence and terror. The Basque daily *El Correo Español*, a conservative paper unsympathetic to Basque separatism, published front-page stories every day in February detailing acts of terrorism and violence in the region and elsewhere. Reports on strikes and terrorism filled more than half the news columns in the issues published in *El Correo Español* during the months before the elections. Only on the day before the voting did the paper carry the texts of the political platforms of the parties supporting regional autonomy. The limited political reporting had previously stressed the national parties' campaigns, highlighting the UCD.

During the first electoral campaign, both *Cambio 16* and *Diario 16* had questioned the origins, membership, and possible connections of GRAPO with the paramilitary and the police. In 1979 these publications focused on charges against ETA, even though 1978 official statistics held ETA responsible for fewer terrorist attacks than GRAPO and one other group. During February 1979, *Cambio 16* devoted three editorials in its four issues to ETA. Only *El País* evenhandedly covered the terrorism of all extremist groups, whether of the right, left, or separatist.

In 1979 the Catholic church campaigned in the conservative press against the leftist parties by denouncing their position on the drafting of the constitution and their defense of divorce and state education. *Ya* published five editorials against the Socialist and Communist parties in February and endorsed Fraga Iribarne's Coalicion Democrática (previously the Alianza Popular) as its first choice and Suárez's UCD as an alternative because both had defended the indissolubility of marriage and private religious education. All this was welcomed by church leaders since the new constitution had declared that Spain no longer designated the Catholic church as the official national church. *El País* demanded the neutrality of the church in the elections. An editorial in *El País*, commenting on a preelectoral statement by the bishops' conference, stated, "the church appears again as a power apparatus defending its interests under a cloak of morality."[17]

Television and the Campaign

El País carried the principal campaign against the government's activities by systematically denouncing the government's alleged manipulation of the electronic media, especially RTVE. Apparently the campaign was neither widely appreciated nor effective. *El País* stressed that in 1979, as two years earlier, Suárez and the UCD controlled, within legal limits, the use of television with its two national channels and a daily audience of about 13 million. Other private newspapers and political parties sporadically joined in this campaign. *Cambio*

Table 11.1 News Coverage of Candidates or Parties on TVE during First Half of Campaign

Parties	Time Allowed	Percentage
UCD	25 minutes, 11 seconds	97.5
PCE	16 seconds	1.0
CD	10 seconds	0.6
PSOE	8 seconds	0.5

Source: *El País*, 18 February 1979.

16, with its wide national circulation and importance, could have contributed to the criticism by *El País*, but it chose not to do so.

Since the new Spanish constitution provided for so many important legal changes when Suárez called for elections immediately after the constitution's approval, there was no time for parliament to enact supplementary legislation. There was, therefore, no Tribunal of Constitutional Guarantees to which *El País* or other media might have turned for help. Free time on the government media followed the rules governing media use adopted for the 1977 elections. The main changes in the system came when the national junta ruled unconstitutional an attempt by the government to limit the time given to smaller parties. Such a development, said the junta, would have discriminated against the regional nationalist parties.[18]

By its control of the administrative committee of RTVE, the government limited regional parties to twenty-six ten-minute periods on UHF, the television channel that can be viewed in only one-half of the country. The PSOE and PCE accepted this manipulation without any protest. As in 1977, only those political parties with candidates in twenty-five of the fifty-two districts would have access to free time on TVE. The majority of the regional nationalistic or separatist parties had candidates only in four to eight districts in their geographical area. These parties were allocated to the second channel (UHF) and given time when the audience was expected to be small. *El Correo Español* condemned the fact that the Basque leftist separatist parties were assigned times from 4:30 to 4:40 P.M. on the second channel.[19] Besides this distribution of free time on television, the government also manipulated the time devoted to political news on the four daily newscasts. *El País* sought to compensate for this discrimination by carrying a daily section from 9 February to 28 February that reported the time given to news provided by the government, the opposition, references, films, and so on.

A reproduction of an analysis of the campaign entitled "UCD Grabbed TVE's News Broadcasts During the First Half of the Campaign" is shown in table 11.1. The table speaks for itself, and the abuse in favor of the government continued until the end of the campaign.

Table 11.2 Pages of Party Advertising on 15 February 1979

Parties	*Ya*	*ABC*	*El País*	*Informaciones*
UCD	3¾	3½	3¾	2
PSOE	½	—	½	¼
CD	1	1¾	1½	½
UN	—	1	1	—
PCE	—	—	¾	—
ORT	—	—	¼	—

Source: First edition of *Ya, ABC, El País,* and *Informaciones,* 15 February 1979.

Spanish law, like French law, exercises no legal control over party financing or expenditures. No newspaper carried out a thorough investigation of the sources of funds or of their expenditure by the various political parties. Perhaps this was because newspapers were afraid their political advertising revenue from the parties would be reduced. It is also true, however, that newspapers, unaided by legally required reporting on campaign financing, would have found it extremely difficult to secure the needed information. EFE's international wire service gave some estimated expenditures on 8 March 1979, stating that UCD had spent approximately $11 million; PSOE, $5.2 million; CD, $8 million; and PCE, $1.6 million.

Table 11.2 shows the advertising space purchased on one day in 1979 in four Madrid dailies, *Ya, El País, ABC,* and *Informaciones.* Assuming the advertisements purchased for 15 February were similar to those purchased on other campaign days, one can estimate the relative cost of press advertising for each of the national parties during the campaign.

As the party in power, the UCD could and did use the official public opinion polling facilities to its own advantage. This abuse was mildly criticized by the private press and by some political parties, especially the PSOE. Only the government could request surveys by the "Public Opinion Institute," an agency within the Ministry of Culture, which is generally responsible during nonelectoral periods for conducting surveys. Poll findings were usually made public, but they could not be released without prior government authorization. On 23 February *El País* condemned "the use of polls conducted by an official organ and their results are known only to the president of the government, Mr. Suárez." In a report from Barcelona two days later, Mr. Suárez admitted having polls that forecast a UCD victory in the upcoming elections. According to *ABC*, secret polls in the hands of the government also predicted a loss of votes by the rightist Coalicion Democratica. Two days later *ABC* quoted Suárez campaign manager Rafael Arias Salgado as saying, "officially none of the polls requested by UCD have been published as yet."[20]

The Press after the Elections

The national newspapers and magazines, particularly those published in Madrid and Barcelona, have been, with few exceptions, the most independent and honest news sources during the period of transition. The press fulfilled a reporting and educational role, which in many instances went beyond the role played by the media in other Western democracies. With all the faults of organization and coverage, the press struggled to assure that the steps taken by the crown and the government were not reversed. The newspapers and magazines were the only information channels that could be utilized by the newly legalized political parties. The press was the democratic protagonist in the absence of an elective parliament. As a consequence of restraints continued from the authoritarian period, many newspapers, magazines, and journalists sometimes suffered from a outmoded, arbitrary system still enforced by the administration in power and by the military.

Unfortunately, the protagonist role of the press did not end with the elections. The slow pace of the democratic development, the limited experience of the politicians, the fears of a destabilization, and even of a military coup left undone some tasks that should be the responsibility of politicians. When the Spanish press can limit itself to reporting the news, to criticizing the politicians and their parties, and to articulating the views first originated by the people and their institutions, then it can indeed be said that in Spain there exists a press that is the equal of those in other democratic societies. When its voice leads the politicians and its reporting restrains the antidemocratic and corrupt of the society, then we can accurately speak of an authentic free press in Spain.

Spanish Politics: Between the Old Regime
and the New Majority

EUSEBIO M. MUJAL-LEÓN

──────In the seven years that elapsed between the death of Francisco Franco in November 1975 and the October 1982 parliamentary election, Spain and its people were protagonists in a remarkable process of democratic transformation. Among the milestones were the appointment of Adolfo Suárez as prime minister in July 1976; the approval of the Law for Political Reform, which gutted the Francoist Fundamental Laws, in December 1976; the legalization of virtually all political parties (including Maoist and Trotskyist ones as well as others with ties to the Basque terrorist movement known as Basque Land and Liberty [ETA]); two national, one municipal, and four regional elections between June 1977 and May 1982; the consensual drafting and approval by popular referendum of a new constitution; and the proclamation of self-government statutes for the Basque country, Catalonia, Galicia, and Andalusia.

This transformation of Spain's political structures did not occur without cost or in a trouble-free environment. Economic stagnation, caused as much by government neglect of economic issues as by an unfavorable international economy, the threat to public order posed by terrorist groups, and the growing disarray in the Union of the Democratic Center (UCD) were serious problems. The disenchantment they generated led to an attempted military coup in February 1981; the occupation of the parliament by a contingent of the Civil Guard ended only when King Juan Carlos refused to bend in his commitment to democracy.

Despite and because of these vicissitudes, Spain attracted the attention of scholars and policymakers. At at time when democracy worldwide was more a hope than a reality, Spain provided an uplifting example. Its transition to democracy, like the developments in Greece and Portugal after 1974, gave hope for the eventual democratization of authoritarian regimes elsewhere, especially in Latin America. More generally, the recent Spanish experience prompted further consideration of the relationship between politics, economics, and democracy. From another perspective, students of European politics found the transformations interesting and relevant to a broader discussion of such issues as the persistence and transformation of traditional cleavage patterns, the relevance and stability of political parties in the late twentieth century, and the articulation of political influence by institutions like the bureaucracy, which are only indirectly accountable to the electorate.[1]

Background

The Franco era died with barely a whimper in June 1977 with the holding of parliamentary elections after forty years of dictatorship. Its demise was the result as much of its successes as of its failures. When Franco launched his military uprising in July 1936, he did so in a highly charged domestic atmosphere of bitter class, religious, and regional cleavages and in an international environment dominated by the rising tide of fascism and the threat of communism.

Spain changed drastically in the ensuing four decades. The roots of this transformation are to be found in the economic and social policies pursued after a February 1957 ministerial reshuffle that introduced a group of technocrats affiliated with Opus Dei into the cabinet and adjunct administrative organs. Responsible for the key economic ministries until the early 1970s, that group instituted important changes and reforms whose objective was to promote growth and productivity by streamlining the economy and integrating Spain into the international economic system, albeit without jeopardizing the regime's authoritarian political structures. The technocrats' policies had a profound effect on Spanish society. The gross national product increased by 75 percent during the 1960s (more than anywhere else in Europe), and per capita income rose from $290 in 1960 to $2,485 in 1975.[2] There were important demographic shifts as well: 2.3 million Spanish workers emigrated to Europe between 1960 and 1973, and more than 4.4 million left the countryside for the cities.[3] Agrarian Spain of 1940, with over 51 percent of its active population engaged in agriculture, had become an industrialized nation by 1976 when this percentage was only 21 percent.[4]

These changes, along with the influx of tourists and intellectual currents from Europe, affected the habits and ways of thinking of Spaniards. Consumerism rose, and religiousness declined. The latter change was of fundamental importance, for Catholicism had been the principal ideological pillar of the regime during and after the Civil War. Under the impetus of Vatican II and of the changes taking place in Spanish society, the church moved toward a position of critical neutrality vis-à-vis the Franco regime.

The processes of economic development and modernization Spain underwent beginning in the 1950s and 1960s led to the formation of a numerous middle class and the emergence of a new working class. Groups claiming to represent the interests of these classes began to assert themselves, formulating demands for political change, the legitimation of dissent, and economic redistribution. Reform of the collective bargaining system in 1958 to permit plant-level negotiations had a deep effect on workers' political participation. This opportunity to negotiate with employers (instead of the state's setting wages) contributed to the development of illegal trade unions—such as the Workers Commissions—and to the radicalization of Catholic apostolic labor organizations. Labor dissent grew at a dizzying pace beginning in the 1960s, with 2,062 "work conflicts" in the years 1963-66, 3,063 in 1967-70, 4,623 in 1971-74, and 3,156 in 1975 alone. By 1975 Spain ranked among Europe's leaders in workdays lost by strikes and other forms of work stoppage.[5] The call for union and political liberties, so basic to the program advocated by labor dissidents in the 1960s and 1970s, was radical in a society that, despite the relaxation of censorship and greater tolerance, was still a dictatorship.

The economic changes taking place in Spain reshaped the profile of the state. It not only became more interventionist but also expanded in size. This growth of the state and the bureaucracy coincided with a shift in the ideology of the regime and in the role of the Falange. The 1957 ministerial reshuffle signaled the decline of the Falange and its occasionally ascetic, revolutionary-sounding rhetoric; but even as the Falange failed in its bid to become the dominant party on the Spanish scene, through the Falangist party (within whose confines all legal political activity took place) it gained a hold on the administrative apparatus. It accomplished this because the party controlled official, vertically organized unions and appointments to political-administrative positions in provincial and local governments. This patronage network became important during the transition to democracy; it served Adolfo Suárez (the Falange's last secretary-general) well when he organized the UCD.

The growth of the bureaucracy and its emergence as a major actor in the political arena resembled developments in other European countries, but the Spanish pattern exhibited special characteristics. With political parties absent and the Falange weakened, the expanded bureaucracy had an increasingly important voice in making political decisions and allocating resources. The broad latitude allowed cabinet ministers, their reliance on civil servants for both their expertise and their connections, and the almost territorial rights of members of the ruling Franco coalition to certain ministries encouraged this political role for the bureaucracy, leading one student of the subject to describe the regime as "not a dictatorship of Franco but . . . a dictatorship of his ministers."[6] Not surprisingly, after 1957 the bureaucracy became the principal source for elite political recruitment, so much so that almost 80 percent of the ministers in the years up to 1975 had previously served in the bureaucracy.[7] The labyrinthine structure of the bureaucratic *cuerpos*, the importance of personal relationships, the lack of coordination, and the absence of any sense of cabinet responsibility encouraged a clientelistic pattern of politics whose continued vitality is still evident in Spain today.[8]

The sociostructural transformations took place in the context of a more general depoliticization and demobilization. Meanwhile, the anti-Franco opposition—composed of traditional organizations such as the Spanish Socialist Workers' party (PSOE), the National Confederation of Labor (CNT), and the Spanish Communist party (PCE) on the left; moderate nationalist groups like the Basque Nationalist party (PNV); and the extreme leftist and regional socialist groups of post-1939 vintage—tried to galvanize and direct the unrest generated by the economic and social dislocations of the early and late 1960s. Nonetheless, the anticipated overthrow of the Franco regime never materialized. The continued weight of the Civil War, popular distrust of the opposition even when it called for the "peaceful" ouster of Franco, the weakness of working-class parties and unions, and the continued physical presence of Franco all worked against that eventuality. Yet, although efforts to force the transformation of the regime in the early 1960s failed, the process of transition from Francoist authoritarianism had begun.

Although Franco remained in power through the late 1960s, his regime had by then lost much of the legitimacy and the sense of purpose that had brought it to power in 1939. The peculiar fusion of traditional Catholic doctrine and Falangism the regime once espoused had dissipated three decades later. The Falange was discredited, the Catholic church was undergoing its own identity crisis, and the developmentalist ideology of the Opus Dei technocrats had come under fire much as its neoliberal counterparts had elsewhere in Europe and North America.

By the early 1970s, although Spaniards still remembered the Civil War, the idea that democracy inevitably breeds chaos and disorder had lost credibility in the face of European developments after World War II. Better off than their predecessors in material possessions as well as in education, Spaniards were less and less inclined to believe that somehow "Spain was different." Furthermore, closer ties between Spain and the rest of the continent in the form of tourism, migration, and economic exchanges increased the attraction of Europe and of democracy. By 1973 a poll found that 60 percent of those surveyed believed Spaniards "should make ourselves heard" and 82 percent felt this could best be accomplished if government officials were elected rather than appointed.[9]

Even though these developments did not result in an immediate and dramatic politicization of the population, they contributed to the disintegration of the Franco regime's legitimacy and the emergence of a democratic ethos,[10] spurring stocktaking within the Francoist elite and stimulating student and worker dissent in the larger cities.[11] Evidence of internal disintegration within the Franco coalition grew in the 1960s, with younger industrialists like Pedro Durán Farrell openly calling for democratization. Factionalism became all the more pronounced in 1973 as Franco became senile and after Admiral Luis Carrero Blanco (head of the government) was assassinated by Basque terrorists. Carrero Blanco was the gray eminence of the regime, the man upon whom Franco relied to ensure an orderly transition and to control the soon-to-be-crowned king. His assassination reopened the debate about the permanence of regime structures and set in motion the struggle for succession within the Francoist *clase política*. Carrero Blanco's death coincided with the economic recession Spain experienced after the oil price hikes in later 1973; neither augured well for holding down inflation or controlling labor unrest.

The overthrow in April 1974 of the nearly fifty-year-old dictatorship in neighboring Portugal deepened the crisis of confidence among the elite and aroused anticipation among Spaniards in general. Although the coup in Portugal had unique causes—above all the radicalization of the Portuguese military, provoked by losing colonial wars—it sent tremors through Spain.[12] But Portugal's importance did not lie only in showing that authoritarian regimes too could be overthrown. The events of 1974 and 1975 showed the Portuguese Communist-Armed Forces Movement were ready to implant a dictatorship and led to the virtual breakdown of discipline in the Portuguese armed forces. Those experiences once again raised the specter of communism (and thus had a negative effect on the PCE's hope for popular support) but also discouraged the Spanish military from assuming too overt a political role, lest its cohesion be destroyed. Portuguese events also demonstrated the willingness of European countries—acting alone, as the Federal Republic of Germany did, or through the European Economic Community (EEC)—to exert pressure in favor of democracy in the Iberian peninsula. Much of the foreign capital that entered Spain in the 1960s and 1970s had been attracted by the stability of the system and by the prospects of eventual Spanish membership in the Common Market. By the early 1970s most European governments and businesses with interests in Spain had concluded that if there were to be social and economic stability in that country, its political structures would have to be reformed.

By the mid-1970s the regime structures in Spain could not be propped up much longer without recourse to force. Neither the opposition nor the regime seemed willing to pay such a high price; indeed, in what was a major change since the 1950s, each side seemed willing to guarantee the other side its survival. The military remained loyal to Franco and to the regime, but it was not entirely immune to the forces at work in Spanish society. With its growing professionalization came a greater hesitation to become involved in the maintenance of domestic public order. The recognition by both regime and opposition politicians that neither was strong enough to overwhelm the other led to mutual restraint and eventual negotiations over future institutional arrangements.[13]

All this remained speculative into the mid-1970s, of course, because regardless of how compelling the situation was, someone had to seize the opportunity. No one was better placed for this task than the man Franco officially chose as his successor in 1969, Juan Carlos. The grandson of Alfonso XIII, Juan Carlos had been educated by tutors appointed by Franco. This and his Borbón heritage (one waggish joke suggested that once in power he would do nothing more than "bourbonate") led many to believe that upon his accession to the throne he would be little more than a figurehead. Instead, Juan Carlos demonstrated rare political skill and judgment by judiciously using the vast powers Franco had placed at his disposal (especially those that made him the real as well as symbolic commander of the armed forces) and by choosing Suárez as prime minister in 1976. Examples of the importance "traditional integrative institutions [have] during a transitional period in which new institutions are emerging,"[14] Juan Carlos and the monarchy were symbols to which most groups in the Franco coalition were willing to adhere and pledge their loyalty. Legitimizing both the past and the future,[15] the king was critical in compelling even the most recalcitrant sectors to support the transformation of the regime as long as the process took place within the framework of the laws made under Franco. His choice of Suárez to lead the government toward the first elections showed keen political acumen. In Suárez he found a man who was part of the new breed of Falangist politician that emerged in Spain in the late 1950s and early 1960s, a pragmatic and career-oriented man young enough to have a political future beyond the Franco regime and yet not burdened by a particularly strong ideology or political preferences.[16] Together King Juan Carlos and Suárez engineered the transition to democracy in Spain.

The 1977 and 1979 Parliamentary Elections

The battle to shape Spanish politics in the post-Franco period began in earnest after the December 1973 assassination of Carrero Blanco and was intensified after the death of the eighty-three-year-old generalissimo himself in November 1975.[17] Four groups were in competition. The first were the *continuistas*. They saw no need to change Spanish political structures; indeed, the most conservative among them wanted to eliminate the corruption associated with a consumer society and restore a pristine form of Falangism. A second group was the *reformista* faction; it included various liberalizing elements within the regime. They looked to the king and the institution of the monarchy as the instruments of reforming the political system and guiding Spain, in controlled fashion, toward political democracy. The moderate third group included several Christian democratic and liberal organizations, which called for a break (or *ruptura*) with Francoist political structures and traditions but envisioned an agreement between reformers within the regime and themselves, with the king playing a major role. What distinguished them from the fourth group—those who not only rejected the legitimacy of the regime but argued (though with decreasing enthusiasm and confidence) that mass mobilizations were the only way to force a break—was their desire to keep change within certain limits, not allowing it to occur too rapidly.

The adroit leadership of King Juan Carlos and Suárez and the Spaniards' determination to avoid the kind of confrontation that led to the Civil War contributed to the victory of the reformists. They were successful in isolating the most conservative groups and in attracting the support of the moderate opposition for a program that promised political liberties. Although those who advocated a dramatic break with Francoist political structures were not strong enough to impose their solution, their pressure (and Suárez's concern with international legitimacy) played an important role in stretching the limits of the reform. This "popular" component complemented what was in many ways the "revolution from above" that cleared the way for elections in June 1977.

The elections confirmed the victory of the reformist wing led by Suárez, whose preeminent role in the transition was rewarded with a 34.4 percent plurality for the Union of the Democratic Center. Taking advantage of the electoral law that Suárez had fashioned, the UCD won 47 percent of the seats in the new Parliament. Its margin over its principal rival, the PSOE, was not as great as many had anticipated, however.

The PSOE, which dated from 1879 but whose clandestine organization had languished until its renewal under Felipe González in the early 1970s, received 29.3 percent of the vote and won 121 seats in the Chamber of Deputies. That showing, as José María Maravall argues in his chapter, owed much to historical memory transmitted intergenerationally in families and communities. But this does not entirely explain the PSOE's performance. It had needed an opportunity to reactivate this memory in the electorate, an opportunity provided as much by the relatively lengthy transition period as by the sound policies of its leaders and the failures and weak democratic credentials of its competitors on the left.

Another notable result of the June 1977 election was the weak showing of the Popular Alliance (AP) and the Communist party. Neither received more than ten percent of the vote, as both suffered from the Spanish electorate's desire to avoid groups that resuscitated unwelcome memories from the past. The Communists and the AP were also hurt by the ability of the UCD and the PSOE to project themselves as the only viable contenders for national power in 1977.

The June 1977 election confirmed the emergence of two broad-based national parties and two distinctly smaller ones. The extreme left groups, running under assumed names because of their formally illegal status, did poorly, although their vote in relation to the Communist total was impressive. Parties of the extreme right received only 0.5 percent of the vote. Only the regional parties in the Basque country and Catalonia blunted the advance of the national parties. In the Basque country the PNV reemerged from nearly four decades of clandestine activity and exile in France to capture 24 percent of the vote and eight of the twenty-six seats in the Chamber of Deputies. In Catalonia the Democratic pact, led by Jordi Pujol, did less well than expected but nevertheless garnered 16 percent of the vote. Elsewhere, however, regional groups and movements proved to have little electoral appeal.

The June 1977 election revealed certain patterns in the Spanish electorate. First, as a number of the chapters in this book indicate, there was a surprising continuity between party votes in the 1930s and those in 1977. Despite the manifold changes in Spanish society—the diminution in intensity and the shift in class, regional, and religious cleavages, as well as the profound changes within the parties and in the party system—there were significant correlations between the 1936 and the 1977 votes. The UCD vote had a 0.45 correlation with the vote for the Spanish Confederation of Autonomous Rightist Groups (CEDA), a putative Christian Democratic party of the 1930s; the vote for the PSOE, the PCE, and the Popular Socialist party (PSP) had a 0.69 correlation with the 1936 Popular Front vote; and the vote for the left in 1977 had a correlation of 0.54 with the PSOE vote in 1936.[18]

Another interesting pattern was the relatively moderate orientation of the Spanish voter. A survey taken in early 1977 showed the distribution of the electorate on a ten-point left-right scale. The mean placement was 5.5, a positioning that compared with the West German (5.8) and the French and Italian (5.0 and 4.3, respectively).[19] Though generally moderate, the Spanish voter also perceived himself as to the left of his parents.[20] Some 40 percent of the voters identified themselves as center and center-left (points three through five), and this group became the object of assiduous wooing by the UCD, the PSOE, and even the Communists.[21] The Socialist electorate overlapped with those of the centrists and of the PCE. Suggesting the competitive dimension of their relationship, the Socialist and Communist votes in particular were correlated strongly at 0.55.[22]

Weak partisan attachments by the electorates were also evident, with measures of party identification uniformly low.[23] Although this was not unexpected in a society where all parties except the Falange had been proscribed, what was especially noteworthy was the low attachment to and high vote for the UCD (compared with either the PSOE or PCE), a tribute to the force of Suárez's personality and to voter support for a position rather than a specific party on the political spectrum. Nevertheless, the phenomenon perhaps foreshadowed the UCD's future difficulties.

The drafting of a new constitution to replace the Fundamental Laws occupied most of the time of the Cortes after 1977. Despite occasionally bitter disagreements over such thorny issues as church-state relations, the form of government (republic or monarchy), the guarantees for private property, the devolution of tax and administrative powers to the regions, a consensus constitution was finally approved in October 1978 and submitted to national referendum in December. Despite a rather high abstention rate in the Basque country and some other parts of Spain, the vote was overwhelmingly favorable.[24]

No legal provision required elections after the enactment of the new constitution, but most political parties felt assured that new elections would in fact be called shortly after the constitutional referendum. Accordingly, they all set about strengthening their organizations and broadening their electoral appeal. For the UCD this required the transformation of the disparate coalition of fourteen parties Suárez had fashioned in June 1977. The analogue to a Christian democratic party in Spain, the UCD was nonetheless distinct from confessional, catchall parties like the Italian *Democrazia Cristiana*. Unable to use such structures as apostolic labor organizations or the parish network of the Catholic church because the episcopate chose not to assume an overt political role during the transition to the post-Franco era, the UCD instead developed from the administrative apparatus (civil governors, municipal governments, and so on) controlled and appointed by the national government. Its brittleness was due not only to the diverse ideologies of the groups composing it, but to the particularistic and personalistic style of the Spanish political elite and the coexistence within its ranks of many who had made their careers under Franco and others who had opposed the regime.[25]

The PSOE sought to exploit the internal contradictions of the UCD, entering not-too-secret discussions with representatives of "progressive" sectors within it like Francisco Fernández Ordoñez with a view to fashioning a parliamentary majority. The PSOE also attempted to join with other parties and groups describing themselves as socialist. The most important of these, Enrique Tierno Galván's Popular Socialist party (PSP), joined the PSOE in May 1978, but the "multiplier" effect this was expected to have on the electoral fortunes of the PSOE in 1979 did not materialize.

Another focus of activity for the PSOE after June 1977 was in the trade unions, where it sought to overcome the initial advantage of the Communist-controlled Workers' Commissions over the General Workers' Union (UGT). Although the syndical elections of early 1978 showed that the Workers' Commissions remained the premier Spanish trade union organization, the UGT had recovered from its atrophy of the late 1960s and won nearly 22 percent (compared with the Workers' Commissions' 34 percent) of the delegates elected. The PSOE thus showed itself capable of holding its own against the Communists in the influential labor sphere. The PCE, for its part, continued to emphasize its moderate "Eurocommunism," dropping the appellation "Leninist" from its program during a much-publicized vote at its Ninth Congress in April 1978.[26]

With the approval of the constitution in December 1978, the stage was set for Suárez's decision to call new elections in March 1979. Contrary to PSOE expectations, Suárez and the centrists won again. The UCD, the PSOE, and the PCE retained the support of 71.0, 76.5, and 75.4 percent of their 1977 voters, respectively, and regional groups like the PNV (with 81.4 percent) and Convergence and Union (70.3) held on to their supporters as well.[27] There was no substantial rise in the votes won by either the PSOE or the UCD, the latter more or less holding its own while the PSOE increased its share marginally from 29.3 to 30.5 percent, or by just over 100,000 votes. The Communists did not improve notably on their 1977 performance; their vote remained concentrated in Barcelona, Madrid, and parts of Andalusia. The parties of the extreme left, campaigning openly this time, won a total of nearly 4 percent of the vote. But for the Popular Alliance, reconstituted under the name Democratic Coalition and with the addition of Alfonso Osorio and José Mariá de Areilza, the elections were a setback. Not only did it lose votes to its right, where Blas Pinar and the ultraconservative *Fuerza Nueva* picked up enough to gain a seat in parliament, but it received less than 6 percent of the vote, losing over a quarter of its 1977 vote to the UCD.

The most notable development in the March 1979 election (reaffirmed in the municipal election a month later) was the consolidation of the regional parties in Catalonia, the Basque country, and Andalusia. Their tally rose from 5.4 percent of the national electorate in 1977 to 9.9 percent in 1979, and the number of seats won in the Chamber of Deputies rose from nineteen to twenty-nine.[28] In Catalonia Convergence and Union dropped slightly from the PDC's 1977 returns (from 16.8 to 16.1 percent) in March but showed its grass-roots strength in April when it gained 80,000 votes while the UCD lost 130,000.[29] The rise of regional parties was dramatic in the Basque country, where the so-called *abertzale* left (the Basque term for independentists) received 22 percent of the vote. The electoral coalition Euzkadi Left received 6.3 percent of the vote, and Herri Batasuna, a party tied to the most radical of the ETA groups, some 13 percent. The PNV dropped slightly, from 24.4 percent in 1977 to 22.6 percent in 1979, but the most serious losses were suffered by the PSOE, which dropped from 25 to 20 percent of the vote in the Basque country. Between the parliamentary election in 1977 and the municipal election in April 1979, the proportion of the Basque vote cast for "ethnic" Basque parties climbed from 35.6 to 55.3 percent.[30] In Andalusia the mistakes committed by the PSOE in dealing with regional claims and the demagogic stance of the Socialist party of Andalusia (PSA) cost the PSOE votes, especially in Málaga, Cadiz, and Córdoba; this redounded to the advantage of the PSA.

Toward the Socialist Alternative

With the approval of the constitution in December 1978 and the second parliamentary election in March 1979, Spain completed an important phase in the transition to democracy. Although a large majority of the population had voted in favor of the constitution, and Suárez and his party had won the parliamentary contest, it was evident that the euphoria democracy had brought was subsiding. Voter turnout had dropped from highs of 77 and 78 percent in December 1976 and June 1977 to 68 percent in the December 1978 referendum and 61 percent in the April 1979 municipal election. With the Cortes now having to flesh out the skeleton provided by the constitution, conflicts came to the fore, not only between the PSOE and the UCD but within the UCD and between the UCD and the PSOE on the one hand and the regional parties on the other. For the left, the Suárez victory in March 1979 brought self-doubt. As one wag put it: "Against Franco, we lived better." Despite a drop in membership, the left at least had national and regional expressions.

Having been in power for nearly four decades, the right now had difficulty consolidating a party presence. The Democratic Coalition and the extreme right had little public audience, many of their potential voters casting a "useful" vote for the UCD. That party was itself torn between the Francoist past that marked so many of its leaders and the credit they deserved for having led Spain to democracy. With conservatives cowed—how many groups surfaced in the post-Franco era calling themselves "social democratic" when they were, in fact, liberals of either a classic or a more recent vintage?—the political spectrum appeared to tilt leftward. Yet, even though those who might have voted for the right moved to support the center in its regional and national manifestations and even though this meant the absence of a sizable party on the right, it did not mean that such a party could not eventually emerge or that the right did not have a social presence. The center and center-right remained fluid, and, for the moment at least, the political base of the right lay more in the party than in what the Spanish refer to as the *poderes fácticos*, the administrative bureaucracy and the military, institutions whose Francoist vestiges had not been purged after 1975.

One thing became apparent after the legislative and municipal elections in early 1979: the weakening of the principal national political parties. There was nothing very surprising about such a development. The twentieth century had seen a diminution in the role of political parties throughout Europe. The shift to executive dominance, the growing complexity of the state (associated with the consolidation of the bureaucracy and the rise of specialized interest groups), the rise of a professional, salaried class for whom the socialization and recruitment functions of the parties were less and less relevant, the personalization of political campaigns—all had contributed to this phenomenon. More specific to Spain was the Franco regime's effort to depoliticize Spaniards that deepened their latent disdain for political parties and politicians. Political parties reappeared in Spain only after a forty-year hiatus. Some were new; others, notably the Socialist and Communist parties, had a long history, but even they had not had an easy time transforming their clandestine structures or adjusting to a society that functioned quite easily without them. Political parties could be adjudged neither the creators of the modern, neocapitalist society with a skeletal welfare state that had emerged under Franco nor were they the principal actors in the transition to democracy. Moreover, numerous social and political groups that, though never allowed to press for explicit recognition, had been informally represented by persons close to Franco or through the patronage networks they controlled were still present, their power only slightly disrupted by the reform the king and Suárez had led. The generally weak associative impulses in Spanish society (not very different from the rest of the Mediterranean), the lingering memory of the Civil War, and the weakening of traditional Catholic and worker subcultures also worked against the parties.[31] Further compounding the problem were the efforts the major parties had made during the transition and constituent processes to arrive at consensual decisions. Such "consociationalism" at the national elite level strongly contributed to the success of the democratization process, but it also lessened public esteem for the parties and their leaders, many of whom were seen as all too eager to strike deals behind closed doors. Of the major party leaders, only González avoided having his image tarnished, and even his reputation for statesmanship and political rectitude provided no organizational boost to the PSOE. Despite a dramatic increase after 1975, general party membership (constituting approximately 4 percent of the electorate) was very low by European standards.[32] Even supposedly mass-based parties like the PSOE and the PCE were weaker organizationally than their counterparts elsewhere in Europe. Compounding these problems for the national parties was the virulence of the regional cleavage, especially in the Basque country and Catalonia. It added a vertical dimension to the party system that was at least partially responsible for the fluctuation in vote totals between national and regional elections.

The problems besetting the parties were perhaps most visible in the UCD. Suárez and the UCD had won the parliamentary elections but had done poorly in the municipal ones. After those elections the Socialists and Communists reached an understanding through which the left (including the PSA in Andalusia) assumed the mayoralties in cities and towns encompassing 70 percent of the population. In early 1980, moreover, the UCD suffered serious losses in regional elections in the Basque country and Catalonia (fourth- and fifth-place finishes, respectively) and embarrassed itself by first supporting, then backing away from, an autonomy statute for Andalusia. These electoral defeats exacerbated internal tensions within the UCD. Suárez, once unassailable, came under attack. Both he and the UCD suffered a loss in public esteem, and disenchantment with them increased. Two surveys taken in 1978 and 1980 showed the proportion of those who thought things had become worse had risen in two years from 12 to 35 percent, while those who thought conditions had stayed the same had dropped from 76 to 46 percent.[33] Spaniards comparing the Suárez government's performance with that of the Franco regime "looked upon [the former] more favorably than the [latter], but not by much."[34] Even if, as McDonough and López Pina suggested, a "reservoir of good will" toward the regime existed, it was also evident that by 1980 Spaniards were increasingly disenchanted, especially with Suárez.

Public confidence in the government sagged as the economy declined. Figures for 1980 and 1981 showed a dramatic rise in unemployment, little domestic investment, and virtually no growth in the gross domestic product. Although this occurred in the context of a more general European and international recession with rising oil prices, Suárez and the UCD could not escape responsibility for the way things were going. Not until early 1980 did the Suárez government unveil a comprehensive economic recovery program. By then it was all too clear that Suárez knew little and cared less about economic questions.

There was, moreover, a problem of political style. Suárez was at his best on television and in face-to-face negotiations. But Spain could not be governed or democracy consolidated by a premier who withdrew to the Moncloa palace, to reemerge only when a crisis seemed imminent, and did not take parliamentary debates seriously or use them to deepen the interest of Spaniards in the democratic process. If Suárez's style had been appropriate and useful during the transition to democracy, there was some question now whether it contributed to democracy's consolidation. Virtually unquestioned during his first three years in office, Suárez became a target for critics in his own party. The UCD— described by one analyst as "the confluence of actors belonging to the two blocs into which Spain was divided, although not representing them jointly"[35] —was less a party that controlled the government than one whose families— Christian Democrats, Social Democrats, ex-Falangists, and Liberals—were at war with one another. Interminable disputes over policy choices and ideological definition exacerbated its factionalism and lessened public esteem for it.

But if the failures and internal tensions within the UCD and the government contributed to the deterioration of the political and social climate during 1980, they did not automatically help the PSOE. At first, the PSOE had more than its share of problems. Although the UCD had done poorly in the March 1980 regional elections, the Socialists had done even worse, losing over 200,000 votes in Catalonia and capturing just over half the votes they had won in the Basque country in 1977. Internal squabbles were widespread, and not only over the proposal First Secretary Felipe González made to drop Marxism from the party program. None questioned his leadership, but scarcely a week went by without some press account of crises and resignations in local and provincial PSOE organizations. A major cause of these tensions was the adjustment required as the party moved from extramural to intramural opposition: many less veteran cadres who were purists on ideological issues objected to concessions made by party leaders in the search for votes.

The crisis affecting the UCD and the PSOE also reverberated in the Communist party. It had done poorly in June 1977, trailing the PSOE by more than a three-to-one margin. Its Eurocommunist image did not prove credible, perhaps because the party and its leader, Santiago Carrillo, revived too many memories from a period (the Civil War) that people wanted to put behind them. The PCE had followed a rather moderate course during the 1970s, eventually dropping its insistence on a rupture. As it became apparent the party would not receive a quick electoral payoff for its Eurocommunism and as international tension between the United States and the Soviet Union grew, however, unrest developed within the PCE. This was understandable since the Communists had had to swallow hard to accept the consensus politics so assiduously preached by Santiago Carrillo. Many militants saw the policy of consensus as a tactical move to allow the PCE to even things up with the Socialists rather quickly. When it did not redound to Communist electoral advantage, the group around Santiago Carrillo found itself under fire both from "Eurocommunist renovators" wanting greater internal democracy and from more hard-liners who desired a return to classic polarization tactics. The result was turmoil in many Communist organizations, with a rapid decline in membership and the expulsion of nearly a dozen Central Committee members by late 1981.

The crisis of the major national parties was at once symptom and cause of a more profound malaise in the authority of the state and the regime. This was evident in the government's failure to channel or encourage meaningful public participation by strengthening municipal and local governments (in which the left was in power and which the UCD had neither the resources nor the desire to see managed well), by encouraging the consolidation of a stable industrial relations system, or by returning basic tax and administrative powers to regions.

The support received by regional parties in the Basque country and Catalonia and the recrudescence of terrorism in 1980 underscored the degree to which Spain was still dogged by the center-periphery cleavage. This had been a longstanding problem, which the Franco regime, by treating all manifestations of regional sentiment or culture as treasonous, had exacerbated. Its repressive policies—forbidding public use of Basque or Catalan or instruction in them, obliging baptismal and marriage certificates to carry only Castilian names—provoked a visceral reaction, especially in the Basque country. There left-wing regionalist sentiment found expression in the various ETA terrorist groups that surfaced in the 1960s. Many hoped that with the installation of democracy and the amnesties for "political" crimes announced by the national government, the Basque problem could finally be resolved. The new constitution and the autonomy statutes granting self-governing powers in administration, education, and police matters raised these hopes, but government indecision and the demands for independence made by radical nationalists shattered them. In this atmosphere, the remaining ETA groups escalated their attacks. Between 1978 and 1980 they killed 206 people, the great majority of whom were military or police officers.[36] A survey taken in the Basque country in November 1979 indicated the depth of the polarization then gripping Basque society: many respondents viewed ETA members with some sympathy, 17 percent believing they were patriots and 33 percent considering them "idealists."[37]

The Suárez government's inability to handle the growth of terrorism (in July 1980 more than 20 percent of those asked in a Gallup poll called it the most important problem facing Spain) weakened it considerably, especially aggravating its relations with the military. Although the armed forces had operated with a good deal of functional and administrative independence from civil authorities under Franco, on political questions their role was above all "to accept rather than to demand, and to obey rather than to govern."[38] As the twilight of the Franco era approached and the coalition he had fashioned disintegrated under the weight of pressures from below and from within, however, the armed forces were thrust into an arbitral role in politics. Their strength lay above all in the approximate balance between *reformistas* and *rupturistas*. King Juan Carlos had played a major part in gaining their acquiescence in the reform program by assuring them that there would be a deliberate and controlled decompression of Spanish society. Since then the government had dealt very carefully (some would say excessively so) with the sensibilities of senior officers and the military hierarchy.

The imposition of civilian control over the military became an especially pressing issue after the February 1981 coup attempt. At the time, with the entire parliament held hostage, only the stalwart attitude of the king and the hesitation of some senior military officers saved the day for democracy. With the so-called 23rd of February syndrome sparking numerous rumors and endless speculation about military intrigues and intentions, the government responded by giving the armed forces an active role in the fight against Basque terrorism and by drafting new legislation (proposed as part of a modernization program linked to NATO entry) to encourage early retirement. In a further precautionary effort aimed at tightening discipline during the trials of those implicated in the February 1981 coup attempt, the government reshuffled the high command. But problems remained. The military tribunals dealt lightly with disciplinary infractions by rightists, and the loyalty of some senior officers (involved in the coup but unindicted) was open to question. Most worrisome was the insubordination of junior officers, some of whom created a clandestine organization to distribute subversive leaflets and establish a national network. Moreover, in December 1981, on the third anniversary of the referendum approving the constitution, one hundred junior and noncommissioned officers signed a manifesto lambasting the treatment that the military, as an institution, had received at the hands of the press. The armed forces, they said, "in order to better fulfill their mission, do not need to be professionalized, democratized, or purged."[39] Only a rapid crackdown by the military hierarchy deterred several hundred other officers (many in the crucial First Military Region encompassing Madrid) from signing the document.

The military was not the only institution to raise its profile amid the deepening public apathy and the spectacle of party bickering. The press—which had helped to disseminate democratic political culture and ideas while political parties were still inchoate or clandestine and had deepened the crisis of the Francoist elite by reporting on its breakup—directed its critical gaze on the political parties and often found them wanting.[40] Some prominent personalities associated with the national daily *El País* went so far as to join various "independents" in exploring the possibility of forging a *partido bisagra* (or bridge party) as the swing party between socialists and the UCD.

Bickering within the UCD and growing restiveness within the military led to the resignation of Suárez just before the February coup attempt. His successor, Leopoldo Calvo Sotelo, a member of a politically influential family, was not involved with any of the factions in the party and was thus broadly acceptable as Suárez's replacement. Yet, precisely because Calvo Sotelo was believed to be a caretaker, the infighting increased. Suárez also rejoined the fray in an effort to reestablish his influence. Personal as well as political squabbles continued to pit Christian Democrats and Liberals against Social Democrats and supporters of Suárez over such issues as state aid to private (Catholic) schools, divorce legislation, abolition of the government's monopoly over television, and entry into NATO. In August 1981 Fernández Ordoñez, the social democratic architect of divorce and fiscal reform legislation and later the founder of the Party of Democratic Action (PAD) as a putative "bridge" party, resigned as minister of justice. As 1981 wore on, the bloodletting within the UCD continued, with Suárez, Calvo Sotelo (who had become party president), and the major UCD "barons" fighting for control of the party machine. Eventually Landelino Lavilla emerged the victor, becoming president of the UCD in July 1982. But his was a Pyrrhic victory. By then the UCD had been reduced to a rump, first by the defection of conservative Christian democratic deputies led by Oscar Lazaga in May and two months later by Suárez when he abandoned the party he had created to form the Social Democratic Center (CDS).

Besieged from within and unable to point to any major successes in domestic or foreign policy (high hopes for rapid Spanish accession into the EEC having been dashed by French opposition to the move), Calvo Sotelo presided over a fraying government. Complicating matters further was the resurgence of the Democratic Coalition (CD). Led by Manuel Fraga Iribarne, the CD won a stunning victory in the October 1981 Galician regional elections where it doubled the share of the vote captured by the AP in national elections just two years before. The UCD total was halved. This increased the pressure from conservatives in the UCD who favored some sort of coalition with Fraga. But Calvo Sotelo, afraid that a formal entente would lead Suárez to walk out of the UCD, preferred to insist on the party's "centrist" option.

The Socialists, for their part, were not particularly eager for early elections. After the February 1981 coup attempt, they pursued a dual strategy, projecting themselves as the only viable alternative to the UCD (and entering into negotiations with Fernández Ordoñez with a view to including him on their list in the next election) while at the same time emphasizing their moderation and willingness to cooperate with the government. In an effort to reassure conservatives in and outside the military of its commitment to national unity, the PSOE joined the UCD in proposing the Organic Law for the Harmonization of Autonomy Process (LOAPA), a legislative package intended to ensure uniformity and coherence in the devolution of powers to the regions. It retained for the central government all powers not explicitly granted to regional administrations. The economic and social program approved at the PSOE congress in October 1981 was mild, stressing moderation, stricter control of credit, and the creation of jobs through public investment programs, while toning down talk of nationalization.

The trials of the officers implicated in the February 1981 coup attempt cast a shadow over Spanish politics in early 1982. For the military, the trials were an extraordinarily sensitive affair: Lieutenant General Luis Milans del Bosch, the highest-ranking officer on trial, was one of the most decorated officers in the Spanish army; by trying him, his peers were in effect rendering retrospective judgment on the uprising many of them had joined in July 1936. Defense efforts to tarnish the king by alluding to his prior knowledge of the coup (a claim they were unable to substantiate) added a further twist to the affair.

The trials provided a backdrop for the Andalusian election, even as they encouraged the major parties to tone down their rhetoric and aggressiveness. The UCD entered the contest at a pronounced disadvantage. A regional unemployment rate of 25 percent, the errors Suárez had committed in handling the Andalusian self-government statute, the squabbling within the centrist camp —all weakened the UCD's appeal to voters who had once seen the party as the principal bulwark against upheaval and disintegration. Although the CD had virtually no organization in the Andalusian provinces, it stood to gain from the

UCD's troubles. Even so, the PSOE was the clear favorite in a region where many of its leaders (Felipe González and Alfonso Guerra, for example) had been born. Yet no one was prepared for the magnitude of their victory. The PSOE outdistanced the combined support for all other parties, winning 52.6 percent of the vote, while the centrists won 500,000 fewer votes than in 1979 (dropping to third place behind the CD).

The PSOE came out of the Andalusian election as the strong favorite to win the next election. The UCD's disastrous showing in the region only increased factional infighting within the party, further lessening its electoral appeal. The Calvo Sotelo government was little more than a caretaker by this point; its only power lay in the ability to decide when to call an early election. Finally, in late August, in a last-ditch effort to weaken the chances for Suárez's new CDS, Calvo Sotelo asked the king to dissolve the Parliament. By then it was not longer a question of whether the PSOE would win the next election, but by what margin.

Conclusion

The seven years after the death of Francisco Franco were years of significant accomplishment for Spain. During that period, Spanish society experienced a virtually unprecedented peaceful transition to democracy and solid foundations were laid for the subsequent consolidation of democracy. Those were the years during which King Juan Carlos, Adolfo Suárez, and the party he created, the UCD, played the leading role in Spanish politics. Suárez and the UCD's victory in the 1977 and 1979 legislative elections reflected voter approval for the way they had led the transition to democracy. Almost immediately after the 1979 elections, however, the UCD began to exhibit the fatal symptoms that would lead to its demise a few years later. Factionalism, once submerged and relatively harmless, became endemic, and Suárez, who had previously been above the fray and in firm command of the coalition, slowly began to lose control of his party. Suárez's personality and idiosyncrasies, his growing political personal isolation, the rise in terrorist violence, and a deepening economic crisis eroded his and the UCD's public image.

The February 1981 coup attempt accelerated the UCD's disintegration and deepened public doubts about the centrists' ability to rule. Although the coup attempt occurred against a backdrop, increased *desencanto* about the parties and politicians, the Spanish public showed no yearning for a return to the past, for a new authoritarian regime. The officers responsible for the coup misunderstood the temper of the population; as the surveys cited by Rafael López-Pintor in the next chapter confirm, there was broad popular support for democracy.

The coup attempt marked a turning point for contemporary Spain and its party system: because it nearly succeeded, the coup weakened the rationale for supporting the UCD. The Centrist party had found favor among the electorate because it promised and delivered democracy without instability. In the wake of the coup attempt, UCD leaders could no longer convince Spaniards (and perhaps themselves) that theirs was the party that could best prevent instability and consolidate democracy in Spain.

Logically, the decline in the UCD's fortunes had a profound effect on the other major parties in the system. Popular Alliance seized the opportunity to project itself as the only viable center-right force in the country. Communist leaders, who had tried so mightily to overcome their party's poor electoral showing by relying on the UCD to keep the Socialists at bay, now found themselves painted into a corner. Eventually, as divisions and confrontations within the PCE intensified, the Socialists lost their only serious competitor on the left.

With their principal competitors in disarray, the Socialists stood on the threshold of power. Of course, the PSOE had made mistakes since 1979, but the party had been less damaged than other groups. On the one hand was the electorate eager to find a party in which to deposit its faith in and support for democracy. On the other, at the prodding of González and other party leaders, the PSOE had toned down its "socialist" credentials, presenting itself as the party of clean and efficient government. The PSOE was the party of change (*el partido del cambio*), but party image-makers stressed that there would be no social or political convulsions, that the PSOE's objective was simply to make things work better.

By mid-1982, then, the Socialist party was ready to reap the rewards of its own efforts and of serendipity. The party retained and intensified the allegiance of its own electorate, but reached out to incorporate those of its nearest ideological and political competitors. The symbols of its historic past, its anti-Franco credentials, and commitment to democratic socialism allowed the PSOE to claim many Communist voters who had become disillusioned by the failed promise of Eurocommunism. To the moderately progressive Centrist voter (and it should be remembered that a plurality of 1979 UCD voters saw their party as positioned on the center-left), a vote cast for the PSOE was at once a vote against the UCD's abandonment of its reformist identity and a vote for modernization, firm government, and a new beginning. Little wonder, then, that the 1982 campaign took on the dimensions of a public fiesta in favor of democracy. For the Socialists, winning in 1982 would be the easy part. Thereafter would come the difficult task of pacifying their divergent constituencies.

The October 1982 General Election and the Evolution of the Spanish Party System

RAFAEL LÓPEZ-PINTOR

On 28 October 1982, the Spanish people were called to their third general election since the restoration of democracy in 1977. This election occurred a few months before the deadline for the legislature that had been elected in March 1979. Contrary to usual parliamentary practice, Prime Minister Leopoldo Calvo Sotelo called the people to the polls even though he had every reason to believe that his party had no chance to win. Apparently he was eager to put an end to the turbulent parliamentary period that had begun in 1980.

During that period there was an unsuccessful vote of no confidence against the regime of Prime Minister Adolfo Suárez in May 1980 after three regional electoral defeats for the government in Andalusia, Catalonia, and the Basque country; then in September a vote of confidence was won by Suárez. In January 1981 Suárez resigned his position as prime minister. In February—while successor his was being chosen in Parliament—there was an attempted coup d'état that failed the next morning. From then until October 1982, the party in government—the Union of the Democratic Center (UCD)—was repeatedly defeated in regional elections in Galicia and Andalusia; it gave rise to four splinter groups and seemed to have lost any ability to keep the government under control. Another planned coup attempt was discovered three weeks before election day.

As for the other political parties, the Spanish Communist party (PCE) also suffered a possibly permanent decline after several internal crises, the weakening of its militancy, and recurrent electoral losses in regional contests. The Spanish Socialist Workers' party (PSOE) and the rightist Popular Alliance (AP) were to benefit from the breakdown of government and the crises of the parties of the center and left. The regional elections of October 1981 in Galicia and of May 1982 in Andalusia anticipated—each in its own way—the outcome of the general election.

Table 13.1 Results of Elections to Spanish Chamber of Deputies, 1977–1982

	1977		
Party	No. of votes	Percent of valid votes	Seats
Spanish Socialist Workers' party (PSOE)	5,367,951	29.3	118
Popular Alliance (AP)	1,516,831	8.3	16
Union of the Democratic Center (UCD)	6,310,151	34.4	166
Spanish Communist Party (PCE)	1,716,810	9.4	20
Social Democratic Center (CDS)	—	—	—
Convergence & Union (CiU)	518,706	2.8	11
Basque Nationalist Party (PNV)	290,297	1.6	8
Basque left radicals (HB, EE)[a]	2,598,189	—	—
Other	2,197,553	14.2	11
Total	18,318,935	100.0	350
Registered voters	23,621,625		

Source: Ministry of the Interior
[a] HB is Herri Batusuna; EE is the Euzkadi Left.

The atmosphere on the eve of the election could be described by the title of one of the latest novels of Gabriel García Marques, *Chronicle of a Death Foretold*. The results were anticipated for months by almost everyone but the "victims"—the UCD and the PCE—whose performance during the preceding year and a half was, to say the least, unrealistic.[1]

The October election was not a "normal" contest in the sense that the party in government was defeated by a swing of a single segment of the voters. The election of 1977 inaugurated the democratic regime and created a constituent assembly. That of 1979 validated the party system that emerged in 1977; yet a "birth crisis" began immediately after the election. The election of 1982 had the flavor of a new era, a political realignment in which the party system would be different.[2]

The Electoral Returns

Twenty-eight parties and coalitions won a share of the vote in 1982, a little more than half the fifty parties that competed in 1979.

The crisis of the UCD gave rise to four splinters, one of which—the Social Democratic Center (CDS)—ran under the leadership of Suárez. One, with a social democratic leaning, ran in coalition with the PSOE. Another, which finally did not run, was liberal. The fourth, in the Christian democratic tradition, joined with the rightist Popular Alliance. Thus the party in government, the

	1979			1982	
No. of votes	Percent of valid votes	Seats	No. of votes	Percent of valid votes	Seats
5,469,813	30.5	121	10,127,092	48.4	202
1,067,732	6.0	9	5,548,336	26.5	107
6,268,593	35.0	168	1,393,574	6.7	11
1,938,487	10.8	23	846,802	4.1	4
—	—	—	604,309	2.8	2
483,353	2.7	8	772,728	3.7	12
275,292	1.5	7	395,656	1.8	8
257,787	1.4	4	310,927	1.4	3
2,171,833	12.1	10	907,358	4.3	1
17,932,890	100.0	350	20,906,782	100.0	350
26,786,042			26,837,212		

Union of the Democratic Center, went to the polls as a residue of the party that had led the transition to democracy in 1977.

The rest of the parties were mainly the same as in 1979, yet with some minor surprises. One of them, Spanish Solidarity, headed by the man who ran into parliament with a gun in 1981, won only 25,000 votes of the more than 21 million cast.

As shown in table 13.1, of the 350 seats in the Chamber of Deputies, the PSOE enlarged its share from 121 to 202 seats (eighty-one more seats than in 1979, and twenty-six more than an absolute majority). The conservative AP increased its seats from nine to 107, achieving the status of the main opposition force. The Communist party fell from twenty-three to four seats, remaining an insignificant parliamentary force. Finally, the UCD fell from 168 to eleven seats, and Suárez's new CDS won only two seats. The bourgeois parties of the historic Catalan and the Basque regions consolidated their position in the system: the Catalan Convergence and Union won twelve seats, four more than in 1979, and the Basque Nationalist party (PNV) won eight, one more than in 1979. Basque radicals—the Euskadi Left and Herri Batasuna—also consolidated their vote, to support the violent independentist forces of the left; they won three seats in the national parliament, with 20 percent of the ballots cast in the region, or 16 percent of the eligible voters. The remaining seat was won by the Left Republican Party of Catalonia (ERC).

Table 13.2 Results of Elections to Spanish Senate, 1977–1982

	Seats		
Party	1977	1979	1982
Spanish Socialist Workers' Party (PSOE)	48	70	134
Union of the Democratic Center (UCD)	105	119	4
Popular Alliance (AP)	2	3	54
Communist party (PCE)	3	1	—
Convergence and Union (CiU)	2	1	7
Basque Nationalist party (PNV)	8	8	7
Herri Batasuna (HB)	—	1	—
Euzkadi Left (EE)	1	—	—
Other	39	5	2
Total	208	208	208

Source: Ministry of the Interior

The PSOE share of the popular vote increased from 30.5 percent in 1979 to 48.4 percent in 1982; AP's vote jumped from 6.0 percent to 26.5 percent. On the other side, the UCD dropped from 35.0 percent to 6.7 percent and the PCE from 10.8 percent to 4.1 percent. The results were far different from those expected in a normal democratic election.

The Senate results moved in the same political direction as in the Chamber of Deputies (see table 13.2). Since senators are elected by a plurality vote rather than by the d'Hondt highest average system of proportional representation, however, the shift of seats was even more striking than in the Chamber. The Socialist membership jumped from 70 seats in 1979 to 134 seats, while the UCD membership dropped from 119 seats to only four. The Popular Alliance rose from three to 54 members. The PCE and the left-wing Basque parties were shut out, but the PNV retained seven of its eight seats and the Catalan Convergence and Union (CiU) increased its membership from one to seven. The remaining two seats were picked up by smaller parties.

Some major conclusions stem from these electoral returns. First, the turnout was the highest of the new Spanish democracy: 79.5 percent, somewhat higher than the turnout at the inaugural election of 1977. This can be considered a plebiscite on the regime itself in spite of economic recession, terrorism, frequent calls to regional elections with lower turnout rates, and several coup attempts, the last uncovered on 2 October, twenty-six days before the election.

Second, the small vote for the UCD and the Suárez splinter showed a massive rejection of the party and leader of the transition period: the new party of Suárez got only 3 percent of the vote; the UCD won 7 percent of the vote and twelve marginal seats, which, except for one in Madrid and one in the Basque country, came from the least-developed provinces (ten in Galicia, northern Castile, and the Canary Islands). The UCD had failed in its quest to become a modern coalitional conservative party.

Third, within the conservative and moderate sectors of society, political hegemony shifted from the transition party, UCD, to the more conservative Popular Alliance, which in previous elections had clearly represented nostalgia for the Franco regime and received a very small share of the vote (only 6 percent) in 1979.

Fourth, and most important, the PSOE, which—like Socialist parties in the recent French and Greek elections—presented itself as a moderate movement for change, received massive support. It secured an absolute majority in the Chamber of Deputies and won almost half the popular vote. In addition to its own old constituencies, the PSOE drew support from the disenchanted of the Communist party and other minor parties of the left and from the more progressive sectors of the center. It also mobilized former nonvoters and newly registered voters. These two groups, however, were also sources of votes for the conservative Popular Alliance.

Finally, the regional parties (except in Catalonia and the Basque country) and extremist national parties of the right or left virtually disappeared from the political scene.

The fluidity of the vote in this election was extraordinary. By combining and contrasting figures from electoral returns and postelection survey research, I have constructed a chart of voting streams, which is summarized in the following paragraphs.[3] About 50 percent of the vote either shifted from one party to another (more than 6 million) or came from former nonvoters (about 2.5 million) and newly registered voters (about 800,000). The change may have involved as many as 10 million persons.

The new PSOE votes included 40 percent of the former nonvoters, 60 percent of new young voters, 40 percent of former UCD voters, 58 percent of former communist voters, and some other minor additions from the extreme left. The "winner of the opposition," the Popular Alliance, won the votes of 60 percent of the former nonvoters, 10 percent of the youth, 40 percent of former UCD voters, and some voters from the extreme right.

Both the PSOE and the AP increased their vote everywhere in the country as the other national parties became marginal political forces. The two center parties, UCD and CDS, and the Communist party were able to win only a minor share of the vote. The vote for all three was spread thin throughout the country and therefore produced few seats. Each won a seat in Madrid. The Communist vote was mostly urban, and the centrist vote mostly rural. The provinces providing the largest percentage of UCD votes were rural Galicia and northern Castile (its largest figure was 31 percent in Orense, its lowest percentage in

Barcelona). The largest vote for the Communists was 11 percent in the historical mining areas of Oviedo, the lowest—less than 1 percent—in several Castilian and Canary Islands provinces.

The PSOE won a plurality of the votes in forty-one of the fifty-two Spanish provinces (see table 13.3). It had an absolute majority of the popular vote in Madrid, the mining and industrial areas of Asturias, the Valencia region, and latifundia areas such as Estremadura, part of La Mancha, and Andalusia (in four of eight Andalusian provinces the PSOE vote was above 60 percent). In Barcelona, Aragon, Santander, Rioja, Murcía, part of La Mancha, and the largest part of Old Castile, the PSOE vote almost reached 50 percent. Only in rural Galicia and the Basque provinces was it under 30 percent—the lowest figure was 26 percent in Guipúzcoa.

The vote for the Popular Alliance was over 40 percent in rural Galicia, Burgos, and Rioja. It reached between 30 and 40 percent in Madrid, most of La Mancha and Old Castile, and the Balearic Islands. It amounted to 20 and 30 percent, respectively, in Andalusia and the Canary Islands. Its smallest share was in industrial Catalonia and the Basque country where the party won between 20 and 30 percent of the votes.

The collapse of the UCD must be explained to understand the dynamics and results of this election: the increased turnout, the PSOE landslide, and the assumption of leadership of the opposition by the AP. Because none of these topics can be treated extensively within the scope of this chapter, I shall comment first very briefly on the causes of increased turnout and then devote the rest of the chapter to an explanation of the breakdown of the center and its electoral consequences.

The higher turnout at this election was the consequence of many factors, which will be thoroughly explored by researchers in the future. Yet, as a working hypothesis, I will argue that increased participation had two main causes —bipolar radicalization of the campaign and fear of violence and civil strife— that stemmed from a long-standing power vacuum following the internal crises of the party in government, recurrent governmental paralysis, military unrest, coup attempts, and uncurbed terrorism. What was more, all of these occurred during the continuing economic recession.

Although the atmosphere of the campaign was restrained, the PSOE's principal competition had undeniably moved toward the right. As the campaign proceeded, the conservative candidate, Manuel Fraga Iribarne, became tougher and more radical in campaigning against the UCD and the PSOE. Since the PSOE was seen as the winner from the beginning of the campaign, this toughness toward its adversary almost certainly attracted antisocialist supporters, if only for utilitarian reasons.[4] The conservative antisocialist appeal seems to have mobilized AP support from some 60 percent of the former nonvoters who voted in 1982.[5]

Table 13.3 Distribution of Seats in the Chamber of Deputies, Spanish Regions and Provinces, 1982

Region and Province	Total	PSOE	AP	UCD	PCE	CDS	CIU	PNV	Other
Andalusia	59	43	15	—	1	—	—	—	—
Almería	5	4	1	—	—	—	—	—	—
Cádiz	8	6	2	—	—	—	—	—	—
Córdoba	7	5	2	—	—	—	—	—	—
Granada	7	5	2	—	—	—	—	—	—
Huelva	5	4	1	—	—	—	—	—	—
Jaén	7	5	2	—	—	—	—	—	—
Málaga	8	6	2	—	—	—	—	—	—
Seville	12	8	3	—	—	—	—	—	—
Aragón	14	9	5	—	—	—	—	—	—
Huesca	3	2	1	—	—	—	—	—	—
Teruel	3	2	1	—	—	—	—	—	—
Zaragoza	8	5	3	—	—	—	—	—	—
Asturias	10	6	3	—	1	—	—	—	—
Balearic Islands	6	3	3	—	—	—	—	—	—
Basque Country	21	8	1	1	—	—	—	8	3
Alava	4	2	1	—	—	—	—	1	—
Guipúzcoa	7	2	—	—	—	—	—	3	2
Vizcaya	10	4	1	—	—	—	—	4	1
Navarre	5	3	2	—	—	—	—	—	—
Canary Islands	13	7	4	2	—	—	—	—	—
Las Palmas	6	3	2	1	—	—	—	—	—
Tenerife	7	4	2	1	—	—	—	—	—
Castile-Leon	35	18	13	4	—	—	—	—	—
Avila	3	1	1	—	—	—	—	—	1
Burgos	4	2	2	—	—	—	—	—	—
León	6	3	2	1	—	—	—	—	—
Palencia	3	2	1	—	—	—	—	—	—
Salamanca	4	3	1	—	—	—	—	—	—
Segovia	3	1	1	1	—	—	—	—	—
Soria	3	1	1	1	—	—	—	—	—
Valladolid	5	3	2	—	—	—	—	—	—
Zamora	4	2	1	1	—	—	—	—	—
Cantabia									
Santander	5	3	2	—	—	—	—	—	—

Table 13.3 continued.

Region and Province	Total	PSOE	AP	UCD	PCE	CDS	CIU	PNV	Other
Rioja									
Logroño	4	2	2	—	—	—	—	—	—
Madrid	32	18	11	1	1	1	—	—	—
Castile-La Mancha	21	13	8	—	—	—	—	—	—
Ciudad-Real	5	3	2	—	—	—	—	—	—
Cuenca	4	2	2	—	—	—	—	—	—
Guadalajara	3	2	1	—	—	—	—	—	—
Toledo	5	3	2	—	—	—	—	—	—
Albacete	4	3	1	—	—	—	—	—	—
Catalonia	47	25	8	—	1	—	12	—	1
Barcelona	33	18	5	—	1	—	8	—	1
Gerona	5	2	1	—	—	—	2	—	—
Lérida	4	2	1	—	—	—	1	—	—
Tarragona	5	3	1	—	—	—	1	—	—
Estremadura	12	9	3	—	—	—	—	—	—
Cáceres	5	4	1	—	—	—	—	—	—
Badajoz	7	5	2	—	—	—	—	—	—
Galicia	27	9	13	5	—	—	—	—	—
La Coruña	9	4	4	1	—	—	—	—	—
Lugo	5	1	3	1	—	—	—	—	—
Orense	5	1	2	2	—	—	—	—	—
Pontevedra	8	3	4	1	—	—	—	—	—
Murcia	8	5	3	—	—	—	—	—	—
Valencia	29	19	10	—	—	—	—	—	—
Alicante	9	6	3	—	—	—	—	—	—
Castellón	5	3	2	—	—	—	—	—	—
Valencia	15	10	5	—	—	—	—	—	—
Spanish Cities in Northern Africa									
Ceuta	1	1	—	—	—	—	—	—	—
Melilla	1	1	—	—	—	—	—	—	—
Total	350	202	107	11	4	2	12	8	4

Source: Ministry of the Interior

There is also evidence that fear of violence, military rule, and eventual civil war was very important in mobilizing young voters and former nonvoters on the left. The coup attempt in February 1981 stirred the fear of violence and possible civil war. Furthermore, the fear was fed by the long and controversial military trials and by new coup attempts. Survey research evidence and qualitative sociopsychological analysis lead to several conclusions. First, fear of civil strife was of paramount importance in the massive support given to the strategy of unrisky transition to democracy after Franco's death. That fear was reborn in 1981 and is still present. Second, military unrest and court-martials did not keep the Spanish people from showing their rejection of military rule. In February 1981 massive demonstrations, larger than any in history, took place in Madrid. A survey I conducted two days after the 1981 coup attempt found only 9 percent of the Spanish people showing some support for the coup. Another survey conducted a few days later after the plot of October 1982 showed that support for the coup had fallen to less than 5 percent of the people. Finally, research on the attitudes of youth during the last few years has invariably shown that desire for peace and support for the constitutional order are its two most cherished values.[6]

These factors explain the higher voting turnout. Yet all of them are also directly related to the power vacuum that originated in the UCD's failure to coalesce as a modern political party and the subsequent governmental inefficiency and paralysis this engendered.

The Collapse of the UCD, or the Story of Failing Leadership

After the 1979 general and local elections the UCD had an absolute majority in the Senate, almost an absolute majority in the Chamber of Deputies, 60 percent of all Spanish mayors belonged to the party, and it controlled the national government. How could such a political force be almost extinguished in three years?

The story of the disintegration began immediately after the 1979 election. It is a story of leadership that failed to meet the challenge of political modernization.[7] The Spanish right as well as the Spanish left had expected that the transition toward democracy would be slow, formalistic, and safe for almost everyone. In practice such a sedate pattern of change creates little public enthusiasm. The entire process of transition was conducted by Suárez through the coalition UCD. The coalition might have become a modern catchall party of the right in the style of the German CDU or the Italian DC, with different wings and much internal politicking and compromising, as in any large modern party. Yet once Suárez was confirmed as prime minister by the first constitutional election of 1979, it became apparent that he was not eager to promote such a party but preferred one of a populistic and autocratic character.[8] The first visible step in this direction was the decision to exclude from the new cabinet those party notables with whom he had built up the 1977 coalition and with whom he had governed since. This decision alarmed the notables and triggered a process of internal conflict—both ideological and tactical—and personal feuds, which have continued even after the recent electoral collapse.[9]

Until the spring of 1980 no one had publicly contested the Suárez leadership. In the wake of a cabinet crisis after the summer of that year, Suárez allowed the notables to rejoin the government, but the damage had been done. The early failure to protect and develop the coalitional partnership was at the heart of most of the UCD difficulties through 1982. Within the government there was no consensus on political and organizational goals. Policy fragmentation and the inability to make policy decisions brought the government to a virtual standstill.

Once it became apparent to Suárez's former partners that they could not democratically coexist under his leadership, the "party's unmaking" was just a matter of rhythm and pace. Nevertheless, the decomposition process was slow, being deterred by the recurring rewards and complexities of holding office.

Party notables and cadres, having perceived that the UCD covenant was no longer binding, began to return to their original ideological and group alliances even while the UCD retained governmental power. The difficulties in agreeing to common ideological and political goals led to sterile pseudoideological debates within the party elite and among cadres. They argued about topics of no serious interest to their voters: whether the UCD was or should be a party of the center left, center right, or pure center. These nominalistic disputes served quite well to mask and unmask personal strategies and interests. Moreover, this ideological approach caused the center to sidestep any important discussions about party organization, constituency orientation, and general policy. There was no serious attempt to strengthen organizational ties to specific constituencies. It was as if the UCD leadership viewed its electorate as homogeneous and anonymous—with an empty profile. From this perspective we can explain two rather frequent occurrences during the period of the UCD government. First, there were the frequently bitter confrontations with specific constituencies before allowing their demands to be fully satisfied. This was the case with medical doctors and school and university professors involving regional devolution negotiations, and in many other problems. Second, the government often confronted various constituencies simultaneously. Sometimes those constituencies disagreed about an issue: on the divorce issue, for example, the government simultaneously confronted the church, the PSOE, and a large part of its own parliamentary group. At other times, the government confronted a number of constituencies and clienteles on various issues: at one time it confronted simultaneously and for different reasons the church, the military, business, and the unions. That this tended to be a style calls for explanation.

Within the area of government, policy definition and implementation were more a matter of the strength and forcefulness of individual ministers than a product of cabinet discussion and negotiation. Conspicuous examples of this were tax reform and divorce policies as tailored by Francisco Fernández Ordoñez who served as a minister under both Suárez and Calvo Sotelo before leaving the UCD to join the PSOE in 1982.

This failure to consolidate a modern party and a democratic style of leadership—a failure of political modernization—can be traced back to early 1980. For analytical purposes I shall distinguish between events at the elite level and trends in mass opinion and electoral behavior.

Significant Events Among the Elite After the 1979 election, Suárez was voted prime minister in parliament without giving the opposition a chance to debate his program. Believing that kind of debate to be constitutionally mandated, the opposition parties strongly disapproved of Suárez's arbitray behavior.

By late 1979 devolution referenda had taken place in Catalonia and the Basque country. The next region to negotiate devolution was Andalusia, where the government and the UCD offended virtually every one by their zigzagging policies. First, the Andalusians were promised a status similar to that of the Basques and Catalans. Then a lower status was offered and defended by the government, causing much dismay among the population and among the cadres of the party. Manuel Clavero, a southern professor who was minister of territorial affairs, resigned first his cabinet position and then his membership in the UCD. Finally, in February 1980 a referendum was called in Andalusia on the devolution issue, on which the Suárez government incredibly called for abstention. The referendum was lost by the government. It was the first serious setback for Prime Minister Suárez and his UCD.

The UCD and the PSOE suffered considerable losses in the March 1980 regional elections in Catalonia and the Basque country. Subsequently the PSOE, which had been the major winner in the Andalusian referendum, tried to recover the political initiative by calling for a parliamentary debate on the political conditions of the nation. By the close of that debate in May, it sought a no-confidence vote against Suárez. Although the vote failed, the performance of the PSOE leader Felipe González in the debate itself was a major public relations victory. His performance—transmitted live for the first time ever to a television audience—was approved by 37 percent of the Spanish public; while only 18 percent preferred Suárez's performance.[10]

UCD notables and founders called Suárez to a meeting in July where they expressed their opposition to the way in which the prime minister was conducting party and government affairs. In September the coalition partners returned to the cabinet, and Suárez asked parliament for a vote of confidence, which he won. Nonetheless, his position became weaker both within the UCD, the government, and among the public: this time only 13 percent of the Spanish public considered his performance during the parliamentary debate the most interesting.[11]

To the most conservative elite sectors of Spanish society it had become clear that defense of their interests meant that they should seek political options other than the UCD and Suárez. One card played by these sectors, the democratic one, was a turn to Fraga's Popular Alliance, which could be revitalized even though it had lost status as the standard-bearer of the right after the 1979 election. The most conservative sectors of the military played the undemocratic card. Thus, it was not the pressure from extreme conservatives that damaged the viability of the UCD, but quite the opposite: it was the failure of the UCD, both as a party and as a government, that encouraged those sectors to seek conservative and even reactionary solutions.

By December 1980 the political conditions and political atmosphere of the country had deteriorated dramatically. One of the most graphic examples was the Christmas greeting of King Juan Carlos on television. For the first time since he became king, he appeared not in a family setting but alone, appealing to the good sense and responsibility of politicians in facing the serious problems of the nation. For the first time, his Christmas speech was almost wholly political.

On 29 January Suárez resigned as prime minister, offering in a televised speech his explanation to the nation that was generally considered neither clear nor reasonable.[12] He proposed as his successor Calvo Sotelo, the number two man in the party from the beginning.

A few days after the Suárez bombshell, the second UCD national convention met in Palma de Mallorca. It was the scene of an open confrontation between followers of Suárez—most of them former Francoists—and the democratic reformers within the party. Most of the reformers had been liberal and Christian democratic opponents of the Franco regime; they were led by Oscar Alzaga, an outstanding member of Parliament who later led one of the UCD splinters on the eve of the election of 1982. The Suárez sector won a very close victory in that conference. They chose as president of the party an obscure and uninspiring politician—Agustín Rodríguez Sahagún—who was ousted by Calvo Sotelo a few months later. Between December 1980 and December 1982 the UCD had four different presidents, as defeat followed defeat.

The frustrated coup d'état that took place while Calvo Sotelo was being chosen prime minister in parliament has already been mentioned. By spring a scandal exploded regarding the selling of poisoned cooking oils that caused about two hundred deaths and had several thousand victims. The political damage of this scandal increased when the minister of health did not resign his cabinet position in spite of public demand.

In September 1981 Fernández Ordoñez, a UCD notable and minister of justice, resigned to found the party of Democratic Action (PAD) that later joined the PSOE.

In October 1981 in an election in Galicia, a northwestern rural region of Spain, the UCD lost heavily, garnering barely more than half of its 1979 vote. Both Suárez and Calvo Sotelo had campaigned actively, and the results of the election severely affected their political positions in the party and the government.[13] A few months after the election, Calvo Sotelo took over the presidency of the UCD but failed to introduce any substantial change in the party structure or dynamics.

Another regional election, this time in Andalusia in May 1982, demonstrated even more clearly the weaknesses of the UCD and the government of Calvo Sotelo. The UCD lost 60 percent of its former vote, and the PSOE obtained a resounding absolute majority.[14]

After this election Calvo Sotelo resigned the presidency of UCD, turning it over to the stylized, self-confident, but ineffective Landelino Lavilla, who would lead his party to an electoral defeat without precedent in contemporary European politics.

By the summer of 1982 Alzaga, the Christian democratic politician, created a new splinter—the Popular Democratic party—which joined the Popular Alliance before the general election. For his part, Suárez founded his own new party—the Democratic Social Center—which claimed to be the "true progressive and reformist party."

Shattered by the October 1982 election, the UCD held its third national convention in December. Its outcome was surrealistic: the party claimed to embrace Christian Democracy reelecting Landelino Lavilla, a man who was by no stretch of the imagination a Christian Democrat and under whose leadership the UCD had collapsed at the polls a month earlier.

The Mass Effects of the UCD Crisis

As has already been noted, after the 1979 election the UCD lost no fewer than six elections. These included:

The referendum for regional autonomy in Andalusia of 28 February 1980. The government and the UCD asked for abstention. The government lost the referendum.

The regional election in the Basque country of 9 March 1980. The UCD lost 54 percent of its 1979 vote, mostly to the regionalist bourgeois Basque Nationalist party (PNV). The PSOE lost 32 percent of its former vote.[15]

The regional election in Catalonia of 20 March 1980. The outcome was similar to that in the Basque provinces. The UCD lost 50 percent of its 1979

Table 13.4 Voting Intentions, by Occupational Sector, 1980 and 1982 (Percentage of Sector)

		December 1980		
	Number of	Intend to vote		
Occupation	cases	UCD	PSOE	AP
Total	25,000	22	19	3
Big business	193	25	14	3
High executive public sector	289	21	17	5
High executive private sector	204	33	18	5
Landowners	124	32	13	5
Liberal professions	121	20	6	10
Middle-small business	1,125	28	15	4
Industry-trade self-employed	621	19	22	7
Farmers not hiring labor	561	38	15	5
Middle technician, public sector	342	24	25	4
Middle technician, private sector	313	27	23	4
Office clerk public sector	308	24	27	3
Office clerk private sector	497	24	27	3
Lower employee public sector	135	34	8	9
Lower employee private sector	171	22	14	0
Sellers of all kinds	514	20	19	2
Foremen	108	22	29	4
Skilled workers	2,254	16	33	2
Unskilled workers	1,379	19	23	2
Rural labor	486	20	28	6
Women out of labor force	8,315	25	15	3
Students over 18	1,542	5	10	1
Retired	2,896	25	14	4

Source: Data bank of the Centro de Investigaciones Sociologicas, where these surveys were conducted.
Note: These samples were representative at the provincial level of the population eighteen and older.

vote (mostly to the regionalist Convergence and Union), and the PSOE lost 31 percent.[16]

A by-election to the Senate in two Andalusian provinces, Seville and Almería, on 18 November 1980. The UCD lost most of its 1979 vote in Seville and in Almería, where the party had been hegemonic. It now received 8 percent of the vote in Seville and 21 percent in Almería.[17]

Regional elections in Galicia on 20 October 1981. As noted earlier, the UCD lost 44 percent of its 1979 vote; the swing did not benefit a regional party

	December 1980			October 1982		
	Intend to vote		Number of	Intend to vote		
UCD	PSOE	AP	cases	UCD	PSOE	AP
12	17	3	25,000	5	25	9
25	10	4	25	2	41	15
13	16	8	48	4	13	17
16	13	12	81	5	18	23
21	12	5	418	4	28	16
8	8	20	599	6	29	15
15	13	5	384	6	17	20
13	16	9	1,172	5	16	13
21	12	4	660	11	17	11
13	19	4	276	7	30	19
16	18	3	293	5	28	10
15	17	5	240	4	23	19
12	28	5	523	6	29	14
26	10	8	131	9	22	11
11	8	1	218	3	30	8
10	15	2	468	5	26	10
8	23	5	100	3	25	9
7	28	2	2,743	3	34	7
6	23	2	1,257	3	30	5
11	21	2	493	4	28	5
14	13	3	8,376	6	20	9
5	18	3	1,100	2	33	14
14	11	4	2,721	6	19	8

Major discrepancies between the two samples can be found, as is usual, among the sectors of the upper social strata.

but the Popular Alliance. The UCD returns anticipated what would happen one year later: a massive swing toward the conservative competitor and the virtual disappearance of the UCD in the urban areas. It looked more and more like a minor, almost irrelevant party.[18]

The regional election in Andalusia on 23 May 1982 that most prefigured the general election in October. The UCD lost 60 percent of its 1979 vote in the region and received very few votes in major towns and cities. The PSOE won an absolute majority, and the conservative AP became the second political force in a region where it had received virtually no previous support.[19]

In both Galicia and Andalusia the disaffection of former UCD voters was very deep. Postelectoral surveys show that while in Catalonia only 13 percent of the swing voters stated they were disenchanted with the party they had voted for in 1979, this percentage was 43 percent in Galicia in 1981 and 52 percent in Andalusia in 1982. In all three cases most of those who switched parties were former UCD voters.[20]

We know from these surveys that the number of swing voters saying that they would support the party they had voted for in regional elections amounted to 19 percent in Catalonia in 1980, 34 percent in Galicia in 1981, and 40 percent in Andalusia in 1982. Moreover, in all three cases most of the other respondents failed to answer the question.[21]

This massive decline in loyalty to the party, although it had been visible in almost every social sector, was most prominent among the urban middle classes. Table 13.4 clearly illustrates the progressive disenchantment with the UCD among people of every social sector, a process that began almost from the day after they cast their ballots in 1979.

The UCD Crisis Viewed through Opinion Trends   There are many indicators of political attitudes that I have used for years to follow the Spanish political process. Here I will focus on three kinds: evaluation of the political situation of the country and voting intentions, ideological self-positioning, and reasons why voters shifted from the UCD to another party.

The data support the following conclusions. First, the evaluation of the political conditions of the country became more and more negative after 1979, paralleling the progressive withdrawal of support for the UCD while support for the PSOE and the AP remained stable or increased. Second, the change in voting intentions was greater than the change in the ideological self-definition of the voters. Finally, the reasons offered by those who changed their political party orientation have more to do with the failure of the UCD to hold firm as party and government than with any significant ideological moves toward either right or left.

As shown in table 13.5, the evaluation of the political conditions in the country became most negative on the eve of the February 1981 coup d'état and during the last two months before the October election. The considerable uncertainty generated trends within the military, the UCD, and the government is clearly reflected in the changes in voting intentions. Yet both the PSOE vote and the AP vote in the election were larger than indicated in preelectoral surveys.

We now know that the voters who switched constituted about 27 percent of the electorate, a proportion far larger than that which realigned itself ideologically.

In fact, the ideological self-identification on an abstract scale from one to

Table 13.5 Voting Intentions and Evaluation of the Political Conditions, 1979 and 1982 (percent)

	June 1979	Jan. 1980	June 1980	Jan. 1981	June 1981	Jan. 1982	June 1982	Sep. 1982	Oct. 1982	Returns 1982
Political conditions are:										
Good or very good	14	12	8	5	5	8	7	5	5	NA
Bad or very bad	18	19	32	42	35	33	28	37	37	NA
Think of voting for a party in next general election different from one voted for in 1979 election	—	7	7	9	8	10	12	18	19	NA
Intend to vote:										
PSOE	—	26	25	19	24	28	30	28	31	36.6
AP	—	4	5	5	4	8	9	12	12	20.1
UCD	—	27	15	13	15	12	10	7	5	5.7
PCE	—	7	3	4	3	4	3	2	3	3.0
No answer, undecided	—	23	31	38	36	31	31	33	34	NA

Source: Regular surveys by the Centro de Investigaciones Sociológicas available at the center data bank.
NA = not applicable. $N = 1,200$.
[a]Percentage of registered voters.

seven shows that a bit more than 10 percent of the voters shifted from a center position; and this evolution was as much toward the right as toward the left (see table 13.6). Moreover, as Wert has acutely pointed out, the UCD voter tended more often than other party voters to place himself in the central position on this scale and in the "no answer" category because the UCD voter was the least ideologically oriented.[22]

Analyzing the data from a scale where labels were attached to ideological positions, a greater ideological displacement can be found, but far below the actual change in the vote. Moreover, the central position on this scale is labeled "centrist of the UCD kind." Consequently, the impressive decrease in the number of people placing themselves in that position is probably more a reflection of a change in voting intentions than of a change in basic ideological orienta-

Table 13.6 Ideological Self-Identification on an Abstract Scale and a Semantic Scale, 1979 and 1982 (percent)

		June 1979	Jan. 1980	June 1980	Jan. 1981	June 1981	Jan. 1982	June 1982	Sep. 1982	Oct. 1982	Dif. June 1979– Oct. 1982	Nov.[a] 1982
Abstract scales												
Left	1	3	1	2	2	1	3	1	1	0	−3	1
	2	7	7	8	8	7	8	7	8	9	+2	10
	3	23	22	26	23	25	26	28	27	26	+3	30
Center	4	30	25	25	22	22	20	17	23	20	−10	17
	5	6	9	7	8	7	11	10	10	13	+7	10
	6	2	3	2	3	3	3	4	4	2	0	3
Right	7	1	1	1	1	0	1	1	0	1	0	1
Don't know; no answer		28	32	29	33	35	28	32	27	29	+1	28
Feel more sympathetic to ideology of:												
Communist		4	3	3	3	3	2	4	3	3	−1	—
Marxist socialist		7	6	7	4	6	5	5	5	5	″2	—
Non-Marxist socialist		18	16	19	16	14	22	22	26	27	¦9	—
Centrist like												
UCD		24	19	16	12	16	10	11	9	5	−19	—
Moderate right		4	7	6	5	5	7	6	11	11	+7	—
Other		9	9	9	9	8	8	6	8	8	−1	—
None[b]		—	—	—	—	22	27	29	13	25	—	—
Don't know; no answer		34	40	40	51	26	19	17	25	16	—	—

Source: Data bank of the Centro de Investigaciones Sociológicas in Madrid, which conducted these surveys.
Note: $N = 1,200$
[a]The November survey was conducted a week after the October election. The sample was 2,400.
[b]This response category was not included until June 1981.

tion. In October the proportion that chose this position was exactly the same as the vote for the UCD a few days later at the polls.

It may therefore be concluded that changes in voting patterns neither resulted in nor caused significant changes in the ideological positions of the voters. That is, the change in voting patterns was more a product of the power vacuum created by a discredited political alternative than of a massive realignment of the electorate toward either right or left.

This conclusion is also supported by the reasons offered on two occasions, before and after the election of October, by voters who switched from the center (see table 13.7). Although the data refer to verbalization of motives or opinions, the point here is that these are consistent with other kinds of data and, most important, fit into the proposition advanced here to explain the results of the election.

Among disaffected voters who intended to vote or actually voted for the PSOE or the AP, there was a common set of motives that explain the change in vote: the UCD's inability to establish a connection between rulers and ruled as well as governmental inefficiency. Specific reasons most often mentioned along these lines by survey respondents are these: lack of governmental authority; poor management of the economy; administrative inefficacy; and inability of leaders to inspire confidence. These reasons reflected the underlying reality of a government unable to govern and of a party whose identity and organization in a political formation, the UCD, that—as Wert has stated—suffered from "an absolute inability to understand its own political goals."[23]

Beyond these common factors there are some differences in motives between those who switched to the PSOE and those to the Popular Alliance. And these are more clearly ideological. Those looking toward the left most often mentioned administrative and political corruption or that the UCD had not defended the popular interest. Among those who leaned to the right, the reasons given more clearly reflected a conservative point of view: that the UCD had not carried out its program; that taxes were too high; that the divorce bill had been approved; that the UCD did not defend the unity of the nation; that terrorism and public disorder prevailed; that the middle classes were not adequately protected.

Concluding Remarks: From Socialist Victory to a New Party System

In looking at the Western scene of the past few years, one is led to think that the PSOE would have won the election even if the UCD had not collapsed. The continued economic recession would have affected the credibility of any government, and this combined with the profound internal crisis of the Spanish Communist party suggest it would not have been difficult for the PSOE to gather the 2 million votes it needed for an absolute majority in parliament.[24]

Table 13.7 Reasons Given for Change in Vote by Former UCD Voters Who Turned to PSOE or AP before and after the Election of 1982, April and November 1982 (percent)

	Switch to PSOE		Switch to AP	
Reasons	April 82	November 82	April 82	November 82
UCD government had no authority	46	77	73	77
Economy worsening	4	75	58	76
UCD leaders not dependable	38	64	51	61
Administration inefficient	37	59	52	55
Things at work worsening	35	58	42	52
UCD people in permanent quarrel	35	60	47	76
Still too much corruption	44	60	—	—
UCD unconcerned about regional problems	34	34	—	—
UCD shifting to the right	34	38	—	—
UCD with banks and fincanciers	31	33	—	—
Tax reform stopped	16	18	—	—
UCD too committed to church	12	12	—	—
Terrorism and insecurity increasing	—	—	62	61
UCD program not implemented	—	—	62	67
Taxes rising	—	—	65	46
Divorce permitted and sexual freedom	—	—	46	45
UCD unable to keep unity of nation	—	—	44	27
UCD shifting to the left	—	—	28	23
Number of cases[a]	903	149	654	126

Source: Data bank of the Centro de Investigaciones Sociológicas, where the surveys were conducted.

Notes: Dash means not applicable.

[a] The national sample of April had 25,000 cases. The number of cases on which percentages have been calculated are those voters for UCD in 1979 who said that they intended to vote either PSOE or AP in the next election. The sample of November CN = 2,400 was taken after the election.

Yet it should be stressed that the way to the unprecedented PSOE victory was well paved by the crisis of the UCD. And this landslide had the additional effect of transferring the hegemony on the right to a party that obtained only 6 percent of the vote in the 1979 election and represented the remnants of the Franco regime.[25] Although unaware of AP's future role, I had argued after the 1979 election that, despite the UCD victory, the Spanish right had not yet found its definitive political articulation and that the Popular Alliance could have an important place in the future.[26]

The Popular Alliance has not changed substantially since 1979, when it was already a more moderate conservative party than in 1977. Its leader, Fraga, is still as mercurial and controversial a personality as before. The AP has gained only the peripheral addition of a UCD Christian Democratic splinter and this can in no way account for its improved electoral showing. The Popular Alliance is an opposition force that has only a slim chance of capturing a parliamentary majority. Its ideology stands too far from the mainstream of Spanish public opinion. Indeed, with the new parliament polarized between the AP and the PSOE, there are very few liberal democrats in the chamber.

This new balance of forces in the parliament poses two challenges to the political system. On the one hand, for the first time a single party has a majority large enough not to have to compromise on every issue, whereas the system had previously operated on opposite assumptions and requirements. On the other hand, if the party system is not to evolve into a dominant single-party system, a masterpiece of political engineering to result in the recomposition of the right is necessary. Furthermore, it must be done from outside parliament, since most of the fourteen representatives of the two national center parties—UCD and CDS—are not politicians who can claim liberal democratic origins. Most of them had worked within the Franco establishment and would have been as well suited to a Popular Alliance ticket. Yet there is hope within parliament among some politicians of the regionalist center parties—especially the Catalans—and the UCD splinter Popular Democratic party. There are liberal democrats who fought the Franco regime, who are not ashamed of being conservatives, and who may have learned how to survive in democratic politics.

The PSOE and its leader, Felipe González, have been the recipients of an unprecedented stream of hope and confidence by the Spanish people. It would be hard for them to govern with less sensitivity and discipline than the UCD had after 1979. Even under harsh economic conditions, if the government can stop terrorism and military unrest, the democratic regime will be stabilized as a parliamentary monarchy, and the civil society will find a way out of its prepolitical fears of war, repression, and uncompromising confrontation.

Conclusion
EUSEBIO M. MUJAL-LEÓN AND
RAFAEL LÓPEZ-PINTOR

───── The process of transition from authoritarianism that began in Spain approximately twenty-five years ago with the Franco regime's decision to pursue an aggressive program of modernization and industrialization has led to the restoration of a parliamentary democracy and the approval of a new constitution. That process, which culminated in the victory of the Spanish Socialist Workers' party (PSOE) in the October 1982 election, has by now developed sufficient impetus that, barring unforeseen economic problems, a large-scale terrorist offensive against military and civilian targets, or a dramatic breakdown in public order, it will be very difficult to reverse.

The Socialist victory and the accompanying collapse of the Union of the Democratic Center (UCD) and the Spanish Communist party (PCE) have redefined the Spanish party system. It has shifted at least temporarily from an imperfect bipolar system—with two large and two small national parties (the former captured 65.5 percent of the vote in March 1979) and several regional groups—to a truly bipolar system with a hegemonic party, an opposition supported by 25 percent of the electorate, and a number of regional parties. In October 1982 the two largest parties captured 74.9 percent of the vote and 88 percent of the seats in the Chamber of Deputies. Of the remaining parties represented in the parliament, only the Basque Nationalist party (PNV) and the Catalan Convergence and Union (CiU) held their own against the Socialist tide. The three other national parties—the UCD, the PCE, and the Social Democratic Center (CDS)—have been reduced to insignificance. They have only seventeen seats in the Chamber, gained from a mere 13.6 percent of the popular vote.

The resounding Socialist victory clears the way for parliamentary efficacy and decisive government (conditions notable for their absence during the last years of UCD rule), but it may also initiate a phase during which there are several "elections without choice." Although Spain may for a time thrive on a

PSOE administration that has a dependable parliamentary majority behind it, the development of a viable democratic alternative—whether from the reemergence of a centrist party or from the broadening of electoral support for the Popular Alliance (AP)—must take place. Undemocratic elements on the right might otherwise gain in strength. Without a democratic opposition, moreover, the Socialists (who will in any case have difficulty in reorganizing the bureaucracy and making it more efficient) might become ensnared in an inelegant clientelism.

The attainment of enduring party alignments has so far eluded Spain. As a number of chapters in this volume indicate, startling continuities with past voting patterns characterized the 1977 and 1979 elections, but in October 1982 major vote shifts occurred. The major gainers were, of course, the PSOE and the Popular Alliance. Benefiting from the coincident disintegration of the UCD and the PCE, the PSOE picked up 4.5 million votes more than in March 1979, a gain of nearly 80 percent. Moreover, in a development that might have profound impact on Spanish democracy during the next decade and that mirrored a parallel development a year and a half earlier in France, the Socialists were successful in attracting the votes of many practicing Catholics. The AP won five times its March 1979 vote, emerging as the major opposition party. The UCD and the Communists were the great losers in October 1982. The UCD dropped from 35.0 to 6.7 percent of the vote (losing 156 seats in the Chamber of Deputies) in one of the most staggering defeats in post–World War II European politics, and the PCE declined from 10.8 to 4.1 percent of the vote. This massive shift of the party system was not accompanied by a polarization of public opinion, however. Rather it corresponded primarily to the incapacity of UCD and Communist elites to overcome bitter internal disputes and to consolidate their constituencies.

Various factors will determine whether this realignment will be permanent and whether a polarization will follow in its wake. Of primary importance will be the policies and choices made by the PSOE and the AP. With the overwhelming mandate it received in October 1982, the PSOE attained electoral support that matched or surpassed that of the major socialist or social democratic parties in post–World War II Europe. Because of the breadth of this vote (and its evident heterogeneity), the PSOE will face a major challenge in articulating policies that satisfy or at least do not alienate this broad coalition of interests. Legislation on education, abortion, or divorce and even the devolution of further powers to the regional governments will tax the Socialists' abilities to govern by consensus. Equally divisive may be the foreign policy-related issues of EEC accession and the decision on possible Spanish membership in NATO. But the determining factor will be the PSOE's success in addressing Spain's economic problems, a task that will require both effective domestic policies and a reinvigoration of the international (and especially the European) economy.

Lack of success in this sphere could not only exacerbate latent divisions within the PSOE (where tensions already exist between the pragmatic modernizers and the more ideological socialists) but also contribute to the polarization of the political scene. Neither the Communists nor the small left-wing regional parties such as the Euzkadi Left and Herri Batasuna represent a major threat to Socialist hegemony on the left, but increased polarization, labor unrest, and continued high unemployment could result in losses for the PSOE.

As the major opposition party, the Popular Alliance can play an important role in the success of democracy in Spain. Much may depend on whether the party's leader, Manuel Fraga Iribarne, opts in favor of a center-directed strategy and whether such an effort reaps electoral reward. There is no way to predict these matters with certainty, but both Fraga's personality and the negative sentiments he elicits from many Spaniards could work against rational choice.

The success of AP in consolidating and expanding its electoral audience will affect the prospects for reconstruction of the center. Despite the disintegration of the UCD, there continues to be a centrist political space in Spain today. The collapse of the UCD was not, as we have noted, the result of electoral polarization. Rather it reflected the failure of a leadership whose political instincts, formed during an apprenticeship served under Franco, could not successfully adapt to the exigencies of normal democratic politics. For nearly two years before the election, the UCD treated the nation to a mad scramble by its "barons" unwilling to give up their official perquisites—"the official car" in the vernacular. Public Health Minister Jésus Sancho Rof, who did not resign even when the death toll from the sale of contaminated cooking oil reached two hundred, personified this approach to government. (Ironically, he was one of the two cabinet members to survive the October 1982 debacle—proof that *caciquismo* was still alive and well in Galicia.) Too many in the centrist elite thought that the electorate owed them a share of power. In their view, they had, after all, saved Spain from another civil war following Franco's death and engineered the transition to democracy: the public had no right to ask for more. Such attitudes complicated the already difficult situation that the UCD as a centrist option faced. Inherently pragmatic and nonideological, the center often appears indecisive, offering compromise between left and right rather than clear-cut choices. In this respect, it may be just as well for Spanish democracy in the long term that the center and right must restructure their alternative from outside the government.

The UCD, reduced after the October 1982 election to thirteen deputies, a tiny fragment of the once strongest party in the Cortes, remained divided thereafter between Christian Democrats who wanted to retain the group's independent identity, and others (like the *azules* led by former Interior Minister Rodolfo Martín Villa) who favored cooperation and eventual fusion with AP.

Ultimately, the UCD abandoned its quest to represent the center, dissolving itself in early 1983. Other claimants to the centrist space had in the meantime also fallen by the wayside. Fernández Ordoñez and his Democratic Action party (PAD) fused with the PSOE. Adolfo Suárez and Agustín Rodríguez Sahagún of the Democratic and Social Center (CDS) retain hopes of constructing a "bridge" party, but in 1985 they remained leaders in search of a party.

Second claimants to the centrist mantle are the Christian Democratic groups, but they are spread across the party spectrum. Nevertheless, the younger Christian democratic members of the UCD who were not too badly tarred by the years in the government and Oscar Alzaga's Popular Democratic party, which ran in coalition with AP in October 1982, may represent the embryo of a future Christian Democratic party in Spain. Although the chances that such a group will become as strong as the Italian Christian Democrats are slim indeed, it may recapture some of the centrist votes that went to the PSOE and thus pave the way for alternation during the 1980s.

Others who might play a role in this venture include Joaquín Garrigues Walker's tiny liberal group as well as centrist regional parties like the Basque Nationalist party and Catalan Convergence and Union (CIU). Their prospects received a significant boost as a result of the April 1984 Catalan regional elections where CIU won an absolute majority of the seats (72 of 135) in the Catalan parliament with 46.6 percent of the vote. This showing—coupled with the 42 percent gained by the PNV in the Basque regional elections months before—spurred a great deal of interest in the proposal for a federated Reformist party whose most visible spokesman was the CIU deputy, Miguel Roca i Junyent. Whether this effort would bear fruit remains unclear, but its pursuit reflects the conviction of many in the center and center-right that, in order to weaken and ultimately defeat the PSOE, a way has to be found to transpose centrist regional strength onto the national arena.

Spanish democracy will be strengthened if the political parties consolidate their organizations and extend their influence over other actors in the society. As evidenced by very low ratios of members to voters and members to the electorate, Spanish parties have had difficulty penetrating the social fabric. The Socialists, for example, are near the bottom of the European list on both scales, and neither the UCD (before its disintegration) nor the AP has a membership that compares with its analogues in other countries. Subcultural or sectoral associations, which in Western Europe have served as conduits for recruiting cadres and extending party electoral bases, are relatively weak as well. Trade unions, for example, retain an important capacity for mobilizing workers, but they have a low membership, variously estimated at between 15 and 20 percent of the active labor force.

As the government, the Socialists have an unprecedented opportunity to increase their influence over such institutions as the bureaucracy and the military. Although the establishment of civilian supremacy is important to the consolidation of Spanish democracy, the danger of a military coup may be a less serious problem for Spain today than many people anticipate, especially if there is no breakdown of public order in the next few years and if the military is reorganized under the aegis of NATO. Indeed, one of Franco's accomplishments may be that he removed the military from active political decision making. More significant perhaps for the longer-term success of Spanish democracy will be the way the Socialists relate to an entrenched and fragmented bureaucracy. With the weakening of the traditional subcultures on which they might rely for support, the Socialists may be tempted to establish political control over the bureaucracy and consolidate their influence in Spanish society by creating new patronage networks. This would not be new: witness the Italian *partitocrazia*, not to mention the practices and style of the UCD. But its adoption by the PSOE would be distinctly counterproductive, not only for the party (whose organization would become dependent on the state) but for Spanish democracy. Party control, in short, must not be allowed to degenerate into a new variant of clientelism.

Spain turned an important corner in October 1982. The uneventful alternation that brought the Socialists to power capped an unprecedented peaceful transition from authoritarianism during which a new constitution was promulgated and national, regional, and municipal elections were held. With the transition now over, the definitive consolidation of Spanish democracy has begun, a phase in which parties outside the government as well as the PSOE will play important roles. While serious obstacles remain, the political experience of the past decade and the deepening public commitment to democracy should ensure the further growth of Spain's democratic institutions and practices.

Appendix A Summary of Spanish National Election Results, 1977–1982 Compiled by Richard M. Scammon

Appendix A   1977 Congress of Deputies

1977 Congress of Deputies

Province	Total Valid Vote	UCD	PSOE	PSUC/PCE	AP/CD	Other
Alava	125,632	38,867	34,638	4,142	7,994	39,991
% Valid Vote		30.9	27.6	3.3	6.4	31.8
Seats	4	2	1	—	—	1
Albacete	168,647	64,285	56,166	13,672	16,034	18,490
% Valid Vote		38.1	33.3	8.1	9.5	11.0
Seats	4	2	2	—	—	—
Alicante	555,677	199,986	216,782	51,094	36,149	51,666
% Valid Vote		36.0	39.0	9.2	6.5	9.3
Seats	9	4	4	1	—	—
Almería	181,427	90,300	49,498	11,757	14,763	15,109
% Valid Vote		49.8	27.3	6.5	8.1	8.3
Seats	5	3	2	—	—	—
Avila	104,873	71,587	14,965	2,406	7,123	8,792
% Valid Vote		68.3	14.3	2.3	6.8	8.4
Seats	3	3	—	—	—	—
Badajoz	319,827	148,593	108,923	22,223	21,844	18,244
% Valid Vote		46.5	34.1	6.9	6.8	5.7
Seats	7	4	3	—	—	—
Balearic Is.	322,490	164,559	74,625	14,140	28,498	40,688
% Valid Vote		51.0	23.1	4.4	8.8	12.6
Seats	6	4	2	—	—	—
Barcelona	2,365,648	358,510	727,199	474,116	75,087	730,736
% Valid Vote		15.2	30.7	20.0	3.2	30.9
Seats	33	5	11	7	1	9
Burgos	194,576	89,005	44,063	4,744	28,445	28,319
% Valid Vote		45.7	22.6	2.4	14.6	14.6
Seats	4	3	1	—	—	—

Province	Total Valid Vote	UCD	PSOE	PSUC/PCE	AP/CD	Other
Cáceres	208,996	115,678	54,886	6,816	19,517	12,099
% Valid Vote		55.3	26.3	3.3	9.3	5.8
Seats		5	4	1	—	—	—
Cádiz	417,442	113,914	153,329	42,254	20,632	87,313
% Valid Vote		27.3	36.7	10.1	4.9	20.9
Seats	8	2	4	1	—	1
Castellón	240,753	85,451	71,236	14,199	14,546	55,321
% Valid Vote		35.5	29.6	5.9	6.0	23.0
Seats	5	2	2	—	—	1
Ciudad Real	251,778	103,493	80,943	16,169	31,361	19,812
% Valid Vote		41.1	32.1	6.4	12.5	7.9
Seats	5	3	2	—	—	—
Córdoba	359,983	117,217	121,757	59,375	33,544	28,090
% Valid Vote		32.6	33.8	16.5	9.3	7.8
Seats	7	3	3	1	—	—
La Coruña	449,996	222,944	78,654	16,929	49,608	81,861
% Valid Vote		49.5	17.5	3.8	11.0	18.2
Seats	9	6	2	—	1	—
Cuenca	126,242	70,744	28,495	7,835	10,327	8,841
% Valid Vote		56.0	22.6	6.2	8.2	7.0
Seats	4	3	1	—	—	—
Gerona	245,990	44,751	60,482	25,127	7,928	107,702
% Valid Vote		18.2	24.6	10.2	3.2	43.8
Seats	5	1	2	—	—	2
Granada	347,811	152,723	111,659	33,697	24,750	24,982
% Valid Vote		43.9	32.1	9.7	7.1	7.2
Seats	7	4	3	—	—	—
Guadalajara	79,071	38,803	16,788	5,415	12,449	5,616
% Valid Votes		49.1	21.2	6.8	15.7	7.1
Seats	3	2	1	—	—	—
Guipúzcoa	329,985	—	93,003	12,179	27,008	197,795
% Valid Votes		—	28.2	3.7	8.2	59.9
Seats	7	—	3	—	—	4
Huelva	196,777	94,184	66,340	10,706	9,822	15,725
% Valid Votes		47.9	33.7	5.4	5.0	8.0
Seats	5	3	2	—	—	—
Huesca	122,560	55,953	33,867	7,443	7,253	18,044
% Valid Votes		45.7	27.6	6.1	5.9	14.7
Seats	3	2	1	—	—	—

Province	Total Valid Vote	UCD	PSOE	PSUC/PCE	AP/CD	Other
Jaén	314,009	104,075	123,368	29,465	27,011	30,090
% Valid Votes		33.1	39.3	9.4	8.6	9.6
Seats		7	3	4	—	—	—
León	269,644	137,632	65,201	12,519	33,391	20,901
% Valid Votes		51.0	24.2	4.6	12.4	7.8
Seats		6	4	1	—	1	—
Lérida	185,392	45,063	27,801	22,659	10,078	79,791
% Valid Votes		24.3	15.0	12.2	5.4	43.0
Seats		4	1	1	—	—	2
Logroño	136,509	56,247	36,157	4,114	19,748	20,243
% Valid Votes		41.2	26.5	3.0	14.5	14.8
Seats		4	2	1	—	1	—
Lugo	166,915	86,960	20,806	2,945	36,331	19,873
% Valid Votes		52.1	12.5	1.8	21.8	11.9
Seats		5	4	—	—	1	—
Madrid	2,302,805	737,699	731,380	247,038	242,077	344,611
% Valid Votes		32.0	31.8	10.7	10.5	15.0
Seats		32	11	11	4	3	3
Málaga	416,947	115,108	166,395	51,951	35,033	48,460
% Valid Votes		27.6	39.9	12.5	8.4	11.6
Seats		8	3	4	1	—	—
Murcia	440,625	179,574	154,167	29,434	29,830	47,620
% Valid Votes		40.8	35.0	6.7	6.8	10.8
Seats		8	4	4	—	—	—
Navarre	259,259	75,255	55,130	6,294	21,884	100,696
% Valid Votes		29.0	21.3	2.4	8.4	38.8
Seats		5	3	2	—	—	—
Orense	162,735	100,833	21,190	2,748	21,638	16,326
% Valid Votes		62.0	13.0	1.7	13.3	10.0
Seats		5	4	—	—	1	—
Oviedo	577,095	177,704	182,743	60,951	77,663	78,034
% Valid Votes		30.8	31.7	10.6	13.5	13.5
Seats		10	4	4	1	1	—
Palencia	102,235	51,787	25,944	3,794	14,784	5,926
% Valid Votes		50.7	25.4	3.7	14.5	5.8
Seats		3	2	1	—	—	—
Las Palmas	282,841	187,254	39,616	7,467	15,944	32,560
% Valid Votes		66.2	14.0	2.6	5.6	11.5
Seats		6	5	1	—	—	—

Appendix A

Province	Total Valid Vote	UCD	PSOE	PSUC/PCE	AP/CD	Other
Pontevedra	352,681	198,949	58,142	11,844	40,157	43,589
% Valid Votes		56.4	16.5	3.4	11.4	12.4
Seats	8	6	1	—	1	—
Salamanca	195,739	110,308	45,240	5,649	15,280	19,262
% Valid Votes		56.4	23.1	2.9	7.8	9.8
Seats	4	3	1	—	—	—
Sta. Cruz de Tenerife	261,413	143,689	52,012	11,054	24,098	30,560
% Valid Votes		55.0	19.9	4.2	9.2	11.7
Seats	7	5	2	—	—	—
Santander (Cantabria)	253,277	100,886	66,796	13,884	36,500	35,161
% Valid Votes		39.8	26.4	5.5	14.4	13.9
Seats	5	3	1	—	1	—
Segovia	85,348	50,752	18,173	2,115	7,442	6,866
% Valid Votes		59.5	21.3	2.5	8.7	8.0
Seats	3	2	1	—	—	—
Sevilla	681,753	221,667	251,000	91,879	42,839	74,368
% Valid Votes		32.5	36.8	13.5	6.3	10.9
Seats	12	5	5	2	—	—
Soria	59,931	35,324	10,755	1,196	3,784	8,872
% Valid Votes		58.9	17.9	2.0	6.3	14.8
Seats	3	3	—	—	—	—
Tarragona	253,056	70,418	59,757	40,850	15,129	66,902
% Valid Votes		27.8	23.6	16.1	6.0	26.4
Seats	5	2	1	1	—	1
Teruel	91,616	46,327	16,302	2,427	14,772	11,788
% Valid Votes		50.6	17.8	2.6	16.1	12.9
Seats	3	2	1	—	—	—
Toledo	267,146	103,102	84,049	21,942	44,397	13,656
% Valid Votes		38.6	31.5	8.2	16.6	5.1
Seats	5	2	2	—	1	—
Valencia	1,073,448	320,010	392,684	100,306	57,950	202,498
% Valid Votes		29.8	36.6	9.3	5.4	18.9
Seats	15	5	7	1	1	1
Valladolid	241,777	103,085	75,173	15,589	20,195	27,735
% Valid Votes		42.6	31.1	6.4	8.4	11.5
Seats	5	3	2	—	—	—

Province	Total Valid Vote	UCD	PSOE	PSUC/PCE	AP/CD	Other
Vizcaya	556,699	90,978	136,474	33,673	36,129	259,445
% Valid Votes		16.3	24.5	6.0	6.5	46.6
Seats	10	2	3	—	1	4
Zamora	127,230	58,237	26,213	2,780	30,693	9,307
% Valid Votes		45.8	20.6	2.2	24.1	7.3
Seats	4	2	1	—	1	—
Zaragoza	441,512	140,154	113,913	22,839	35,298	129,308
% Valid Votes		31.7	25.8	5.2	8.0	29.3
Seats	8	3	3	—	—	2
Ceuta	24,218	8,804	7,886	—	—	7,528
% Valid Votes		36.4	32.6	—	—	31.1
Seats	1	1	—	—	—	—
Melilla	18,949	10,723	5,186	966	2,074	—
% Valid Votes		56.6	27.4	5.1	10.9	
Seats	1	1	—	—	—	—
Total	18,318,935	6,310,151	5,367,951	1,716,810	1,516,831	3,407,192
Percentage		34.4	29.3	9.4	8.3	18.6
Seats	350	165	118	20	16	31*

Source: "Advances of the Ministerio del Interior" and data supplied by José Ignacio Wert Ortega, Centro de Investigaciones Sociológicas, Madrid.

Parties that are listed in the "other vote column that obtained seats are: 11 PDC/CiU—6 in Barcelona, 2 in Gerona, 2 in Lérida, 1 in Taragona; 6 PSP/US—1 in Cádiz, 3 in Madrid, 1 in Valencia, 1 in Zaragoza; 8 PNV—1 in Alava, 3 in Guipúzcoa, 4 in Vizcaya; 2 UC/DCC—2 in Barcelona; 1 EE—in Guipúzcoa; 1 EC—in Barcelona; 2 Center. Independents—1 in Castellón, 1 in Zaragoza

PDC/CiU —Democratic Pact for Catalonia/Convergence and Union
PSP/US —Popular Socialist Party/Socialist Union
PNV —National Basque Party
UC/DCC —Union of the Center/Christian Democrats of Catalonia
EE —Basque Left
EC —Catalan Left

Appendix B

1979 Congress of Deputies

Province	Total Vote	Total Valid Vote	UCD	PSOE	PSUC/PCE	AP/CD	Other
Alava	119,892	116,120	29,625	24,891	3,877	7,205	50,522
% Valid Vote			25.5	21.4	3.3	6.2	43.5
Seats			4	2	1	—	—	1
Albacete	168,862	168,757	65,883	65,465	20,945	8,224	8,240
% Valid Vote			39.0	38.8	12.4	4.9	4.9
Seats			4	2	2	—	—
Alicante	560,985	553,088	207,570	218,137	62,018	28,917	36,446
% Valid Vote			37.5	39.4	11.2	5.2	6.6
Seats			9	4	4	1	—	—
Almería	184,487	182,537	80,854	67,782	13,534	8,067	12,300
% Valid Vote			44.3	37.1	7.4	4.4	6.7
Seats			5	3	2	—	—
Avila	103,007	101,306	67,001	20,341	3,661	6,995	3,308
% Valid Vote			66.1	20.1	3.6	6.9	3.3
Seats			3	6	—	—	—
Badajoz	332,132	328,319	146,699	122,680	30,873	11,194	16,873
% Valid Vote			44.7	37.4	9.4	3.4	5.1
Seats			7	4	3	—	—
Balearic Is.	314,850	299,197	146,927	88,232	14,575	27,554	21,727
% Valid Votes			49.1	29.5	4.9	9.2	7.3
Seats			6	4	2	—	—
Barcelona	2,337,310	2,284,843	387,543	694,847	436,908	84,195	681,350
% Valid Votes			17.0	30.4	19.1	3.7	29.8
Seats			33	6	12	7	1	7
Burgos	183,336	179,223	95,425	41,394	7,189	14,759	20,456
% Valid Votes			53.2	23.1	4.0	8.2	11.4
Seats			4	3	1	—	—

Province	Total Vote	Total Valid Vote	UCD	PSOE	PSUC/PCE	AP/CD	Other
Cáceres	210,287	207,196	97,592	78,670	10,777	8,490	11,667
% Valid Votes			47.1	38.0	5.2	4.1	5.6
Seats		5	3	2	—	—	—
Cádiz	422,011	412,986	121,800	124,693	43,824	13,465	109,204
% Valid Votes			29.5	30.2	10.6	3.3	26.4
Seats		8	2	3	1	—	2
Castellón	243,601	239,508	111,359	85,727	17,361	8,382	16,679
% Valid Votes			46.5	35.8	7.2	3.5	7.0
Seats		5	3	2	—	—	—
Ciudad Real	245,254	242,449	100,896	95,996	19,171	11,659	14,727
% Valid Votes			41.6	39.6	7.9	4.8	6.1
Seats		5	3	2	—	—	—
Córdoba	373,958	369,329	110,734	111,237	70,554	20,909	55,895
% Valid Votes			30.0	30.1	19.1	5.7	15.1
Seats		7	3	3	1	—	—
La Coruña	438,702	428,981	200,120	76,873	20,213	50,588	81,187
% Valid Votes			46.7	17.9	4.7	11.8	18.9
Seats		9	6	2	—	1	—
Cuenca	124,380	122,140	64,273	38,654	10,049	7,388	1,776
% Valid Votes			52.6	31.6	8.2	6.0	1.5
Seats		4	3	1	—	—	—
Gerona	240,660	235,908	58,939	66,328	22,261	7,927	80,453
% Valid Vote			25.0	28.1	9.4	3.4	34.1
Seats		5	2	2	—	—	1
Granada	360,710	357,610	131,107	128,002	45,384	16,958	36,159
% Valid Votes			36.7	35.8	12.7	4.7	10.1
Seats		7	3	3	1	—	—
Guadalajara	79,020	78,009	36,361	18,155	6,699	8,417	8,377
% Valid Votes			46.6	23.3	8.6	10.8	10.7
Seats		3	2	1	—	—	—
Guipúzcoa	334,960	328,073	50,551	59,863	10,034	3,419	204,206
% Valid Votes			15.4	18.2	3.1	1.0	62.2
Seats		7	1	2	—	—	4
Huelva	186,498	184,072	68,756	65,302	12,913	6,080	31,021
% Valid Votes			37.4	35.5	7.0	3.3	16.9
Seats		5	3	2	—	—	—

Appendix B

Province	Total Vote	Total Valid Vote	UCD	PSOE	PSUC/PCE	AP/CD	Other
Huesca	119,688	117,354	56,449	40,885	7,724	5,280	7,016
% Valid Votes			48.1	34.8	6.6	4.5	6.0
Seats			3	2	1	—	—	—
Jaén	332,590	328,982	111,209	137,861	42,466	11,752	25,694
% Valid Votes			33.8	41.9	12.9	3.6	7.8
Seats			7	3	3	1	—	—
León	260,967	256,278	124,085	71,533	15,157	29,313	11,190
% Valid Votes			50.4	27.9	5.9	11.4	4.4
Seats			6	4	2	—	—	—
Lérida	174,756	171,591	54,540	42,937	18,340	5,509	50,265
% Valid Votes			31.8	25.0	10.7	3.2	29.3
Seats			4	2	1	—	—	1
Logroño (La Rioja)	136,419	134,093	64,735	39,245	4,810	18,686	6,617
% Valid Votes			48.3	29.3	3.9	13.9	4.9
Seats			4	3	1	—	—	—
Lugo	161,880	159,120	79,964	27,920	2,441	30,731	18,064
% Valid Votes			50.3	17.5	1.5	19.3	11.4
Seats			5	3	1	—	1	—
Madrid	2,334,229	2,304,953	764,830	769,328	301,496	198,345	261,954
% Valid Votes			33.2	33.4	13.5	8.6	11.4
Seats			32	12	12	4	3	1
Málaga	420,027	413,172	120,201	148,497	53,036	16,304	75,134
% Valid Votes			29.1	35.9	12.8	3.9	18.2
Seats			8	3	3	1	—	1
Murcia	460,782	452,938	178,229	178,621	36,090	25,903	34,095
% Valid Voters			39.3	39.4	8.0	5.7	7.5
Seats			8	4	4	—	—	—
Navarre	257,039	252,243	83,302	55,399	5,619	—	107,923
% Valid Votes			33.0	22.0	2.2	—	42.8
Seats			5	3	1	—	—	1
Orense	153,860	143,391	75,271	23,292	3,829	26,901	14,098
% Valid Votes			52.5	16.2	2.7	18.8	9.8
Seats			5	3	1	—	1	—
Oviedo (Asturias)	545,179	536,168	177,459	200,346	73,444	46,365	38,254
% Valid Votes			33.1	37.4	13.8	8.6	7.1
Seats			10	4	4	1	1	—

Province	Total Vote	Total Valid Vote	UCD	PSOE	PSUC/PCE	AP/CD	Other
Palencia	101,141	98,733	51,069	25,888	4,517	9,351	7,908
% Valid Votes			51.7	26.2	4.6	9.5	8.0
Seats		3	2	1	—	—	—
Las Palmas	296,753	286,736	171,842	41,616	8,245	8,607	56,426
% Valid Votes			59.9	14.5	2.9	3.0	19.7
Seats		6	4	1	—	—	1
Pontevedra	296,770	290,298	137,769	49,213	16,111	37,046	50,159
% Valid Votes			47.5	17.0	5.5	11.7	17.3
Seats		8	5	2	—	1	—
Salamanca	199,991	193,888	104,328	51,866	7,837	14,992	14,865
% Valid Votes			53.8	26.8	4.0	7.7	7.7
Seats		4	3	1	—	—	—
Sta. Cruz de Tenerife	250,940	245,740	139,908	53,604	11,560	11,204	29,464
% Valid Votes			56.9	21.8	4.7	4.6	12.0
Seats		7	5	2	—	—	—
Santander	264,658	258,132	108,552	78,512	17,140	—	53,928
% Valid Vote			42.1	30.4	6.6	—	20.9
Seats		5	3	2	—	—	—
Segovia	84,354	82,869	49,375	19,216	3,450	5,458	5,370
% Valid Votes			59.6	23.2	4.2	6.6	6.5
Seats		3	2	1	—	—	—
Sevilla	698,818	691,090	191,099	203,468	110,731	32,428	153,364
% Valid Votes			27.7	29.4	16.0	4.7	22.2
Seats		12	4	4	2	—	2
Soria	56,808	54,913	33,756	14,187	1,550	5,567	1,853
% Valid Votes			57.8	25.8	2.8	10.1	3.4
Seats		3	2	1	—	—	—
Tarragona	251,668	247,224	69,926	71,417	35,283	9,998	60,600
% Valid Votes			28.3	28.9	14.3	4.0	24.5
Seats		5	2	2	1	—	—
Teruel	87,304	83,902	46,775	22,886	2,737	6,971	4,533
% Valid Votes			55.7	27.3	3.3	8.3	5.4
Seats		3	2	1	—	—	—
Toledo	268,645	265,201	110,700	85,288	28,961	14,933	25,319
% Valid Votes			41.7	32.2	10.9	5.6	9.5
Seats		5	3	2	—	—	—

Province	Total Vote	Total Valid Vote	UCD	PSOE	PSUC/PCE	AP/CD	Other
Valencia	1,092,817	1,075,518	364,174	394,813	145,141	47,017	124,372
% Valid Votes			33.9	36.7	13.5	4.4	11.6
Seats		15	6	7	2	—	—
Valladolid	239,215	235,404	93,062	71,230	18,229	19,706	33,177
% Valid Votes			39.5	30.3	7.7	8.4	14.1
Seats		5	3	2	—	—	—
Vizcaya	566,307	552,056	88,431	105,481	31,942	23,484	302,718
% Valid Votes			16.0	19.1	5.8	4.3	54.8
Seats		10	2	2	—	—	6
Zamora	123,222	119,568	61,025	27,143	3,506	19,603	8,291
% Valid Votes			51.0	22.7	2.9	16.4	6.9
Seats		4	3	1	—	—	—
Zaragoza	431,656	423,095	153,457	113,600	34,000	22,969	99,069
% Valid Votes			36.3	26.8	8.0	5.4	23.4
Seats		8	4	3	—	—	1
Ceuta	21,484	21,132	11,020	7,502	—	1,669	941
% Valid Votes			52.1	35.5	—	7.9	4.5
Seats		1	—	—	—	—	—
Melilla	17,686	17,457	9,035	3,750	793	848	3,031
% Valid Votes			51.8	21.5	4.5	4.9	17.4
Seats		1	1	—	—	—	—
Total	18,272,555	17,932,890	6,268,593	5,469,813	1,938,487	1,067,732	3,188,265
Percentage			35.0	30.5	10.8	6.0	17.8
Seats		350	168	121	23	9	29

Source: "Las Elecciones Legislativas del 1 de Marzo de 1979," Centro de Investigaciones Sociológicas, Madrid.

The figures included in "other" vote column for parties that received seats in the 1979 Congress of Deputies is as follows:

  483,353 PDC/CiU—8 elected: six in Barcelona, one in Gerona, one in Lérida
  378,964 UN—1 elected in Madrid
  325,842 PSA—5 elected: two in Sevilla, one in Málaga, two in Cádiz
  275,292 PNV—7 elected: four in Vizcaya, one in Guipúzcoa
  123,452 ERC/FNC—1 elected in Barcelona
    85,677 EE—1 elected in Guipúzcoa
    58,953 UPC—1 elected in Las Palmas
    38,042 PAR—1 elected in Zaragoza
    28,248 UPN—1 elected in Navarra
The AP–CD vote includes UFPV in the Basque Region

PDC/CiU = Democratic Pact for Catalonia-Convergence and Union
UN = National Union
PSA = Andalusian Socialist Party
PNV = National Basque Party
HB = Herri Batasuna
ERC/FNC = Catalan Republican Left/National Front
EE = Basque Left
UPC = Canary People's Union
PAR = Aragonese Regional Party
UPN = Union of the Navarrese People

Appendix C

1982 Congress of Deputies

Province	Total	Total Valid Vote	PSOE/PSC	AP/PDP	UCD	PCE/PSUC	CiU	Other
Alava	149,794	145,377	51,674	27,974	—	1,573	—	64,156
% Valid Votes			35.5	19.2	—	1.1	—	44.1
Seats			4	2	1	—	—	—	1
Albacete	196,992	192,021	103,328	55,666	16,755	8,874	—	7,398
% Valid Votes			53.8	29.0	8.7	4.6	—	3.9
Seats			4	3	1	—	—	—
Alicante	665,188	648,463	352,632	189,040	46,940	26,531	—	33,320
% Valid Votes			54.4	29.2	7.2	4.1	—	5.1
Seats			9	6	3	—	—	—
Almería	212,708	206,645	119,903	48,280	23,294	5,504	—	9,664
% Valid Votes			58.0	23.4	11.3	2.7	—	4.7
Seats			5	4	1	—	—	—
Avila	114,016	111,075	34,142	37,193	11,218	1,947	—	26,575
% Valid Votes			30.7	33.5	10.1	1.8	—	23.9
Seats			3	1	1	—	—	—	1
Badajoz	371,664	363,846	209,114	85,296	30,647	15,368	—	23,391
% Valid Votes			57.5	23.4	8.4	4.2	—	6.4
Seats			7	5	2	—	—	—
Balearic Is.	372,330	354,391	144,232	134,444	37,148	5,962	—	32,605
% Valid Votes			40.7	37.9	10.5	1.7	—	9.2
Seats			6	3	3	—	—	—
Barcelona	2,716,287	2,671,594	1,292,672	385,967	40,222	131,314	560,555	260,864
% Valid Votes			48.4	14.4	1.5	4.9	21.0	9.8
Seats			33	18	5	—	1	8	1
Burgos	218,622	211,990	79,626	90,969	20,609	3,737	—	17,049
% Valid Votes			37.6	42.9	9.7	1.8	—	8.0
Seats			4	2	2	—	—	—	—

Province	Total	Total Valid Vote	PSOE/PSC	AP/PDP	UCD	PCE/PSUC	CiU	Other
Cáceres	240,936	235,104	123,902	57,736	29,832	3,831	—	19,803
% Valid Votes			52.7	24.6	12.7	1.6	—	8.4
Seats			5	4	1	—	—	—
Cádiz	493,229	483,928	308,571	97,314	22,728	20,749	—	34,566
% Valid Votes			63.8	20.1	4.7	4.3	—	7.1
Seats			8	6	2	—	—	—
Castellón	270,118	261,293	130,200	73,826	33,547	8,280	—	15,440
% Valid Votes			49.8	28.3	12.8	3.2	—	5.9
Seats			5	3	2	—	—	—
Ciudad Real	285,326	279,112	151,168	79,037	29,443	7,627	—	11,837
% Valid Votes			54.2	28.3	10.5	2.7	—	4.2
Seats			5	3	2	—	—	—
Córdoba	435,097	420,958	243,428	90,023	28,414	37,555	—	21,538
% Valid Votes			57.8	21.4	6.7	8.9	—	5.1
Seats			7	5	2	—	—	—
La Coruña	523,019	511,030	196,359	180,619	66,689	9,113	—	58,250
% Valid Votes			38.4	35.3	13.0	1.8	—	11.4
Seats			9	4	4	1	—	—
Cuenca	135,447	132,333	59,676	42,502	20,163	4,257	—	5,735
% Valid Votes			45.1	32.1	15.2	3.2	—	4.3
Seats			4	2	2	—	—	—
Gerona	272,099	266,150	91,228	35,178	5,994	8,431	96,306	29,013
% Valid Votes			34.3	13.2	2.3	3.2	36.2	10.9
Seats			5	2	1	—	—	—
Granada	409,109	404,125	234,154	97,554	27,897	28,636	—	15,884
% Valid Votes			57.9	24.1	6.9	7.1	—	3.9
Seats			7	5	2	—	—	—
Guadalajara	91,174	88,917	34,212	33,748	12,049	3,392	—	5,516
% Valid Votes			38.5	38.0	13.6	3.8	—	6.2
Seats			3	2	1	—	—	—
Guipúzcoa	391,237	383,003	99,972	31,308	—	4,844	—	246,879
% Valid Votes			26.1	8.2	—	1.3	—	64.5
Seats			7	2	—	—	—	5
Huelva	223,318	219,736	139,420	45,755	17,174	7,976	—	9,411
% Valid Votes			63.4	20.8	7.8	3.6	—	4.3
Seats			5	4	1	—	—	—
Huesca	135,567	129,660	63,103	33,945	19,234	3,314	—	10,064
% Valid Votes			48.7	26.2	14.8	2.6	—	7.8
Seats			3	2	1	—	—	—

Appendix C

Province	Total	Total Valid Vote	PSOE/PSC	AP/PDP	UCD	PCE/PSUC	CiU	Other
Jaén	367,372	363,117	207,754	83,833	32,456	26,829	—	12,245
% Valid Votes			57.2	23.1	8.9	7.4	—	3.4
Seats		7	5	2	—	—	—	—
León	306,217	295,834	133,206	94,506	46,170	5,856	—	16,096
% Valid Vote			45.0	31.9	15.6	2.0	—	5.4
Seats		6	3	2	1	—	—	—
Lérida	203,403	200,158	70,821	31,832	11,484	5,495	56,188	24,338
% Valid Vote			35.4	15.9	5.7	2.7	28.1	12.1
Seats		4	2	1	—	—	1	—
Logroño	159,966	154,909	67,781	64,778	11,545	2,491	—	8,314
% Valid Votes			43.8	41.8	7.5	1.6	—	5.4
Seats		4	2	2	—	—	—	—
Lugo	194,639	190,387	53,263	88,462	34,567	1,391	—	12,704
% Valid Votes			28.0	46.5	18.2	.7	—	6.7
Seats		5	1	3	1	—	—	—
Madrid	2,791,248	2,726,787	1,439,137	891,372	92,508	137,459	—	166,311
% Valid Votes			52.8	32.7	3.4	5.0	—	6.1
Seats		32	18	11	1	1	—	1
Málaga	513,864	506,922	315,092	118,369	19,435	26,935	—	27,091
% Valid Votes			62.2	23.4	3.8	5.3	—	5.3
Seats		8	6	2	—	—	—	—
Murcia	541,158	531,107	270,552	189,542	34,354	20,065	—	16,494
% Valid Votes			50.9	35.7	6.5	3.8	—	3.1
Seats		8	5	3	—	—	—	—
Navarre	305,693	296,126	112,186	76,255	31,245	2,144	—	74,296
% Valid Votes			37.9	25.8	10.6	.7	—	25.1
Seats		5	3	2	—	—	—	—
Orense	182,217	176,496	50,619	63,801	52,282	1,620	—	8,174
% Valid Votes			28.7	36.1	29.6	.9	—	4.6
Seats		5	1	2	2	—	—	—
Oviedo (Asturias)	630,947	616,816	339,575	181,965	—	53,017	—	42,259
% Valid Votes			55.1	29.5	—	8.6	—	6.9
Seats		10	6	1	—	1	—	—
Palencia	118,129	115,203	49,756	44,965	12,330	2,679	—	5,473
% Valid Votes			43.2	39.0	10.7	2.3	—	4.8
Seats		3	2	1	—	—	—	—

Province	Total	Total Valid Vote	PSOE/PSC	AP/PDP	UCD	PCE/PSUC	CiU	Other
Las Palmas	346,873	333,551	109,366	97,701	45,905	—	—	80,579
% Valid Votes			32.8	29.3	13.8	—	—	24.2
Seats			6	3	2	1	—	—	—
Pontevedra	421,897	412,471	126,228	155,556	76,575	8,070	—	46,042
% Valid Votes			30.6	37.7	18.6	2.0	—	11.2
Seats			8	3	4	1	—	—
Salamanca	224,454	216,878	100,534	64,972	29,951	2,611	—	18,810
% Valid Votes			46.4	30.0	13.8	1.2	—	8.7
Seats			4	3	1	—	—	—
Sta. Cruz de Tenerife	327,099	317,752	130,249	78,174	61,436	—	—	47,893
% Valid Votes			41.0	24.6	19.3	—	—	15.1
Seats			7	4	2	1	—	—
Santander	311,415	300,397	135,987	117,567	16,265	9,265	—	21,313
% Valid Votes			45.3	39.1	5.4	3.1	—	7.1
Seats			5	3	2	—	—	—
Segovia	94,734	91,700	34,375	35,483	9,680	1,348	—	10,814
% Valid Votes			37.5	38.7	10.6	1.5	—	11.8
Seats			3	1	2	—	—	—
Sevilla	813,157	789,564	496,543	176,054	30,004	57,272	—	38,691
% Valid Votes			62.2	22.0	3.8	7.2	—	4.8
Seats			12	8	3	—	1	—
Soria	63,458	60,461	21,639	22,820	11,453	715	—	3,834
% Valid Votes			35.8	37.7	18.9	1.2	—	6.3
Seats			3	1	1	1	—	—
Tarragona	292,738	286,076	120,880	51,098	12,535	13,313	59,679	28,571
% Valid Votes			42.3	17.9	4.4	4.7	20.9	10.0
Seats			5	3	1	—	—	1	—
Teruel	96,743	94,351	38,834	31,779	15,770	1,124	—	6,844
% Valid Votes			41.2	33.7	16.7	1.2	—	7.3
Seats			3	2	1	—	—	—
Toledo	300,743	292,711	138,169	98,244	28,433	12,849	—	15,016
% Valid Votes			47.2	33.6	9.7	4.4	—	5.1
Seats			5	3	2	—	—	—
Valencia	1,224,632	1,192,533	635,522	350,281	52,768	63,026	—	90,936
% Valid Votes			53.3	29.4	4.4	5.3	—	7.6
Seats			15	10	5	—	—	—

Province	Total	Total Valid Vote	PSOE/PSC	AP/PDP	UCD	PCE/PSUC	CiU	Other
Valladolid	289,846	279,175	144,409	88,057	20,704	9,622	—	16,383
% Valid Votes			51.7	31.5	7.4	3.4	—	5.9
Seats		5	3	2	—	—	—	—
Vizcaya	678,998	660,952	196,674	79,866	—	14,537	—	369,875
% Valid Votes			29.8	12.1	—	2.2	—	56.0
Seats		10	4	1	—	—	—	5
Zamora	139,372	131,289	47,804	47,504	24,725	1,386	—	9,870
% Valid Votes			36.4	36.2	18.8	1.1	—	7.5
Seats		4	2	1	1	—	—	—
Zaragoza	513,479	494,755	255,402	156,800	34,044	16,492	—	32,017
% Valid Votes			51.6	31.7	6.9	3.3	—	6.5
Seats		8	5	3	—	—	—	—
Ceuta	26,117	25,571	11,698	7,647	1,870	188	—	4,141
% Valid Votes			45.7	30.0	7.3	.7	—	16.2
Seats		1	1	—	—	—	—	—
Melilla	23,351	22,981	10,291	5,551	3,083	188	—	3,868
% Valid Votes			44.8	24.2	13.4	.8	—	16.8
Seats		1	1	—	—	—	—	—
Total		21,427,236	20,906,781	10,127,092	5,548,335	1,393,574	846,802	772,728	2,218,250
Percent			48.4	26.5	6.7	4.1	3.7	10.6
Seats		350	202	107	11	4	12	14

Source: Alejandro Munoz Alonso, *Las Elecciones del Cambria* (Madrid: Editorial Argos Vergara, 1984).

The AP/PDP column includes votes cast by the following coalitions:
AP–PDP–PDL–UCD in Alava, Guipúzcoa, and Vizcaya
AP–PDP–UV in Alicante; Castellón and Valencia
AP–PDP–PAR in Huesca, Teruel, and Zaragoza
AP–PDP–UPN in Navarra
The UCD vote includes UCD–CC in Barcelona, Lerida, and Tarragona
The figures included in the "other" vote column for parties that received seats in the 1982 Congress of Deputies is as follows:

604,172 CDS—2 elected: one in Avila, one in Madrid
395,656 PNV—8 elected: one in Guipúzcoa and four in Vizcaya
210,601 HB—2 elected: one in Guipúzcoa and one in Vizcaya
138,116 ERC—one elected in Barcelona
100,326 EE—one elected in Guipúzcoa

CDS = Democratic and Social Center
PNV = National Basque Party
HB = Herri Batasuna
ERC = Catalan Republican Left
E   = Basque Left

Notes

Preface

1 Juan J. Linz, "The Party System in Spain: Past and Future," in Seymour Martin Lipset and Stein Rokkan, eds., *Party Systems and Voter Alignments: Cross-National Perspectives* (New York: Free Press, 1967), p. 245. This essay is but one of many extraordinarily insightful, detailed chapters Linz has written about the Civil War and the authoritarian regime that followed it.
2 Ibid.
3 Ibid.
4 Juan J. Linz, "Opposition in and under Authoritarian Regime: The Case of Spain," in Robert A. Dahl, ed., *Regimes and Opposition* (New Haven, Conn.: Yale University Press, 1973), p. 211.
5 For an excellent comparison of the 1931 and 1977-78 constituent Cortes, see the article by Richard Gunther and Roger A. Blough, "Religious Conflict and Consensus in Spain: A Tale of Two Constitutions," *World Affairs*, 143, no. 4 (Spring 1981): 366-412.
6 Samuel P. Huntington, *Political Order in Changing Societies* (New Haven, Conn.: Yale University Press, 1968), pp. 7-8.

Representative Government in Spain

1 The outstanding empirical study of the early twentieth-century Spanish electoral system is Javier Tusell, *Oligarquía y caciquismo en Andalucía (1890-1923)* [Oligarchy and caciquismo in Andalusia] (Barcelona: Planeta, 1976), but see also R. W. Kern, *Liberals, Reformers, and Caciques in Restoration Spain 1875-1909* (Albuquerque: University of New Mexico Press, 1974). The chief study of electoral campaigns and results under the old liberal system is Miguel M. Cuadrado, *Elecciones y partidos políticos de España (1868-1931)* [The elections and political parties of Spain (1868-1931)] (Madrid: Taurus, 1969).
2 There is no comprehensive history of the nineteenth-century liberal system in Spain. The best general account of the entire period is Raymond Carr, *Spain, 1808-1939* (Oxford: Oxford University Press, 1965). See also Stanley G. Payne, *A History of Spain and Portugal* (Madison: University of Wisconsin Press, 1973), vol. 2; Miguel Artola, *Partidos y programas políticos, 1808-1936* [Parties and political programs, 1808-1936] (Madrid: Aguilar, 1974); and Diego Sevilla Andrés, *Historia política de España, 1800-1967* [Political history of Spain, 1800-1967] (Madrid: Editora Nacional, 1968).
3 There is no adequate political or historical study of the Primo de Rivera regime. For a cogent new scholarly reassessment, see Shlomo Ben-Ami, "The Dictatorship of Primo de Rivera: A Political Reassessment," *Journal of Contemporary History* 12, no. 1 (January 1977): 45-84. There is a broader historical treatment by Stanley G. Payne, *Ejército y sociedad en la España liberal, 1808-1936* [Army and society in liberal Spain, 1808-1936] (Madrid: Akal Editor, 1977), 265-364.

4   The first attempt at a republic was the abortive Federal Republic of 1873-74.
5   On the development of the revolutionary process in Spain, see Stanley G. Payne, *The Spanish Revolution* (New York: W. W. Norton, 1970).
6   The best general treatment of the rightist forces in Republican Spain is R. A. H. Robinson, *The Origins of Franco's Spain* (Pittsburgh: Pittsburgh University Press, 1970). The failure of a genuine Christian Democratic party to emerge among the Catholics amid the polarization of the 1930s is examined by Javier Tusell, *Historia de la democracia cristiana en España* [History of Christian democracy in Spain] (Madrid: Editorial Cuadernos para el Diálogo, 1974). The middle-of-the-road radicals are extensively studied in Octavio Ruiz Manjón, *El Partido Republicano Radical* [The Radical Republican party] (Madrid: Editorial Tebas, 1976).
7   Payne, *Spanish Revolution*, p. 216. On the agrarian prerevolution in rural Spain, see E. E. Malefakis, *Agrarian Reform and Peasant Revolution in Spain* (New Haven, Conn.: Yale University Press, 1970).
8   The outstanding one-volume history of the conflict is Hugh Thomas, *The Spanish Civil War*, 3d ed., rev. and exp. (New York: Harper and Row, 1977). The classic account from the viewpoint of the moderate democratic left is Gabriel Jackson, *The Spanish Republic and Civil War* (Princeton, N.J.: Princeton University Press, 1965). The best right-wing treatment is Ricardo de la Cierva, *Historia ilustrada de la guerra civil española* [Illustrated history of the Spanish Civil War], 2 vols. (Barcelona: Ediciones Danae, 1971). The best treatments of Communist policy are Burnett Bolloten, *The Grand Camouflage* (New York: Praeger, 1961), and David T. Cattell, *Communism and the Spanish Civil War* (Berkeley: University of California Press, 1955).
9   The best biography of Franco in English is J. W. D. Trythall, *El Caudillo* (New York: McGraw-Hill, 1970). By far the most outstanding of the apologetic Spanish biographies is Ricardo de la Cierva, *Francisco Franco: Un siglo de España* [Francisco Franco: A century of Spain] (Madrid: Editora Nacional, 1973). Philippe Nourry, *Franco: La conquête du pouvoir, 1892-1937* [Franco: The conquest of power, 1892-1937] (Paris: Denoel, 1976), offers a perspicacious treatment of the formative phase of Franco's career.

Shaping the Constitution

Some of the ideas expressed in this essay were the result of debates on the Spanish constitution held at the Gesellschaft für Auslandskunde and the Spanish Institute in Munich, in February 1979, and at the Law School of the University of Valladolid. I would also like to thank Ambassador Mayer-Lindenberg, Manuel Muñoz Cortes, and my law students. Finally, Alfonso Ortí's lucid comments have always been of great help to me.

1   At the outset of our constitutional process, unfortunately, we did not have at our disposal a design as well thought out and fully developed as the blueprint by James Madison at the time of the American Constitutional Convention. The framers of the Weimar constitution, whatever its shortcomings, had Hugo Preuss's systematic *Denkschrift*, and the Fundamental Law of the Federal Republic of Germany was the product of extensive debate within the parties. On the United States, see C. Herman Prichett, *The American Constitution* (New York: McGraw-Hill, 1968), and Carl J. Friedrich and Robert McCloskey, *From the Declaration of Independence to the Constitution* (Indianapolis: Bobbs Merrill, 1954). Regarding Weimar, see Hugo Preuss, *Das Wert von Weimar, Aufbau und Verteidigung, in Staat, Recht, und Freiheit, aus 40 Jahren deutscher Politik und Geschichte* [Building and defending the Weimar political system, in the state, law, and freedom, from forty years of German politics and history] (Hildesheim: George Olms Verlagsbuchhandlung, 1964). On Bonn's Fundamental Law, see Werner Sorgel, *Konsensus und Interessen: Eine Studie*

zur Entstehung des Grundgesetzes für die Bundesrepublik Deutschland [Consensus and interests: An essay on the origins of the German Federal Republic's Fundamental Law] (Stuttgart: Ernst Klett Verlag, 1969). The level of improvisation in the Spanish drafting process recalls the writing of the Fifth Republic constitution. See Stanley H. Hoffman, "The French Constitution of 1958: I. The Final Text and its Prospects," *American Political Science Review* (March 1959); Nicholas Wahl, "The French Constitution of 1958: II. The Initial Draft and its Origins," *American Political Science Review* (March 1959); Henry W. Ehrmann, "Die Verfassungsentwicklung im Frankreich der Funften Republik" [Constitutional evolution in the France of the Fifth Republic], *Jahrbuch des offentlichen Rechts*, Neue Folge, vol. 10 (Tübingen: J. C. B. Mohr [Paul Siebeck], 1961). Whereas in France it was primarily the Union for the New Republic (UNR) that improvised its responses to the issues, in Spain all parties did so.

2 The Socialist party has always regarded freedom as essential to internal party life. Party discipline is enforced in decisions of political organs or when a vote comes up, but the party has never sought to influence the professional or intellectual work of its members.

3 See Juan J. Linz, "The Spanish Party System," in Seymour Martin Lipset and Stein Rokkan, eds., *Party System and Voter Alignments* (New York: Free Press, 1967). See also the following works by Antonio López Pina, "Spain: From Dictatorship to Constitutional Monarchy," in *Proceedings, Workshops of the European Consortium for Political Research* (Berlin, 1977); "Das spanische Parteiensystem," *Berichte* (Munich, May-June 1977); *La españa democrática y europa* (Madrid: Editorial Cambio 16, 1977); *Poder y clases sociales* (Madrid: Ediciones Tecnos, 1978).

4 See López Pina, *La españna democrática*.

5 See Twenty-seventh PSOE Congress (Madrid: Edicíon del Partido Socialista Obrero Español, 1977).

6 Chamber of Deputies, *Minutes*, 27 July 1977.

7 Name given to the military movement against the Second Republic led by General Franco. Chamber of Deputies, *Minutes*, no. 59, 5 May 1978.

8 Ibid.

9 Ibid.

10 Ibid.

11 Ibid. *Pacto foral* means a pact based on the old charters (*fueros*); see further footnote 21.

12 Chamber of Deputies, *Minutes*, no. 60, 8 May 1978.

13 Seven deputies drafted the first constitutional proposal, which became the working document of the Constitutional Committee. The revised text was later debated and voted on article by article by the full Chamber of Deputies and then by the Senate. Before this took place, more than one thousand amendments had been presented.

14 In the spring of 1978 Tierno Galván's Popular Socialist party merged with the PSOE, of which Tierno Galván became honorary president.

15 The minutes demonstrate how much Peces-Barba's approach toward the constitution represented only the Christian perspective within the socialist parliamentary party. Several other approaches were also represented, by Deputies Luis Gómez Llorente and Jóan Reventós (socialist historical legacy), Senator Fernández Viagas (theory of justice and law), and Senator López Pina (political theory of the constitution and the political regime). Beyond the party working groups each contributed to the parliamentary debates and thus enriched the contribution of the socialists.

16 Quotations from the Spanish constitution in this chapter are from the English edition published by the Servicio Central de Publicaciones/Presidencia del Gobierno (no. 180, extra/SEPARATA, Madrid, October-December 1978). A few details of style have been altered (in this quotation the word "Spanish" has been capitalized), and some terms have been

338   Notes: Shaping the Constitution

substituted to conform to usage in this book (prime minister has been used instead of president of government, for example, and Chamber of Deputies instead of Congress of Deputies).

17 Chamber of Deputies, *Minutes*, no. 64, 11 May 1978.
18 Senate, *Minutes*, no. 39, 18 August 1978.
19 The Law for Political Reform (discussed in more detail in the next chapter) provided for the legal dismantling of the Francoist regime. It was announced on television by Prime Minister Suárez on 11 September 1976, ratified by the Cortes on 18 November 1976, and approved in a referendum on 15 December 1976.
20 Senate, *Minutes*, no. 55, 14 September 1978.
21 The Basque nationalists' position is grounded in the special status enjoyed by the Basque country under the ancien régime. Absolutist theorists from Bodin to Mariana spoke of basic laws in each kingdom that the monarch had to uphold. The root of the Basque claims grew from the monarch's oath to respect the provinces' status, in return for which he demanded allegiance from his subjects. The privileges accorded Vizcaya, Guipúzcoa, and Alava, which related mainly to military service and taxes, were part of the complex infrastructure of rights and duties that characterized society under the ancien régime.

Spain's liberal constitution of 1837 clashed with the privileges of the Basques on several points. Article 6, for example, stated that the obligation of every Spaniard was "to take up arms in defense of his country" and "to contribute according to his means to the expenses of the state." In 1839, after the First Carlist War, the liberal regime passed a law confirming "the priveleges of the Basque and Navarre regions, provided they do not run counter to the constitutional unity of the monarchy." This committed the government to proposing modifications in the *fueros*—old charters—that would reconcile the provinces' traditional rights and privileges with the general interests of the nation and respect for the constitution.

Throughout the nineteenth century the supporters of regional privilege, as well as reactionary traditionalists like the Carlists, opposed, sometimes violently, the liberalizing and modernizing tendencies promoted by progressive forces.

22 The Cortes approved the Statutes of Autonomy for the Basque Country and Catalonia— Organic Laws of 18 December 1979. The statutes concede a very broad area of jurisdiction to the autonomous institutions within the framework of a federal regime, the only important reservation being that of sovereignty. In June 1980 the Cortes approved the Organic Law for Financing of Autonomous Communities. In May and June 1981, at the request of the government, a commission of experts drafted a report to serve as a basis for the Organic Law for the Harmonization of the Autonomy Process. Article 150.3 of the constitution states: "The state may enact laws establishing the principles necessary for harmonizing the rule-making provisions of the self-governing communities, even in the case of matters over which jurisdiction has been conferred upon the latter, when this is necessary in the general interest. It is incumbent upon the Cortes General, by an absolute majority of the members of each Chamber, to evaluate this decision."

In accordance with this article, the government sent a communication to the Cortes including a copy of the proposed organic law. On 29 September the Chamber of Deputies approved the law with an absolute majority, and the plenary session of the chamber made a concrete pronouncement of a series of harmonizing principles, the first of which refers to the cooperation between state authorities and those of the autonomous communities. A second principle affects relations among the autonomous communities and provincial councils. The preparation of standards or programs of national accountability will also be subject to harmonization, as will be organization and jurisdiction of legal corporations that represent economic or professional interests. Last but not least, the new law also seeks to harmonize the thorny question of civil service.

23 Chamber of Deputies, *Minutes*, no. 69, 18 May 1978.
24 Article 27 states:
    (1) Everyone is entitled to education. Freedom of instruction is recognized.
    (2) Education shall have as its objective the full development of the human personality compatible with respect for the democratic principles of coexistence and for fundamental rights and liberties.
    (3) The public authorities guarantee the right of parents to ensure that their children receive religious and moral instruction compatible with their own convictions.
    (4) Basic education is compulsory and free.
    (5) The public authorities guarantee the right of everyone to education, through general planning of education, with the effective participation of all parties concerned and the setting up of teaching establishments.
    (6) The right of individuals and legal entities to set up teaching establishments is recognized, provided they are compatible with respect for constitutional principles.
    (7) Teachers, parents, and, when appropriate, pupils shall participate in the control and management of all the centers maintained by the administration with public funds, under the terms to be laid down by the law.
    (8) The public authorities shall inspect and standardize the educational system to guarantee compliance with the law.
    (9) The public authorities shall help teaching establishments that meet the requirements to be laid down by the law.
    (10) The autonomy of the universities is recognized, under terms to be laid down by the law.
25 See the speech by Olarra, senator by royal appointment, in the plenary session of the Senate. Senate, *Minutes*, no. 61, 28 September 1978.
26 See Ernst Fraenkel, *Representative und plebiscitäre Komponente im Verfassungssystem* [Representative and plebiscitary components of the constitutional system] (Tubingen: J. C. B. Mohr [Paul Siebeck], 1958).
27 The powers of the Senate as stated in the constitution include the establishment of investigative commissions (article 76.1); legislative initiative (articles 87.1 and 89.2); the right to veto bills (article 90.2); the right to question members of the government (article 111.1); under special circumstances, the use of the state's coercive power over nationalities and regions (article 155.1); and the distribution of funds to compensate for regional inequalities (article 158.2).
28 See Senator López Pina's speech in Senate, *Minutes*, no. 62, 29 September 1978.
29 See López Pina, "En torno a la ley electoral," and Antonio López Pina, *Estructuras electorales contemporaneas* [Contemporary electoral structures] (Madrid: Tecnos, 1970).
30 See López Pina, in Senate, *Minutes*, no. 62.
31 Peter McDonough, Antonio López Pina, and Samuel H. Barnes, "The Spanish Public in Political Transition," *British Journal of Political Science* 2 (January 1981): 49–79; and Peter McDonough and Antonio López Pina, "Cleavages in Spanish Politics: Regionalism, Religiosity, and Social Class," in Russell J. Dalton, Paul Allen Beck, et al., eds., *Electoral Change in Advanced Industrial Democracies— Dealignment or Realignment?* (Princeton, N.J.: Princeton University Press, 1984).

Electoral Rules and Candidate Selection

1 See, for example, the testimony of G. Carcassone and P. Subra de Bieusses, *L'Espagne ou la démocratie retrouvée* [Spain or democracy rediscovered] (Paris: Enaj, 1978), p. 11. We

340   Notes: Electoral Rules and Candidate Selection

mention this because the restoration of democracy in Spain has awakened hope in countries under authoritarian regimes, especially in Latin America, that they might follow the Spanish example, which, unfortunately, may not always be possible.

2   See Jorge de Esteban, "Desarrollo político y régime constitucional español" [Political development and the Spanish constitutional system], *Sistema* (May 1973), pp. 77ff.
3   J. de Esteban and L. López Guerra, *De la dictadura a la democracia* [From dictatorship to democracy] (Madrid: Facultad De Derecho, 1979), pp. 3ff.
4   See J. de Esteban and L. López Guerra, *La crisis del estado franquista* [The crisis of the Francoist state] (Barcelona: Labour, 1977), pp. 118ff.
5   See Juan J. Linz, "An Authoritarian Regime: Spain," in E. Allardt and Y. Littunen, eds., *Cleavages, Ideologies, and Party Systems* (Helsinki: Westmarck Society, 1964).
6   Robert A. Dahl, *Polyarchy* (New Haven, Conn.: Yale University Press, 1971).
7   This process is outlined in J. de Esteban, S. Varela, L. López Guerra, J. L. García Ruíz, and F. J. García Fernández, *Desarrollo político y constitución española* [Political development and the Spanish constitution] (Barcelona: Ariel, 1973).
8   See Maurice Duverger, *Lettre ouverte aux socialistes* [Open letter to the socialists] (Paris: Albin Michel, 1976), p. 144.
9   See de Esteban and López Guerra, *De la dictadura*, p. 145.
10 In Franco's Cortes, a portion of the representatives (*procuradores*) were elected by heads of families and married women after 1967. See table 1.4 in the first chapter of this volume.
11 See de Esteban and López Guerra, *De la dictadura*, p. 207.
12 See the well-known works by Maurice Duverger, Georges Lavau, Giovanni Sartori, and Douglas W. Rae. The influence of this assumption during the drafting of the electoral law may be seen in *Ley electoral y consecuencias políticas* [Electoral law and political consequences] (Madrid: Citep, 1977).
13 See de Esteban and López Guerra, *De la dictadura*, p. 236.
14 See de Esteban et al., *El proceso electoral* [The electoral process] (Barcelona: Labour, 1977), p. 374.
15 Beginning with the elections of 1 March 1979, the three island provinces elected a total of sixteen senators in accordance with article 69 of the constitution already in effect.
16 On the proposals presented by the opposition, see de Esteban and López Guerra, *De la dictadura*, pp. 215ff. See also F. de Carreras and J. M. Vallés, *Las elecciones* (Barcelona: Blume, 1977), p. 312.
17 For example, the minimum of two representatives per province and matters regarding ineligibility. De Esteban et al., *El proceso electoral*, p. 375, argues that it would have been more equitable to have stipulated one representative per province, which would logically have benefited opposition.
18 For the first time in more than one hundred years, there are today no Spanish political exiles.
19 According to Carcassone and Subra de Bieusses, *L'Espagne ou la democratie retrouvée*, p. 62, if the number of ineligibilities were a criterion for democracy, Spain would be a shining example.
20 Note that in the French Fifth Republic, under General de Gaulle's constitution, membership in the executive branch is incompatible with membership in the legislative branch.
21 Cf. A. de Miguel, *Sociologia del franquismo* [A sociology of Francoism] (Barcelona: Euros, 1975).
22 Cf. F. González Ledesma et al., *Las elecciones del cambio* [The elections of change] (Barcelona: Plaza-Janes, 1977), p. 126.
23 For an explanation of the d'Hondt highest-average formula, see Douglas W. Rae, *The*

Political Consequences of Electoral Laws, rev. ed. (New Haven, Conn.: Yale University Press, 1971), pp. 31-33. Although the d'Hondt method produces inequalities that benefit the large parties, the omission of remainders is what most hurts minorities. See M. Caciagli, "Le nouve elezioni politiche in Spagna" [The new political elections in Spain], *Il Mulino* (March 1979), p. 290. See also de Esteban et al., *El proceso electoral*, p. 374.

24 The decree does, however, allow the presentation of lists for senatorial elections, and this was done in some districts. See P. Pérez Tremps, "La ley para la reforma política" [The law for political reform], *Revista de la Facultad de Derecho de la Universidad Complutense* 54 (1978): 154.

25 This view is expressed in de Esteban et al., *El proceso electoral*, p. 374.

26 See Pérez Tremps, "La ley para la reforma política," pp. 154-55.

27 See L. Sánchez Agesta, *Ley electoral* [Electoral law] (Madrid: Ediciones Revista Derecho Privado, 1977), p. 36.

28 He alluded to this in the inauguration speech to the Cortes in July 1977.

29 See J. de Esteban, F. M. García Fernández, E. Espin, *Esquemas del constitucionalismo español* [Outlines of Spanish constitutionalism] (Madrid: Servicio de publicaciones de la Facultad de Derecho de la Universidad de Madrid, 1977).

30 More discussion of this point may be found in J. de Esteban and López Guerra et al., *El regimen constitucional espanol* [The Spanish constitutional system] (Barcelona: Labor, 1980).

31 The most noticeable influences are those of the Portuguese constitution of 1974, the Italian constitution of 1947, the German constitution of 1949, and the French constitution of 1958.

32 Only the Basque representatives rejected the text. This exception underlines the fact that the Basque problem is the only serious threat to Spanish democracy.

33 The Organic Electoral Law had not been written as of June 1981. Organic laws must be approved by an absolute majority of votes in the chamber.

34 According to data gathered in December 1978, 2,489,655 eighteen-year-olds participated in the elections of 1 March 1977.

35 In Spain television is a state monopoly, though radio is both public and private.

36 The PSOE and the Popular Socialist party were legalized on 17 February 1977. The Spanish Communist party had to wait until 9 April 1977.

37 The Popular Alliance was a coalition of several parties headed by former Franco ministers. It was founded in October 1976 and held its first congress in March 1977. See Andrés de Blas, "UCD, PSOE, PCE, y AP: Las posiciones programáticas" [UCD, PSOE, PCE, and AP: Programmatic positions] in Raúl Morodo et al., *Los partidos políticos en España* [Political parties in Spain] (Barcelona: Labour, 1979), pp. 156-86.

38 See the warning call of Ricardo de la Cierva, "A dónde nos lleva el colapso del Centro?" [Where is the collapse of the center taking us?], *El País*, 20 April 1977.

39 See Fernando Alvarez de Miranda (later Speaker of the Chamber of Deputies), "El difícil parto del Centro Democrático" [The difficult birth of the Democratic Center], *El País*, 15 May 1977. The Democratic Center changed its name to UCD (Unión del Centro Democrático).

40 The groups that became part of the EE included the ANV, EIA, ES, ESEI, LAB, and MCE. The PDC incorporated Convergencia Democrática de Catalunya (Democratic Convergence of Catalonia, CDC), headed by Jordi Pujol and Esquerra Democrática de Catalunya (Catalan Democratic Left, EDC), headed by Ramón Trías Fargas.

41 See *El País*, 5 April 1977, for the PSOE-PSC agreement.

42 In March 1977 the government-sponsored FSI (Federacíon Social Independiente, or Independent Social Federation) was created. It included many supporters and friends of Prime

Minister Suárez. They later joined the Union of the Democratic Center, but most of Suárez's political friends remained "independents without party."

43 See "Candidaturas: Decide la Moncloa" [Candidacies: The Moncloa decides], *Blanco y Negro*, May 11-17, 1977; and "El desembarco de la Moncloa" [The landing of the Moncloa], 14 May 1977. Veteran members of the UCD expected that Suárez would propose only six or seven candidates. Instead, he named more than one hundred. In some places, like Catalonia, the center parties left the UCD, whose lists had to be composed of "independents."

44 See J. García de Madariaga, "Porque nos fuímos del Centro" [Why we left the center], *El País*, 13 May 1977. See also *El País*, 31 January 1979.

45 *El País*, 5 April 1977.

46 In some districts, however, the PCE supported the candidates presented by the PSP.

47 *El País*, 28 January 1979.

48 During the Franco regime, several newspapers belonged to the government or to official organizations. The democratic regime closed some of those newspapers and threatened to eliminate all of the state-owned press.

49 Pedro J. Ramírez, *Asi se ganaron las elecciones 1979* [How the 1979 elections were won] (Madrid: Prensa Española, 1979), p. 86. Ramírez gives an interesting journalistic account of the campaign, with some bias in favor of the UCD. Also interesting is his previous book, *Asi de ganaron las elecciones 1977*.

50 J. García Morillo, "El desarrollo de la campana" [The campaign], in *Las Elecciones legislativas del 1 de Marzo de 1979* (Madrid: Centro de Investigaciones Sociologicas, 1979), written under the direction of J. de Esteban and L. López Guerra, p. 194.

51 Ibid., p. 193.

52 See the case of Laureano López Rodó, a former Franco minister, in Barcelona. *El País*, 17 January 1979.

53 García Morillo, "El desarrollo de la campaña," p. 195.

54 On the UCD organization, see P. Bofill Abeilhe, "La estructura interna" [Internal structure], in Morodo, *Los partidos políticos*, pp. 187-223.

55 García Morillo, "El Desarrollo de la campana," pp. 191-92.

56 Ramírez, *Asi se Ganaron*, p. 73. Also *El País*, 3 February, gives the following composition of the electoral committee: president, Adolfo Suárez; Members: Rafael Arias Salgado (general secretary of the UCD), Rodolfo Martín Villa (interior minister), Fernando Abril Martorell (minister for economic affairs), his brother, Joaquin Abril, and M. Nuñez.

57 Thus Ramírez, *Asi se ganaron*, p. 112.

58 Ibid, p. 72.

59 *Informaciones*, 2 January 1979.

60 Ramírez, "Asi se Ganaron," p. 106; *Informaciones*, 2 January 1979. "El aparato administrativo amenzado por las dimisiones" [The administration threatened by resignations], *Informaciones*, 3 January 1979. *Informaciones*, 6 January 1979 lists twenty administration officials authorized to resign.

61 See J. Oneto, "La campana de invierno" [The winter campaign], *Cambio 16*, 4 February 1979, p. 15.

62 *El País*, 19 January 1979.

63 García Morillo "El Desarrollo de la campaña," pp. 192-93; Ramírez, *Asi se ganaron*, pp. 108-10. See also the regional press, *El Correo Gallego*, 23 January and February 1979, *Diario de Pontevedra*, 4 February 1979, and the national press, *Diario 16*, 22 January 1979, *El País*, 23 January 1979, and so on.

64 See *El Periódico de Madrid*, 20 January 1979.

65 See Bofill Abeilhe, *La estructura interna*, and García Morillo, "Formación de candida-

turas." See also the interesting letter from the campaign coordinator for the Badajoz province published in *Hoy* (Badajoz), 24 January 1979.
66 *El País*, 2 January 1979.
67 García Morillo, "El desarrollo de la campaña," pp. 191–92.
68 The Confederal Committee, the highest national organ of the UGT, did not unanimously vote to support the PSOE in the elections. Several members were in favor of supporting other parties of the left. *Pueblo*, 13 February 1979. There were problems with the UGT in Vizcaya, Teruel, León, Jaén, and so on. See *El País*, 7 February 1979, and *Informaciones*, 8 January 1979.
69 Modesto Seara was initially nominated for the Senate, but he declined to run.
70 *El País*, 23 January 1979.
71 *El Periódico de Madrid*, 20 January 1979.
72 García Morillo, "El desarrollo de la campaña," p. 193.

The Transition from Below

1 According to the eighth transitory provision of the constitution, the prime minister could choose either to resign after the approval of the constitution—after which it would be up to the king to open the process of consultation with parliamentary leaders to propose a prime minister to the Chamber of Deputies—or to dissolve the Cortes and call for elections. Adolfo Suárez made the second choice, and on 29 December 1978, he announced the dissolution of the Cortes, with legislative elections to be held by 1 March and local elections by 3 April.
2 A set of political and economic agreements signed by the main political forces. After a personal initiative of Prime Minister Adolfo Suárez in the fall of 1977 and long negotiations, an agreement was reached between the UCD, the PSOE, the PCE, the Popular Socialist party (PSP), and the AP (the AP signed only the economic agreement). The main trade unions also signed the economic agreements, which included a promise of moderation in salary demands. See *Los pactos de la Moncloa: Texto completo del acuerdo sobre el programma de saneamiento y reforma de la economía y del acuerdo sobre el programa de actuación jurídica y política* [The Moncloa Agreements: Complete text of the agreement on the program of economic recovery and reform and of the agreement on the program of judicial and political action] (Madrid: Presidencia del Gobierno, 1977).
3 The main events in that regard were the provisional establishment of the Generalitat of Catalonia (by government decree) under the presidency of Josep Tarradellas, who returned from exile to take office in September 1977, and the establishment—provisional as well—of a General Council in the Basque country in December 1977. At the same time, during 1977 and 1978, the political forces negotiated the content of the statutes on regional self-government to be passed after the constitution. In other regions, with no previous experience of self-government, some steps were taken toward a provisional arrangement of autonomy.
4 One of the first acts of Parliament, in October 1977, was to pass an Amnesty Act intended to complete a cycle of measures implemented by the government in September 1976 and March 1977 forgiving any offense with a political motive. The only exception was denial of the request for reincorporation into the service of those army officers who had been condemned for belonging to the Democratic Military Union (UMD). The reason for that denial was military pressure.
5 The statistics on deaths from political violence illustrate the trend:

	Killed by ETA (Basque leftist separatist)	Killed by GRAPO (Marxist-leninist group)	Killed by extreme Right	Killed by Police and Civil Guard	Total
1968	2	0	0	0	2
1969	1	0	0	0	1
1970	0	0	0	1	1
1971	1	0	0	2	3
1972	6	0	0	1	7
1974	18	0	0	0	18
1975	14	7	0	2	23
1976	18	2	1	22	43
1977	11	8	8	23	50
1978	64	6	4	15	89
1979	67	29	10	20	126

Source: Rafael López-Pintor, "Los condicionamientos socioeconómicos de la acción política en la transición democratica" (Socioeconomic effects of political action during the transition to democracy), Revista Española de Investigáciones Sociológicas, 15 (1981): 21.

6 The elections were held during 1978 according to a schedule agreed upon by the Ministry of Labor and the main trade unions. Nationally the Workers' Commissions (*Comisiones Obreras*, affiliated with the Communists), won, followed by the General Workers' Union (*Unión General de Trabajadores*, affiliated with the Socialists). *Independientes* and *no afiliados* (different kinds of independent unions of workers) did rather well and together received roughly the same number of votes as the winner. See Victor Pérez Díaz, *Clase obrera, partidos y sindicatos* [Working class, parties and unions] (Madrid: Fundación INI, 1979).

7 On the eve of approval of the constitution, an intended coup d'état against the government, headed by Lieutenant Colonel Antonio Tejero under the name Operation Galaxy, was discovered and aborted. The verdict of the military court was ridiculous and provoking to democratic forces: six months in prison for Tejero. Two and a half years later the same officer headed the contingent of the Civil Guard that seized government and Parliament for eighteen hours in the most serious plot the system has been confronted with.

8 See Rafael López-Pintor and Ricardo Buceta, *Los españoles de los años 70: Una versión sociológica* [Spaniards in the decade of the 1970s: A sociological version] (Madrid: Tecnos, 1976); Antonio López Pina and Eduardo López Aranguren, *La cultura política de la España de Franco* [The political culture of Franco Spain] (Madrid: Taurus, 1976); Manuel Gomez-Reino et al., "Sociológia politica" [Political sociology], in FOESSA: *Estudio sociologico sobre la situación social de España* [FOESSA: Sociological study on the Spanish social situation] (Madrid: Euroamérica, 1976).

9 See Francisco Alvira et al., "La ideologia política" [Political ideology], in *La reforma política: La ideologia politica de los Espanoles* [Political reform: The political ideology of the Spanish people], (Madrid: Center for Sociological Studies, 1977); the most conclusive and insightful account of public opinion during the transition to democracy is Rafael López Pintor, "El estado de la opinión pública española y la transición a la democracia" [The state of Spanish public opinion and the transition to democracy], *Revista Espanola de Investigaciones Sociologicas*, no. 13 (1981): 7–47; see also Peter McDonough et al., "The Spanish Public in Political Transition," *British Journal of Political Science* 2 (1981).

10   See Alvira et al., "La ideologia política," p. 17. The poll was conducted by the Center for Sociological Research, using a sample of 976 people.
11   The turnout for the referendum was as follows:

Electoral census:	22,644,290	
Participation:	17,599,562	77.7%
Vote:		
Yes	16,573,180	94.2%
No	450,102	2.6%
Blank and null	576,280	3.3%
Abstention:	5,044,728	22.3%

Source: Central Electoral Commission.

The Democratic Opposition Platform (which included the main opposition parties and independent personalities) had campaigned for abstention. The ground for this position was not the substance of the bill (with which they basically agreed) but the lack of guarantees of political participation under fair conditions of the left and liberal parties in subsequent elections.

12   See Alvira et al., "La ideología política," p. 34. The poll was conducted by the Center for Sociological Research, using a sample of 1,008 people.
13   López-Pintor, "El estado de la opinión pública," p. 27.
14   The Popular Alliance won 8.21 percent of the vote (sixteen seats), and the fascist National Alliance of the Eighteenth of July got 0.62 percent and no seats; together they won 8.83 percent of the vote.
15   See José María Maravall, "Transición a la democracia: Alienamientos políticos y elecciones en España" [Transition to democracy: Political alignments and elections in Spain], *Sistema* 36 (1980): 86–89.
16   The percentages of votes won by the main "national" parties were as follows:

Right and Center		Left	
AP	8.2	PSP-US[a]	4.5
UCD	35.1	PSOE	29.2
		PCE	9.2
Total	43.3	Total	42.9

[a] Socialist Unity.

17   The UCD won 165 of the 350 seats in the Chamber of Deputies and was therefore eleven seats short of an absolute majority. The parliamentary situation of the party was rather comfortable for passing ordinary legislation: given the political diversity of the opposition groups in Parliament, the UCD could reasonably count on the abstention of the left or the right to win a relative majority. Nevertheless, on some occasions, the government was defeated on minor points either by the unanimous vote of all the opposition groups or by the absence of a significant number of its parliamentarians. See Victor Márquez Reviriego, *Apuntes parliamentarios: La tentación canovista* [Parliamentary notes: the "canovista" temptation] (Madrid: Saltes, 1978).
18   As Maravall points out, the 1977 election was the best electoral performance for the PSOE since its birth in 1878. In the last election of the Second Republic, the PSOE captured 21.4 percent of the seats in Congress; in the 1977 election, 33.7 percent. See José María Mara-

vall, "La alternativa socialista: La política y el apoyo electoral del PSOE" [The socialist alternative: the policies and electoral support of the PSOE], *Sistema* 35 (1980): 3.
19   The strategy of Manuel Fraga in this period was somewhat ambiguous. On the one hand he desperately made efforts to accommodate to the new democratic situation: for instance, in an unprecedented gesture he introduced Santiago Carrillo when the latter was for the first time invited to give a lecture at the conservative Club Siglo XXI [Twenty-first Century Club]. On the other hand, he frequently returned to his old authoritarian style and held opinions and attitudes on the borderline of the new political order. The returns of the 1979 election clearly suggest that this strategy had negative consequences for the party and its leader.
20   The Workers' Commissions and the UGT sat at the negotiating table for the economic agreement of the Moncloa Agreements and finally signed it (see footnote 6). The Confederation of Business Organizations (CEOE) participated indirectly, holding separate meetings with the government and the trade unions.
21   See John F. Coverdale, *The Political Transformation of Spain after Franco* (New York: Praeger, 1979), pp. 91–94, for an excellent critical discussion of the contents of the Moncloa Agreements.
22   See López-Pintor, "Los condicionamientos," p. 18.
23   In fact, as many recent polls show, once the tax reform became law, its evaluation became more and more negative among the population.
24   See Coverdale, *Political Transformation of Spain*, pp. 113–34, for a summary of the constitutional process; an analysis of the results of the constitutional referendum can be found in Juan Linz et al., *Informe sociológico sobre el cambio político en España, 1975-81* [Sociological report on the political change in Spain, 1975-1981] (Madrid: Euroamerica, 1981), pp. 311–36.
25   Coverdale, *Political Transformation of Spain*, p. 114.
26   The results of the vote in the Chamber of Deputies and in the Senate were as follows:

	Chamber	*Senate*
Absent	5	9
Yes	325	226
No	6	5
Abstention	14	8
Total	350	248

Source: El País, 1 November 1978.

27   These were the returns at the national level:

Electoral census:	26,561,819	
Participation:	17,972,511	(67.7%)
Vote		
Yes	15,782,639	(87.8%)
No	1,423,184	(7.9%)
Blank and null	766,688	(4.3%)
Abstention:	8,589,308	(32.3%)

Source: Central Electoral Commission

28   See Linz et al., *Informe sociológico*, p. 623.

29 For a detailed analysis of the referendum in the Basque provinces, see ibid., pp. 315ff.
30 A recent book on the transition period, written by two journalists of the liberal newspaper *El País*, is titled "From Consensus to Disenchantment." The title adequately summarizes the stance of the newspaper for which the authors worked during this period. See Bonifacio de la Cuadra and Soledad Gallego, *Del Consenso al desencanto* [From consensus to disenchantment] (Madrid: Saltes, 1981).
31 See footnote 5 on the increase of deaths from political violence. There was growing concern among the population about delinquency. In a survey conducted for the Center for Sociological Research in June 1978, 36 percent declared that they felt insecure in the streets, and 26 percent declared that security had decreased in the last year. See *Revista Española de Investigaciones Sociologicas* 4 (1978): 223–78.
32 Survey conducted by Consulta S.A. and published by *Cambio 16* on 9 January 1977.
33 Surveys conducted by the Center for Sociological Research in the last months of 1981 and the first months of 1982 found a much lower percentage of the population who evaluated the political situation as "very good" or "good" (from 10 to 13 percent).
34 The abundance of surveys on voting intentions contrasts with the relative scarcity of more in-depth research on political attitudes. Politicians and pollsters overestimated the importance of such predictive polls and neglected the collection of more structural information.
35 See Maravall, "La alternativa socialista," p. 18, for a critical analysis of the results.
36 The mean score on the left-right scale was 5.64 in July 1976 and 5.53 in January 1977, according to surveys carried out by DATA. At first glance, it might seem that there was an impressive shift leftward between 1977 and 1978. But the shift, rather than reflecting deep changes in the distribution of political attitudes, could be explained by the increasing acceptability of the term "left."

The Democratic Center and Christian Democracy in the Elections of 1977 and 1979

1 See especially the following articles by Juan Linz: "An Authoritarian Regime: Spain" in Erik Allardt and Yrjö Littunen, eds., "Cleavages, Ideologies, and Party Systems: Contributions to Comparative Political Sociology, Transactions of the Westermarck Society," vol. 10 (1964); "From Falange to Movimiento Organization," in Huntington and Moore, eds., *Authoritarian Politics in Modern Society: The Dynamics of One Party Systems* (New York: Basic Books, 1970); "Opposition in and under an Authoritarian Regime: The Case of Spain," in Robert Dahl, ed., *Regimes and Oppositions* (New Haven: Yale University Press, 1973).
2 These included Christian Social Democracy, led by José María Gil Robles; the Christian Democratic Left, led by another former minister of the Republican era, Manuel Giménez Fernández; the Spanish Union, a liberal group headed by Joaquín Satrústegui; and the Social Party of Democratic Action, founded by an old Falangist, Dionisio Ridruejo. See Javier Tusell, *La oposición democrática al franquismo, 1939-62* [The democratic opposition to Francoism, 1939-62] (Barcelona: Editorial Planeta, 1977).
3 On the Tácito team, see Alfonso Osorio, *Trayectoria política de un ministro de la Monarquía* [Political trajectory of a minister of the monarchy] (Barcelona: Editorial Planeta, 1980).
4 The EDC included not only the followers of Gil Robles (Christian Social Democracy, in 1975 renamed Popular Democratic Federation) and of Ruiz Giménez, but also the Basque Nationalist party (PNV), one of whose leaders from the republican period — José Antonio de Aguirre — had been an important advocate of cooperation between European Chris-

tian Democrats, and the Democratic Union of Catalonia, a Catholic nationalist party founded in the 1930s that had survived underground throughout the Francoist period. A local party from Valencia also joined. For the recent history of the Christian Democratic groups see: Jaime Gil Robles, *Federación Popular Democrática* [The Popular Democratic Federation] (Barcelona: Editorial Avance, 1976); Joaquín Antuna, Carlos Bru, Jaime Cortezo, and Eugenio Nasarre, *Izquierda Democrática* [The Democratic Left] (Barcelona: Editorial Avance, 1976); Alvaro Santamarina, *Joaquín Ruiz Giménez: Perfil humano y político* [Joaquín Ruiz Giménez: Personal and political profile] (Madrid: Editorial Cambio 16, 1977). See also José María Gil Robles, *Un final de jornada* (Madrid: n.p., 1977), which quotes the memorandum sent to the king, campaign speeches, and an analysis of the defeat of the leading Christian democrat.

5 On the liberals, see *Partido Democráta: Federación de partidos demócratas y liberales* [The Democratic party: A federation of democratic and liberal parties] (Madrid: Unión editorial, 1977); Executive Committee of the Democratic Party of Castile, *Partido Democrata* [The Democratic party] (Barcelona: Editorial Avance, 1976); Lorenzo Contreras, *Joaquín Satrústegui: Perfil humano y político* [Joaquín Satrústegui: Personal and political profile] (Madrid: Editorial Cambio 16, 1977); Ramon Pi, *Joaquín Garrigues Walker: Perfil humano y político* [Joaquín Garrigues Walker: Personal and political profile] (Madrid: Editorial Cambio 16, 1977).

6 On Ridruejo's party, see *Dionisio Ridruejo: De la Falange a la oposición* [Dionisio Ridruejo: From the Falange to the opposition] (Madrid: Editorial Taurus, 1976). Other social democrats joined the Social Democratic Federation, founded shortly after Suárez became prime minister with Francisco Fernández Ordoñez as its president. See Francisco Fernández Ordoñez, *Qué son los socialdemócratas?* [What are social democrats?] (Barcelona: Editorial La Gaya Ciencia, 1976).

7 A little before the fall of the Arias government, thirty-two members of the opposition (of whom, significantly, fifteen were identified afterward with the UCD) had issued a statement very critical of Suárez—but later, when Democratic Coordination came to speak unfavorably of Suárez, a similar group pointed out how much the government's attitude had changed.

8 Unpublished poll for the Konrad Adenauer Stiftung.

9 Results of the poll in *Revista Española de Opinión Pública* 48 (April-June 1977): 395ff.

10 Some previously isolated figures also participated in this group, notably Victor Carrascal and Rodríguez Solar.

11 Gil Robles and Satrústegui were cool toward the alliance, and the UDE was still exclusively Francoist.

12 Gil Robles made these remarks at a meeting in Madrid at the end of 1976 attended by some two thousand representatives of Spanish Christian democratic groups as well as, among others, the Belgian prime minister and a French minister. European Christian democracy did not decisively support the small Spanish groups: on the contrary, the Germans insisted that their Spanish counterparts should try to open their ranks to sectors previously linked with Francoism, and numerous foreign participants praised the Suárez government, about which the Spaniards remained cool.

13 The principal source on the 1977 election is the Madrid press: above all the dailies *El País*, *Ya*, *ABC*, *Informaciones*, and *Diario 16*. Also important have been interviews with participants in the events described, especially Fernando Alvarez de Miranda, José Luis Alvarez, Iñigo Cavero, Antonio Fontán, and Juan Antonio Ortega Díaz Ambrona. See also Pedro J. Ramírez, *Así se ganaron las elecciones* [How the elections were won] (Barcelona: Editorial Planeta, 1977); and Pedro Calvo Hernando, *Juan Carlos, escucha: Primer balance de España sin Franco* [Listen, Juan Carlos: A first assessment of Spain without

14 Franco] (Madrid: Ultramar ediciones, 1976). Documents issued by the various political groups have also been consulted and will not be cited in detail.

14 Areilza's version of what happened is given in José Oneto, *José María de Areilza: Perfil humano y político* [José María de Areilza: Personal and political profile] (Madrid: Editorial Cambio 16, 1976). See also José María de Areilza, *Diario de un ministro de la Monarquía* [Diary of a minister of the monarchy] (Barcelona: Editorial Planeta, 1977).

15 These were the Agrupación Regional Extremeña [Estremaduran Regional Group, AREX] (Sánchez de León), the Partido Liberal Social Andaluz [Andalusian Social Liberal party] (Manuel Clavero), the Independent Galician party (José Luis Meilán Gil), the Unión Canaria [Canary Union] (Lorenzo Olarte), and the Democratic Union of Murcia (Antonio Pérez Crespo).

16 This happened in Estremadura, where AREX took seven of twelve slots and Juan Antonio Ortega, one of the secretaries of the Popular party, resigned, and in Galicia, where the primacy conceded to the Independent Galician party led some anti-Francoist groups to withdraw. The predominance of the PSLA in Andalusia was less exclusive. There were also tensions in Valencia and Navarre.

17 Civil governors had a hand in candidate selection in other parts of Spain too. In Jaén the governor gave the list a very conservative cast; in Valencia the governor promoted a group called ANEPA, of Francoist origin, which also called itself the Popular Center.

18 In Catalonia the Democratic Union allied itself before the election with a group called the Catalan Center, made up of liberal and democratic businessmen without previous political affiliation. It had hopes of becoming the Catalan and Catalanist expression of the Suárez center (which did not happen) or of allying itself with the Democratic Pact for Catalonia of Jordi Pujol. Though it was the party identified most closely with Christian Democracy, the Democratic Union did not seem to represent an option of consequence. The Galician Popular party, another regional variant of Christian Democracy, entered the elections in alliance with a small group called the Social Democratic party, of very similar non-Marxist complexion. Perhaps the most surprising alliance was that in Albacete between elements of Ruiz Gimenez's Democratic Left and parts of the Popular Socialist party of Enrique Tierno Galván. In Aragon the local Christian Democrats ran their list in competition with both the UCD and the EDC. In Soria the Christian Democratic Team ran its own list, as did the Popular party of the Canaries, which had been interested in a possible link with the Christian Democrats, and the miniscule non-nationalist Christian Democracy of Catalonia.

19 As opinion polls showed, Suárez was the first or second choice of a full 49 percent of the voters—as compared with a mere 19 percent for Felipe González. These data are contained in an unpublished poll prepared for the Konrad Adenauer Stiftung.

20 For a commentary on the election results, see Javier Tusell, "Un primer análisis de los resultados electorales" [A preliminary analysis of the election results], and Juan Linz, "Un sociólogo ante la primera elección democrática [A sociologist looks at the first democratic election], in *La Corona y la nueva sociedad española ante un ano histórico: Ciclo de conferencias pronunciadas en el Club Siglo XXI durante el curso 1976-1977* [The Crown and the new Spain in a historic year: Twenty-first Century Club lectures, 1976-1977] (Madrid: Fomento Editorial, 1977).

21 Interestingly enough, the correlation between the PSOE vote in the two elections is even greater: .59. See Javier Tusell, "Las elecciones del Frente Popular en España," *Cuadernos para el Diálogo*, 1971.

22 The Andalusian Regionalist Union took a maximum of four percent in Cádiz; Agrarian Social Action garnered only 2.6 percent in Jaén; and in Teruel, Logroño, and Ceuta, small centrist groups obtained a few votes.

23 On the Madrid results see *Nuestra Bandera*, the theoretical journal of the Communist

party in Spain, vol. 87, and *Diario 16* 12, no. 7 (1977).
24 Gil Robles, *Un final de jornada.*
25 See Raul Morodo et al., *Los partidos políticos en España* (Political parties in Spain] (Barcelona: Labor, 1979).
26 See the Catholic daily *Ya*, especially the editorial of 13 January 1979.
27 See in particular, *La reforma política: La ideología política de los españoles* [Political reform: The political ideology of the Spanish people] (Madrid: Centro de Investigaciones Sociológicas, 1977); Francisco Alvira et al., *Partidos politicso e ideologías en España: Un análisis de la evolucion de la ideología política de los españoles* [Political parties and ideologies in Spain: An analysis of the evolution of the political ideology of the Spanish people] (Madrid: Centro de Investigaciones Sociológicas, 1978). Also used were studies still unpublished in 1981.
28 The principal source on the election campaign was the Madrid press. See also Pedro J. Ramírez, *Así se ganaron las elecciones 1979* [How the 1979 elections were won] (Madrid: Prensa Española, 1979). Also Jorge de Esteban and Luis López Guerra, *Las elecciones legislativas del 1 Marzo 1979* [The legislative elections of 1 March 1979] (Madrid: Centro de Investigaciones Sociológicas,
29 Notably Jesús Sancho Rof, subsecretary of the interior, José Luis Leal, subsecretary for economics, and Eduardo Merigó, subsecretary for public works.
30 See, for example, José María Gil Robles in *ABC*, 14 January 1979.
31 There were regional differences in turnover. In Catalonia only one in six of the candidates running in March 1979 had run in 1977.
32 *La solución a un reto* [Solution to a challenge] (Madrid: Union Editorial, 1979).
33 See Guillermo Medina, a UCD candidate in Seville, in *El País*, 3 February 1979.
34 *Ya*, 14 February 1979.
35 *Ya*, 27 February 1979.
36 Official returns published by the Central Electoral Junta under the title *Elecciones generales del primero de Marzo 1979: Actas de escrutinio general* [General elections of 1 March 1979: Records of the general election] (Madrid, 1979). Preliminary returns were released by the Ministry of the Interior, and the National Institute of Statistics published final returns by district some months after the election. All of this is a great improvement over the 1977 election, for which no final electoral returns have ever been published. Appendix B in this volume gives the preliminary returns for 1977 and the Central Election Junta's returns for 1979, by province.
37 Unpublished survey for the Konrad Adenauer Stiftung.
38 There are several recent monographs and regional studies of Spanish electoral sociology based on the results of the 15 June elections. See *Perspectiva Social*, no. 10, Institut Catolic d'Estudis Socials de Barcelona: Sospedra et al., *Las Elecciones del 15 de Junio en la circunscripción de Valencia* [The 15 June elections in the district of Valencia] (Valencia: University of Valencia Secretaría de Publicaciones, 1978); Estudis electorals a cura de l'équip de sociología electoral (UAB), "Sobre les eleccions legislatives del 1977" [On the legislative elections of 1977] (Barcelona: mimeograph, April 21-22, 1978); *Publicaciones de la Fundació Jaume Bofill* [Publications of the Jaume Bofill Foundation] (Barcelona: n.p., December 1978); Antonio Checa Godoy, *Las elecciones de 1977 en Andalucía [The 1977 elections in Andalusia]* (Granada: Aljibe, 1978); Montserrat Terradas i Batlle, *Les elecciones del 15 de juny a les comarques gironines: Análisi geografico* (Gerona: Universidad Autónoma de Barcelona, Colegi Universitari de Girona, 1978).
39 For a general interpretation, see José María Maravall, "Political Cleavages in Spain and the 1979 General Election," *Government and Opposition* 14, no. 3 (Summer 1979).

The Socialist Alternative

1 On the distribution of the 1936 vote see Juan J. Linz, "The Party System of Spain: Past and Future," in Seymour Martin Lipset and Stein Rokkan, eds., *Party Systems and Voter Alignments* (New York: Free Press, 1967), pp. 197-282; Juan J. Linz and J. de Miguel, "Hacia un análisis regional de las elecciones de 1936 en España" [Toward a regional analysis of the 1936 elections in Spain], *Revista Española de la Opinió Pública* 48 (1977):27-68; Javier Tusell, "The Popular Front Elections in Spain, 1936," in Stanley G. Payne, ed., *Politics and Society in Twentieth Century Spain* (New York: New Viewpoints, 1976), pp. 93-119.
2 Good analyses of the dilemma of revolution and reform in the history of the PSOE may be found in S. Juliá, *La izquierda del PSOE* [The left of the PSOE] (Madrid: Siglo XXI, 1977); A. de Blas, *El socialismo radical en la 2ª República* [Radical socialism in the Second Republic] (Madrid: Tucar, 1978); A. Balcells, *Teoría y práctica del movimiento obrero en España* [Theory and practice of the working-class movement in Spain] (Valencia: Fernando Torres, 1977).
3 There were thirteen ordinary congresses in exile (1944, 1946, 1947, 1950, 1952, 1955, 1958, 1961, 1964, 1967, 1970, 1972, and 1974) and one extraordinary congress (1951).
4 This persistence is noted by H. Pacheco, "El socialismo español y la realidad española" [Spanish socialism and Spanish reality], *Nuevos Horizontes*, vol 5-6 (1968). This magazine expressed the views of E. Tierno-Galván and his group of supporters, who were then trying to set up a Socialist party of the Interior (PSI), independent of the organization of the PSOE.
5 Among these delegates were some present-day leaders of the PSOE and UGT, including Carmen García Bloise and Manuel Garnacho.
6 This group included Ana María Ruiz Tagle, Rafael Escuredo, Antonio Gutierrez Castaños, Alfonso Guerra, Luis Yáñez, Guillermo Galeote, Alfonso Fernándes Torres, Alfonso Fernández Malo, Manuel del Valle, Miguel Angel Pino, and Felipe González.
7 Particularly important was a strike in Siderúrgica Sevillana—the first strike to be led by the UGT in Seville for many years. Other strikes that were important in the increasing activity of this socialist group took place in Astilleros Españoles, Los Certales, Aguirrezabala, Recalux, and Montajes Nervión.
8 Strikes took place at the Renault factory in Valladolid, the Firestone factory in Burgos, and the Bazán shipbuilding company in Bilbao.
9 Contacts with Asturian Socialists were ensured through Agustín González, contacts with the Basque socialists through Nicolás Redondo (Vizcaya) and Enrique Múgica (Guipúzcoa).
10 "Entrevista a F. González" [Interview with F. González], *Leviatán*, 2d period, no. 1 (1978), pp. 25-26.
11 Ibid., p. 19.
12 The zones were: the north (Vizcaya, Alava, and Santander), the northwest (Asturias and Galicia), Pyrenees (Guipúzcoa, Navarre, and Aragón), the center (Madrid, Valladolid, Salamanca, and Burgos), the east (Catalonia, Valencia, Alicante, and the Balearic Islands), and the south (Andalusia, Estremadura, and the Canaries).
13 Pascual Tomás, the general secretary of the UGT, had died in 1969.
14 Among the ten were the main leaders of the interior: Felipe González, Nicolas Redondo, Enrique Múgica, and Pablo Castellano.
15 In the new executive committee González was press secretary, Pablo Castellano was secretary for international relations, Nicolas Redondo was secretary for political relations, Enrique Múgica was secretary of organization. Other members of the executive included Alfonso Guerra, Guillermo Galeote, and Carmen García.

16 These zones were in the Basque country (Alava, Vizcaya, and Guipúzcoa), Asturias, Catalonia, Valencia (Alicante and Valencia), Castille (Madrid and Valladolid), and Andalusia (Seville and Córdoba); informal groups existed in Cádiz, Granada and Huelva, Galicia, Rioja, and Salamanca.
17 This was a document issued by González, Guerra, Múgica, Redondo, and Castellano, in Guipúzcoa in September 1974.
18 *XXVII Congreso del Partido Socialista Obrero Español* [Twenty-seventh Congress of the Spanish Socialist Workers' party] (Barcelona: Avance, 1977), pp. 115-16.
19 Ibid., pp. 159-324 for the economic reform program; p. 117 for the strategy of mobilization.
20 There is a good description of the building up of interparty agreement on the transition in R. Carr and J. P. Fusi, *Spain: Dictatorship to Democracy* (London: Allen & Unwin, 1979), chaps. 10, 11.
21 The classic discussion of this type of party system and its internal dynamics is provided by Giovanni Sartori, *Parties and Party Systems* (Cambridge: Cambridge University Press, 1976), chaps. 6, 8.
22 See this view expressed in *Memoria I.—gestión de la Comisión Ejecutiva Federal* [Memo I—report of activities of the Federal Executive Committee], Twenty-eighth Congress of the PSOE, May 1979, p. 21.
23 The views of the PSOE on the Moncloa Agreements are expressed in the speech of Felipe González to the Cortes on 27 October 1977; the editorial in *El Socialista*, 16 October 1977; PSOE Secretariat for Information and Press, document no. 73, 31 October 1977; report of the Grupo de Economistas del PSOE, "El acuerdo económico de la Moncloa: Análisis y valoracíon" [The economic agreement of the Moncloa: Analysis and evaluation], no date.
24 See Marx and Engels's series of articles "Revolutionary Spain," written in 1852 for the *New York Daily Tribune* and reprinted in their book *Revolution in Spain*.
25 It seems that the PSOE regarded the UCD electorate as largely inconsistent, while the PCE thought that the PSOE vote had been "disposable" and "transitory." See the analysis of the 1977 elections in G. Carcassone and P. Subra de Biasses, *L'Espagne ou la democratie retrouveé* [Spain or democracy rediscovered] (Paris: Enaj, 1978), p. 215, passim.
26 A fascinating analysis of the dynamics of polarized pluralism in Spain, showing both multilateral competition and centrifugal tendencies as causing grave problems for governmental stability, can be found in Juan J. Linz, "Il sistema partitico spagnolo" [The Spanish party system], *Rivista Italiana di Scienza Politica*, vol. 3 (1978).
27 The correlation between increase in the Socialist vote and low population density is .50. For a more extended analysis of the 1979 elections, see J. M. Maravall, "Political Cleavages in Spain and the 1979 General Election," *Government and Opposition* 14, no. 3 (1979).
28 On this strategy, see, for example, Comité Federal, *Informe de gestión* [Report of activities], 1-2 July 1978, p. 96; and A. Guerra, "Estrategia de poder" [Strategy for Power], *Leviatán*, 2d period, no. 1 (1978), pp. 52-53.
29 My data refer to complete censuses for 138 municipalities with 11,962,012 voters (around fifty-seven percent of the electorate), which include forty-six of the fifty-two provincial capitals and twenty additional cities with more than 50,000 inhabitants.
30 Felipe González, opening speech to the Twenty-eighth Congress of the PSOE, 17 May 1979, mimeo., p. 31.
31 Of the 11,962,012 registered voters, 6,613,439 did vote (55.3 percent, which is similar to the rate of electoral participation for the whole electorate). The data for municipalities have been grouped by province to facilitate comparisons with the general election results.
32 The Italian Communist party in the 1950s and 1960s and the French Socialist party in the 1970s grew through a similar process. On the PCI, see Sidney Tarrow, "Communism in Italy and France: Adaptation and Change," in Donald L. M. Blackmer and Sidney Tarrow, eds.,

Communism in Italy and France (Princeton, N.J.: Princeton University Press, 1975); on the PS, Roland Cayrol and Jérôme Jaffré, "Socialist Leaders, Followers, and Voters and the Social Structure of France," in K. Lawson, ed., *Political Parties and Linkages*, forthcoming.

33 It is thus questionable whether the decline of the PSI was due to losses on its right or on its left. The Morandista period of communist-socialist alliances ended in a decrease of 8.2 percentage points from 1946 to 1953, while the *Centro-Sinistra* period of Christian Democratic-Socialist alliances from 1963 onward led to a loss of 4.2 points between 1963 and 1972. The losses, however, hurt the Socialists more than the Social Democrats (from 1963 to 1972 the PSDI vote declined by only 0.9 percentage points). Fractionalism, oligarchies, lack of leadership, the practice of *sottogoverno*, the absence of a convincing socialist political alternative, all have been offered as explanations, but they hardly account for the progressive *effacement* of the PSI. Such an explanation would be very welcome by PSOE leaders and, a fortiori, by the PCE. A useful study of the PSI's decline, which shows the contrast with the PSOE's development, is that of A. Panebianco, "Analisi di una sconfitta: Il declino del PSI" [Analysis of a defeat: The decline of the PSI], in A. Parisi and G. Pasquino, eds., *Continuità e mutamento elettorale in Italia* [Electoral continuity and change in Italy] (Bologna: Il Mulino, 1977), pp. 145-84.

34 The ecological correlation between the UCD vote in June 1977 and the CEDA vote in February 1936 is .46. Juan J. Linz discusses the difference between "cultural" and "organizational" continuity in "Il sistema partitico spagnolo."

35 Seymour M. Lipset and Stein Rokkan, "Cleavage Structures, Party Systems, and Voter Alignments—an Introduction," in Lipset and Rokkan, eds., *Party Systems and Voter Alignments: Cross-National Perspectives* (New York: Free Press, 1967), p. 50.

36 David Butler and Donald Stokes, *Political Change in Britain* (London: Macmillan, 1969), chap. 2. For partisan stability over time in the United States (despite fluctuations in presidential elections), see two books by Angus Campbell, Phillip E. Converse, Warren E. Miller, and Donald Stokes: *The American Voter* (New York: John Wiley and Sons, 1960), and *Elections and the Political Order* (New York: John Wiley and Sons, 1966).

37 Phillip E. Converse, "Of Time and Partisan Stability," *Comparative Political Studies*, no. 2 (1969).

38 Samuel H. Barnes, *Representation in Italy: Institutionalized Tradition and Electoral Choice* (Chicago: University of Chicago Press, 1977), p. 68. Geographical analyses of political continuity in Italy's case may be found in M. Dogan, "Political Cleavage and Social Stratification in France and Italy," in Lipset and Rokkan, *Party Systems*, pp. 129-95, and G. Galli, "Il bipartitismo imperfetto: Communisti e democristiani" [Imperfect bipartism: Communists and Christian democrats], in P. Farnetti, ed., *Il sistema politico italiano* [The Italian political system] (Bologna: Il Mulino, 1973), pp. 263-85.

39 On the emergence of the PCI and the DC as the dominant organizations in the "socialist" and the "Catholic" subcultures after 1945, see G. Poggi, *L'organizzazione partitica del PCI e della DC* [The party organization of the PCI and the DC] (Bologna: Il Mulino, 1968).

40 For example, Giacomo Sani, "Determinants of Party Preference in Italy: Toward the Integration of Complementary Models," *American Journal of Political Science*, no. 18 (1974); and, by the same author, "Mass Level Response to Party Strategy: The Italian Electorate and the Communist Party," in Blackmer and Tarrow, *Communism in Italy and France*, pp. 456-503, and "Political Traditions as Contextual Variables: Partisanship in Italy," *American Journal of Political Science*, no. 20 (1976).

41 H. M. Blalock, *Causal Inferences in Nonexperimental Research* (Chapel Hill: University of North Carolina Press, 1964).

42 Maravall, *Dictatorship and Political Dissent*, chaps. 3, 4, 6.

43 The survey was carried out by the PSOE Secretariat of Organization in May-June 1979. I was able to add a few questions and to analyze the questionnaries directly, for which I am grateful to Alfonso Guerra, Carmen García Bloise, Javier Guerrero, and José-Félix Tezanos. The sample was 295 delegates, roughly twenty-seven percent of the total.

44 Thus, Lagroye et al. have shown that ninety percent of PCF militants and ninety-one percent of PS militants came from leftist families, concluding, "A strong politicization of the family mileu leads them to adhesion and even more to militancy." J. Lagroye, G. Lord, L. Mouneir-Chazel, and J. Polard, *Les militants politiques dans trois partis français* [Political militants in three French parties] (Paris: Pedone, 1976), p. 44.

45 For France, see G. Dupeux and P. E. Converse, "Politicization of the Electorate in France and the United States," in *Public Opinion Quarterly*, no. 26 (1962); for Italy, Barnes, *Representation in Italy*, chap. 5, and Sani, "Mass Level Response to Party Strategy," pp. 491-92.

46 Sani, "Mass Level Response to Party Strategy," p. 491.

47 For example, P. Preston, "The Anti-Francoist Opposition: The Long March to Unity," in P. Preston, *Spain in Crisis* (Hassocks, Sussex: Harvester Press, 1976), p. 153; or L. G. San Miguel, "Para una sociología del cambio político y la oposición en la España actual" [For a sociology of political change and opposition in today's Spain], *Sistema* 4 (1974):102.

48 O. Kirchheimer, "The Transformation of the Western European Party Systems," in Joseph LaPalombara and Myron Weiner, eds., *Political Parties and Political Development* (Princeton, N.J.: Princeton University Press, 1966), pp. 184-200.

49 Cayrol and Jaffré, "Socialist Leaders." Also Louis Harris survey, *Le Matin*, 10 February 1978; and A. du Roy, "Qui est socialiste en France?" [Who is a socialist in France?], *L'Express*, 14 April 1979, pp. 75-78. Sidney Tarrow has also shown the increasing social heterogeneity of support for the PCI (as compared with the PCF) in "Communism in Italy and France," pp. 596-606.

50 Data in table 6.7 are from two surveys. One was carried out by the Centro de Investigaciones Sociólogicas (CIS) in July-August 1978 using a national sample of 5,348 individuals representative of the Spanish adult population, the other by EMOPUBLICA for the PSOE in May 1979, using a national sample of 4,175 individuals also representative of the Spanish adult population. I was able to carry out computer analysis of the results of both surveys and to introduce several questions to the questionnaire of the second. I must thank J. Diéz Nicolás, F. Alvira, and U. Martínez-Lázaro for their help concerning the first survey, G. Galeote and J. F. Tezanos for their help in the second survey.

51 I refer to the survey by the Centro de Investigaciones Sociológicas mentioned in footnote 50 and one by Pérez-Díaz. Pérez-Díaz indicates that 48 percent of industrial workers voted PSOE, 19.5 percent PCE, and 19.5 percent UCD. See Perez-Díaz, "Orientaciones politicas de los obreros españoles hoy" [Political orientations of Spanish workers today] *Sistema*, 29-30 May 1979, p. 162. According to the CIS survey, 49 percent of the skilled workers and 46 percent of unskilled workers voted for the PSOE, as against 32 and 34 percent who voted UCD and 9 and 15 percent who voted PCE.

52 See speech of Felipe González to the Twenty-eighth Congress of the PSOE, mimeographed, 17 May 1979; also I. Sotelo, "Socialismo y Marxismo" [Socialism and Marxism], *Sistema*, 29-30 May 1979, pp. 15-26.

53 A. Parisi and G. Pasquino, "20 Giugno: Struttura politica e comportamento elettorale," in Parisi and Pasquino, *Continuità e mutamento elettorale*, pp. 31-34.

54 The classic statement of this argument was Seymour M. Lipset, *Political Man* (New York: Doubleday, 1960), chap. 2. See also V. R. Lorwin, "Working Class Politics and Economic Development in Western Europe," *American Historical Review* 63, no. 2 (1958): 338-51.

55 For example, Barnes, *Representation in Italy*, pp. 97-116, 179-80, footnote 5 to chap. 7,

and Samuel H. Barnes, "Left, Right, and the Italian Voter," *Comparative Political Studies*, no. 4 (1971); also G. Sartori, *Parties and Party Systems* (Cambridge: Cambridge University Press, 1976), chap. 10.
56   See Butler and Stokes, *Political Change in Britain*, chap. 9; R. Inglehart and H. D. Klingmann, "Party Identification, Ideological Preference, and the Left-Right Dimension among Western Mass Publics," in I. Budge, I. Crewe, and D. Farlie, eds., *Party Identification and Beyond* (New York: John Wiley and Sons, 1976).
57   Barnes, *Representation in Italy*, p. 102; E. Deutsch, D. Lindon, and P. Weill, *Les familles politiques* [Political families] (Paris: Pedone, 1966).
58   See, for example, González, speech to the Twenty-eighth Congress, pp. 20-21; A. Guerra, interview in *Saida*, 10 December 1977; idem, "Democracia y socialismo en el sur de Europa" [Democracy and socialism in Southern Europe], in *Conferencia de Partidos Socialistas del sur de Europa* [Conference of Socialist parties of Southern Europe] (Madrid: PSOE, 1977), pp. 50-55, passim; idem., "Estrategia de poder," pp. 46-49; J. Solana, speech to Federacion Socialista Madrileña, 22 June 1979. This view on strategy was already expressed at the Twenty-seventh Congress of the PSOE, December 1976, where joint parliamentary and extraparliamentary action was defended, as well as mass and participatory democracy.
59   See, for instance, Guerra interview in *Saida*, p. 17.
60   The tensions between an eventual socialist government (and a fortiori of a coalition government with the UCD, even if it included some sort of participation of the PCE) and the political expectations of the PSOE militants (possibly also some of the voters), were evident soon after the 1977 elections. See, for example, the documents *Desarrollo de la resolucíon del Comité Federal* [Development of the resolution of the Federal Committee], PSOE, 1-2 July 1978, and *Informe de gestión* [Report of activities], Comité Federal del PSOE, July 1978, p. 96.
61   Other important explanations are the political frustrations that had developed within the party from the politics of constitutional and economic compromise after the autumn of 1977 and the organizational difficulties of adjusting from a membership of 8,000 (Twenty-seventh Congress) to a membership of 150,000 (Twenty-eighth Congress).
62   See my discussion of these strategic dilemmas in J. M. Maravall, "The Limits of Reformism: Parliamentary Socialism and the Marxist Theory of the State," *British Journal of Sociology* 30, no. 3 (1979). For the term "constitutional radicalism," see R. D. Putnam, "The Italian Communist Politician," in Blackmer and Tarrow, *Communism in Italy and France*, for example, pp. 214-16.

The Spanish Communists and the Search for Electoral Space

1   *Cuadernos para el Diálogo*, 28 May 1977.
2   See, for example, Santiago Carrillo's report to the PCE Central Committee in July 1976 entitled *De la clandestinidad a la legalidad* [From clandestinity to legality] (n.p., n.d.), pp. 9-11.
3   The "Proyecto de acuerdo constitucional del PCE" appeared in the theoretical journal *Nuestra Bandera*, 86 (March-April 1977): 57-59.
4   *Mundo Obrero*, 20 April 1977.
5   *Diario 16*, 30 April 30 1977.
6   For a consideration of the PSOE's resurgence, see my chapter "The Spanish Left: Present Realities and Future Prospects," in William E. Griffith, ed., *The Western European Left* (Lexington: D. C. Heath, 1979).

7   The phrase appeared in the principal report approved at the Third Conference of the Madrid provincial organization in April 1976 (mimeographed), p. 18. There is some question whether Communist leaders really believed what they were saying after a certain point, but they continued to make such statements.
8   See the article by Angel Mullor, the PCE Central Committee press secretary, in *El País*, 11 June 1977.
9   *Mundo Obrero*, 16 June 1977.
10 Ibid., 22 June 1977.
11 A complete version of his report to the Central Committee session in late June may be found in *Mundo Obrero*, 29 June 1977.
12 For an analysis of the changes in Spanish communist policy since 1956, see my chapter "The Domestic and International Evolution of the Spanish Communist Party," in Rudolf L. Tökés, ed., *Eurocommunism and Détente* (New York: New York University Press, 1978).
13 These are from the results of a survey by DATA, S.A., cited by Juan Linz in "A Sociological Look at Spanish Communism," in George Schwab, ed., *Eurocommunism: The Ideological and Political-Theoretical Foundations* (Westport, Conn.: Greenwood Press, 1980), p. 250.
14 Santiago Carrillo, *"Eurocomunismo" y estado* ["Eurocommunism" and the state] (Barcelona: Editorial Grijalbo), p. 212.
15 For example, *El País*, 31 May 1977, and *Mundo Obrero*, 25 May 1977.
16 Jaime Ballesteros, "El Partido Comunista en los umbrales de la democracia" [The Communist party in the shadows of democracy], in *Nuestra Bandera* 85 (n.d.): 13–18.
17 *El País*, 11 May 1977.
18 The figures are those of Victor Pérez-Díaz, *Clase obrera, partidos y sindicatos* [Working class, parties, and trade unions] (Madrid: Fundación del Instituto Nacional de Industria, 1980), p. 109. There are other estimates, however. José María Maravall, "Political Cleavages in Spain and the 1979 General Election," *Government and Opposition*, p. 305, suggests approximately sixty percent of the Comisiones' voters in 1978 voted PSOE in 1977. Samuel Barnes, Antonio López Pina, and Peter McDonough, *British Journal of Political Science*, p. 76, indicate the PCE received 3 percent of the UGT vote and 46 percent of that from Comisiones voters. The PSOE, they indicate, captured 75 percent of the UGT and 24 percent of the Comisiones' vote.
19 A detailed discussion of these initiatives may be found in my "The PCE in Spanish Politics," *Problems of Communism* 27 (July-August 1978): 15–37.
20 *La Calle*, 17–23 April 1979, p. 8.
21 See José Felix Tezános, "Analisis sociopolítico del voto socialista en las elecciones de 1979" [Sociopolitical analysis of the socialist vote in the 1979 elections], *Sistema* 31 (July 1979): 111.
22 This was Fernando Claudín in *El País*, 15 March 1979.
23 *Mundo Obrero*, 27 February 1979.
24 Ibid., 2 March 1979.
25 José Felix Tezános, "El espacio político y sociológico del socialismo" [The political and sociological space of socialism], *Sistema* 32 (September 1979): 54. The PCE had improved on its 1977 performance in this regard. Then it had received seventy-five percent of its vote from men and only twenty-five percent from women. See Mónica Threlfall, "Socialismo y electorado femenino" [Socialism and the feminine electorate], ibid., p. 23.
26 Tezános, "El espacio político," p. 54.
27 Ibid., p. 56.
28 Ibid. The breakdown was 24.6 percent skilled and 6.8 percent unskilled. For the PSOE, it was 18.3 and 6.0 percent, respectively.

29 Victor Peréz Díaz, *Clase obrera*, p. 162.
30 José María Maravall, "Political Cleavages," p. 24.
31 *Diario 16*, 27 March 1978, and *El País*, 28 March 1978, covered the controversies during their reporting of the March 1978 provincial and regional meetings.
32 *Mundo Obrero*, 16 June 1977.
33 Emilio López (Beltza), *Nacionalismo vasco y clases sociales* [Basque nationalism and social classes] (San Sebastián: Editorial Txertoa, 1976), p. 138.
34 Ibid.
35 See *Hacia el III Congreso del Partido Comunista de Euzkadi* [Toward the Third Congress of the Basque Communist party] (n.p., n.d.), p. 24.
36 The figures may be found in an unabridged manuscript version of the chapter by Linz cited in note 13. See pp. 63-68.
37 *El País*, 12 June 1977.
38 *Triunfo*, 7 January 1978, noted that between 1962 and 1973 the proportion of the active population engaged in agriculture in Galicia dropped from 62.9 percent to 52.7 percent.
39 For an interesting analysis, see Cesar E. Díaz López, "Algunas Hipótesis explicativas de los resultados electorales en Galicia" [Some hypotheses explaining the election results in Galicia], in Equip de Sociología Electoral, eds., *Sobres les eleccions legislatives del 1977* (Barcelona: Fundació Jaume Bofill, 1978), pp. 81-101.
40 Javier Alfaya, "Galicia: La explicación no es unicamente el miedo" [Galicia: Fear is not the only explanation], *Argumentos* (July 1977), p. 27,
41 José María Maravall, "Spain: Eurocommunism and Socialism," *Political Studies*, p. 229.

Francoist Reformers in Democratic Spain

1 For an account of the parties making up the Popular Alliance, see Manuel Fraga Iribarne, *Alianza Popular* (Bilbao: Albia, 1977), pp. 9-10.
2 The Popular Alliance's founding manifesto can be found in the Madrid morning paper *El País*, 10 October 1976, p. 8.
3 For a study of the Franco regime as an example of limited pluralism, see Juan Linz, "An Authoritarian Regime: Spain," in Erik Allardt and Y. Littunen, eds., *Cleavages, Ideologies, and Party Systems* (Helsinki: Transactions of the Westermack Society, 1974), pp. 291-341.
4 Later five of the seven member parties united in a single party called the Popular Alliance while maintaining the federation under the same name.
5 For a critical account of this development, see Jose Luis Martínez and Soledad Gallego, *Los 7 magníficos* [The magnificent seven] (Madrid: Cambio 16, 1977), pp. 157, 158, 202-7.
6 Ibid., p. 157.
7 Fraga is the author of more than fifteen books of political science and political journalism. His overview of himself emerges clearly and consistently from several recent sources, including his book *Alianza Popular*, pp. 49-51, and the interview in *El País* of 12 June 1977, pp. 18-19. Fraga's last television speech before the 1977 election was also illustrative. For a critical biography of Fraga, see Martinez and Gallego, *Los 7*, pp. 157-208.
8 The information that Fraga resigned and was not left out by Suárez was leaked to the press and has not been denied by competent sources. See Martínez and Gallego, *Los 7*, p. 15.
9 Public confrontations on this subject have been frequent in the last couple of years in the daily press, lectures, and so on. For an assessment of the First Development Plan by an American scholar, see Charles Anderson, *The Political Economy of Modern Spain: Policy-Making in an Authoritarian System* (Madison: University of Wisconsin Press, 1970).
10 Opinion polls in the 1960s showed that Fraga was widely known to the general public and

11 See Fraga, *Alianza*, p. 54.
12 Martínez and Gallego, *Los 7*, p. 145.
13 See excerpts from a speech by Fernández de la Mora in the 1970s in ibid., p. 151.
14 For an assessment of this aspect of the campaign, see the Madrid daily *Informaciones*, 14 June 1977, p. 8.
15 This was seated by Fernández de la Mora in Barcelona, the second largest city in Spain. See Martínez and Gallego, *Los 7*, p.
16 See the Madrid daily *Ya*, 12 June 1977, p. 12.
17 *El País*, 29 June 1977, p. 13.
18 Martínez and Gallego, *Los 7*, pp. 30-31.
19 See the manifesto in Fraga, *Alianza*, pp. 11-47. Programmatic statements by Fraga can also be found in *El País*, 12 June 1977, p. 7, and pp. 18-19 of the Sunday supplement of the same issue.
20 These are excerpts from advertising material in the daily press, radio broadcasting, and wall stickers of different cities, including Madrid.
21 See *El País* 15 May 1977, p. 13.
22 *Informaciones*, 14 June 1977, p. 8.
23 This was the opinion expressed by Javier Tusell in his lecture at the Madrid Club Siglo XXI on 21 June 1977.
24 *El País*, 10 June 1977, p. 8. This editorial contains some of the hardest criticisms made of the leaders of the Popular Alliance, denouncing them as responsible for the last decade of Francoism and for the corruption and violence so characteristic of it.
25 Tussell, Club Siglo XXI, 21 June 1977.
26 See declarations by these politicians in Martínez and Gallego, *Los 7*, pp. 34, 132, 133.
27 See survey data in the magazine *Cambio 16*, no. 284, 22 May 1977, p. 18, and no. 288, 19 June 1977, p. 20. See also data from the largest published survey in Spain (15,000 interviews) in *El País*, 12 June 1977, p. 1. The findings of this last survey were the closest to the actual returns for every party.
28 *Cambio 16*, 3 June 1974; and *El Europeo*, 19 April 1975.
29 According to preelectoral surveys conducted in February 1979, only about 40 percent of former Popular Alliance voters intended to vote for the Democratic Coalition, and a shift toward the center and the extreme right was likely. Although "no answer" percentages were high, this pattern of intentions was basically consistent with returns. This information comes from the Centro de Investigaciones Sociologicas data bank.
30 For the historical background, see Juan Linz, "The Party System of Spain," in Seymour M. Lipset and Stein Rokkan, eds., *Party Systems and Voter Alignments* (New York: Free Press, 1967), pp. 197-282. Professor Linz emphasized this point in his lecture at the Madrid Club Siglo XXI on 23 June 1977.
31 Linz discussed this point at the Club Siglo XXI meeting on 23 June 1977.

Catalan Nationalism and the Spanish Elections

1 José Agustín Goytisolo, *Poetas catalanes contemporáneos* [Contemporary Catalan poets] (Barcelona: Seix Barral, 1968), p. 5.
2 Oriol Pi-Sunyer, "The Maintenance of Ethnic Identity in Catalonia," in Oriol Pi-Sunyer, ed., "The Limits of the Integration: Ethnicity and Nationalism in Modern Europe," *Research Reports* (October 1971), p. 112.

3   Pi-Sunyer, "Maintenance of Ethnic Identity," p. 118. Another sociologist who has emphasized the importance of this "internal colonialism" and of social disequilibrium in developing countries is the Mexican Pablo González Casanova. See his "Sociedad plural y desarrollo: El caso de México" [Plural society and development: The Mexican Case] *América Latina*, no. 4 (October-December 1962): 31-51. This subject was later developed in one of his best-known books, *La democracia en México* [Democracy in Mexico] (Mexico: Era, 1965).
4   Pi-Sunyer, "Maintenance of Ethnic Identity," p. 118.
5   Jaume Vicens i Vives, *Noticia de Catalunya* [Report from Catalonia] (Barcelona: Destino, 1962), p. 23.
6   Enric Prat de la Riba, *La nacionalidad Catalana* [The Catalan nationality] (Valladolid: Imprenta Castellana, 1917), p. 90.
7   Luis Durán i Ventosa, "Regionalisme i federalisme" [Regionalism and federalism], cited in Albert Balcells, *Cataluna contemporanea (1900-1939)* [Contemporary Catalonia, 1900-1939] vol. 2 (Madrid: Siglo XXI, 1974), p. 69.
8   Pierre Vilar, *Catalunya dins l'Espanya moderna* [Catalonia in modern Spain] vol. 1 (Barcelona: Ediciones 62, 1964), pp. 35-45.
9   H. H. Gerth and C. Wright Mills, eds., *From Max Weber: Essays in Sociology* (New York: Oxford University Press, Galaxy, 1958), p. 176.
10 See Juan J. Linz, "Early State-Building and Late Peripheral Nationalisms against the State: The Case of Spain," in S. N. Eisenstadt and Stein Rokkan, eds., *Building States and Nations: Analysis by Region* (Beverly Hills, Calif.: Sage Publications, 1973), p. 99.
11 An insightful exposition of the whole process may be found in Martí Rizal (José A. González Casanova's pseudonym), "Cataluña en la España moderna" [Catalonia in modern Spain], *Diario de Barcelona*, 2 August 1977. This is the first of a series of six articles published by him under the comprehensive title "Historia de la cuestión Catalana," [History of the Catalan question]. The series provides an excellent historical analysis.
12 At the end of the sixteenth century the distribution of land and population of the four Hispanic kingdoms was as follows:

	Area (km^2)	Population	Density
Castile	378,000 (65.2%)	6,910,000 (72.9%)	18.2
Aragon	100,000 (17.2%)	1,180,000 (12.4%)	11.8
Navarre	12,000 (2.1%)	145,000 (1.5%)	12.1
Portugal	90,000 (15.5%)	1,250,000 (13.2%)	14.0

Inside the kingdom of Aragon the population distribution was: Aragon, 310,000; Catalonia, 340,000; Majorca, 80,000; and Valencia, 450,000. See Joan Reglá, *Introducció a la historia de la corona d'Aragó* [Introduction to the history of the crown of Aragon] (Palma de Mallorca: Moll, 1969), p. 86.
13 The Generalitat, or Diputació, is a Catalan institution that dates back to the late Middle Ages. The Generalitat developed in the principality of Catalonia out of the committees appointed by the Cortes (the Catalan Parliament) to organize the collection of subsidies granted the king. It became a standing committee of the Cortes and consisted of three Diputats and three Oidors (auditors and accountants). The Generalitat has traditionally been considered by the Catalans as the defender of Catalonia's liberties. For a historical analysis of this institution, see John Elliot, *Imperial Spain, 1469-1716* (Harmondsworth: Penguin, 1970), pp. 29-31.
14 *Fuero* is a Castilian term (*fur* in Catalan), derived from the Latin *forum*. It is applied to any right, privilege, or charter that recognizes the legal customs and usages of a territory.

Originally, in Roman times, the Iberian peninsula was divided into *fora*, or jurisdictions, each with its proper established law. Every free subject could demand that he be governed in accordance with the customs and usages of his proper forum. By the fourteenth century Catalan *furs* and *usatges* had already developed into a sort of general code of local validity.

15   The Decree of Nueva Planta (29 June 1707) abolished all the *fueros* of the former crown of Aragon (which included Catalonia) and subjected all territories to Castilian laws and jurisprudence.

16   Ibid., p. 385.

17   Ibid., p. 387.

18   Albert Balcells, *Cataluña contemporánea I, (siglo XIX)* [Contemporary Catalonia I, nineteenth century] (Madrid: Siglo XXI, 1977), p. 59.

19   See *Diario de las sesiones de Cortes, Congreso de los Diputados, Legislatura de 1916* [Daily of Parliament sessions, Congress of Deputies. Legislature of 1916] vol. 2, no. 22 (Session of 7 June 1916) (Madrid: Ramona Valesco, 1916), p. 446.

20   See *La Vanguardia Española* (Barcelona), 15 February 1939.

21   See Josep Termes, "El federalisme català en el periode revolucionari de 1868-1873" [Catalan federalism in the revolutionary period of 1868-1873], *Recerques*, no. 2 (Barcelona: Ariel, 1972), pp. 33-69; Antoni Jutglar, *Federalismo y revolución: Las ideas sociales de Pí y Margall* [Federalism and revolution: Social ideas of Pí and Margall] (Barcelona: Publications from the chair of General History of Spain). Also Antoni Jutglar, *Pí y Margall y el federalismo espanol* [Pí and Margall and Spanish federalism], 2 vols. (Madrid: Taurus, 1975).

22   "The so-called war autonomy was the culmination of the 1932 Statute." This refers to the *Estatuto de Cataluña* of 15 September 1932, which recognized Catalonia as an autonomous region inside the Spanish Second Republic (article 1). "War conditions and revolutionary processes led to a unilateral proclamation of Catalan autonomy, necessary for the military defense of the region and the preservation of the revolution. Workers' groups—particularly the anarchists—made the cause of Catalan autonomy their own since, by proclaiming and implementing autonomy, they ensured the existence of an adequate formal-legal framework for their social revolution. All the nationalizing measures—in particular, collectivation of Catalan industry—were protected from state Republican powers in Madrid and afterwards in Valencia. The climax of the autonomist movement had been reached." Rizal, "El catalanismo de izquierdas" [Leftist Catalanism], *Diario de Barcelona*, 7 September 1977.

23   Many regulations published in the *Boletín Oficial del Estado* [State Official Bulletin] prove how real this cultural and linguistic repression was. Just a few examples: on 18 May 1938, an order forbade the use of any language other than Castilian for civil registration of citizens; on 21 May 1938, an order did the same for titles, statutes, and all legal documents; when the Civil War was over, another order (16 May 1940) prohibited the use of any language other than Castilian for industrial documents; a decree of 2 June 1945, declared Castilian the unique and compulsory language of primary school; and an order of 11 January 1945, forbade Catalan names for merchant ships. The Insitut Catalá d'Estudis Politics i Socials [Catalan Institute of Social and Political Studies], a scholarly institution that worked underground in Barcelona, has published the complete *Catalunya sota el régim franquista: Informe sobre la persecució de la llengua i la cultura de Catalunya pel régim del general Franco* [Catalonia under the Franco regime: Report on the persecution of Catalan language and culture by the government of General Franco] (Paris: Ediciones Catalanes de Paris, 1973). See also Jesus Ynfante's work on the enrichment of local oligarchies under the Franco regime, *Los negocios de Porcioles: Las sagradas familias de Barcelona* [The businesses of Porcioles: Sacred families in Barcelona] (Toulouse: Monipodio, 1974).

24   Juan F. Marsal, *La sombra del poder: Intelectuales y política en España, Argentina, y*

México [The shadow of power: Intellectuals and politics in Spain, Argentina, and Mexico] (Madrid: Edicusa, 1975), pp. 224-25.
25 José A. González Casanova, "El voto de los Barceloneses" [How the Barcelonians voted], *Tele-expres*, 22 June 1977.
26 Esteban Pinilla de las Heras, "Resultados electorales en Cataluña" [Electoral results in Catalonia], *El Correo Catalán*, 22 June 1977.
27 *Constitution of 1977*, article 99.
28 Formally it is the king who dissolves the Cortes or either of its houses at the proposal of the prime minister. See the constitution of 1978, article 115.1.
29 They were (1) the referendum on the Law of Political Reform, 15 December 1976, (2) the general election of 15 June 1977, (3) the constitutional referendum, 6 November 1978, and (4) the general election of 1 March 1979.
30 See Esteban Pinilla de las Heras, "De la política de interés general a la política de intereses concretos" [From a policy of general interest to the policy of specific interests], *El Correo Catalán*, 4 March 1979, p. 4.
31 Tarradellas kept alive the spirit of the Generalitat during his long exile in France. On 23 October 1977, he returned in triumph to Catalonia once the Suárez government had provisionally restored the Generalitat by royal decree in September 1977. See Royal Decree 41/1977, *Boletín Oficial del Éstado* [Official State Bulletin], 5 October 1977.
32 Article 2 of the 1978 constitution reads: "The constitution is based on the indissoluble unity of the Spanish nation, the common and indivisible country of all Spaniards, and recognizes and guarantees the right of self-government of the nationalities and regions of which it is composed and solidarity among them all."
33 Organic Law 4/1079, *Boletín oficial del éstado* [Official State Bulletin], 22 December 1979, pp. 29363-70.
34 Ibid., article 12, p. 29364.
35 Juan J. Linz, "Politics in a Multi-lingual Society with a Dominant World Language, the Case of Spain," in Jean-Guy Savard and Richard Vigneault, eds., *Les états miltilingues: Problemes et solutions* [Multilingual states: Problems and solutions] (Quebéc: Université Laval, 1975).

Regional Nationalism and the Elections in the Basque Country

1 Ramón Tamames, *Introducción a la economía española* [Introduction to the Spanish economy], 9th ed. (Madrid: Alianze Editorial, 1974), pp. 420-21.
2 Juan Linz, "Early State-Building and Late Peripheral Nationalism against the State: The Case of Spain," in S. N. Eisenstadt and Stein Rokkan, eds., *Building States and Nations*, vol. 2 (Beverly Hills, Calif.: Sage Publications, 1973), p. 87.
3 The province of Madrid has ranked first among all Spanish provinces in per capita income in recent years, but its prosperity is due principally to its political preeminence.
4 Jorge Nadal, *La población española* [The Spanish population] (Barcelona: Ariel, 1966), p. 190.
5 Salustiano del Campo et al., *La cuestión regional española* [The Spanish regional question] (Madrid: Edicusa, 1977), p. 125.
6 Linz, "Early State-Building," p. 85.
7 Campo, *La cuestión regional española*, p. 213.
8 Linz, "Early State-Building," p. 85.
9 Milton M. da Silva, "Mobilization and Ethnic Conflict: The Case of the Basques," *Comparative Politics* (January 1975), pp. 244-45.

362   Notes: The Elections in the Basque Country

10 This section relies heavily on Jaime Vicens Vives, *Approaches to the History of Spain* (Berkeley: University of California Press, 1967); Stanley Payne, "Catalan and Basque Nationalism," *Journal of Contemporary History* 6, no. 1 (1971): 15-51; and Linz, "Early State-Building," pp. 32-116.
11 Paul H. Lewis, "The Spanish Ministerial Elite, 1938-1969," *Comparative Politics* (October 1972), pp. 102-3.
12 Fomento de Estudios Sociales y de Sociologia Aplicada, *Estudios sociológicos sobre el estado social de España* [Sociological studies on the social condition of Spain] (Madrid: Euramérica, 1975), table Tc 3.12, p. 58.
13 *Euzkadi*, sometimes written *Euskadi*, is the Basque name for the Basque country.
14 For a full discussion of political developments between the 1977 and 1979 elections, see John F. Coverdale, *The Political Transformation of Spain after Franco* (New York: Praeger, 1979).

The Media and the Elections

1   I.N.O.P. (National Institute of Public Opinion), Ministry of Culture, May 1977. Released by the Information Coordination Office.
2   *5 Días* (Five Days Economic Journal), Madrid, 14 February 1979.
3   Instituto Oficial de Radio y TV (Official Institute of Radio and TV), poll published in *ABC*, 15 February 1979, p. 14.
4   Law of 13 July 1940. Cortes Bulletin.
5   "Ley de Prensa e Imprenta" (Publications and Printing Law), 1966.
6   Article 2, Publications and Printing Law, 1966.
7   Royal Decree Law 9008, April 1977, B.O.E. (Official Register), modifying several aricles of the 1966 Press Law.
8   Editorial page, *Diario 16*, 13 April 1977.
9   *El País*, 13 June 1977, Sofemasa Poll.
10 Editorial page, *El País*, 22 June 1977.
11 Editorial page, *El Imparcial*, 11 February 1979.
12 *Sabado Gráfico*, April 1979, E.B.R., pp. 34-35.
13 *El País*, 14 February 1979.
14 *El Correo Español* (Bilbao), 9 February 1979.
15 *El Correo Español*, 27 February 1979.
16 *Ya*, "GRAPO, 1 October Armed Resistance Groups, and MPAIAC, Canary Islands Separatists," 18 February 1979.
17 *El País*, 10 February 1979.
18 *El País*, 4 and 11 February 1979. In the United Kingdom, as in a number of other democracies, smaller parties are given time in proportion to their strength while regional parties are restricted to broadcasting in the area of their support.
19 *El Correo Español*, 18 February 1979.
20 *ABC*, 25 February 1983.

Spanish Politics: Between the Old Regime and the New Majority

1   There have been a substantial number of conferences and research projects on these topics. Among the most significant conferences are "Prospects for Democracy: Transitions from Authoritarian Rule in Latin America and Latin Europe," sponsored by the Latin America

Program of the Woodrow Wilson International Center for Scholars, Smithsonian Institution, Washington, D.C.; "Transitions from Authoritarianism in Southern Europe and Latin America," sponsored by the Centro de Investigaciones Sociológicas, Madrid; and "Transitions to Democracy in Southern Europe," sponsored by the Social Science Research Council, New York. Major research projects include the *Informe sociológico sobre el cambio político en España, 1975-1981* [A Sociological Report on Political Change in Spain, 1975-1981] (Madrid: Editorial Eurámerica, 1981), prepared by Juan Linz, Manuel Gómez Reino, Francisco Orizo, and Darío Vila [hereafter cited as FOESSA 1981]; and the numerous monographs and papers prepared by Samuel H. Barnes, Peter McDonough, and Antonio López Pina as part of their project on "Parliamentary Monarchy and Political Legitimacy in Spain."

2 Frederick Pike, "The New Corporatism in Franco's Spain and Some Latin American Perspectives," in Pike and Thomas Stritch, eds., *The New Corporatism* (Notre Dame: University of Notre Dame Press, 1974), pp. 179-80.

3 José Féliz Tezanos, *Estructura de clase y conflictos de poder en la Espana postfranquista* [Class structure and power conflicts in post-Franco Spain] (Madrid: Editorial Cuadernos para el Diálogo, 1978), pp. 138-43.

4 Ibid., p. 186.

5 Ibid., p. 313, 319.

6 The quotation is from Ramón Salgado-Araujo, *Mis conversaciones privadas con Franco* [My private conversations with Franco] (Barcelona: Editorial Planeta, 1976). It is cited in Carlos Alba, "The Organization of Authoritarian Leadership: Franco Spain," in Richard Rose and Ezra Suleiman, eds., *Presidents and Prime Ministers* (Washington, D.C.: American Enterprise Institute, 1980), p. 267.

7 Alba, "Authoritarian Leadership," p. 274.

8 These points are made in Kenneth Medhurst, *Government in Spain: The Executive at Work* (Oxford: Pergamon Press, 1973). Also of interest is the discussion by Angel Viñas in his "La administración de la política económica exterior de España, 1936-1979" [The Administration of Foreign Economic Policy in Spain, 1936-1979] *Cuadernos Económicos de* ICE 13 (1980): 169-72.

9 Richard Gunther, *Public Policy in a No-Party State* (Berkeley and Los Angeles: University of California Press, 1980), p. 40.

10 Rafael López-Pintor, *La opinion pública española: Del franquismo a la democracia* [Spanish public opinion: From Francoism to democracy] (Madrid: Centro de Investigaciones Sociológicas, 1982).

11 As to the latter, an outstanding analysis may be found in José María Maravall, *Dictatorship and Political Dissent: Workers and Students in Franco's Spain* (London: Tavistock Publications, 1978).

12 For succinct and knowledgeable discussions of the Portuguese situation, see Kenneth Maxwell, "The Transition in Portugal," Latin American Program of the Woodrow Wilson International Center for Scholars, Working Papers, no. 81; and Philippe Schmitter, "Liberation by *Golpe*: Retrospective Thoughts on the Demise of Authoritarian Rule in Portugal," *Armed Forces and Society* 2, no. 1 (November 1975): 5-33.

13 As suggested by the discussion on "mutual guarantees" in Robert Dahl, *Polyarchy: Participation and Opposition* (New Haven and London: Yale University Press, 1978), pp. 217-18. On the military in Spain, see Joaquín Romero Maura, "After Franco, Franquismo: The Armed Forces, the Crown, and Democracy," *Government and Opposition* 2, no. 1 (Winter 1976): 35-64; Manuel G. García, "The Armed Forces: Poor Relation to the Franco Regime," in Paul Preston, ed., *Spain in Crisis* (London: Harvester Press, 1976); and Med-

hurst, "The Military and the Prospects for Spanish Democracy," in *West European Politics* (February 1978), pp. 42–59.

14. The quotation is from Seymour Martin Lipset, *Political Man* (New York: Doubleday, 1960), p. 66. Juan Linz saw the king "as an arbitrator in the situation, as the focus of loyalty for the armed forces, as a symbol of continuity for some and hope for others, and as a decisive actor without running the risks of holding executive power." From his Note entitled "Some Comparative Thoughts on the Transition to Democracy in Portugal and Spain," in Jorge Braga de Macedo and Simon Serfaty, eds., *Portugal since the Revolution* (Boulder, Colo.: Westview Press, 1981), pp. 25–46, at p. 29.

15. This formulation may be found in a thought-provoking essay by Guiseppe de Palma, "Derecha, izquierda, o centro? Sobre la legitimación de los partidos y coaliciones en el sur de Europa," [Right, left, or center? On the legitimation of parties and coalitions in southern Europe], *Revista del Departamento de Derecho Político* (Universidad Nacional de Educacion a Distancia, Madrid) 4 (Fall 1979): 136.

16. A useful biographical sketch is in Gregorio Morán, *Adolfo Suárez: Historia de una ambición* [Adolfo Suárez, A history of an ambition] (Barcelona: Editorial Planeta, 1979).

17. Assessments of the transition include Shlomo Ben Ami, *La revolucion desde arriba: Espana 1936–1979* [Revolution from above: 1936–1979] (Barcelona: Riopiedras Ediciones, 1980), pp. 273–324; Rafael López-Pintor, "Transition Toward Democracy in Spain: Opinion Mood and Elite Behavior," Latin American Program of the Woodrow Wilson International Center for Scholars, Working Papers, no. 80; José María Maravall, "Transición a la democracia: alienamientos políticos y elecciones en España" [Transition to democracy: Political alignments and elections in Spain] *Sistema* 36 (May 1980): 65–105; Carmen de Elejabeitia et al., *Lucha política por el poder* (Madrid: Elías Querejeta Ediciones, 1976); and Raymond Carr and Juan Pablo Fusi, *Espana: De la Dictadura a la Democracia* [Spain: From dictatorship to democracy] (Barcelona: Editorial Planeta, 1981), pp. 269–300.

18. FOESSA 1981, p. 343.

19. Ibid., pp. 372–73.

20. Peter McDonough, Antonio Lopez Pina, and Samuel H. Barnes, "The Spanish Public in Political Transition," *British Journal of Political Science* 2, no. 2 (1981): 54. Also relevant are the discussions on the backgrounds of delegates to party congresses and candidates for the Chamber of Deputies and the Senate by several of the contributors to this volume.

21. FOESSA 1981, p. 372.

22. Ibid., p. 394.

23. McDonough, López Pina, and Barnes, "Spanish Public in Transition," pp. 51, 55–56, 61–65, 68. I have also benefited from lectures by and conversations with Samuel H. Barnes on this point.

24. A detailed analysis of the constitution is contained in Oscar Alzaga, *La constitución española de 1978* [The Spanish constitution of 1978] (Madrid: Ediciones del Foro, 1978) as well as in the work of Jorge de Esteban and Luis López Guerra.

25. On the UCD, see the important work by Carlos Huneeus, "La union de centro democratico: Un partido consociacional" [The Union of the Democratic Center: A consociational party], *Revista de Politica Comparada*, no. 3 (Winter 1980–81): 163–92. On patrons and clients, see Alex Weingrod, "Patrons, Patronage, and Political Parties," *Comparative Studies in Society and History*, 10 (July 1978): 377–400.

26. For an analysis of Spanish Communist strategy since the 1950s, see my *Communism and Political Change in Spain* (Bloomington: Indiana University Press, 1983).

27. José Féliz Tezanos, "El espacio político y sociológico del socialismo español" [The political and sociological space of Spanish socialism], *Sistema* 31 (October 1979): 68.

28 José María Maravall, "Political Cleavages in Spain and the 1979 General Election," *Government and Opposition* 14, no. 3 (Fall 1970): 69.
29 For detailed results, see *Comunicació* (Barcelona), no. 2 (April 10), 1982.
30 Robert Clark, "Recent Voting Trends in Spain's Basque Provinces," unpublished manuscript, pp. 22-23, and the chapter in this volume by Coverdale. Clark has written two books—*The Basques: The Franco Years and Beyond* (University of Nevada Press, 1979), and a history of the ETA (University of Wisconsin Press, 1984)—which are required reading for those interested in the Basque question. Similarly, the book by Stanley Payne entitled *Basque Nationalism* (University of Nevada Press, 1975).
31 FOESSA 1981, p. 627.
32 For an extended and useful discussion of trends in this area, see José Ramon Montero Gubert, "Partidos y participación política: Algunas notas sobre la afiliación política durante la etapa inicial de la transición española" [Parties and political participation: Some notes on political affiliation during the initial phase of the Spanish transition] *Revista de Estudios Políticos* (Madrid), September-October 1981, pp. 33-72.
33 Peter McDonough and Antonio López Pina, "Democracy and Disenchantment in Spanish Politics," in Paul Allen Beck et al., eds., *Mass Politics in Industrial Societies* (Princeton: N.J.: Princeton University Press, forthcoming), p. 36.
34 Peter McDonough and Antonio López Pina, "Authoritarian Brazil and Democratic Spain: Toward a Theory of Political Legitimacy," paper presented at the Eighth National Meeting of the Latin American Studies Association, Pittsburgh, Pennsylvania, 5-7 April 1979, p. 44.
35 Huneeus, "La unión," p. 175.
36 Robert Clark, "Patterns of Insurgent Violence in Spain's Basque Provinces," paper delivered at the 1981 Southwestern Political Science Association meeting in Dallas, Texas, 25-28 March 1981, p. 10.
37 FOESSA 1981, p. 522.
38 García, "The Armed Forces," p. 27.
39 *El País*, 6 December 1981.
40 On the role of the press, see Kenneth Maxwell, ed., *The Press and the Rebirth of Iberian Democracy* (Westport, Conn.: Greenwood Press, 1983).

The October 1982 General Election and the Evolution of the Spanish Party System

1 Survey data predicting a PSOE victory and an unprecedented UCD defeat were published in newspapers and magazines during 1982. Moreover, key social and political actors had their own surveys, which, so far as I know, agreed with the published surveys.
2 As Juan J. Linz has noted, "Modern Spanish political history is characterized by discontinuities." With this sentence Linz begins a long chapter on the Spanish party system that emerged from the elections of 1977 and 1979. At the end of the chapter he says: "It is the indeterminacy of the future electoral strength, ideological and programmatic positions, and organizational articulation as mass parties of the PSOE and the UCD that makes it so difficult to advance any solid prediction about the future dynamics of Spanish democratic politics." See Juan J. Linz, "The New Spanish Party System," in Richard Rose, ed., *Electoral Participation: A Comparative Analysis* (London: Sage Publications, 1980), pp. 101-90.
3 This comes from a postelectoral report available at the data bank of the Centro de Investigaciones Sociológicas in Madrid.

4 As stated above, all opinion surveys agreed that the PSOE would win the election. Moreover, not only were a majority of the people thinking of voting for the PSOE, but the electorate was almost unanimous in believing that the PSOE was likely to win the election. See opinion surveys from Centro de Investigaciones Sociológicas at its data bank in Madrid.
5 This comes from the same source as in footnote 3.
6 These findings stem from unpublished studies available at the data bank of the Centro de Investigaciones Sociológicas: the four-year collection of Continued Qualitative Research, the project on urban youth directed by Carlos Moya, and the project on youth values directed by José Juan Toharia and Manuel García Ferrando.
7 See my *La opinión pública española del franquismo a la democracia* [Spanish public opinion from Francoism to democracy] (Madrid: Centro de Investigaciones Sociológicas, 1982), chaps. 2, 3; or my "Transition toward Democracy in Spain: Opinion Mood and Elite Behavior" (Washington, D.C.: Wilson Center, Smithsonian Institution, 1980), Working Paper, no. 80.
8 One of the most outstanding Spanish columnists, Juan Tomás de Salas, discussed "the Franco-Leninist traits of Suárez politics" in *Cambio 16* (20 September 1982), p. 3.
9 Even after the convention of December 1982, it was not clear whether the UCD would survive the personal differences of the few remaining members.
10 These data come from the data bank on Centro de Investigaciones Sociológicas.
11 There is still one more sorry aspect about the public perception of Suárez: during the parliamentary debate before choosing Felipe González as prime minister in November 1982, the performance of Suárez was considered "most interesting" by only 2 percent of the public. The positive evaluation of Lavilla in the same debate was 4 percent. Ibid.
12 See the newspapers of the time. The opinion of the media was unanimous. The speech was considered cryptic.
13 For detailed information about this election, see my *La Opinión Pública*, pp. 134–35.
14 Ibid.
15 Ibid.
16 Ibid.
17 José Ignacio Wert, "El electorado de UCD: Una version sociológica" [The UCD electorate: A sociological version] unpublished paper (Madrid, 1982).
18 For a detailed analysis of these electoral processes, see this author's *La Opinión Pública*, pp. 134–43. The residual character of what remained of the UCD's electoral support was dramatically evident in a November 1982 postelectoral survey: only in rather marginal areas and social sectors of the country did the UCD receive a somewhat higher vote than its national average of 7 percent. These were municipalities with fewer than 2,000 inhabitants (there, 12 percent of the vote went to the UCD), among people with no education or incomplete primary school (9 percent), the retired (10 percent), and those in ancillary occupations (10 percent). The data come from the Centro de Investigaciones Sociológicas in Madrid.
19 See *La Opinión Pública*, pp. 134–43.
20 Ibid.
21 Ibid.
22 Wert, "El electorado."
23 Ibid.
24 This might have been enough to get an absolute majority under the Spanish electoral system.
25 See my chapter on the Popular Alliance, "Francoist Reformers in Democratic Spain," written in 1979 for this book.
26 Ibid., last paragraph.

Index

Ansón, Rafael, 265
Arias Navarro, Carlos, 24, 50, 94

Basque country: amnesty and autonomy, 55, 73, 131, 135, 228, 233-34, 240, 243, 244, 250, 252, 274; Basque Land and Liberty (ETA), 24, 26, 234-35, 236, 244-45, 274; Basque Nationalist party (PNV), 29, 38, 61, 64, 81-83, 233, 234, 238-39, 240, 246, 249, 250, 251, 252, 277, 295, 296, 305; campaign 1977, 61-63, 233-39; campaign 1979, 64, 244-50; Catholicism, 231, 232; Constitutional Commission, 34; economy, 227, 230; Herri Batasuna, 29, 244-51; historical roots, 229-33; industry and trade, 227, 230; nationalist sentiment, 29, 139, 227, 228-29, 230-33, 242-52; public opinion, 76-77, 81-83, 228-29; terrorism, 24, 26, 29, 139, 228, 232-33, 240, 245; transition to democracy, 233-39; under Franco, 231-33; voter behavior, 235-39, 241-44, 245, 246-49, 250-51, 283-84

Calvo Sotelo, Leopoldo, 101-3, 289, 290-91, 293, 304-5
Campaign 1977 and results: Basque country, 61-63, 233-39; Catalonia, 213-19; center parties, 107-16; Communist party (PCE), 26, 62, 63, 64, 162-64, 280-81; Democratic Center, 107-9; electoral rules and candidate selection, 54-58, 60-64; media, 107, 253, 260-64, 265-67; national parties, 61-64; Popular Alliance (AP), 188, 190-91, 196-99, 280; public opinion, 76-77, 85-87, 124-27; regional parties, 61-63, 233-51; Spanish Socialist Workers' party (PSOE), 26, 61-64, 137; Union of the Democratic Center (UCD), 62, 63
Campaign 1979 and results: Basque country, 64, 244-50; Catalonia, 219-23; Communist party (PCE), 66-67, 172-87, 283;

Democratic Coalition (CD), 66-67, 199-200; electoral rules and candidate selection, 64-72; media, 118, 121, 253, 268-69; public opinion, 83, 86, 87, 124-27; Spanish Socialist Workers' party (PSOE), 28, 70-72, 140, 283-84; Union of the Democratic Center (UCD), 67-70, 116-27, 283, 284
Candidate selection process: election 1977, 61-64; election 1979, 64-72, 119-20; party lists, 60-61; qualifications, 54-55
Carrero Blanco, Luis, 24, 278
Carrillo, Santiago, 162, 163, 164, 166, 171, 173, 174, 176, 287
Catalan nationalism: 9-10, 206-7, 213-14, 224; amnesty and autonomy, 7-8, 55, 73, 214, 223-25; campaign 1977, 61-63; Civil War, 213; Constitutional Commission, 34; historical background, 206-13; media, 221, 224; Organic Law for the Harmonization of the Autonomy Process (LOAPA), 225; party lists, 214-16; Pujol, Jordi, 117, 214, 218, 221, 281; regional parties, 61-62; transition to democracy, 214-23; voter behavior, 216-21, 283-84
Catholicism: Basque country, 231, 232; change, 49, 165, 169, 175, 275, 277, 281, 282, 285, 315; Christian Democratic movement, 88-128; church-state relations, 7-8, 27, 33, 39, 282; Constitutional Commission, 39; education, 39, 169, 289; labor, 276; media, 90, 91, 123, 257, 262, 270; Opus Dei, 189, 257, 275, 277; Spanish Confederation of Autonomous Rightist Groups (CEDA), 8-10, 14, 281; Tácito, 90-91, 93, 96, 97
Christian Democracy: Christian Democratic Left (IDC), 93, 95-96, 97; Christian Democratic Team of the Spanish State (EDC), 92; de Areilza, José María, 96-97; Democratic Coordination, 92-93, 95; Democratic Left (ID), 92-93, 96; Federa-

tion of Democratic and Liberal Parties (FPDL), 93; Gil Robles, José María, 92, 96, 98, 116; Liberal Party (PL), 93; media, 90-91, 97; Osorio, Alfonso, 91, 96; Popular Christian Democratic Party (PPDC), 96, 98; Popular Democratic Federation, 92; Popular Party (PP), 95-97; public opinion, 95; Ruiz Giménez, Joaquín, 90, 93, 95, 96, 98, 116; Spanish Democratic Union (UDE), 96; Spanish Social Democratic Union (USDE), 94; Spanish Union (UE), 93; Tácito, 90-91, 93, 96-97; transition to democracy, 90-94, 116-19. *See also* Democratic Center, Democratic Coalition (CD), Popular Alliance (AP)

Civil War, 13-18, 48, 160-61, 213

Communist party (PCE): campaign 1977 and results, 62, 63, 64, 160-65, 168, 280-81; campaign 1979 and results, 28, 66-67, 161, 172-85, 283; Carrillo, Santiago, 162, 163, 164, 166, 171, 173, 174, 176, 287; Civil War memories, 161, 166; Constitutional Commission, 34; decline, 251, 278, 283, 287, 292, 293, 294, 295, 296, 297-98, 311, 314-16; economic program, 162; Eurocommunism, 161, 166-67, 170, 176, 182, 285, 287, 292; foreign relations, 170-71, 176; Ibárruri, Dolores, 166-67, 177; legalization, 95, 164; media, 103, 164, 166, 173, 266; National Confederation of Labor (CNT), 9-10, 11, 15, 16, 130, 277; public opinion, 78, 168, 169; terrorism, 165; trade unions, 165, 168-69, 173-74, 176-77, 179, 183, 187, 282-83; transition period, 162, 166, 167-68, 277, 278, 285; voter turnout, 160, 174-76, 177, 178, 180-85

Constitution of 1978: 58-59, 282; autonomy, 27; church-state relations, 27, 39; Constitutional Commission, 30; economic order, 39-42; form of government, 36; issues, 31-35; in practice, 45-47; Law for Political Reform, 30, 51-54; legislative power, 44-45, 51; parliamentary debates, 34-35; party spokesmen, 34-35, 171; public opinion, 79-83; rationalist view, 35; representation and plebiscites, 42-44; sociological view, 35-36; sovereignty, 36-37; strategy of consensus, 31-32; territorial organization, 37-38; traditional view, 35-36

Coup attempt, 46, 274, 288, 289, 291-92, 293, 301, 304

de Areilza, José María, 96-97, 99-100, 108, 283

Democratic Center: Calvo Sotelo, Leopoldo, 101-3; campaign 1977 and results, 107-9; de Areilza, José María, 99-100, 108; Federation of Democratic and Liberal Parties, 98; Gil Robles, José María, 98, 100-101, 108; media, 100, 103; Osorio, Alfonso, 99; party lists, 99-103, 104-7; Popular Christian Democratic party (PPDC), 101; Popular Democratic party, 98; Popular party (PP), 98; public opinion, 98; Ruiz Giménez, Joaquín, 98, 101, 109; Spanish Democratic Union (UDE), 98, 101; Suárez, Adolfo, 99-104

Democratic Coalition (CD): campaign 1979 and results, 66-67, 188, 200, 283, 284; de Areilza, José María (Liberal Action), 195-96; electoral program, 199-200; Falange, 189; Fraga Iribarne, Manuel (Democratic Reform), 188, 190-92; Martínez Estreuelas, Cruz (Spanish People's Union), 194-95; public opinion, 201; Opus Dei, 189, 193; Osorio, Alfonso (Progressive Democratic party), 196; transition to democracy, 189, 191, 192; voter turnout and distribution, 188, 201-4. *See also* Popular Alliance (AP), Christian Democracy

d'Hondt system, 57, 137, 142, 296

Economy: consumerism, 275; EEC, 28, 198, 278, 315; effect on state, 275-76; Constitutional Commission, 39-42; growth of, 28, 48, 227; industrialization, 227, 275; labor, 276, 277, 282-83; labor-management agreements, 45; PSOE, 282, 290; Suárez, Adolfo, 286; transition to democracy, 26, 28, 48-49; under Franco, 21

Electoral rules: campaign duration and funding, 57-58; candidate selection, 54-55, 56-57, 60-72; Constitution of 1978, 58-59; d'Hondt system, 57, 137, 142, 296; electoral procedures Decree of 18 March 1977, 54-58; Law for Political Reform, 51-54, 59; party legalization, 56; suffrage, 59-60; transition to democracy, 48-50

Fraga Iribarne, Manuel, 188, 190, 191, 257, 264, 290, 298, 304, 313, 316

Francoism: Arias Navarro, Carlos, 24, 50, 94; background, 88-92; Carrero Blanco, Luis, 24, 278; Civil War, 15-18, 48, 160-61, 213, 277, 280; decline, 27; Falange, 18-20, 189, 276-77; German-Italian support, 19-20; in Basque country, 231-33; King Juan Carlos, 24; media, 253-57; regime, 18-25, 277-78; relations with United States, 21

General election, October 1982: Chamber of Deputies' returns, 294-97; Communist party (PCE) decline, 293, 294, 296, 297-98, 311, 314-15; conclusions about returns, 296-97; new party system, 311-13; party fluidity, 297-301, 308-11; Popular Alliance (AP), 292, 294, 295, 296, 297, 298, 307, 311, 313; public opinion, 308-11; regional parties, 295, 297, 303, 308; Senate returns, 296; Spanish Socialist Workers' party (PSOE) landslide, 296, 297-98, 311-13; television, 303, 304; timing of, 293, 303-5; Union of the Democratic Center (UCD), collapse, 294-95, 296, 297, 301-5, 314-17; voter turnout, 296

González, Felipe: confidence in, 95, 285, 287, 303, 313; constitutional process, 31; PSOE renewal, 280, 292

Gutiérrez Mellado, Manuel, 28, 267

Juan Carlos, King: politician, 190, 280, 304; transition to democracy, 25-26, 46, 49, 274, 279-80, 288; under Franco, 24

Labor and trade unions: 8, 10, 28, 41, 73, 276; Communist party (PCE), 66-67, 168-69, 173, 174, 176-77, 179, 183, 185, 187, 272-83; emigration and immigration, 60, 228, 249-50, 275, 277; General Workers' Union (UGT), 71-72, 130-33, 136, 137, 256, 282-83; labor-management-government agreements, 45-46; National Confederation of Labor (CNT), 9-10, 11, 15, 16, 130, 277; strikes, 14, 21, 135; Workers' Commissions, 174, 176, 179, 183, 283

Lavilla, Landelino, 96, 122, 305

Media: 289; Ansón, Rafael, 265; censorship, 60, 173, 255-62; Catholic church, 90, 91, 123, 262, 270; election 1977, 260-61; election 1979, 268-69; informing citizens, 253; government control and subsidies, 253, 255-57, 265-68, 271; military, 262; party and union press, 103, 130, 256; public opinion, 254, 255, 264, 268-69, 272; radio and television, 57, 64-65, 107, 199, 253, 265-67, 270-72; regional press, 259, 261, 269; Suárez and UCD, 121, 123, 261, 263, 265, 272; terrorism, 263, 269-70; transition to democracy, 253-54, 258-64, 271-73, 289

Military: 197-98, 278-79, 288-89, 290, 291-92; Civil War, 14-18; coup attempt, 274, 288; democratization period, 27-28; Gutiérrez Mellado, Manuel, 28, 267; institutional change, 49, 318; King Juan Carlos, 28; media, 27-28, 289; NATO, 28, 198, 289, 315; Royal Decrees for the Armed Forces, 37; under Franco, 18-19, 20, 21; Moncloa Agreements, 45, 73, 77-79, 138-40, 170

Organic Law for the Harmonization of the Autonomy Process (LOAPA), 46, 225, 290

Popular Alliance (AP): 283, 294; as opposition party, 293, 298, 315, 316; Catholicism (Opus Dei), 189-90, 193; coalition members, 191-96, 280; Constitutional Commission, 34, 51; de Areilza, José María, 283; De la Fuente, Licinio (Social Democracy), 194; Fernández de la Mora, Gonzalo (Spanish National Union), 195; Fraga Iribarne, Manuel, 188, 191-92, 290, 298, 304, 313, 316; Franco and Falange, 189-91, 199; election 1977, 108, 188, 191, 196-99; López Rodó, Laureano (Regional Action), 193; media, 118, 196-97, 199, 264; public opinion, 78, 81, 201; Silva, Federico (Spanish Democratic Action), 194; television, 199; Thomás de Carranza, Enrique (Popular Social Union), 195; transition to democracy, 188, 189, 190-91; voter turnout, 188, 201, 236, 283, 295, 296, 297, 298. *See also* Democratic Coalition (CD), Christian Democracy

Public opinion: 315; consensus, 77-83; constitutional process, 79-83; electoral behavior, 76-77; evolution to democracy,

73-76, 118; Law for Political Reform, 74-75, 95; media, 264, 268-69, 272; Moncloa Agreements, 78-79; national parties, 76, 80; political figures, 95; regional parties, 76; transition process, 83-87, 98
Pujol, Jordi, 117, 214, 218, 221, 281

Regional elections, 140, 144, 274, 283, 284-86, 291, 305-8
Regional parties, 61-62, 126, 140, 178-81, 226-52, 277, 281, 283-84, 285-86, 295, 297, 303, 308, 314, 316, 317
Regional nationalism: Basque country, 29, 139, 178-79, 226-52; Catalonia, 9-10, 179-81, 206-7, 213-14

Social Democratic Center (CDS), 289, 294, 296, 297, 317
Spanish Socialist Workers' party (PSOE): 277, 280, 281-82, 283-84, 286-87, 291, 293, 295; amnesty, 131-35, 137, 234-35; as opposition party, 137; campaign 1977, 61-64, 137, 234-37; campaign 1979, 28, 64, 70-72, 140, 246, 248; Constitutional Commission, 34-35; foreign relations, 166; General Workers' Union (UGT), 71-72, 130-34, 136, 137, 139, 256; González, Felipe, 133, 134, 137, 142, 280, 285, 287, 292, 303, 313; Guerra, Alfonso, 291; historical background, 7, 129-34; labor affiliations, 130, 131, 135, 283; media, 137, 256, 266; Moncloa Agreements, 138-40; October 1982 landslide, 296, 297-98, 311-13, 315; Organic Law for the Harmonization of the Autonomy Process (LOAPA), 225, 290; public opinion, 76, 80; television, 304; transition to democracy, 134-36, 138, 146-48, 158-59; voter profiles, 146-58; voter turnout, 129, 137, 140-45
Suárez, Adolfo: 25-26, 274, 276, 281, 282; campaign 1977 and results, 102-16; campaign 1979 and results, 116-27; Catholic vote, 108-9; democratic center, 99-103; failing leadership, 285-86, 288-89, 290,
293, 301-4; media, 107, 261, 263, 265, 267, 272; public opinion, 95; resignation, 293; Social Democratic Center (CDS), 289, 294; transition to democracy, 25, 50, 276, 279-80, 285, 291

Terrorism: 24, 26, 29, 139, 165, 178, 179, 228, 232-33, 240, 245-52, 263, 274, 278, 287-88
Transition to democracy: 48-50, 88-102, 274-92; candidate selection, 60-72; Civil War, 13-18; Constitution of 1978, 30-47, 58-60; democratization, 25-29; electoral rules, 48-60; Franco regime, 18-25; Law for Political Reform, 51-54; Moncloa Agreements, 45, 73, 138-39; Organic Law for the Harmonization of the Autonomy Process (LOAPA), 46, 225, 290; political opinion, 73-87; Popular Front Elections of 1936, 10-13; reform and *ruptura*, 32, 165, 279-80, 288; Second Republic, 6-10; U.S. relations, 28

Union of the Democratic Center (UCD): 281, 282; Calvo Sotelo, Leopoldo, 293, 304-5; campaign 1977 and results, 63, 102-16, 234-36, 239; campaign 1979 and results, 28, 67-70, 116-27, 244-51, 283, 284; candidate selection, 119-20; centrist coalitions, 94-102; Constitutional Commission, 34-35; economic program, 286; Garrigues, Joaquín, 93, 96, 98, 102, 103, 122; Lavilla, Landelino, 96, 122, 305; Law for Political Reform, 95; media, 263, 266, 272, 304; Organic Law for the Harmonization of the Autonomy Process (LOAPA), 290; party collapse, 274, 284, 286, 289, 291-92, 296-97, 301-5, 314-17; Perez Llorca, José Pedro, 97, 119, 123; public opinion, 76, 80, 95, 308-11; regional elections, 285-86, 290-91, 293, 295, 305-8; Suárez, Adolfo, 26, 94-95, 274, 276, 281, 282, 293, 301-5; voter defection, 287, 297, 305-8, 311, 314-15

Contributors

JOHN F. COVERDALE has received his law degree and has spent one year as a clerk for a federal district judge in Washington, D. C. He is a former associate professor of history at Northwestern University and the author of *The Political Transformation of Spain After Franco*. He has also published on civil strife in the Basque country during the nineteenth century.

JORGE DE ESTEBAN is currently the Spanish Ambassador to Italy. He is a former professor of law at the University of Madrid and is the author of numerous works on Spanish politics and political systems. He served as a member of the Provincial Electoral Committee of Madrid during the 1977 elections and of the Central Electoral Committee during the 1979 elections. Among his books are *Political Development and the Spanish Constitution* and *Political Parties in Contemporary Spain*, which he coauthored with Luis López Guerra.

LUIS LÓPEZ GUERRA is professor and chairman of the department of constitutional law at the University of Extremadura. He is the author of *Electoral Campaigns in the West*. He also coauthored (with Jorge de Esteban) a book on the Spanish constitution and has published an analysis of the March 1979 Spanish parliamentary elections.

ANTONIO LÓPEZ PINA, professor of law at the Universidad Autónoma, was elected to the Spanish Parliament in 1977. He has written widely on the constituent process and political legitimacy in contemporary Spain. He is currently working on a book entitled *Structural Conflicts and Institutional Order: Labor Politics in Spain*.

RAFAEL LÓPEZ-PINTOR is a professor at the Universidad Autónoma in Madrid. He is a former director of the Research Department of the Spanish Institute of Public Opinion and was director of the Center of Sociological Research (CIS) from 1979 to 1982. He has written numerous books, among which is *Spanish Public Opinion: From Francoism to Democracy*.

JOSÉ MARÍA MARAVALL has been minister of education since 1982. He is a former professor of sociology at the Universidad Complutense de Madrid and a member of the executive committee of the Spanish Socialist Workers' party (PSOE). He has also been senior lecturer in sociology at Warwick University and research fellow at St. Anthony's College, Oxford. Among his publications are *Dictatorship and Dissent* and *The Transition to Democracy in Spain*.

JUAN F. MARSAL, original author of the Catalan chapter, was professor and chairman of the department of sociology at the Universidad Autónoma at Barcelona. After his death, his assistant Javier Roiz concluded Marsal's work on the 1977 elections and added the analysis of the 1979 elections. Among Marsal's books are *Dependence and Independence: The Alternatives of Latin American Sociology in the Twentieth Century* and *Intellectual Currents Under Franco*.

EUSEBIO M. MUJAL-LEÓN is associate professor of government at Georgetown University and the author of numerous articles on Spanish and Portuguese politics, the most recent of which appeared in *West European Politics* and *Foreign Policy*. His book *Communism and Political Change in Spain* was published by Indiana University Press in 1983. He is currently a visiting fellow at the Center of International Studies at Princeton University at work on a project about Soviet-Latin American relations.

Contributors

STANLEY PAYNE is Hillsdale Jaime Vicens Vives professor of history at the University of Wisconsin at Madison. He has written widely on Spanish history. Among his most recent books are *Fascism: Comparison and Definition* and *Spanish Catholicism: An Historical Overview*.

JAVIER ROIZ is adjunct professor of political science at the Universidad Complutense de Madrid. He was a visiting fellow at Princeton University from 1975 to 1977. His most recent work is *Empirical Investigation of Collective Behavior* (forthcoming).

JUAN ROLDÁN ROS has been director of Radio El País since early 1984. Prior to this, he was a correspondent in Washington, D.C., for the Spanish news agency EFE. He subsequently worked on the UCD press campaign, then as a journalist on the staff of the Madrid daily, *El País*.

RICHARD M. SCAMMON, coauthor of *This U.S.A.* and *The Real Majority*, is director of the Elections Research Center in Washington, D.C. He has edited the biennial series *America Votes* since 1956.

JAVIER TUSELL GÓMEZ is currently professor of contemporary history at the Universidad Nacional Educacion a Distancia. Until 1978 he was a professor of contemporary history at the University of Valencia. He then became director general of fine arts in the ministry of culture until 1982. Among his books are *Democratic Opposition to Francoism, Oligarchy and Caciquism in Andalusia*, and *The History of Christian Democracy in Spain*.

JOSÉ IGNACIO WERT ORTEGA teaches political sociology at the Universidad Autónoma in Madrid. He is a member of the Madrid city council, elected on the PDP (Popular Democratic party) ticket. He was director of studies at RTVE, the Spanish national broadcasting system until 1979 when he became head of the technical cabinet at the Center for Sociological Research. He has published numerous articles on electoral behavior and on the media.

Library of Congress Cataloging-in-Publication Data
Main entry under title:
Spain at the polls, 1977, 1979, 1982.
"An American Enterprise Institute book."
Bibliography: p.
Includes index.
1. Elections—Spain—Addresses, essays, lectures.
2. Representative government and representation—
Spain—Addresses, essays, lectures. 3. Political
parties—Spain—Addresses, essays, lectures. 4. Spain—
Politics and government—1975– Addresses, essays,
lectures. I. Penniman, Howard Rae, 1916–
II. Mujal-León, Eusebio, 1950– . III. American
Enterprise Institute. IV. Title.
JN8371.S63 1985   324.946′044   85-20523
ISBN 0-8223-0663-8
ISBN 0-8223-0695-6 (pbk.)